The ACT® FOR DUMMIES®
4TH EDITION

by Michelle Rose Gilman and Veronica Saydak
Suzee Vlk
Author of *The SAT I For Dummies,*
The GRE Test For Dummies,
The GMAT For Dummies

WILEY
Wiley Publishing, Inc.

The ACT® For Dummies®, 4th Edition

Published by
Wiley Publishing, Inc.
111 River St.
Hoboken, NJ 07030-5774
www.wiley.com

Copyright © 2005 by Wiley Publishing, Inc., Indianapolis, Indiana

Published by Wiley Publishing, Inc., Indianapolis, Indiana

Published simultaneously in Canada

No part of this publication may be reproduced, stored in a retrieval system, or transmitted in any form or by any means, electronic, mechanical, photocopying, recording, scanning, or otherwise, except as permitted under Sections 107 or 108 of the 1976 United States Copyright Act, without either the prior written permission of the Publisher, or authorization through payment of the appropriate per-copy fee to the Copyright Clearance Center, 222 Rosewood Drive, Danvers, MA 01923, 978-750-8400, fax 978-646-8600. Requests to the Publisher for permission should be addressed to the Permissions Department, John Wiley & Sons, Inc., 111 River Street, Hoboken, NJ 07030, (201)748-6011, fax (201)748-6008, or online at http://www.wiley.com/go/permissions.

Trademarks: Wiley, the Wiley Publishing logo, For Dummies, the Dummies Man logo, A Reference for the Rest of Us!, The Dummies Way, Dummies Daily, The Fun and Easy Way, Dummies.com and related trade dress are trademarks or registered trademarks of John Wiley & Sons, Inc. and/or its affiliates in the United States and other countries, and may not be used without written permission. ACT is a trademark or registered trademark of ACT. All other trademarks are the property of their respective owners. Wiley Publishing, Inc., is not associated with any product or vendor mentioned in this book.

LIMIT OF LIABILITY/DISCLAIMER OF WARRANTY: THE PUBLISHER AND THE AUTHOR MAKE NO REPRESENTATIONS OR WARRANTIES WITH RESPECT TO THE ACCURACY OR COMPLETENESS OF THE CONTENTS OF THIS WORK AND SPECIFICALLY DISCLAIM ALL WARRANTIES, INCLUDING WITHOUT LIMITATION WARRANTIES OF FITNESS FOR A PARTICULAR PURPOSE. NO WARRANTY MAY BE CREATED OR EXTENDED BY SALES OR PROMOTIONAL MATERIALS. THE ADVICE AND STRATEGIES CONTAINED HEREIN MAY NOT BE SUITABLE FOR EVERY SITUATION. THIS WORK IS SOLD WITH THE UNDERSTANDING THAT THE PUBLISHER IS NOT ENGAGED IN RENDERING LEGAL, ACCOUNTING, OR OTHER PROFESSIONAL SERVICES. IF PROFESSIONAL ASSISTANCE IS REQUIRED, THE SERVICES OF A COMPETENT PROFESSIONAL PERSON SHOULD BE SOUGHT. NEITHER THE PUBLISHER NOR THE AUTHOR SHALL BE LIABLE FOR DAMAGES ARISING HEREFROM. THE FACT THAT AN ORGANIZATION OR WEBSITE IS REFERRED TO IN THIS WORK AS A CITATION AND/OR A POTENTIAL SOURCE OF FURTHER INFORMATION DOES NOT MEAN THAT THE AUTHOR OR THE PUBLISHER ENDORSES THE INFORMATION THE ORGANIZATION OR WEBSITE MAY PROVIDE OR RECOMMENDATIONS IT MAY MAKE. FURTHER, READERS SHOULD BE AWARE THAT INTERNET WEBSITES LISTED IN THIS WORK MAY HAVE CHANGED OR DISAPPEARED BETWEEN WHEN THIS WORK WAS WRITTEN AND WHEN IT IS READ.

For general information on our other products and services, please contact our Customer Care Department within the U.S. at 877-762-2974, outside the U.S. at 317-572-3993, or fax 317-572-4002.

For technical support, please visit www.wiley.com/techsupport.

Wiley also publishes its books in a variety of electronic formats. Some content that appears in print may not be available in electronic books.

Library of Congress Control Number: 2005925494

ISBN-13: 978-0-7645-9652-0

Manufactured in the United States of America

10 9

4B/SW/QX/QV/IN

About the Authors

Michelle Rose Gilman

"I get up every morning determined to both change the world and have one heck of a good time. Sometimes this makes planning the day difficult." — E.B. White

Michelle Rose Gilman is proud to be known as Noah's mom (Hi Noah!). A graduate from the University of South Florida, Michelle found her niche early and at 19 was already working with emotionally disturbed and learning-disabled students in hospital settings. At 21 she made the trek to California and there she found her passion for helping teenage students become more successful in school and life. What started as a small tutoring business in the garage of her California home, quickly expanded and grew to the point where traffic control was necessary on her residential street. Today, Michelle is the Founder and CEO of Fusion Learning Center, a private school and tutoring/test prep facility in Solana Beach, CA, serving over 2,000 students per year. She has taught tens of thousands of students since 1988. She created the Mentoring Approach to Learning and is the author of various books on self-esteem, writing, and motivational topics. Michelle founded the Addiction and Recovery Division at Fusion and has overseen dozens of programs focused on helping kids become healthy adults. She currently specializes in motivating the unmotivatable adolescent, comforting their shell-shocked parents, and assisting her staff of 27 teachers. Michelle lives by the following motto:

"There are people content with longing; I am not one of them."

Veronica Saydak

Veronica graduated from the University of San Diego with a Bachelors Degree in English. She found her real education in travel and seeing the world. She has traveled to over 12 countries, studying various cultures through their literature and lifestyles. She has been a highly coveted English teacher, specializing in writing, for over 4 years. Currently, Veronica is the Director of Student Development at Fusion Learning Center, where she is responsible for program development, staff supervision, and teaching her students on a one-to-one basis. As an administrator, Veronica specializes in the emotional well-being of over 400 students. Her wit and humor might not solve the world's problems but it definitely makes the world feel lighter. Veronica takes the following advice from one of her favorite authors, Goethe:

"Certain defects are necessary for the existence of individuality."

Suzee Vlk

"I'm not a complete idiot. Parts of me are missing."

Although more likely to admit to being a used-car salesperson, Suzee Vlk was a test prep specialist from 1975 to her death in 2003, working her way through graduate business school and law school teaching courses in ACT, SAT I, GRE, GMAT, and LSAT preparation. By her own description, she found the paranoia and take-no-prisoners mindset required for doing well on the ACT a big help in developing cutthroat tactics to use in the boardroom or courtroom. Eventually, she became president of Suzee Vlk Test Prep and taught thousands of students in dozens of courses at universities and private corporations. She wrote material used in SAT and GRE preparation software and videos. Her prep books for the ACT and other standardized exams have been published worldwide. Suzee lived by the following motto, which she delighted in sharing with others:

"Madness takes its toll. Please have exact change ready."

Dedication

This book is humbly dedicated to the thousands of students who have, over the years, passed through Fusion Learning Center. When the teacher is ready, the right student appears. You have taught us well. And to the memory of Suzee Vlk, the original author, whose humor, wit, and intelligence live on in these pages.

Acknowledgments

We would like to thank agent Bill Gladstone of Waterside Productions in Cardiff, California, for giving us the opportunity to revise the 4th Edition of this book. Special thanks to Christopher Burger (the Book Fairy), for being a delightful perfectionist, and who meticulously reviewed and updated the math sections. Thanks to Shawn Hicks and Karina Gillick for their invaluable input. Many thanks also go to Kathy Cox and our editors at Wiley, Natalie Harris and Neil Johnson. Thanks also to Christina Wolfe for always feeding us, and Nicholas Angelo for his daily dose of silliness.

It's important for us to acknowledge the staff and students of Fusion Learning Center, Solana Beach, California, for their encouragement and their ability to distract us from our seriousness. Also, gratitude to our patient friends and family who continually heard, "We'll see you after this book is done." We're now ready to party!

Publisher's Acknowledgments

We're proud of this book; please send us your comments through our Dummies online registration form located at www.dummies.com/register/.

Some of the people who helped bring this book to market include the following:

Acquisitions, Editorial, and Media Development

Project Editor: Natalie Faye Harris

Acquisitions Editor: Kathy Cox

Copy Editor: E. Neil Johnson

General Reviewers: Don and Diana Garner

Senior Permissions Editor: Carmen Krikorian

Editorial Manager: Michelle Hacker

Editorial Assistants: Courtney Allen, Melissa Bennett

Cartoons: Rich Tennant, www.the5thwave.com

Composition

Project Coordinator: Nancee Reeves

Layout and Graphics: Carrie Foster, Lauren Goddard, Denny Hager, Stephanie D. Jumper, Lynsey Osborn

Proofreaders: Leeann Harney, Betty Kish, Carl William Pierce, Dwight Ramsey

Indexer: Infodex Indexing Services Inc.

Publishing and Editorial for Consumer Dummies

Diane Graves Steele, Vice President and Publisher, Consumer Dummies

Joyce Pepple, Acquisitions Director, Consumer Dummies

Kristin A. Cocks, Product Development Director, Consumer Dummies

Michael Spring, Vice President and Publisher, Travel

Kelly Regan, Editorial Director, Travel

Publishing for Technology Dummies

Andy Cummings, Vice President and Publisher, Dummies Technology/General User

Composition Services

Gerry Fahey, Vice President of Production Services

Debbie Stailey, Director of Composition Services

Contents at a Glance

Introduction 1

Part I: Coming to Terms with Reality: An Overview of the ACT 7
Chapter 1: Getting Your ACT Together: The Format 9
Chapter 2: Succeeding on the ACT 15
Chapter 3: Reading the Admissions Committee's Mind: What Colleges Want 21

Part II: Serving Your "Sentence": English Review and Test 25
Chapter 4: Glamour Grammar: The Five-Star Review 27
Chapter 5: Misspellers of the World, Untie! Mastering the English Test 41
Chapter 6: It's Not What You Say, It's How You Say It: English Practice Questions 47

Part III: Writing the Writing Test Rightly: You Have a Choice 53
Chapter 7: ACT Write: The First Words on Essay Writing 55
Chapter 8: Write Right: The Writing Test Review 65
Chapter 9: Practicing Promptly with Practice Prompts: Essay Practice Examples 75

Part IV: Don't Count Yourself Out: The Math Review and Mini-Test 77
Chapter 10: Ogling More Figures than a Beauty Pageant Judge: Geometry Review 79
Chapter 11: Catching Some (X's, Y's, and) Z's: Algebra and Other Sleeping Aids 99
Chapter 12: Reviewing Miscellaneous Math You Probably Already Know 117
Chapter 13: Numb and Number: Acing the Mathematics Test 131
Chapter 14: More Fun Than a Root Canal: Mathematics Practice Questions 137

Part V: Time to Read the Riot ACT: The Reading Test 143
Chapter 15: This, Too, Shall Pass(age): Sailing through the Reading Test 145
Chapter 16: Where Are CliffsNotes When You Need Them? Reading Practice Questions ...151

Part VI: Proven to Cause Brain Defects in Laboratory Rats: The Science Reasoning Test 157
Chapter 17: Frankenstein to Einstein: Excelling on the Science Reasoning Test 159
Chapter 18: Faking Atomic Ache Won't Get You Out of This: Science Practice Questions 169

Part VII: I'd Rather Wait for the Movie: Full-Length Practice ACTs 179
Chapter 19: How to Ruin a Perfectly Good Day, Part I: Practice Exam 1 181
Chapter 20: Practice Exam 1: Answers and Explanations 227
Chapter 21: How to Ruin a Perfectly Good Day, Part II: Practice Exam 2 265
Chapter 22: Practice Exam 2: Answers and Explanations 311

Part VIII: The Part of Tens 351
Chapter 23: Ten Wrong Rumors About the ACT 353
Chapter 24: Ten Differences between the ACT and the SAT 357

Index 359

Table of Contents

Introduction 1
    About This Book... 1
    You Can Run, but You Can't Hide 1
    How This Book Is Organized... 2
        Part I: Coming to Terms with Reality: An Overview of the ACT 2
        Part II: Serving Your "Sentence": English Review and Test 2
        Part III: Writing the Writing Test Rightly: You Have a Choice 3
        Part IV: Don't Count Yourself Out: The Math Review and Mini-Test 3
        Part V: Time to Read the Riot ACT: The Reading Test............................... 3
        Part VI: Proven to Cause Brain Defects in Laboratory Rats:
            The Science Reasoning Test 3
        Part VII: I'd Rather Wait for the Movie: Full-Length Practice ACTs 3
        Part VIII: The Part of Tens 3
    Icons Used in This Book 4
    Where to Go from Here.. 4
    Making a Commitment... 5

Part I: Coming to Terms with Reality: An Overview of the ACT 7

Chapter 1: Getting Your ACT Together: The Format 9
    I'd Forget My Head If It Wasn't Attached: What to Take to the ACT 9
    What Not to Take to the ACT... 10
    Normal Is Boring: Unusual Circumstances 11
    Anything's Better than Nothing: Guessing for Points 11
    Your Number's Up: Scoring 12
    So How Do I Know that I'm a Genius? What Scores Mean 12
    What Do They Want from Me? What Is Tested? 12
    Practice Makes Perfect: Repeating the Test 13

Chapter 2: Succeeding on the ACT 15
    Four Stress-Busters to Help You Survive the ACT 15
        Counting to four 15
        Stretching 15
        Practicing visualization 16
        Thinking positively 16
    Nine Points to Always Double-Check 16
        Exponents 16
        Common-sense connections 16
        Decimal places.. 17
        Operations signs... 17
        Political correctness... 17
        -ing and other beware! words 17
        Context 17
        Grammar.. 17
        Completed answer grid 17
    Ten Dumb Things You Can Do to Mess Up Your ACT 18
        Losing concentration... 18
        Panicking over time.. 18
        Messing up numbering on the answer grid 18

  Rubbernecking..19
  Cheating..19
  Worrying about previous sections..19
  Worrying about the hard problems 19
  Transferring information from problem to problem or section to section 20
  Forgetting to double-check 20
  Looking back and doing "coulda-shoulda" 20

Chapter 3: Reading the Admissions Committee's Mind: What Colleges Want 21

  What's the Number One Thing That Colleges Look For?..............................21
  How Important Is the ACT, Really? 21
  Do Schools Care Whether I Repeat the ACT?..22
  Can I Take the ACT Instead of the SAT I? 22
  If I Mess Up Big-Time on the ACT, What Can I Do to Compensate? 22
  What Classes Do You Recommend That I Take as a Senior? Junior? Sophomore?.........22
  How Helpful Are Charity Work and Sports?..23
  What Should I Say on the College Essay?..23
  What Will They Ask Me in the Interview, and What Should I Say? 23
  How Can I Decide Which School Is Best for Me?..24
  What's the Biggest Mistake Most Students Make in College Planning? 24

Part II: Serving Your "Sentence": English Review and Test 25

Chapter 4: Glamour Grammar: The Five-Star Review 27

  Subject-Verb Agreement...27
  Pronouns 29
  Adjectives and Adverbs 30
  Sentence Structure..31
  Parallelism 32
  Comparisons 32
  Diction 33
    affect/effect 33
    amount/number...33
    anxious/eager..34
    assure/ensure 34
    between/among 34
    complement/compliment 35
    eminent/immanent/imminent 35
    everyday/every day 35
    farther/further 35
    flaunt/flout...36
    founder/flounder 36
    good/well..36
    if/whether..36
    imply/infer...37
    it's/its 37
    less/fewer...37
    lie/lay 37
    phase/faze 38
    prescribe/proscribe 38
    principle/principal 38
    rise/raze/raise 39
    stationary/stationery 39
    who/whom..39

Miscellaneous Mistakes 39
    hardly 39
    hopefully 40
    if . . . would 40
    in regards to . . . in regard to 40
    where . . . that 40

Chapter 5: Misspellers of the World, Untie! Mastering the English Test 41

Seeing Is Believing: The Format of the Test 41
    The passages 41
    The questions 42
    The answer choices 42
Being Boxed In: The Box Questions 42
What Do They Want Outta Me? What the English Usage Questions Test 43
Maximizing the Gain, Minimizing the Pain: Questions Worth Looking For 44
    Looking for short, diction-type questions 44
    Going for pure grammar 44
    Ignoring superfluous info 45
Their Pain, Your Gain: Traps That Others Have Fallen Into 46

Chapter 6: It's Not What You Say, It's How You Say It: English Practice Questions 47

Part III: Writing the Writing Test Rightly: You Have a Choice 53

Chapter 7: ACT Write: The First Words on Essay Writing 55

Rattle Your Writing with Some Loose Screws 55
    Thought diarrhea: Writing before you think 56
    The attack of the clock: Panicking about time 56
    Being too relaxed: Not noticing your time limit 56
    Expressing your inner poet: Using creativity as a crutch 56
    Big words with big consequences: Using words you don't know 56
    Expecting perfection in 30 minutes: Being overcritical of yourself 57
    Speaking another language: Dude, they want to read English 57
    Being a wimp: Not taking a solid stand 57
    You are not an island: Forgetting that people really read this stuff 57
    Do not do not repeat yourself: 'nuff said 58
    Leaving the bathroom with TP on your shoe: Not editing your essay 58
Making the Grade: How the ACT Folks Are Going to Score You 58
Example Essays and Their Scores 58
    1 — 1 is the loneliest number: How not to be a 1 59
    2 — 2 little 2 late: Steer clear of coming in second 59
    3 — Still on the wrong side of the tracks 60
    4 — The grass is greener on this side 60
    5 — Star material: Five-star winners 61
    6 — You unlocked the code: A perfect score 62

Chapter 8: Write Right: The Writing Test Review 65

Keeping It Simple: Making a Judgment 65
Fightin' with Their Words: Incorporating the Question 66
Putting Up Your Dukes: Deciding Your Position and Writing About It 67
Throwing a Good First Punch: The Hook 67

The Proof Is in the Pudding: Proving Yourself..69
    Specific examples..69
    Variety of examples...69
Hamburger Writing: The Organization of the Essay..70
    Top Bun: The introduction...70
    The Three Meats: Example paragraphs...70
    Transitions 71
    The Bottom Bun: Conclusion..71
Wielding the Red Pen: Editing and Proofing...72
    Relax, you've already learned it..72
    Top four editing techniques...72
This Was Not a Prescription: Handwriting..73

Chapter 9: Practicing Promptly with Practice Prompts: Essay Practice Examples 75

Writing Prompt #1..75
Writing Prompt #2..76

Part IV: Don't Count Yourself Out: The Math Review and Mini-Test 77

Chapter 10: Ogling More Figures than a Beauty Pageant Judge: Geometry Review 79

You Gotta Have an Angle..79
Triangle Trauma..82
    Similar figures..84
    Area...85
    Pythagorean theorem..85
    Pythagorean triples...86
Thanks 4 Nothing: Quadrilaterals...87
    Quaint quads: Bizarre quadrilaterals...89
    Leftovers again: Shaded-area problems..89
Missing Parrots and Other Polly-Gones..90
    One interior angle..90
    Volume...91
    Total surface area (TSA)...92
I'm Too Much of a Klutz for Coordinate Geometry..93
Running Around in Circles..94

Chapter 11: Catching Some (X's, Y's, and) Z's: Algebra and Other Sleeping Aids....99

The Powers That Be: Bases and Exponents..99
Keep It in Proportion: Ratios..101
Things Aren't What They Seem: Symbolism...102
Abracadabra: Algebra..105
    Solve for x in an equation..105
    Curses! FOILed again...106
    Fact-or Fiction: Factoring...108
Too Hip to Be Square: Roots and Radicals...108
    Addition and subtraction..109
    Multiplication and division...109
    Inside out...110

Probably Probability..110
    Rule 1: Create a fraction 110
    Rule 2: Multiply consecutive probabilities..111
The Stats Don't Lie: Statistics...111
    Median 112
    Mode 112
    Range 112
Don't Soak Your Head: SOH CAH TOA..113
How to Use All This Junk: Trigonometric Ratios of Angles 115
No Nervous Breakdowns, Please 116

Chapter 12: Reviewing Miscellaneous Math You Probably Already Know 117

DIRTy Math: Time, Rate, and Distance 117
It All Averages Out: Averages 118
    Missing term average problem 119
    Weighted averages 119
Percentage Panic...120
Ready, Sets, Go: Number Sets...122
Prime and Composite Numbers 123
I'm All Mixed Up: Mixture Problems 124
Greed Is Great: Interest Problems 124
All Work and No Play: Work Problems 125
Smooth Operator: Order of Operations 126
Measuring Up: Units of Measurement 126
Broken Hearts, Broken Numbers: Fractions 128
    Adding or subtracting fractions 128
    Multiplying fractions..128
    Dividing fractions 129
    Working with mixed numbers...129

Chapter 13: Numb and Number: Acing the Mathematics Test 131

What You See Is What You Get: The Format and Breakdown...................131
Absence Makes the Heart Grow Fonder: What Isn't on the Mathematics Test.............132
Getting into the Grind: The Approach..133
Time Flies When You're Having Fun: Timing Tips.....................................134
    Skim for your favorite questions 134
    Start in the middle when plugging in the answer choices 134
    Kindly refrain from showing off everything you know 134
    Put aside two minutes to fill in the remaining ovals..........................135
Do's, Don'ts, and Darns: What to Do and Not Do in the Math Test 135
    Do get the lead out 135
    Don't start working until you've read the entire problem 136
    Do reread the problem with your answer inserted 136
    Don't strike out over a difficult question early on 136

Chapter 14: More Fun Than a Root Canal: Mathematics Practice Questions 137

Part V: Time to Read the Riot ACT: The Reading Test 143

Chapter 15: This, Too, Shall Pass(age): Sailing through the Reading Test 145

Facing Forty (Questions): The Reading Test 145
    Timing 146
    Scoring 146
    Reading strategies 146

The ACT For Dummies, 4th Edition

I've Been Meaning to Ask You Something: The Questions..148
    Main idea 148
    Details 148
    Tone, attitude, and inference 148
    Vocabulary in context 149
    Negative or reverse questions 149
Tips and Traps 149

Chapter 16: Where Are CliffsNotes When You Need Them? Reading Practice Questions 151

Passage 1 151
Passage 2 154

Part VI: Proven to Cause Brain Defects in Laboratory Rats: The Science Reasoning Test 157

Chapter 17: Frankenstein to Einstein: Excelling on the Science Reasoning Test 159

I'm Mad, but I'm No Scientist: What Do I Need to Know? 159
Too Graphic for Words: The Format 159
Chalk Talk: Developing a Game Plan 160
The Android's Favorite: Data Representation 160
    After the game plan: Executing the play 161
    Going for pay dirt: The "data-analysis" question 162
That's It in a Nutshell: Research Summaries 163
    Purpose 163
    Experimental design 163
    Just tell me what you want: Question styles 164
Warring Factions: Conflicting Viewpoints 165
Asking for Trouble: Question Styles 166
Parting Is Such Sweet Sorrow: The Conclusion 167

Chapter 18: Faking Atomic Ache Won't Get You Out of This: Science Practice Questions 169

Passage 169
Initial Analysis 171

Part VII: I'd Rather Wait for the Movie: Full-Length Practice ACTs 179

Chapter 19: How to Ruin a Perfectly Good Day, Part I: Practice Exam 1 181

Answer Sheet 182
English Test 185
Mathematics Test 195
Reading Test 203
Science Reasoning Test 211
Getting Down to the Nitty-Gritty: Subscores 223
Score One for Our Side: The Scoring Key 223
Answer Key 225

Chapter 20: Practice Exam 1: Answers and Explanations 227
- English Test 227
- Mathematics Test 235
- Reading Test 248
- Science Reasoning 254

Chapter 21: How to Ruin a Perfectly Good Day, Part II: Practice Exam 2 265
- Answer Sheet 266
- English Test 269
- Mathematics Test 280
- Reading Test 288
- Science Reasoning Test 296
- Getting Down to the Nitty-Gritty: Subscores 307
- Score One for Our Side: The Scoring Key 307
- Answer Key 309

Chapter 22: Practice Exam 2: Answers and Explanations 311
- English Test 311
- Mathematics Test 320
- Reading Test 332
- Science Reasoning Test 338

Part VIII: The Part of Tens 351

Chapter 23: Ten Wrong Rumors About the ACT 353
- You Can't Study for the ACT 353
- Different States Have Different ACTs 353
- The ACT Has a Passing Score 354
- The ACT Tests IQ 354
- If You Don't Know the Answer, Choose A or F 354
- You Should Never Guess 354
- The ACT Is Easier than the SAT I 354
- The ACT Is the Same as the Achievement Test 355
- You Have to Write an Essay 355
- You Can't Take Both the SAT I and the ACT 355

Chapter 24: Ten Differences between the ACT and the SAT 357
- The ACT Emphasizes English Grammar; The SAT I Emphasizes Vocabulary 357
- The ACT Has an Optional Essay Question; The SAT I Has a Required Essay Section 357
- The ACT Questions Are All Multiple-Choice; SAT I Math Questions Aren't 357
- The ACT Tests Science Reasoning; The SAT I Doesn't 358
- The ACT Doesn't Penalize You for Guessing; The SAT I Does 358
- The ACT Has Five Long Sections; The SAT I Has Ten Short Sections 358
- The ACT Has No Experimental Sections; The SAT I Has One 358

Index 359

Introduction

Welcome to *The ACT For Dummies,* 4th Edition. This is a nondiscriminatory, equal-opportunity book. You're welcome to participate whether you are a genius or (like us) you need a recipe to make ice. Besides, the title is not a slam at you. You're not the dummy; the test is (and we've heard it called worse, believe us — especially the Friday night before the exam).

About This Book

The goal of this book is to show you exactly how to survive this ridiculous situation. No matter how excellent your high school teachers are (or were), they prepared you for the Real World, a world that, alas, has very little connection to the ACT. High school teachers can give you a good foundation in grammar, reading, science, and math skills (the areas tested on the ACT), but think of them as the friendly old GPs, the general practitioners whose job is to keep you well or handle the little day-to-day problems. What do you do when you have a crisis that's making you really sick, like the ACT? We like to think of *The ACT For Dummies,* 4th Edition, as a loony but gifted specialist you can call in when the situation is desperate.

No one wants to deal with the eccentric specialist for too terribly long. The goal of this book, just like the goal of the expert, is to come in with the Code Blue crash cart, deal with the situation, and then leave rapidly with as few lives destroyed as possible. This book has one goal: to prepare you for the ACT — period. It is not our heart's desire to teach you every grammar rule ever created or every math formula Einstein knew. No extra "filler" material is included in this book to make it look fat and impressive on bookstore shelves. If you want a thick book to use as a booster seat for the vertically challenged, go find *War and Peace.* If you're looking for something that you can use to prepare you for the ACT as quickly and painlessly as possible, again we say to you, welcome to *The ACT For Dummies,* 4th Edition.

You Can Run, but You Can't Hide

There is no escaping the ACT. Many colleges require you to take this entrance exam before they will even look at your application. Some colleges will accept scores from either the ACT or the SAT. (It just so happens that Wiley publishes an *SAT I For Dummies* book as well, should you choose to take that exam.) Many students decide to take both tests to see which one they do better on. Is that a good idea? Absolutely. If you have the option of taking either the ACT or the SAT, take both.

Many colleges emphasize ACT scores to compensate for grade inflation. That is, some high schools may give you an A for doing the same level work that would gain you a C in other high schools. It's certainly not fair that a person at an "easy" high school has a 4.0 while a student at a more demanding high school has a 3.0 for doing the same work. Because the ACT is the same for everyone (students nationwide take the exact same exam), colleges can use the scores to get inside your head and see what's really there. Think of this as an opportunity, not a crisis: A good ACT score can overcome a low GPA. In just a few hours one fine Saturday morning, you can make up a little for years of messing up in school.

In *The ACT For Dummies,* 4th Edition, you find out which types of questions are on the exam, which questions to work on carefully, and which to guess at quickly (good news: The ACT has no penalty for wrong answers; you should guess at absolutely every question you don't know), the approach to each type of question, and, perhaps most important, some traps that are built into each question style. We have been test-prep tutors for many years and have developed a list of the "gotchas" that have trapped thousands of students over the years. Let us see whether we can make them trap you, as well.

This book is also full of the substantive information that you need to know, including grammar rules and geometry, algebra, and arithmetic formulas. Naturally, we include some truly sick humor, on the principle that, as you're groaning at our jokes, you won't notice that you're suffering from the questions. (Hey, as the mushroom said to his friends, "Of course, everyone likes me. I'm a fun-gi!")

Note to nontraditional students: The days of high school may be just a fading memory for you (along with your thin waistline and full head of hair). We recognize that not everyone taking the ACT is a high school junior or senior. Maybe you took a few years off to build your career or to nurture a family (or to pay your debt to society) and are now having to go back and review what you thought you had left behind years ago. As the Walrus said, "I weep with you; I deeply sympathize." It can be totally frustrating to have to deal with the subjunctive or pluperfect or quadratic equations all over again. Postpone your nervous breakdown. Things aren't as dismal as they look. You'll probably be surprised how quickly material comes back to you as you go through this book. If you need more hands-on instruction such as private tutoring, call a high school or community college. Someone there will almost certainly be able to recommend a low-cost course or a tutor. The local library can also give you some help.

How This Book Is Organized

The ACT For Dummies, 4th Edition, is organized into seven parts to help you quickly get right to the chapters you need.

Part 1: Coming to Terms with Reality: An Overview of the ACT

Part I is an overview of the exam, explaining what it tests, how the scoring works, and so on. You also get some tips on how to do well on the test, plus an overview of what colleges want from you.

Part II: Serving Your "Sentence": English Review and Test

Part II introduces the English portion of the ACT, explaining the format of the questions, suggesting how best to prepare for the test, and presenting a grammar review that refreshes your memory on all the piddling little points you once knew but have long forgotten.

Part III: Writing the Writing Test Rightly: You Have a Choice

Okay, so you really don't have to take the ACT writing test. However, considering that many colleges and universities require the writing ACT, we recommend you study the chapters in this section very carefully and plan to do some writing!

Part IV: Don't Count Yourself Out: The Math Review and Mini-Test

The Math materials show you strategies for doing well on this portion of the exam. As a "gift with purchase," you also get three math reviews: geometry, algebra, and miscellaneous math.

Part V: Time to Read the Riot ACT: The Reading Test

Sure you can read, but can you read fast enough to get through all the reading passages and answer all the questions? This part gives you strategies for doing so, saving you time and brain cells.

Part VI: Proven to Cause Brain Defects in Laboratory Rats: The Science Reasoning Test

This part introduces you to a test unique to the ACT: Science Reasoning. Here, you find out how to analyze the various types of science passages and graphs, plus get techniques for doing your best on each type. You also find tips to help you recognize your own strengths and weaknesses and make the best use of your time.

Part VII: I'd Rather Wait for the Movie: Full-Length Practice ACTs

This is the part you've either been waiting for or dreading. Here, you find two full-length ACTs that look similar to the real deal. Although these questions are not identical to what you'll see on the ACT, they're close enough for good practice.

Part VIII: The Part of Tens

Assuming you've survived all that excitement, the book finishes up with the good stuff, The Parts of Tens. These are lists of ten points (sometimes nine, sometimes eleven — no one wants to be too stuffy) to remember. There's much good stuff in this part, and it's also a lot of fun to read.

Icons Used in This Book

Some information in this book is really, really important. We flag it by using an icon (and if Icon, hey, anyone con . . .). For example, if we know of a particular trap that most students fall for, I put a Traps & Tricks icon next to the explanation. If we have some time-saving tips, an icon goes next to them, as well. Here are the examples of the icons:

Burn this stuff into your brain or carve it into your heart; it's the really important material. If you skip or ignore the Heads Up icons, you won't get your money's worth out of this book.

These are the "gotchas" that can kill you before you know that you're dead. Pay special attention to the cheesy notes marked with this mousetrap.

Follow the arrow to score a bull's-eye by using these shortcut tips.

This icon marks sample problems.

This icon points out information pertaining to international students — which questions are worth doing and which ones are "guess and go on."

This little ragged edge shows up on chapter pages containing practice tests and questions. Keep an eye out for it if you want to find those practice sessions quickly!

Where to Go from Here

You've probably heard the joke about the student who was debating over whether to buy a book at the bookstore. The sales clerk, eager to make his commission, proclaims, "Buy this book — it'll do half the work for you!" The student brightens up and exclaims, "Great! I'll take two!"

As much as we wish we could simply transfer test-taking material into your brain in one dump, we realize that learning it takes effort on your part. Meet us halfway. We've done our job by showing you what and how to learn; now it's your turn. We suggest two ways to use this book:

- First, fine-tune your skills. Maybe you're already a math whiz and just need help with the English grammar. Go right to the English portion. Maybe you're a grammar guru who wouldn't know a nonagon if you met one in a dark alley. The math review is for you.

- Second, start from scratch. Lock yourself into your room, lay in a sack of food and some sharpened pencils, and go through this book word for word. Don't worry; it's not

Introduction

as bad as it seems. Actually, starting from scratch is the preferred method. Many students make what we call the "mediocre mistake": They are good at one section, mediocre at a second, and dismal at the third. They spend all their time in their worst section and barely look at the sections that they're mediocre or good in. Big mistake! If you spend two hours studying something that's totally incomprehensible to you, you may improve your score a few points. If you spend two hours studying your mediocre material, you may improve your score by ten or twelve points. Ten points that you gain in your mediocre section are just as valuable — and a heck of a lot easier to gain — than ten points you gain in your weakest section. Humor us and read the book from cover to cover. You'll pick up some great material . . . and a few new jokes along the way.

Making a Commitment

In the real world, you have classes, family obligations, sports practices, and, if you're lucky, a social life. How on earth are you going to fit studying for the ACT into your schedule? The answer is that you have to commit to this project and make it a priority. How many hours exactly should you carve out of your schedule? Here is what we suggest.

This book features two full-length ACTs. Each ACT takes 2 hours and 55 minutes, not including breaks. You may take about an hour to review your errors on each exam. (Not that you'll make that many mistakes, but we'd like you to review the answer explanations to every question, not just to the ones you miss. Doing so provides you with yet another opportunity to see shortcuts you may not have noticed or traps you luckily avoided.)

Basically, therefore, each exam should take you 4½ hours, for a total of 9 hours. In addition, this book has five general parts (English, writing, math, reading, and science), each of which should take you about an hour. At the end of each part is a short practice exam requiring about 30 minutes to take and review. Therefore, each of these chapters is an hour and a half, for a total of 7½ hours.

This book features a very important grammar review that we strongly suggest you spend at least 2 hours on. Even if you are good at grammar, this section features all sorts of persnickety grammar rules, just the type that (with your luck) you'd get caught on during the ACT. And finally, the book features three math reviews: geometry, algebra, and arithmetic, each of which should take you about an hour. Here's the final timetable:

Activity	Time
Five Parts and sets of practice questions at 1½ hours per part/set	7½ hours
Two practice exams at 4½ hours per exam	9 hours
Three math review chapters at 1 hour per chapter	3 hours
One grammar review chapter at 2 hours	2 hours
Time spent groaning in pain at authors' lame jokes	10 minutes
Time spent firing off letter complaining about authors' lame jokes	10 minutes (or sending us your better ones!)
TOTAL TIME	21 hours, 50 minutes

Fear not: You don't have to do all 21 hours and 50 minutes at once. The book is designed so that you can start at any unit at any time. You don't have to have finished the general math chapter, for example, before you go through the general reading chapter.

Okay, are you ready? Are you quivering with anticipation, living for the moment when you can pick up your yellow No. 2 pencil and head for the thrills of a lifetime? (Or are you thinking, "These authors got to get a life!"?) Listen, you're going to take the ACT anyway, so you may as well have a good time learning how to do so. Laughing while learning is the whole purpose of this book. Take a deep breath, rev up the brain cells, and go for it! Good luck. Just remember that for you, ACT can come to stand for Ace Conquers Test!

Part I
Coming to Terms with Reality: An Overview of the ACT

The 5th Wave   By Rich Tennant

"THEY'RE MOVING ON TO THE READING COMPREHENSION QUESTIONS. THAT SHOULD DAZE AND CONFUSE THEM ENOUGH FOR US TO FINISH CHANGING THE TIRE AND GET THE HECK OUT OF HERE."

In this part...

The reality is that you have to take the ACT. Reality bites. But by knowing what the ACT looks like and what you can expect, you may be able to bite back. Although you are undoubtedly eager to get right to studying for the ACT (Hello, what planet am *I* from?), please take a few minutes to go through this introductory material. Think of the ACT as a blind date: Knowing a little bit about what you'll encounter can lower your anxiety level at least a smidgen.

In addition, this part features a chapter that gives you vital info about how to beat stress, avoid careless mistakes, and recognize common ways you may mess up their scores. Saving the best for last, this part also has an interview with an independent college counselor who presents answers to the question, "What do the colleges want from me?"

Chapter 1

Getting Your ACT Together: The Format

In This Chapter
▶ Packing your bags: What to take to the ACT
▶ Avoiding dead weight: What not to take to the test
▶ Dealing with unusual circumstances: What to do if you're someone special
▶ Chancing it with sophisticated scoring: What's that about dumb-luck guessing?
▶ Looking right before your eyes: What's on the ACT
▶ Examining the strange but true: Horrible (but hilarious) tales of the ACT

Are you the type who jumps in the cold water all at once instead of just dipping your toe in a little at a time? If so, do we have a table for you! Table 1-1 gives you an overview of the ACT and shocks you with the entire kit and caboodle all at once.

Table 1-1	ACT Breakdown by Section	
Test	*Number of Questions*	*Time Allotted*
English	75	45 minutes
Mathematics	60	60 minutes
Reading	40	35 minutes
Science Reasoning	40	35 minutes
Optional Writing	1	30 minutes

If you add up the numbers, you find that you have 216 questions to answer in 205 minutes; 205 minutes is 3 hours and 25 minutes, or nearly 3½ hours. You get one ten-minute break between tests two and three (the Mathematics and the Reading tests). If you opt to not take the optional writing test, then you get to happily walk out right after the Science test. If you include the time in the classroom spent giving out the tests, explaining the directions, checking your ID, and so on, your whole morning is shot. You may as well figure on giving up 4 to 4½ hours for this test.

I'd Forget My Head If It Wasn't Attached: What to Take to the ACT

If you can't borrow the brain of that whiz kid in your calculus class, you're stuck using your own. In addition, be sure that you have the following with you:

- **Admission ticket:** By about two weeks before the exam, you should have received your ticket in the mail. If you don't have the ticket by then or if you got it but lost it, call the ACT at 319-337-1270.

- **Pencils:** Take a bunch of sharpened No. 2 pencils with you. You may also want to take a big eraser (nothing personal, everyone makes mistakes) and a small pencil sharpener.

- **Map or directions:** Go to the test center a few days before the actual exam, and scope out your driving route and parking area. Often, the ACT is given at colleges that have parking lots far, far from the test rooms. Drive to the college a few days in advance, park your car, and see just how long it takes you to get to the room. You don't need the stress of having to run to the test room at the last minute.

- **Clothing:** Rumor has it some weird kids are lobbying for a special Nude ACT. Until it becomes available, you need to have some sort of external covering. Take a few extra layers. The heat often is turned off for the weekend in many classrooms (the ACT is usually offered on a Saturday), and the room can be freezing cold. Alternately, in the summer, schools turn off the air conditioning, making the room boiling hot. Dress in layers and be prepared for anything.

- **Photo ID:** Showing the birthmark your boyfriend thinks is so cute isn't going to cut it with the proctor. You need to bring a photo ID (student ID, driver's license, passport, military ID, FBI Most Wanted mug shot, whatever). If you don't have a photo ID, you can bring a letter of identification from your school. (The ACT registration booklet goes into detail about what this letter entails; we won't bore you with that information here.)

- **Eyeglasses:** Students frequently forget their reading glasses at home and then squint for the next four hours. The ACT itself is enough of a headache; you don't need eyestrain, as well. And if you wear contacts, be sure to bring cleaning/wetting solution in case you have to take the lenses out and reinsert them. (Hey, all those tears can really mess up your lenses!)

- **A snack:** True, your break is only ten minutes between tests two and three, but that's enough time to gobble down something to jump-start your brain. We often suggest taking an energy bar or some peanuts, something with protein and carbohydrates. Scarfing down a candy bar is actually counterproductive; your sugar levels rise only momentarily and then drop down below where they were before you had your chocolate fix.

- **A watch:** If your watch has an alarm, turn it off so that you don't disturb the other students. If you don't know how to do so, borrow another watch. The proctor will take a beeping watch away from you.

- **A calculator:** ACT gurus finally joined the 20th century and agreed to allow students to use calculators. Although the ACT information bulletin has an entire quarter page detailing which calculators can and cannot be used, for all practical purposes, you can use any calculator (yes, even a graphing calculator) as long as it doesn't make a noise. You may not use a laptop computer (don't laugh; you'd be surprised by how many of my students want to bring one to the test!) or a pocket organizer.

What Not to Take to the ACT

Believe it or not, you shouldn't take some things to the test, such as the following:

- **Books and notes:** Last-minute studying won't do you much good. Forget the books; you won't be allowed to take them into the test room with you. (Just be sure to tell this to your parents. We once had a student whose mother drove all the way to the test center with her daughter's ACT prep book, thinking the girl needed it for the test. The mom actually pulled the girl out of the test to give her the book, resulting in the girl's nearly being disqualified from continuing.)

> ### The watch game: Using your watch to simplify the test
>
> Here's the deal. The proctor — whom you're pretty sure you saw on *America's Most Wanted* last week — tells you at 8:47 that you may begin a 45-minute section. You have 75 questions. The time is now 9:29, and you're on question 30. How are you doing for time? Can you relax and slow down, or are you entering Panic City?
>
> Who needs this kind of stress? It's like adding on another whole math problem. Don't strain your brain; make life easier by resetting your watch. What's your lucky number? Three? When the proctor tells you to begin, set your watch for 2:15. That way, you're counting down the minutes to your lucky number. A glance at your watch tells you how many minutes you have left. Who cares what the time is outside in the real world? You can use your watch as a stopwatch for the exam, not as a timepiece.

- **Scratch paper:** You may not bring your own scratch paper, and no scratch paper will be given to you during the exam. Fortunately, the exam booklet has plenty of blank space on which you may do your calculations.

Normal Is Boring: Unusual Circumstances

Not everyone takes the ACT under the same conditions. You may have a special circumstance that can allow you to change the date of the ACT or the way you take your exam. Here is a brief list of special circumstances and how they affect your ACT.

- **Learning disabilities:** If you have a diagnosed learning disability, you may be able to get special accommodations. You may have extended time, but you must specifically request this on your application form. Please note that in order to get special testing, you must have been diagnosed LD professionally and must have a current, individualized plan at school. Talk to your counselor for further information.

- **Physical disabilities:** If you have a physical disability, you may be allowed to take a test in a special format — in Braille, large print, or on audiocassette. If your disability is physical, do not complete a registration folder; write to the ACT Universal Testing and receive a form called "Request for ACT Assessment: Special Testing." This booklet explains your options.

- **Religious obligations:** If your religion prohibits you from taking a test on a Saturday, you may test on an alternate date. The ACT registration bulletin specifies dates and locations in each state.

- **Military duty:** If you're an active military person, you don't complete the normal registration form. Instead, ask your Educational Services Officer about testing through DANTES (Defense Activity for Nontraditional Educational Support).

Anything's Better than Nothing: Guessing for Points

Scoring on the ACT is very straightforward:

- You get one point for every answer you get right.
- You get zero points for every answer you omit.
- You get zero points for every wrong answer.

Part I: Coming to Terms with Reality: An Overview of the ACT

> The ACT is absolutely wonderful in that it does not penalize you for wrong answers. (The SAT subtracts a fraction of a point for every question you miss. The ACT does not.) Therefore, guessing on the ACT obviously works to your advantage. Never leave anything blank. We suggest that you save a couple of minutes at the end of each section just to go through the test and make sure that you've filled in an answer for every single question.

Your Number's Up: Scoring

We once had a frustrated student tell us that the scores on the ACT looked like measurements to him: 34, 29, 36. However, the ACT has four scores, which makes for a very strange set of measurements! The ACT scores are nothing like high school scores based on percentages. They are not even like the more familiar SAT scores that range from 200 to 800. The ACT scores are as follows:

- Each test (English, Mathematics, Reading, and Science Reasoning) goes from 1 (low) to 36 (high). The Writing scores go from 1 (low) to 6 (high).
- You also have a composite score, which is the average of the four test scores.
- Three of the tests have subscores. The subscores in English, Mathematics, and Reading range from 1 to 18. Don't assume that the subscores determine the total score. That would be too easy and too logical. The subscores are determined independently and do not necessarily add up to the total score in a section.
- A percentile score tells you where you rank in your state and nationwide.

So How Do I Know that I'm a Genius? What Scores Mean

Look at the percentiles. Just knowing you got a 26 doesn't tell you much. You need to know whether a 26 is a 50th percentile, a 75th percentile, or a 99th percentile. If you got a 36, be prepared to be accepted at any college nationwide!

What Do They Want from Me? What Is Tested?

The following subjects are tested on the ACT:

- **English:** The ACT tests English grammar. You are expected to know the fundamentals of usage, diction, and rhetorical skills. For example, you must understand sentence construction — what makes a run-on and what makes a fragment. You need to know how to distinguish between commonly confused words, like *affect* and *effect* or *principal* and *principle*. You must be able to use the proper forms of words, distinguishing between an adjective and an adverb. If you don't have a strong grammar background (you probably have been studying literature for the past few years and haven't had grammar since about the seventh grade), don't panic. This book features a gruesomely exhaustive grammar review with just about everything you'll need to know.

  Surprisingly, the ACT English Test is one of the strongest portions of this exam for international students. You learned all these picky grammar points as you learned English. You may be much more comfortable with the rules than native English speakers are.

- **Mathematics:** The ACT requires basic skills in arithmetic, geometry, and algebra. If you have had two semesters of algebra, two semesters of geometry, and a general math background, you can answer probably 90 percent of the questions. Unfortunately, the ACT also tests a little bit of trigonometry. If you have not had trigonometry, don't worry. This book gives you the few things you need to know. In addition, the test has only a few trig questions (usually just four), and they are often so close to the end that many students don't even get to them anyway. Trig should be the least of your worries.

   You don't have to know calculus. The ACT has no calculus questions. Happy day!

 - **Reading:** You are expected to be able to read a passage in a relatively short amount of time and answer questions based upon it. Your reading skills are probably pretty set by now. If you are 17, you are not going to change the way you've been reading for the past 12 years. However, this fact does not mean you cannot improve your reading *score*. Chapter 12 shows you tricks that you can use to improve your speed and tells you how to recognize and avoid traps built into the questions.

 - **Science Reasoning:** You are not required to have any specific science background. The passages may test chemistry, biology, botany, physics, or any other science, but you do not have to have had those courses. The test gives all the information you need to answer the science questions in the passages or in diagrams, charts, and tables.

 - **Optional Writing Test:** You are not required to take this test, but we suggest that you do. The ACT folks added this section to test your writing ability (an extremely important component for college success). Don't worry, you've been writing for years. And the ACT people know that you can't possibly write a perfect essay in a measly 30 minutes. What they will be focusing on is your thesis, your organization, and your ability to support your thoughts.

Practice Makes Perfect: Repeating the Test

Are you allowed to repeat the ACT? Yes. Should you repeat the ACT? Probably. Decide whether to repeat the ACT based on your answers to the following questions:

 - **What errors did I make the first time around?** If your mistakes were from a lack of knowledge, that is, you just plain didn't know a grammar rule or a math formula, you can easily correct those mistakes with studying. However, if you made mistakes because you were careless or if you daydreamed during the exam, that may be a personality quirk that you're not going to change. Very few people who are careless test-takers change their test style overnight.

 - **Why do I want to repeat the test?** Is your ego destroyed because your best friend got a better score than you did? That is probably not a good enough reason to retake the ACT. Do retake the exam if you are trying to get a minimum qualifying score to enable you to get into a college or into a scholarship program.

 - **Can I go through this all over again?** How seriously did you take studying the first time around? If you gave it all you had, you may be too burned out to go through that again. On the other hand, if you just zoomed through the booklet and didn't spend much time preparing for the test, you have a second chance to show your stuff.

 - **Were the mistakes caused by factors that were not my fault?** Maybe you were in a fender-bender on your way to the exam, or perhaps you stayed up late the night before in an argument with your parents or your boyfriend or girlfriend. If you just weren't up to par when you took the exam, definitely take it again, and this time be sure to get a good night's sleep the night before.

Chapter 2

Succeeding on the ACT

In This Chapter
▶ Mellowing, chilling, and relaxing before and during the ACT
▶ Giving careless mistakes the raspberry by knowing ten critical points to double-check
▶ Identifying and sidestepping ten easy ways to mess up your score

On the wall of my office, we have a padded cushion that is imprinted with the words, "BANG HEAD HERE!" We've found that most of our students use it either to reduce stress (we guess one headache can replace another!) or — much more commonly — to express their exasperation over unnecessary, careless (we're trying not to say it, but okay — dumb!) mistakes. Going through the material in this chapter about how to relax and how to recognize and avoid common mistakes can prevent your having to be a head-banger later.

Four Stress-Busters to Help You Survive the ACT

Most people are tense before a test, with butterflies dancing in their stomachs. The key is to use relaxation techniques that keep your mind on your test and not on your tummy.

Counting to four

Breathing is grossly underrated. Breathing is good. Take a deep breath until your belly expands, hold it for four counts, and then expel the air for four counts. Try not to take short, shallow breaths, which can cause you to become even more anxious, because your body is deprived of oxygen.

Stretching

Rotate your head around to stretch out and relax your neck muscles. (We suggest keeping your eyes closed while doing this so the proctor doesn't think that you're trying to cheat.) Hunch and roll your shoulders to help relax your back and spine. You'll be sitting for more than three hours, so maintaining good posture is crucial. Shake out your hands like you have a writer's cramp. Imagine that all your tension and stress is going out through your fingertips. Extend and push out your legs like you're pushing something away with your heels. Point your toes back toward your knees and hold that position for a count of three.

Practicing visualization

Don't do this during the test; you just waste time and lose concentration. However, before the exam or during the break, practice visualization. Close your eyes and imagine yourself in the test room cheerfully looking at questions that you know the answers to, filling in the bubble grids to the right answers, finishing early, and double-checking your work. Picture yourself leaving the exam room all uplifted, and then five weeks later, getting your scores and rejoicing. Think of how proud of you your parents are. Imagine getting an acceptance letter from the college of your dreams. Picture yourself driving a fire-engine-red Ferrari ten years from now, telling the *Time* magazine reporter in the passenger seat that your success started with your excellent ACT scores. The goal is to associate the ACT with good feelings.

Thinking positively

Any time you feel yourself starting to panic or thinking negative thoughts, make a conscious effort to say to yourself, "Stop! Don't dwell on anything negative." And then switch over to a positive track. Suppose that you catch yourself thinking, "Why didn't I study this math more? I saw that formula a hundred times but can't remember it now!" Change the script to, "I got most of this math right; if I leave my subconscious to work on that formula, maybe I'll get it, too. No sense worrying now. Overall, I think I'm doing great!"

Nine Points to Always Double-Check

One father's favorite thing to say before his child takes a test is, "Always double-check! If your mother and I had double-checked before we left the hospital with you, we might have brought home a normal child . . . ."

Mental and emotional child abuse aside, that dad has a point. Double-checking is integral to getting what you want. The test-makers know what types of careless mistakes students make, so they build those mistakes into the test. This section shares some of the most common areas in which test-takers get sloppy.

Exponents

Make sure that as you multiplied like bases, you added the exponents ($x^5 \times x^5 = x^{10}$), and that as you divided like bases, you subtracted the exponents ($x^9 \div x^3 = x^6$). Forgetting this and just multiplying ($x^5 \times x^5 = x^{25}$) or dividing ($x^9 \div x^3 = x^3$) instead of adding or subtracting is all too easy to do.

Common-sense connections

Think about what a math question is asking. If you are asked to find the weight of a child, and your answer is 400 pounds, something went haywire somewhere. If McCaela is bicycling, and you deduce that she bikes at a rate of 220 mph, sign that woman up for the Olympics!

Decimal places

If a question has two or more answers with the same digits, you know that the decimal point is being tested. If the choices are .05, 0.5, 5, 50, and 500, double-check that your decimal point is in the right place.

Operations signs

Double-check all operations signs (+, –, ÷, and ×) when you move from one side of the equal sign to the other side.

Political correctness

The grammar and reading portions of the ACT contain very few correct, negative-sounding answers. If a passage talks about people, especially those in a minority group, it never says nasty things about them. The entire ACT is sweetness and light; if your answer is petty and mean-spirited, it is probably wrong.

-ing and other beware! words

Always double-check the words that give you trouble: *lie* or *lay* and *affect* or *effect,* for example (see Chapter 4). Pay close attention to the *-ing* words as well.

Context

When you're taking the English and Reading tests, read a few sentences before and after the sentence you're working on. You won't get tripped up by an answer choice that seems correct in the sentence but isn't because of text that precedes or follows the sentence.

Grammar

To double-check your work, insert your answer into the sentence and read it again. Does your answer still make sense?

Completed answer grid

If you've read through this book, you've seen the following information a gazillion times, but it bears repeating: *Wrong answers on the ACT are not penalized.* You lose no points for a mistake. Therefore, it behooves you to answer every question, even if you have to make wild guesses to do so. When you see that you have only a minute or two left, fill in an answer for every question left in the test. You may pick up several points for lucky guesses.

Ten Dumb Things You Can Do to Mess Up Your ACT

Throughout this book, you discover techniques for doing your best on the ACT. We're sorry to say, however, that there are just as many techniques for messing up big-time on this test. Take a few minutes to read through them now to see what dumb things people do to blow the exam totally. By being aware of these catastrophes, you may prevent them from happening to you.

And no — no booby prize is awarded to the student who makes the greatest number of these mistakes.

Losing concentration

When you're in the middle of an excruciatingly boring reading passage, the worst thing you can do is to let your mind drift off to a more pleasant time (last night's date, last weekend's soccer game, the time that you stole your rival school's mascot and set it on the john in the principal's private bathroom). Although visualization (picturing yourself doing something relaxing or fun) is a good stress-reduction technique, it stinks when it comes to helping your ACT score. Even if you have to pinch yourself to keep from falling asleep or flaking out, stay focused. The ACT is less than five hours of your life. You've probably had horrible blind dates that lasted longer than that, and you managed to survive them. This, too, shall pass.

Panicking over time

Every section on the ACT begins with directions and a line that tells exactly how many questions are in the section and, therefore, how many minutes you have per question. It isn't as if this is some big mystery. You can waste a lot of time and drive yourself crazy if you keep flipping pages ahead, counting up how many more questions you have to do. You can do what you can do; that's all. Looking ahead and panicking only wastes time and is counterproductive.

Messing up numbering on the answer grid

Suppose that you decide to postpone doing question number 11, hoping that inspiration will strike. But now you accidentally put the answer to question 12 in the blank for question 11 . . . and mess up all the numbers from that point on. After you answer question 30 and suddenly realize that you just filled in bubble number 29 and have one bubble left — *aaargh!* Stroke City! It's easy for me to say, "Don't panic," but chances are that your blood pressure will go sky-high, especially when you eyeball the clock and see that only one minute remains.

If you have a good eraser with you (which is one of the things I suggested in Chapter 1 that you bring with you), the wrong answers on the answer grid should take only a few seconds to erase. But how on earth are you going to resolve all those problems and reread and reanswer all the questions? You're not; you're going to thank your lucky stars that you bought this book and took the following advice: When you choose an answer, *circle that answer in your test booklet first* and *then* fill in the answer on the answer grid. Doing so takes you a mere nanosecond and helps you not only in this panic situation, but also as you go back and double-check your work.

Throughout this book, we remind you that random guesses can't hurt you on the ACT because there is no penalty for wrong answers. Never leave a bubble blank. Make a random guess. Fill in the bubble; then put an arrow in the margin of the test booklet (*not* on the answer grid) to remind yourself to review that question. Because you have all the bubbles filled in, you won't make a numbering error like we described earlier in this section.

Rubbernecking

Rubbernecking is craning your neck around to see how everyone else is doing. Forget those bozos. You have too much to do on your own to waste precious seconds checking out anyone else. You don't want to psych yourself out by noticing that the guy in front of you is done with his section and is leaning back whistling while you're still sweating away. Maybe the guy in front of you is a complete moron and didn't notice that the booklet has yet another page of problems — so he did only half the section. After the exam booklet is put in front of you, don't look at anything but it and your watch until time is called.

Try not to sit by the clock in the classroom. Because everyone looks at the clock constantly, you may become self-conscious, thinking that you're being checked out. People staring at you every few seconds can be quite distracting. You need to keep your mind entirely on what you're doing, instead of continually looking up and catching someone's eye.

Cheating

Dumb, dumb, *dumb!* Cheating on the ACT is a loser's game — it's just plain stupid. Apart from the legal, moral, and ethical questions, let's talk practicality: You can't predict what types of grammatical mistakes will show up in the questions; what are you going to do, copy a textbook on the palm of your hand? All the math formulas that you need can't fit onto the bottom of your shoe. Copying everything that you *think* you may need would take more time than just learning it. Besides, the ACT tests critical reasoning skills, not just rote memorization. The test never asks a question as straightforward as, "How many degrees in a triangle?" The questions require thinking and reasoning, not just copying down a formula. Short of having a brain transplant, cheating is impractical.

Worrying about previous sections

Think of the ACT as five separate lifetimes. You are reborn four times and so get four more chances to "do it right." Every time the proctor says, "Your time is up. Please turn to the next test and begin," you get a fresh start. The ACT rules are very strict: You cannot go back to a previous section and finish work there or change some of your answers. If you try to do so, the proctor will catch you, and you'll be in a world of hurt. But suppose that you're too ethical even to consider going back to earlier material. There's still the problem of *worrying* about the previous test. If you're now working on math, you shouldn't be wracking your brain trying desperately to remember what that frustrating, it's-on-the-tip-of-my-tongue grammar rule was. Forget one test as soon as you enter the next. Think of it as you would think of a new boyfriend or girlfriend in your life: out with the old, in with the new.

Worrying about the hard problems

The ACT contains some incredibly hard problems and questions. Forget about 'em. Almost no one gets them right, anyway. A ridiculously few total 36's are scored every year, and if you get into the 30s, you're in a superelite club of only a few percent of the thousands and thousands of students who take the ACT annually. Just accept the fact that you either won't get to or can't answer a few of the hard questions and learn to live with your imperfection. If you do go fast enough to get to the hard questions, don't waste too much time on them. Scan them; if you can't think of how to begin, choose an answer at random. Then go back and double-check your easy questions. Keep reminding yourself that every question counts the same in a section, whether that question is a simple 1 + 1 = 2 or some deadly word problem that may as well be written in Lithuanian.

Transferring information from problem to problem or section to section

Each question exists in its own little world. If $x = 17$ in question number 15, it does not necessarily equal that in question number 16 (unless a note says something like, "Questions 15 and 16 refer to the following information"). Now that sounds incredibly simplistic, but it's surprising how many people transfer information from problem to problem. This practice is especially prevalent in dealing with symbolism questions. If you learn in a symbolism question that △ = 25, it is highly unlikely that it will be equal to 25 in another triangle problem.

Forgetting to double-check

If you finish a test early, go back and double-check the *easy* and *medium* questions. Don't spend more time trying to do the hard questions. If a question was too hard for you five minutes ago, it's probably still too hard for you. Your brain capacity probably hasn't doubled in the last few minutes. If you made a totally careless or dumb mistake on an easy question, however, going back over the problem gives you a chance to catch and correct your error. You're more likely to gain points by double-checking easy questions than by staring open-mouthed at the hard ones. **Remember:** Every question counts the same. A point you save by catching a careless mistake is just as valuable as a point you earn, grunting and sweating, by solving a mondo-hard problem.

Looking back and doing "coulda-shoulda"

Don't discuss the questions with your friends in the bathroom during break. They don't really know any more than you do. Your friends may all tell you that they got answer A for question five — but maybe answer A was the trap answer and they all fell for it. If you get depressed because you chose answer B, you're only hurting yourself. Maybe B was right all along, and you alone brilliantly recognized and circumnavigated the trap. Why put yourself through this grief? The same is true after the exam. Forget the postmortem. You did what you did; no sense fretting about it until you get your scores back.

Chapter 3

Reading the Admissions Committee's Mind: What Colleges Want

In This Chapter
- Pinpointing what the colleges *really* want from you
- Masterminding the right mix of academics, sports, and extracurricular activities
- Preparing for the all-important essay and interview
- Eliminating the biggest mistake most anxious applicants make

The number one question that we're asked by our students is, "What do colleges want outta me?" We took that question to an expert, Jill Q. Porter, M.S., of La Jolla, California. An independent college counselor, Jill has helped thousands of students get into the schools that best meet their needs and fulfill their dreams. She visits dozens of colleges every year, talks with the admissions officers, and knows what's important to them. She's great at debunking some of the rumors that make the rounds. Here are her answers to 11 of the most important questions a student recently posed in an interview.

What's the Number One Thing That Colleges Look For?

"Grades and the level of coursework. If you get straight *A*'s but you take basket weaving and lint picking, schools aren't going to be impressed. If you take five solids, like physics, calculus, Spanish, history, and English lit, and get a few *A*'s and a few *B*'s, schools are going to be very impressed. It isn't just the grades but the difficulty level of the classes that's important."

How Important Is the ACT, Really?

"The ACT is crucial. Do you think the colleges would spend so much time and money separating students by their ACT scores if the schools didn't consider the scores important? The colleges need to have some universal measure of skills, something that can put all students on an equal footing. Some kids don't have the chance to take calculus in their high schools, or they go to schools that just plain don't offer AP (Advanced Placement) classes. By having everyone take the same test, schools have a fairer and more equitable frame of reference."

Do Schools Care Whether I Repeat the ACT?

"The answer to this question depends on the college. The very top-tier colleges don't expect you to take the ACT six or seven times and may be dubious if you do so. Twice is enough for the top schools. Second-rung schools don't mind if you take the ACT three or four times. Check directly with the individual school to find out its policy."

Can I Take the ACT Instead of the SAT I?

"Many schools in the Midwest accept ACT scores in lieu of SAT I scores. Other schools let you take both exams and evaluate both scores. My suggestion is that you plan to take both exams. You want to keep your options open. What if you suddenly decide you want to go to a different college, one you hadn't considered before? By the time you realize you need an SAT score, it may be too late to take the test. Automatically plan on taking both tests, if possible."

It just so happens that your friendly neighborhood bookstore has copies of *The SAT I For Dummies* (Wiley) to help you prepare for that exam. Could life *get* any better?

If I Mess Up Big-Time on the ACT, What Can I Do to Compensate?

"Adjust your expectations. Reality is the name of the game when it comes to college planning. Although we'd all love to go to Status U., most of us have to settle for less. If you do very badly on the ACT and don't have time to take it again, there's nothing you can do but look at another school. You always have the option of transferring after your first or second year.

"Keep in mind that schools do get last-minute openings. Even if you think your ACT score absolutely disqualifies you from your Dream School, send in the application and try to get on a wait list. You never know how lucky you can get."

What Classes Do You Recommend That I Take as a Senior? Junior? Sophomore?

"In general, the more challenging and complete your course load, the more likely you are to get accepted by a good college. And let me warn you: You can't slack off your senior year. Many students tell me that they work superhard their junior year and then take easy classes their senior year because it's too late for the colleges to get those grades. Wrong. Some schools don't send out confirmation notices until the end of March of the senior year. That means they get the first-semester grades and know whether you've signed up for and then dropped classes your senior year. Remember, the application form is a legal contract. If you write that you're taking a bunch of hard classes, which you actually stayed in for a day and dropped, you're lying to the college, and that's called fraud.

"Enough of scaring you. Here's what most colleges are looking for: three years of math (four is even better); four years of English; two to three years of language (any language is fine; you won't get extra points for taking a 'classy' language like Latin); two to three years of science; and two years of social studies. As far as the math goes, you don't have to take calculus unless you're trying to get into a math, engineering, or architecture program. And physics isn't required by all colleges, either."

How Helpful Are Charity Work and Sports?

"Colleges *expect* you to have some sort of community involvement. The key is doing something you enjoy. Don't sign up to work at a preschool if you don't have patience with small children, for example. The newspaper is always full of organizations requesting volunteers; somewhere, there's a perfect match for you. In my opinion, it's more important to be very involved with one charity than to sign up for ten different charities just to have them on your application form. The schools aren't dumb; they'll know what you're doing.

"As for sports, they show you're well rounded. You don't have to play varsity sports, just be involved in something, even intramurals. A word of caution: Sports are *not* more important than grades. Don't let your athletics stand in the way of your academics."

What Should I Say on the College Essay?

"I stress individuality. Show the colleges who you really are. College admissions officers read hundreds, maybe even thousands, of essays every year. They don't award points when you say what you obviously think the college wants to hear. They're impressed when you let your personality shine through. If you're archconservative and take pride in campaigning for rightwing candidates, mention your experiences. If you are really into pyramid power, channeling, and New Age stuff, talk about that. The key is to write about something you enjoy.

"And it goes without saying that your writing should be well organized and grammatically correct. With spell-checkers (both mechanical and that type called 'parents'), there's no excuse for turning in a sloppy essay."

What Will They Ask Me in the Interview, and What Should I Say?

"Colleges have two basic types of interviews, those done by alumni and those done by college staff. The alumni interviews tend to be a little less formal, but that doesn't mean you don't have to take them seriously.

"In both types of interviews, the most important thing is to show you are seriously interested in *this* school. Demonstrate that you've done your homework. By that, I don't mean bring in your algebra scratch paper, but indicate that you've done your background reading on the college. Mention some programs you find impressive or something about the history of the school. Above all, be very careful not to annoy the interviewer by asking some trite question that's already been answered in the promotional literature. For example, asking 'How many students are on campus?' is lame when that number is given in the school bulletin. Ask questions that relate to your personal goals in college."

How Can I Decide Which School Is Best for Me?

"This is the big question. First, be realistic. Everyone wants to go to the best schools in the country, but we can't all get accepted there. Although you should have one Dream School just for fun, be prepared by having several more realistic schools as backups.

"Next, look at affordability. Be absolutely sure that you can afford a school before you go through all the visitations and applications (which cost money). You may think you'll get a scholarship and financial aid, but they are getting harder and harder to acquire and rarely cover all the costs. Figure out just exactly how much you have to contribute, and then have a realistic talk with your parents about how much they can help. Yes, you can get a job during school, but that money usually goes toward daily expenses and fun, not tuition and books. You may be able to work only part-time, remember.

"Of course, the physical comfort of a school is vital. By that I mean, would you enjoy living in that particular city and on the campus? If you're a big-city sophisticate, you may not want to live in a small college town in the Midwest that has few of the extras you grew up with. If you are a laid-back, small-town type, life in the big city may be so distracting that you don't concentrate on your studies. And you have to like the campus, too, because you'll probably live on it for at least a few years.

"And last, I always recommend thinking about long-range internships and job opportunities. If you want to be a schoolteacher, for example, does the college have a good student-teaching program? Are there jobs in the community for teachers after you graduate? Many students fall in love with the city in which a school is located and want to stay there after they graduate. You're only in high school now and may not be thinking as far ahead as graduation and job hunting, but they should be a vital part of your decision on colleges."

What's the Biggest Mistake Most Students Make in College Planning?

"Relying on misinformation. The school grapevine and rumor mill are always working. I have students come to me who are convinced that they can have a mediocre ACT score and still get into their Dream School 'because a friend of a friend at school, this guy who plays water polo, did it.' Check your facts. You may want to believe what you hear, but trust me, much of it will be wrong. Read the school bulletin. Talk to the admissions office or to an alumnus of the school. Talk to your high school guidance counselor or get help from an independent counselor.

"The second biggest mistake is choosing a college based solely on how much money it will give you in scholarships or financial aid. Although money is critical, it need not be your only reason for attending a school. Somewhere out there, you can find a school you love, one that fits you to a *T*. You don't have to settle for the first school that offers you money, thinking that you won't find anything better. Your college experience is something you'll remember forever. It will affect your friendships, your career, and the rest of your life. Don't just settle for 'good enough'; look for 'just right.'"

Part II
Serving Your "Sentence": English Review and Test

In this part . . .

Lurking in the dark alleyways of the ACT is your first opponent, the English Test, one of four separate tests that you have to battle. The information in this part can help you to win the fight (or at least lessen the slaughter!).

Remember those persnickety grammar rules you thought you'd left behind forever? Surprise! They're baaaaaack. This part refreshes your memory of those rules with a grammar review — one that uses enough stupid examples and silly jokes to keep you from dozing off. Following the grammar review is a chapter that tells you what the exam actually looks like, which questions are worth doing, and which questions you may as well just guess at wildly. Finally, the last chapter in this part is an abbreviated English test: a dozen questions to make sure that what you've learned and reviewed is forever imprinted in your brain. Life just couldn't get any better.

Chapter 4

Glamour Grammar: The Five-Star Review

In This Chapter
- Distinguishing commonly confused twosomes
- Identifying the most frequently tested grammar concepts
- Learning to "agree with" verbs and pronouns

The English Test portion of the ACT tests standard, written English. What's that? That's what I call Arrogant English — stuck-up, highfalutin English. In the real world, you can use slang and casual English and communicate perfectly well with your buddies, but on the ACT, you have to use the formal English that you were taught in school. When you knock on a friend's door, for example, you call out, "It's me!" Right? On the ACT, you have to choose, "It is I."

About half of the ACT English Test questions test rhetorical skills — your general writing style and organization. That's the stuff you use every time you pick up a pen or turn on your word-processing program. The other half of the questions test what most people lump together in the general category they call English: punctuation, sentence structure, and basic grammar, including diction errors, subject-verb agreement, modifiers (adjectives and adverbs), and so on. That's the stuff you probably forget (or intentionally purge from your brain) ten minutes after being tested on it.

This chapter gives you a basic grammar review that brings back those thrilling days of yesteryear when you knew how to use the subjunctive and actually cared about the differences between adjectives and adverbs. The review starts off with the really easy stuff, but please don't get too bored and drop out. The harder, picky stuff comes later, and chances are that's the stuff you really need. Besides, to reward you for hanging in there and suffering through this quagmire, I've put in quite a few trivia points and a couple of jokes as bonuses.

You do not — I repeat, *do not* — have to fear encountering something like the pluperfect. I am very careful not to use technical terms throughout this material. Only teachers care about the technical names for this stuff. All *you* need to know is how to use the right rules, not what to call things.

Subject-Verb Agreement

1. A singular subject takes a singular verb.

Mozart's music *is* (not are) beautiful.

2. **A plural subject takes a plural verb.**

    The <u>works</u> of Mozart and Brahms *are* (not is) beautiful.

    (By the way, do you know what Mozart and Brahms are doing these days? *De*composing!)

3. **A compound subject — two or more subjects often connected by the word *and* — takes a plural verb.**

    <u>A symphony and a fugue</u> *are* (not is) beautiful.

4. **The following words are always plural and therefore require plural verbs:**

    - *few:* <u>Few</u> people *take* (not takes) only the ACT and not the SAT.
    - *both:* <u>Both</u> the ACT and the SAT *are* (not is) entrance exams to college.
    - *several:* <u>Several</u> of my friends *have* (not has) taken the ACT and the SAT.
    - *many:* <u>Many</u> of my friends *wish* (not wishes) they had never heard of the ACT.

5. **The following words are always singular and require singular verbs:**

    - *each:* <u>Each</u> question on the ACT *has* (not have) the potential to be a trick question.
    - *every:* <u>Every</u> question *is* (not are) to be approached with trepidation and paranoia.

    The *every* words — *every*one, *every*body, *every*thing, *every*where — are always singular.

6. **The following words may be singular or plural, depending on what follows them:** *some, any, most, all,* **and** *none.*

    - *some*, plural: <u>Some</u> of the <u>jokes</u> in this book *are* (not is) beyond hope and should be given a decent burial.
    - *some*, singular: <u>Some</u> of the <u>humor</u> in this book *is* (not are) inexcusable.

    TIP: You can remember these words with the acronym S.A.M.A.N., the first letters of the words. Think of the sentence, "S.A.M.A.N. (Say, man), can you tell me which words are sometimes singular and sometimes plural?"

7. **The following collective nouns look plural but are singular and require a singular verb:** *group, public, club, government, union, organization,* **and** *collection.*

    The <u>public</u> *is* (not are) constantly exposed to my sense of humor. My <u>collection</u> of jokes *is* (not are) not always fully appreciated.

    TIP:
8. **A prepositional phrase does not affect subject-verb agreement.**

    When you see a prepositional phrase, draw a line through it and simply read the noun (subject) next to the verb.

    That irate <u>group</u> ~~of test-takers~~ *is* (not are) bombarding the proctor with tomatoes.

    (Did you remember from Rule #7 that *group* is singular even though it may look plural?)

    Five words are exceptions to Rule #8: Do not ignore prepositional phrases containing the S.A.M.A.N. words.

    <u>All</u> of the dancers *are* (not is) wearing new leotards today; <u>all</u> of their time *is* (not are) spent complaining about the price of workout clothes.

    Trivia: Do you know who invented the leotard? It was created by and obviously named after Jules Leotard, a French trapeze artist.

9. **Some nouns have irregular singular and plural forms.**

Singular	Plural
criterion	criteria
curriculum	curricula
bacterium	bacteria
phenomenon	phenomena
medium	media
datum	data

```
Television is my favorite news medium; I get my news from several media.
```

(I love the quote from humorist Fred Allen: "TV is called a medium because it is so rarely well done!")

When in doubt about whether a word is singular or plural, remember that, in general (but not always), the plural form of the word ends in a vowel (*data, criteria*) while the singular form of the word ends in a consonant (*datum, criterion*).

10. **The second subject in an *either/or* or *neither/nor* construction determines whether the verb is singular or plural.**

```
Neither Kimberly nor her parents are (not is) on the cruise.
```

```
Neither her parents nor Kimberly is (not are) able to afford cruise tickets.
```

(Did you hear what happened when the pink cruise ship rammed into the purple one? All the passengers were marooned.)

Many people are so concerned with the subject-verb agreement of *neither/nor* that they forget that *neither* and *nor* belong together and that *either* and *or* belong together. In other words, the constructions *neither/or* and *either/nor* are wrong. Double-check whenever you see these words.

Pronouns

The next time your grammar teacher asks you to name two pronouns, you can be a smart aleck and shout out, "Who, me?"

1. **A *pronoun* (a word that takes the place of the noun) must have the same number (singular or plural) as the noun or noun phrase it is replacing.**

```
Everybody is on his (not their) best behavior during a college interview.
```

You would probably be wealthy if you had a dollar for each time you've heard someone say, "Yeah, everybody is trying their best." Because the construction *everybody . . . their* is so commonly used, it sounds correct. Red-flag this expression. Whenever you see the word *everybody*, triple-check the pronoun to make sure that it is singular.

2. A pronoun must have the same gender (feminine, masculine, or neuter) as the noun it is replacing.

```
The ewe is slowly making her way home from the pasture.
```

Because a ewe is a female sheep, use the female pronoun *her*.

3. A pronoun must have clarity (that is, you must be able to tell which noun the pronoun is replacing).

```
Matthew asked Franklin to pick up his laundry off the floor.
```

Did Matthew want Matthew's laundry picked up, or did Matthew want Franklin's laundry picked up? This reference is unclear — and thus makes the sentence a poor one.

An unclear pronoun reference often requires major reconstructive surgery. In this example, the entire sentence must be rewritten. Here's one possibility:

```
Matthew, disgusted at seeing Franklin's laundry on the floor, picked it up.
```

(Now you know perfectly well that the pronoun *it* is referring to Franklin's heap of clothes, not Matthew's.)

4. A pronoun must be in the proper case: subjective (I, you, he, she, it, we, they), objective (me, you, him, her, it, us, them), or possessive (my, mine, your, yours, his, her, hers, its, our, ours, their, theirs).

A pronoun following any form of the verb *to be,* such as *is, are, was,* and *were,* is going to be in the subjective form. This form often sounds pretentious and bizarre (a sure clue that it's probably correct on the ACT!). Following are common constructions:

It is I.   It was she who . . .

It was he.   This is he.

It could be they.   It was they.

```
I finally confessed to my family that it was I who put the dent in the bumper of the car.
```

Adjectives and Adverbs

1. Place an adjective (which modifies a noun or pronoun) or an adverb (which modifies a verb, adjective, or adverb) as close as possible to the noun or pronoun it is modifying.

That rule isn't followed in this sentence:

```
WRONG: Nancy and Frank left the neighborhood they had lived in for ten years reluctantly.
```

This sentence sounds as if Nancy and Frank had been reluctant to live in the neighborhood, when in fact they were reluctant to leave. Change the sentence so that *reluctantly* comes just before *left:*

```
RIGHT: Nancy and Frank reluctantly left the neighborhood they had lived in for ten years.
```

2. **An adverb (which modifies a verb, adverb, or adjective) often answers the question "How?" and may end in *-ly*.**

   How do I study? I study reluctantly.

3. **Place *not only* and *but also* in parallel positions within a sentence.** People often place *not only* and *but also* incorrectly. Following is an example of a wrong way to use these expressions:

   WRONG: Angelique not only was exasperated but also frightened when she locked herself out of the house.

   See the problem? In this wrong example, the phrase *not only* comes before the verb *was,* but the phrase *but also* comes before the adjective *frightened.*

   RIGHT: Angelique was not only exasperated but also frightened when she locked herself out of the house.

   Not only and *but also* precede the adjectives *exasperated* and *frightened,* respectively.

Sentence Structure

1. **A run-on sentence (two or more independent clauses incorrectly joined) must be changed.** The following is a run-on:

   WRONG: Jessimena was furious when she went to the party on the wrong day, she went home and yelled at her boyfriend, who had given her the wrong information.

   You can choose from five ways to correct a run-on:

   - **Make two separate sentences.**

     Jessimena was furious when she went to the party on the wrong day. She went home and yelled at her boyfriend, who had given her the wrong information.

   - **Use a semicolon to separate independent clauses.**

     Jessimena was furious when she went to the party on the wrong day; she went home and yelled at her boyfriend, who had given her the wrong information.

   - **Use a semicolon, conjunctive adverb, and comma (as in this construction: *; therefore,*) to separate the clauses.**

     Jessimena was furious when she went to the party on the wrong day; therefore, she went home and yelled at her boyfriend, who had given her the wrong information.

   - **Use a subordinating conjunction (such as *because*) with one of the clauses.**

     Because Jessimena was furious when she went to the party on the wrong day, she went home and yelled at her boyfriend, who had given her the wrong information.

   - **Use a comma and a coordinating conjunction (as in this construction: *, and*) between the two clauses.**

     Jessimena was furious when she went to the party on the wrong day, and she went home and yelled at her boyfriend, who had given her the wrong information.

2. **A sentence fragment (an incomplete sentence) must be changed to reflect a completed thought.**

   ```
   WRONG: Wendy, singing merrily to herself as she walked to class, unaware
   that the professor was at that very moment preparing a pop quiz.
   ```

   ```
   RIGHT: Wendy, singing merrily to herself as she walked to class, was
   unaware that the professor was at that very moment preparing a pop quiz.
   ```

Parallelism

Parallelism (also called parallel structure) means that objects in a series must be in similar form.

```
WRONG: I spent my weekend working on a jigsaw puzzle, doing chores around
the house, and finally got out on Sunday evening to play a set of tennis.
```

Rewrite the sentence so that the verbs are in the same form:

```
RIGHT: On the weekend, I worked on a jigsaw puzzle, did chores around the
house, and finally got out on Sunday evening to play a set of tennis.
```

or

```
RIGHT: I spent my weekend working on a jigsaw puzzle and doing chores
around the house, finally getting out on Sunday evening to play a set of
tennis.
```

TIP: Items in a series may be nouns, verbs, adjectives, or entire clauses. However, nonparallel verbs are the items that most commonly have errors. When a clause contains more than one verb, watch out for this particular error.

Comparisons

1. **Use the *-er* form (called the comparative form) to compare exactly two items; use the *-est* form (called the superlative form) to compare more than two items.**

   ```
   I am taller than my brother Beau, but Darren is the tallest member of our
   family.
   ```

   A particularly difficult comparison uses the words *latter* and *last*.

   ```
   My boyfriend asked whether I would like to go to Chicago, where the
   temperature was -5 degrees, or to Los Angeles, where the temperature was
   80 degrees. I told him that I preferred the latter (not last).
   ```

   Trivia: Did you know that the name *Chicago* is derived from a Native American term that means "place that stinks of onions"?

   TRAPS & TRICKS: Comparisons may trap you when you refer to twins. Remember that *twins* indicates two people. The following is a good trick question:

   ```
   WRONG: Myron and Mayor Thibadeau are identical twins, but Myron is the
   oldest by five minutes, a fact that he never lets Mayor forget.
   ```

The error is in the comparison because there are only two twins.

> RIGHT: Myron is the *older* by five minutes.

2. Compare only similar objects or concepts.

> WRONG: The motor skills of a toddler are more advanced than a baby.

The problem with the preceding sentence is that it is comparing *motor skills* to a *baby*. Its intention is to compare a toddler's motor skills to a baby's motor skills. Following are two ways to correct the error:

> RIGHT: The motor skills of a toddler are more advanced than those of a baby.

or

> RIGHT: A toddler's motor skills are more advanced than a baby's.

Diction

I like to refer to diction errors as *twosomes* because they are errors that you make when you swap two (or sometimes three) commonly confused words. This section lists the most commonly confused words, along with short-and-sweet definitions and examples.

affect/effect

To *affect* is to influence or concern.

> A good ACT score will positively *affect* your chances of admission to college.

(It will positively *influence* your chances.)

Effect means cause or result.

> A good ACT score will have a positive *effect* on your chances for admission (a positive *result*).

> A good score will *effect* a change in which schools you consider (cause a change).

Affect has another, little-known meaning. To *affect* also means to pretend.

> When I want to get out of meeting with my friends to study for the ACT, I often *affect* a headache (pretend to have a headache).

amount/number

Amount modifies a singular noun.

> I have a large *amount* of respect for the poetry of Dorothy Parker.

Number modifies a plural noun.

> A *number* of times I have read her poem that contains the lines, "The lads I've met in Cupid's deadlock / were, shall we say, born out of wedlock?"

anxious/eager

Anxious means worried or doubtful.

> Meg was *anxious* about the call from her mechanic, knowing that her Tercel probably needed some repairs.

Eager means joyously anticipating.

> The mechanic was *eager* to work on Meg's car, because he needed cash.

Tercel Trivia: They don't just make up these names for cars, you know. A tercel is a small male hawk. Maybe the carmakers wanted to give drivers the idea of being free-flying and soaring like a hawk.

assure/ensure

To *assure* means to convince.

> Quentin talked fast, trying to *assure* his girlfriend that the heart-shaped necklace in his locker was, in fact, a belated birthday present for her.

To *ensure* is to make certain.

> To *ensure* that his girlfriend believed him, Quentin called a friend, who pretended she was the salesgirl who had sold the item to Quentin.

between/among

Be*tw*een (note the *tw*) compares exactly <u>tw</u>o things.

> I have difficulty choosing *between* cherry Jell-O and chocolate pudding.

Among compares more than two.

> I go crazy when I have to choose *among* the desserts in a smorgasbord.

Trivia: Can you name five Jell-O flavors that flopped? Apple, celery, salad, cola, and (ugh!) mixed vegetables.

The word *between* is often followed by *and:* I have difficulty choosing between this *and* that. A trap answer may have a sentence asking you to choose between this *or* that; the *or* is wrong.

complement/compliment

Complement means to complete.

> The buzz haircut *complemented* the image that Chan wanted to project as a no-nonsense guy.

Compliment means to praise.

> Chan's girlfriend was eager to *compliment* him on his new look.

eminent/immanent/imminent

Eminent means outstanding, distinguished.

> Dr. Regis Weiss is an *eminent* oncologist, well respected by his peers.

Immanent means inherent, innate.

> I think that compassion probably is an *immanent* trait in a good physician; it doesn't seem possible that someone could take a course to learn how to be caring.

Imminent means about to happen.

> When I saw Dr. Weiss shaking his head at me as I stood on the scale, I knew a lecture about weight management was *imminent*.

TIP: Think of imminent as "in-a-minute." Something imminent is about to happen in a minute.

everyday/every day

As one word, *everyday* means usual or customary.

> I wore my *everyday* clothes for a quick trip to the grocery store, little realizing that I'd run into Brad Pitt next to the kumquats.

Every day as two words means each 24-hour period.

> From now on, I'm going to go to the store *every day* to get fresh fruit.

(After all, everyone needs fruit, kumquat may . . . .)

farther/further

Farther refers to measurable distance.

> I made a mistake on the test when I said that Morocco is *farther* from Egypt than it is from New York.

Further refers to a figurative degree or quantity that can't be measured.

> Obviously, I need to study my geography *further*.

flaunt/flout

Flaunt means to show off.

> Brittany was thrilled to get her engagement ring and couldn't wait to *flaunt* it to her friends at school.

Flout means to show scorn or contempt.

> Her fiancà was furious that Brittany had *flouted* their agreement to keep their engagement a secret for the next few months.

founder/flounder

To *founder* is to sink, fail, or collapse.

> Reports estimate that one of every two new businesses *founders* within the first three years.

To *flounder* is to thrash about.

> A new business owner, desperate for advice, will *flounder* wildly, running from government bureau to government bureau attempting to get help.

good/well

Good is an adjective that modifies a noun.

> You're doing a *good* job learning these rules.

Well is an adverb that modifies verbs, adverbs, and adjectives and usually answers the question *how*.

> How do you study? You study very *well*.

Well also refers to physical condition.

> By the time you leave the ACT, huffing, puffing, sweating, and fretting, you may not be feeling very *well*.

if/whether

If introduces a condition.

> *If* the teacher allows an open-book exam, I will be ecstatic.

Whether compares alternatives.

> I don't know *whether* I could pass a normal, closed-book exam.

TIP: *If* usually sounds correct even when it is wrong. Personally, even though I know better, I hear myself saying, "I don't know *if* I can make it tonight," when I know I should say, "I don't know *whether* I can make it tonight." Try *whether* first. If it sounds right, it probably is right.

imply/infer

To *imply* means to suggest indirectly.

```
I didn't mean to imply that your dress is ugly when I asked you whether
you bought it at an upholstery store.
```

To *infer* is to conclude or deduce, to read a meaning *in*to something.

```
Based on the evidence, the officer inferred that the man was guilty.
```

it's/its

It's (notice the apostrophe) means *it is*.

```
It's good to know the distinction between these two words.
```

Its (without an apostrophe) is possessive.

```
The ACT is ruthless in its insistence that it's important to know the
difference between these two words.
```

less/fewer

Less modifies a singular noun.

```
I have less patience with problems than I should have.
```

Fewer modifies a plural noun.

```
I would make fewer careless mistakes in math if only I had the patience
to finish each problem completely.
```

lie/lay

To *lie* is to recline.

```
I lie down in the afternoon for a nap to reduce stress.
```

To *lay* is to place.

```
I lay a cold washcloth on my head every time I get a headache from
studying for the ACT.
```

TIP: Do you often get *lie* and *lay* confused? I have an easy way to remember them. To *lie* is to recline. Listen for the long *i* sound in l*i*e and the long *i* sound in rec*li*ne. When I lie down, I recline. To *lay* is to place. Listen for the long *a* sound in l*ay* and the long *a* sound in pl*a*ce. Now I lay me down to sleep. Now I place me down to sleep.

Few people know how to conjugate these words correctly. Memorize the following:

- *Lie, lay, have lain:* Today I *lie* down, yesterday I *lay* down, every day I *have lain* down.
- *Lay, laid, have laid:* Today I *lay* my keys on the table, yesterday I *laid* my keys on the table, every day this week I *have laid* my keys on the table.

Notice how confusing the past tense of *lie* is because it is the same as the present tense of *lay*. Do not use the past tense of *lie* as *lied*. The sentence "I *lied* down yesterday" is egregiously incorrect.

phase/faze

Phase means stage or time period.

```
College years are just one phase of your life.
```

Faze means to upset, bother, or disconcert.

```
Do not let the pressure of the ACT faze you.
```

Many students look at the word *faze* and immediately assume that it is misspelled. The ACT contains *no* misspelled words. If you think that a word is misspelled, you are in error. (My favorite is *judgment*. Most people misspell the word as *judgement*, but there is no *judge* in *judgment* in American English.)

prescribe/proscribe

Do you know the distinction between the words *prescribe* and *proscribe*? To *prescribe* is to recommend.

```
I prescribe that you learn these two words.
```

To *proscribe* is to outlaw or forbid.

```
I proscribe your believing that the ACT has typographical errors.
```

principle/principal

Principle means rule.

```
The principles of justice upon which our country is founded apply to all.
```

Principal means first in authority or importance.

```
The principal reason democracy works, in my opinion, is that it gives
everyone an equal opportunity to succeed.
```

Princip<u>le</u> means ru<u>le</u>. Note that they both end in *-le*. If the word does not appear to mean rule, it can't be principle; choose *principal*. The English language has many uses of the word *principal*, including investment principal, the principal reason I telephoned you, and the principal of a high school.

rise/raze/raise

Rise means to ascend.

> It is time to *rise* when your mother yanks the covers off the bed.

Raze means to tear down.

> When she threatens to *raze* the bedroom around your head, you know that she means business.

Raise means to lift. (It also has several other meanings.)

> You wearily *raise* your body, ready to face another day.

stationary/stationery

Stationary means unmoving.

> The little girl tried to remain *stationary*, hoping that the birds would come up to her and eat out of her hand.

Stationery is writing paper.

> The little girl used her new *stationery* to write a letter telling her grandmother about the birds.

TIP: *Stationary* means something that *stays*. Note the letter *a* in st*a*y and the letter *a* in station*a*ry. *Stationery* is something you write a letter on. Note the letter *e* in station*e*ry and the letter *e* in l*e*tter.

who/whom

Who is a subject and does the action.

> *Who* wants to study on a weekend?

Whom is an object and receives the action.

> I don't know *whom* to ask for help in deciding my major.

Miscellaneous Mistakes

This section reveals some of the miscellaneous grammar mistakes that many people make every day. In the real world, you can live with these mistakes; on the ACT, they're deadly.

hardly

Hardly is negative and often shows up in a trap double-negative question. Do not say, "Ms. Hawker has *hardly nothing* to do this weekend after she finishes the ACT and is looking forward to vegging out in front of the TV." The correct version is, "Ms. Hawker has *hardly anything* to do this weekend after she finishes the ACT and is looking forward to vegging out in front of the TV."

hopefully

Use *hopefully* only where you can plug in the words *full of hope*.

```
Hearing the telephone ring, Alice looked up hopefully, thinking that
Steve might be calling her to apologize for sending her flowers on his
ex-girlfriend's birthday.
```

Many people use the word *hopefully* incorrectly as a substitute for "I hope." The sentence "*Hopefully,* my ACT score will improve" is wrong. Your score won't improve unless you learn to say, "I hope that my ACT score will improve."

if . . . would

Do not place *if* and *would* in the same clause. A common error is to say, "*If* I *would* have studied more, I would have done better." The correct version is, "*If* I *had* studied more, I would have done better," or, "*Had* I studied more, I would have done better."

in regards to . . . in regard to

The English language has no such expression as *in regards to*. Dump the *s;* the proper expression is *in regard to*.

```
We need to have a heart-to-heart talk in regard to your making this
mistake.
```

where . . . that

Do not confuse *where* with *that*. *Where* refers only to physical location. Saying, "Did you hear *where* Principal Denges ran off to Tahiti with his secretary?" is wrong. The correct structure is, "Did you hear *that* Principal Denges ran off to Tahiti with his secretary?"

Chapter 5

Misspellers of the World, Untie! Mastering the English Test

In This Chapter
- Understanding the format of the passages with "phantom" questions
- Distinguishing the must-do easy questions from the brain-straining difficult ones
- Avoiding falling for the ACT traps . . . or creating your own

When you open your ACT booklet, the first thing you see is the English Test. Your still-half-asleep brain and bleary eyes encounter 5 passages and 75 questions. Somehow, you're to read all the passages and answer all the questions within 45 minutes. This test is definitely one part of the ACT on which you have to hustle.

Seeing Is Believing: The Format of the Test

The ACT English Test passages look like standard reading comprehension passages, the kind you've seen on tests for years. The difference is that these passages have many underlined portions. An underlined portion can be an entire sentence, a phrase, a word, or even just a punctuation mark. (You may want to take a quick look right now at the practice test in Chapter 6 to see what a passage looks like. I'll wait.)

Okay, you're back. Here are the details about what you get and what you're expected to do with it.

The passages

The five passages can cover a variety of topics. You may get a fun story that's a personal anecdote — someone talking about getting a car for his 16th birthday, for example. Or you may encounter a somewhat formal scientific passage about the way items are carbon-dated. Some passages may discuss history; some, philosophy; others, cultural differences among nations. Some passages are fiction, such as excerpts from novels, old and new. One type of passage is not necessarily more difficult than another. You don't need to use specific reading techniques for these passages (as you do with standard reading comprehension passages). Just read and enjoy. (Yeah, right.)

Although these English passages are not reading comprehension passages per se, you do need to pay at least a little bit of attention to content rather than just to the underlined portions. Why bother? Because a few of the questions at the end of the passages are reading comp–type questions, asking you about the purpose of the passage or what a possible conclusion might be. More about those in the "Being Boxed In: The Box Questions" section of this chapter.

The questions

The English Test has no questions. Well, let me rephrase that before I get your hopes up too high. You will not usually be faced with what you consider specific questions in the standard interrogatory form. You will not see "Which of the following is an adjective?" or "The purpose of the subjunctive is to do which of these?" Instead, the "question" is simply an underlined portion of the exam. Your job is to determine whether that underlined portion is correct as is or whether one of the alternate answer choices is preferable.

The answer choices

The answer choices are A, B, C, and D (for the odd-numbered questions) and F, G, H, and J (for the even-numbered questions). Choices A and F are always "NO CHANGE." You select that if the original is the best of the versions offered. Occasionally, choice D or J will say, "OMIT the underlined portion." Choose that answer when you want to dump the whole underlined portion and forget that you ever saw it. (And no, you can't do that with the entire test!)

The other choices are often variations on a theme. For example, if the underlined portion has the word *lay* in it, the answer choices might be

   F. NO CHANGE

   G. lie

   H. lain

   J. lying

Being Boxed In: The Box Questions

Usually at the end of a passage — but sometimes, quite annoyingly, within the passage itself — you see a small box with a number in it, like this: 49. That box indicates what most students think of as a reading comprehension–type question. Here are a few examples:

If the purpose of this essay was to convey the author's opinion about the morality of the death penalty, did the author accomplish the purpose?

   A. Yes, because the reader understands the author's philosophy of right and wrong.

   B. Yes, because the author specifically refers to the church's teachings on the subject.

   C. No, because the passage never addresses fundamental religious issues.

   D. No, because the author never discusses life imprisonment as an alternative to the death penalty.

Notice that here you have to understand not only what the passage said but also whether it went far enough. This "Did the author accomplish his purpose?" question is pretty common. To answer it, you usually have to comprehend the passage as a whole pretty well.

Given the topic and the tone of the passage, was the author's use of the pronoun "I" proper?

   F. Yes, because the only examples he cited were from his own life.

   G. Yes, because he was projecting his personal feelings onto the topic.

   H. No, because a formal essay should not be written in the first-person singular.

   J. No, because using "I" prevents the readers from becoming involved with the topic.

Chapter 5: Misspellers of the World, Untie! Mastering the English Test

TIP

In this case, you're expected to get a feel for the tone of the passage as a whole. I suggest that, as soon as you read the question, you decide whether using "I" was appropriate — *before* you even look at the answer choices. If you don't have at least some idea in your brain *before* you look at the answer choices, they all will look good. I often have students read them and say, "Choice F is true. Well, wait a minute, I agree with choice G, too. And now that I think of it, I could make a case for H. No, no, wait a minute: It's definitely choice J. I think." Don't get yourself so confused. Predict an answer of your own before you get bamboozled by the test's answers.

Here's an example of the type of box question I like least: the structure or reorganization question.

EXAMPLE

To make the passage a coherent whole, paragraph 4 should be placed

    A. where it is now.

    B. at the beginning of the passage.

    C. after paragraph 2.

    D. at the end of the passage.

Notice how much time this type of question takes up. In the passage, each paragraph is numbered. You have to go back and reread the entire passage, thinking about which order of paragraphs would make the most sense. Most of the time, you have to read the passage repeatedly, first with this order of paragraphs and then with that order. You really don't have the time to do so.

TIP

My suggestion is that you make a quick guess at this question and come back to it later if you have the time. (Never leave any question blank: Remember, the ACT does not penalize you for guessing.)

What Do They Want Outta Me? What the English Usage Questions Test

The questions fall into two basic categories. Just over half the questions cover topics of usage or mechanics. These questions include sentence structure (whether a sentence is a fragment or a run-on), grammar and usage (just about everything most people think of as English, such as adverbs, adjectives, and so on), and punctuation (don't worry; this isn't superhard, mostly just semicolons). Just under half the questions test rhetorical skills, organization (reordering the sentences in the passage), style (which expression, slang or formal, is appropriate within the passage), and strategy ("This passage would be most appropriate in which of the following types of books . . . ?").

TIP

Some questions are much more doable than others. For example, most students would agree that a simple grammar question asking about a pronoun reference or subject-verb agreement is easier than an organization question expecting you to put the paragraphs of the entire passage in order. In the practice tests in this book (see Chapters 16 and 18), I emphasize these more doable questions, giving a slightly greater percentage of them than you might find on the real ACT. Why? Because I want you to be absolutely, positively able to get these questions correct in a heartbeat. They are the basics, the foundation of your test. If you can get the easy and medium-difficulty questions right, you'll already have a good score. Getting the harder questions correct will be the icing on the cake.

Maximizing the Gain, Minimizing the Pain: Questions Worth Looking For

The biggest complaint I hear from my students about the English Test is not that it's too hard but that it's too long. Five passages, 75 questions, and only 45 minutes to finish is pretty daunting. This section gives you a few strategies to help you to get the most bang for your buck.

Looking for short, diction-type questions

A diction error is a wrong word choice. Obvious errors, such as *lie/lay, phase/faze,* and *affect/effect* are not tested as frequently as they used to be, but when they show up, they are easy questions to answer correctly. One diction error that does show up repeatedly is *its/it's*. Here's an example:

Barney told the club that <u>it's policy of discriminating</u> against redheads was probably illegal and certainly unethical.

   A. it's policy of discrimination

   B. it's discrimination policy

   C. its discriminating policy

   D. its discrimination

The possessive pronoun *its* has no apostrophe ("The cat was licking its paw.") *It's* (with an apostrophe) means *it is*. This example requires the possessive, *its*. Eliminate choices *A* and *B*. Choice *D* more directly expresses the thought of the sentence than does choice *C*. *Correct Answer:* **D**.

We put many questions like this one into the practice exams simply because they are the most doable questions. You have no excuse for missing a diction question. All you have to do is memorize the common diction twosomes (conveniently presented for your viewing pleasure in Chapter 4).

Going for pure grammar

A grammar question may test subject-verb agreement, pronoun reference, or a multitude of other concepts that you probably think of as English. Following is an example. (Keep in mind that on the real test, this question is part of a passage, not an isolated sentence.)

A full case of sodas, when opened by a horde of thirsty athletes who have been running laps, <u>don't go</u> very far.

   F. NO CHANGE

   G. do not go

   H. doesn't go

   J. doesn't get to go

What's the subject of the sentence? *A case.* That's singular, requiring the singular verb *doesn't*. Eliminate choices F and G immediately. Choice J is totally ridiculous, adding unnecessary words and making the sentence awkward. *Correct Answer:* **H**.

Did you see the trap in this sentence? Some students think that either *sodas, athletes,* or *laps* — all of which are plural — is the subject (especially *laps*, because it is right next to the verb). In that case, they think that the verb has to be plural, too, and choose F. You didn't fall for that cheap trick, did you?

If English is not your first language, the diction and grammar questions are the key to your getting a good score in this section. When you studied English, you probably memorized rule after rule after rule, just the kinds of things that these questions test. In this situation, you actually have an advantage over American kids who haven't been tested on this stuff since the seventh grade. (In many American high schools, students start learning literature in the eighth or ninth grades and no longer focus on pure grammar.) Spend time studying the grammar and diction rules in Chapter 4, and then head for these types of questions, especially if you're running short of time.

Ignoring superfluous info

Some sentences feature redundancies, such as "red *in color*" or "the reason was *because.*" Others offer irrelevant or unnecessary information, as in the following example.

Taking a class in a foreign language can be very rewarding. You never know when you will use the knowledge. You may someday visit a country that uses that language or meet someone from that nation. Even if you never actually practice the language, you can learn more about the way languages are developed and words are created. Many students agree that they learned more English grammar by studying a foreign language than they did in English classes. <u>You could also learn both Spanish and French at the same time, for example.</u> Most teachers of a foreign language emphasize sentence structure and grammar. It is an axiom among language teachers that students who are good writers in their native languages learn foreign languages quickly.

   A. NO CHANGE

   B. For example, you could also learn both Spanish and French at the same time.

   C. At the same time, for example, you could learn both Spanish and French.

   D. OMIT the underlined portion.

Choices A, B, and C are saying basically the same thing. All they do is shuffle the words a little bit. None of them adds anything to the paragraph. The underlined sentence seems to go off on a tangent, as you can see by the fact that the next sentence continues the previous idea, the role of grammar in foreign language classes. Dump the whole underlined sentence.

Which is better: The tortoise or the hare?

Question: Is it better to go slowly and do a good job on four passages, never getting to the fifth, or should I try to get through all five passages?

Answer: I advocate trying to get through all five passages. On average, each passage has 15 questions. I don't think you can afford to blow off that many questions. Keep reminding yourself of how different these passages are from standard reading comprehension passages. With very few exceptions, you don't have to answer "substance" questions, such as, "With which of the following would the author agree?" If you're short on time, skip the box questions (which sometimes require a lot of time, thought, and suffering) and the longer questions requiring you to rewrite an entire sentence, and zoom on to the next passage.

Do not leave any answers blank. If you don't get to that last passage, at least fill in an answer for every question. The ACT has no penalty for guessing. Out of 15 questions, you're pretty sure to get at least a few right even with random guessing, and every little bit helps.

Their Pain, Your Gain: Traps That Others Have Fallen Into

I've tutored for the ACT for a couple of decades now. By this point, I think I've seen students fall for every trap the test-makers could think of — and some they probably never considered! Watch out for these most commonly tumbled-into traps:

- **Forgetting the NO CHANGE option:** Because the first answer choice (choice A for odd-numbered questions, choice F for even-numbered questions) is always NO CHANGE, students tend to gloss over it. Don't forget that you always have the option to keep things exactly the way they are.

- **Automatically choosing "OMIT the underlined portion" each time it occurs:** Although you may be tempted to shorten this section by screaming, "Dump it! Just dump the whole stupid thing!" every chance you get, don't fall into that habit. When you see the OMIT answer (either choice D or choice J), realize that it has the same one-in-four chance of being right as the other answers have. Consider it, but don't make it a no-brainer choice.

- **Automatically selecting the "other" diction or grammar choice:** When a student sees *who* in a sentence, she is often tempted to change it immediately to *whom*. Yet if that same sentence said *whom* to begin with, that same student would immediately change it to *who*. The temptation to *do* something, anything, is very strong. Don't change just for the sake of change.

- **Wasting time on the box questions:** Students sometimes ask me what I have against the box questions. Nothing, really. Some of the box questions, like the attitude ones ("Would this essay be appropriate for a group of university professors?"), can be quite simple. But others can be incredibly time-wasting and frustrating. I refer specifically to my least-favorite type of question, the "order of the sentences" or "order of the paragraphs" ("Which of the following would be the most logical sequence of sentences in paragraph 4?"). Usually, you have to read and reread and reread the paragraph, changing and rearranging the sentences again and again. And even then, students argue that the organization seems subjective: "Why does Sentence 4 go before Sentence 2? I think it sounds better the other way!" You may be able to get the question right, but at what price? How much time do you chew up? How many more of the easy questions could you have gotten right in that time?

- **Ignoring the big picture:** Some questions are style questions. A style question expects you to sense the overall picture, to know whether the tone of the passage is friendly so that you can appropriately use a slang expression (for example, *totally lame*) or whether you need to be a bit more formal (*useless* rather than *totally lame*). If you focus on only the underlined portions and don't read the passage as a whole, you can easily miss this type of question.

> **TIP:** Even if a question doesn't seem to expect you to understand the entire passage, you should still read a few sentences ahead of the question. How you correct a run-on or a fragment, for example, may depend on how the next few sentences are structured.

Chapter 6

It's Not What You Say, It's How You Say It: English Practice Questions

In This Chapter
- Seeing the English questions in context
- Recognizing what doesn't fit in
- Using — not abusing — the language

On the real ACT, the passage is on the left side of the page, and the questions are on the right side (see the Chapters 16 and 18). For this one brief test, I put the questions after the passage. That way, you can read the answer explanations with the questions.

DIRECTIONS: Below are five paragraphs containing underlined portions. Alternate ways of stating the underlined portions follow the paragraphs. Choose the best alternative. If the original is the best way of stating the underlined portion, choose NO CHANGE.

You also see questions that refer to the passage or ask you to reorder the sentences within a passage. These questions are identified by a number in a box. Choose the best answer.

Passage

[1]

[1] Marian Anderson possibly <u>will have</u> <u>the greatest</u> influence opening doors and gaining well-deserved
              1   2

opportunities for other Black singers than anyone else to date <u>so far</u>. [2] Anderson, born in Philadelphia,
                                                             3

Pennsylvania, had an early interest in music. [3] She <u>learns</u> to play the piano and was singing in the
                                                             4

church at the age of six. [4] She gave her first concert at age eight<u>, when she was still a young child</u>.
                                                                                    5

[2]

[5] In 1925, Anderson won a concert hosted by the New York Philharmonic, beating out <u>no less than</u>
                                                                                                                       6

300 singers. [6] <u>It launched her career but,</u> America was not quite ready for her fantastic voice, person-
                    7

ality, or color.

[3]

[7] In 1936, <u>asked</u> to give a performance at the White House. [8] She confessed that this occasion
               8

was the first time that she had really been nervous <u>to sing</u>. [9] She and Eleanor Roosevelt became
                                                                         9

<u>close friends, but</u> this friendship became evident with the Daughters of the American Revolution Affair.
   10

Part II: Serving Your "Sentence": English Review and Test

[4]

[10] The DAR refused to let Anderson perform in Constitution Hall in 1939. [11] The White House made arrangements for Ms. Anderson to sing on the steps of the Lincoln Memorial in D.C. instead.

[5]

[12] In 1977, First Lady Rosalynn Carter presented Marian Anderson with a Congressional Gold Medal, the first Black to receive such an honor. [13] Later she was inducted into the Women's Hall of Fame in Seneca Falls, New York.

11

1. A. NO CHANGE
   B. has had
   C. has
   D. is having

To understand the tense of the passage, you have to read a few sentences ahead. Doing so makes it clear that Marian Anderson accomplished her singing several decades earlier. (The passage mentions such dates as 1936 and 1977.) Therefore, the verb needs to be in the past tense. *Correct answer:* **B.**

(Alas, not all of us sing as well as Ms. Anderson. My own singing is so bad that the governor declared my last opera a disaster aria!)

2. F. NO CHANGE
   G. a greater
   H. one of the greatest
   J. a great

You need to read the entire sentence before deciding on an answer. If you read "the greatest influence" all by itself, it sounds correct. However, if you continue to read the sentence, you find the comparative "than." You cannot say "the greatest influence than" but rather "a greater influence than." *Correct answer:* **G.**

Be very careful to read the entire sentence. You may save a few seconds by reading only the underlined portion, but you will sacrifice a lot of points.

3. A. NO CHANGE
   B. dating so far
   C. so far dated
   D. OMIT the underlined portion

To date and *so far* are redundant; they mean the same thing. You can use one or the other, but not both. (Quick! Notify the Department of Redundancy Department!) *Correct answer:* **D.**

Many students tend to choose "OMIT the underlined portion" every time they see it, reasoning that it would not be a choice unless it were correct. Not so. If you decide to omit the underlined portion, be especially careful to reread the entire sentence. Often, omitting the underlined portion makes nonsense out of the sentence.

Chapter 6: It's Not What You Say, It's How You Say It: English Practice Questions

4. F. NO CHANGE

   G. has been learning

   H. learned

   J. is learning

Because Marian Anderson is no longer six years old, the sentence requires the past tense, *learned*. **Hint:** If you aren't sure of the tense, check out the rest of the sentence. You are told that Ms. Anderson "was singing," meaning the situation occurred in the past. *Correct answer:* **H.**

Notice that choices G and J both have the -ing verb *learning*. Often, -ing verbs are trap answers. They are frequently clumsy, awkward, and unnecessary. Although not *all* -ing verbs are wrong, check them carefully.

5. A. NO CHANGE

   B. still a young child

   C. still young

   D. OMIT the underlined portion

A person who is eight is still a young child — duh! The underlined portion is superfluous, unnecessary. Eliminate it. The period is necessary to finish the sentence. *Correct answer:* **D.**

Speaking of children and sentences reminds me of a friend of mine. He got so tired of seeing cutesy bumper stickers that said things like "My child was honor citizen of the month at Sweetums Preschool" that he created his own bumper sticker. His back fender now reads, "My child was Inmate of the Month at State Prison!"

6. F. NO CHANGE

   G. less than

   H. fewer than

   J. no fewer than

Fewer modifies plural nouns, as in fewer brain cells, for example. *Less* modifies singular nouns, like less intelligence. Because the noun *singers* is plural, use the word *fewer*. *Correct answer:* **J.**

If you chose H, you fell for the trap. You forgot to reread the sentence with your answer inserted. The meaning of the whole sentence changes with the phrase "fewer than 300 singers." In that case, you are denigrating, or lessening, the winner's accomplishment. The tone of the passage is one of respect. The author is impressed that Ms. Anderson beat out "no fewer than 300 singers." Keep in mind that you must make your answers fit the overall tone or attitude of the passage. If a passage is complimentary, be sure that your answers continue in that vein.

7. A. NO CHANGE

   B. Launching her career,

   C. Her career was launched, but

   D. Upon launching it (her career),

Part II: Serving Your "Sentence": English Review and Test

> **TIP:** Be very suspicious of that two-letter rascal *it*. Always double-check *it* out because *it* is so often misused and abused. *It* must refer to one specific thing: "Where is the book? Here *it* is." In question 7, *it* doesn't refer to any one object but to Ms. Anderson's winning the contest. Dump choice A. Choices B and D sound as if America launched Ms. Anderson's career: "Upon launching it . . . America was not quite ready . . . ." Be sure to go back and reread the entire sentence with your answer inserted. *Correct answer:* **C.**

> **TIP:** Beware of *-ing* words. They often result in a misplaced modifier, changing the meaning of the sentence. Misplaced modifiers and bad grammar in general can result in some pretty funny sentences. A few of every grammar teacher's favorites, taken from newspaper headlines, are
>
> Iraqi Head Seeks Arms
>
> Two Convicts Escape Noose; Jury Hung
>
> Police Discover Crack in Australia

8. F. NO CHANGE

    G. she was asked

    H. upon being asked

    J. asking

The original is a fragment, an incomplete sentence. The sentence has no subject. *Who* was asked? *She* was asked. *Correct answer:* **G.**

> **TIP:** Choice H has the dreaded word *being*. People often use *being* incorrectly; you should make it one of your red-flag words, words that you immediately double-check. Choices H and J both have the same problem that the original has: They lack a subject.

9. A. NO CHANGE

    B. about singing

    C. of singing

    D. and singing

The word *nervous* is usually followed by the word *about*. You are nervous *about* something, not nervous *to* or *by* something. (How do you feel about the ACT? You may be frightened or intimidated by it or scared of it, but if it makes you nervous, you are nervous about it.) *Correct answer:* **B.**

> **HEADS UP:** This sentence is one of the few times when an *-ing* verb is correct, not a trap. Always double-check *-ing* verbs, but don't automatically assume that they are wrong. Watch out for an exception, like this one. (I believe it was Yogi Berra who said, "You can observe a lot by watching.")

10. F. NO CHANGE

    G. close friends, and

    H. close friends — which

    J. close and friendly,

The clause "but this friendship became evident . . ." makes no sense in the context. Use *but* only to indicate dissent or change; use a comma and the word *and* to indicate a short pause. *Correct answer:* **G.**

Chapter 6: It's Not What You Say, It's How You Say It: English Practice Questions

11. **A.** NO CHANGE
  B. Medal, being the first Black
  C. Medal; the first Black
  D. Medal; she was the first Black

The original sounds as if the medal were the first Black to receive such an honor. The sentence obviously means to say that Ms. Anderson was the first Black to receive the honor. Note that the semicolon separates two independent sentences; each sentence could stand alone. *Correct answer:* **D.**

Did the word *being* in choice B catch your eye? *Being* is a red-flag word, one that is frequently misused. You should double-check it every time you see it.

12. If the author of this passage were to add the following lines to the article, where would they be most logically placed?

It was an era of color prejudice, a time when people were still legally excluded from jobs, housing, and even entertainment merely because of their race. Thus, the early promise of success seemed impossible until something amazing for the times happened.

  F. At the end of sentence 2
  G. At the end of sentence 6
  H. At the end of paragraph 3
  J. In the middle of paragraph 5

Because the first sentence of the addition talks about color prejudice, look in the passage for something mentioning color. That is specifically discussed only in sentence 6. *Correct answer:* **G.**

Be sure to go back to the passage and reread the entire paragraph with the new lines inserted to make sure that they make sense.

This question just wastes time, requiring you to understand both the structure and the content of the passage. You have to go back and reread the passage four times, once with each answer choice inserted in the indicated position. If you didn't really understand the passage or if you just skimmed it to get the grammar points, your best bet is to make a quick guess. *Remember:* The ACT does not penalize you for wrong answers. Guessing at any question that has you stumped is to your advantage.

Part III
Writing the Writing Test Rightly: You Have a Choice

The 5th Wave   By Rich Tennant

"I always get a good night's sleep the day before a test so I'm relaxed and alert the next morning. Then I grab my pen, eat a banana and I'm on my way."

In this part . . .

That's write — er — right! You *do* have a choice with the ACT writing test. The test is optional, so you can choose between spending an extra 30 minutes getting writer's cramp, or risking having your future college or university become rather disappointed in you — because there's a very real chance that they'll require this section of the ACT. It's up to you, of course, but our advice is to read the following chapters very carefully and opt to take the writing test. When it comes to the writing test, better safe than sorry!

Chapter 7

ACT Write: The First Words on Essay Writing

In This Chapter

▶ Learning the ten major writing errors to avoid in your writing

▶ Understanding the ACT scoring system

▶ Viewing sample essays

The writing portion of the ACT is optional, meaning you have the choice of spending an extra 30 minutes at the testing center (How lucky for you!). Although it's optional, three-quarters of the colleges and universities require this section of the ACT, so it's in your best interest to take this section. Taking this part of the test and assuming your college is going to require it is better than not having a score to submit. In other words, take the darn test. You have *nothing* to lose if your university doesn't want it, and *everything* to lose if it does. In this chapter you'll find out about frequent pitfalls you can expect in writing and what scoring system the ACT people use, and you'll read sample essays that have received scores ranging from one to six.

If you're already an excellent writer, which most of you probably are, this chapter gives you the added confidence you need to understand the ACT essay. If you're not the greatest writer, as many students are not, don't despair. That's what we're here for. This chapter teaches you the writing skills and builds up your confidence so you can use them! Seeing how other people have done it makes beginning to write easier. As a result, we included sample essays with low scores for you to laugh at (don't worry, we don't include their names) and essays with high scores for you to learn from. Generally, test-takers are provided with a point-counterpoint topic and asked to write about one side or the other. For information on how the essay test is administered, see Chapter 8.

Rattle Your Writing with Some Loose Screws

Relax. You've been writing since first grade, you have something to say, and this test is a way to prove that. All you need is a quick refresher. Although you may be scared to death of putting your ideas on paper with your name clearly indicated at the top (ooooohh, how we hate to be judged), relax, your name is only on the first page and the ACT scoring folks don't know what you look like. Before you start, though, here are some things to consider and remember to keep you from making the most common mistakes in essay writing. Keep these things in mind, and you'll write the best darn essay ever.

We know you can do it. Here we go . . .

Thought diarrhea: Writing before you think

If you have no destination, you're bound to get lost. The most important part of your essay is having structure and a clear idea of where you're going. If you put your pen to the paper without knowing what the heck you're going to say, you can bet your bottom dollar that the ACT folks won't know what you're saying either. Plan, plan, plan. Thought diarrhea, or writing just to be writing, leads to loose essays, and no one wants to read that mess. Besides that kind of running off at the ink pen makes your writing stink. Creating a solid essay that has a clear organizational plan, however, will get you a high score.

The attack of the clock: Panicking about time

Writer's block, when you simply can't think of anything to put down, often occurs in stressful situations and frequently is caused by a time crunch. You have 30 full minutes to complete the writing portion of the ACT. That's plenty of time to read the question, organize your thoughts, write, and do a quick edit. We suggest that taking 2 minutes to read the question, 3 minutes to write your thesis and hook, 5 minutes to organize your thoughts, 17 minutes to write, and 3 minutes to edit and proofread is an easy breakdown of the 30 minutes. Panicking takes 30 minutes just to get over, and by then, your time's up!

Being too relaxed: Not noticing your time limit

Be aware of your time but don't panic. We know, that's easier said than done. But remember that the ACT people know that you don't have enough time to write the great American novel. However, they expect you to produce a good, concise essay in the time that's allotted. It's important for you to start right away, use your time wisely, and stick to the time schedule. You won't have any time for deep, inner reflection, so don't waste it. You have a time limit; stick to it.

Expressing your inner poet: Using creativity as a crutch

College admissions offices are looking for your creative individualism, but the folks at the ACT are looking for an essay. The ACT writing test gives you a prompt, or topic, to write about. It is very specific, but it isn't the time to write a novel, a journal entry, or a poem. Although you may think you're being creative and impressive, the real creativity lies in impressing them with your writing skills. The ACT writing test is the time to conform to the model of what the test-makers want (which is an organized, thought-out essay that answers the question that they originally asked you), but you still can throw a dose of *you* into the essay by using unique examples. The structure and the language of the essay need not be in a creative format. Do what the test-makers want, so you get the score you want.

Big words with big consequences: Using words you don't know

Nobody can be Shakespeare, especially in 30 minutes, not even Bill himself. When writing the ACT, you won't have the thesaurus button on your word processor in front of you. The worst thing you can do is use words that you think sound good, but you're not really sure what they mean. Instead of trying to use words that you don't know, impress the ACT readers with your thoughts and your ability to communicate clearly. Using words you don't know or quite understand, may give the ACT graders a laugh, but *you* won't be laughing when you see your score.

Expecting perfection in 30 minutes: Being overcritical of yourself

Nobody writes the perfect essay in 30 minutes. Nobody! The graders know that. Trying to be obsessively perfect does you more harm than good. If you spend too much time critiquing yourself, the ACT graders won't have anything to critique. You still can get a perfect score in 30 minutes, if you follow the suggestions and format in this book. Watch your time, stay organized, express yourself clearly (and in your own words) and you *can* get the perfect score, even though you can do better when given more time.

Speaking another language: Dude, they want to read English

We all know that speaking is much easier than writing. However, this test is neither the time nor the place to impress the test-makers with your street vocabulary, dude. Whatever you do, don't drop it like it's hot, don't think you're too cool for school, don't think you're kinda-like the, like, greatest, or like "ohmygod" this is so cool, or else it's your bad. In other words, you're not I'ming, you're not talking to your best friends, and you're not trying to communicate on the playground. You are writing for a bunch of old fogies who have no idea what the latest slang means, dude. (By the way, don't ever use "dude" in your essay, dude.) Make sure that you're using words that your grandparents understand.

Being a wimp: Not taking a solid stand

Our definition of wimp is being indecisive. If you don't take a solid position with your writing, you're going to get knocked down by the graders. You may read a question and think you can justify it in a few different ways, but nobody ever plays for two opposing teams. Don't be scared of picking a side even though you don't believe it. Sometimes you have to lie. The ACT people won't know that you're lying. They only care that you sound confident and that you can support yourself. Choose your thesis based on the amount of ideas you have to back it up, and your solid thesis and back-up punches will give you a winning score.

You are not an island: Forgetting that people really read this stuff

The weekend before the ACT, you may be picketing your local politician, participating in a hunger strike for the dying kids in Africa, or living in the trees to save the forests from corporate logging. However, the ACT essay is not a forum for political activism. Remember, the people who score your essay come from all walks of life. You don't want to become too controversial and risk angering the reader so that it can affect your score. Remember that real people are reading your essay from their points of view and your score may reflect their counterviews. Steer clear of controversy.

Do not do not repeat yourself: 'nuff said

One of the biggest mistakes that you can make on the ACT writing test is saying the same thing again and again in different words. Don't try to lengthen your essay by repeating yourself. The test-graders got it at the first sentence. If you find yourself repeating sentences for lack of things to say, then you've chosen the wrong topic. The way to avoid this mistake is by organizing your thoughts and coming up with specific and different examples to prove your thesis *before* writing your essay.

Leaving the bathroom with TP on your shoe: Not editing your essay

The most embarrassing thing that can happen to you on that perfect first date is your date noticing that you have toilet paper sticking to your shoe. Date over. To counteract potential faux pas like that, make sure that you double-check you shoes before leaving the bathroom — hence a skill that can be applied to your ACT writing. (At last, a real-world skill you can finally use.) Leave yourself time to proofread and check your essay for any obvious sentence structure errors, spelling mistakes, lack of clarity, punctuation, repetition, and illegible handwriting. It helps you to avoid veritable TP that's stuck to your writing. Proofreading and editing are the essential double-checking that you need to do before you walk out the door.

Making the Grade: How the ACT Folks Are Going to Score You

You'll be happy to know that you personally receive not one, but two, yes two, trained readers who will score your essay. And it gets better . . . if the first two don't agree, you personally receive a third, yes third, reader all to yourself. Aren't you special? The ACT guys sure think you are. Not only will you be fortunate enough to receive a numerical score, you even have the pleasure of reading the graders' individual comments on your writing. And yes, those comments appear on your high school and college reports. So, we better get cracking . . . .

Here's the skinny on the scoring:

Two readers read your essay and each assigns a numerical grade from 1 to 6. The sum of those ratings is a student's Writing Test Subscore (2 to 12). If you take the writing test, the ACT people report the score as a Combined English/Writing Score. The English test contributes two-thirds and the writing test contributes one-third toward the combined English/Writing score. If you choose not to take this writing test, your score is reported only as the English subscore. The absence of the writing test score won't affect your score in any other area.

Example Essays and Their Scores

The ACT essay is scored from one to six. One is the lowest score you can achieve, and a six is the highest score. One of the best ways to avoid the common mistakes associated with receiving the lower scores is to read examples of all possible grades. After reading the examples

Chapter 7: ACT Write: The First Words on Essay Writing 59

we've created, you will have a much better idea what to avoid in your writing. This next section explains what it takes to get the highest possible scores on your essay. You also get a chance to see samples of each scored essay so that you're better prepared. Feel free to laugh at the ones with lower scores. We did.

The ACT gives you a long-winded prompt for you to write about. Here's the prompt and six sample essays:

> Example Prompt
>
> In some high schools, many teachers and parents have encouraged the school to adopt a dress code that sets guidelines for what students can wear in the school building. Some teachers and parents support a dress code because they think it will improve the learning environment in the school. Other teachers and parents do not support a dress code because they think it restricts the individual student's freedom of expression. In your opinion, should high schools adopt dress codes for students?

In your essay, take a position on the question. You may write about either one of the two points of view given, or you may present a different point of view on this question. Use specific reasons and examples to support your position.

Remember it doesn't matter which side you choose to write about. Picking one or the other won't matter in the ACT graders' eyes. All that matters is that you pick one side and support your opinion.

1 — 1 is the loneliest number: How not to be a 1

I think students should have a dress code. There is a lot of gangsters at my school that where there pants to low and I don't really like it. If we had a dress code they wouldn't be allowed to do it. Girls should be able to wear shirts that show their stomach though since it looks good and everyone else likes it. There should also be a dress code for really stupid fashion. This should be imposed on teachers too. And principles. I think this is only fair. Why should we have to be the only ones who who have to have a dress code.

Being number 1 may be great for high school football, but it isn't great on your ACT test. This writer answered the question and chooses a side, but she did not support or back up her statement. Not only does she not support herself, she goes off on a tangent and wanders throughout the essay. Her lack of focus, irreverent examples, and her manner or writing like she speaks is going to get her a 1 on the test. Oh, and by the way, the number of spelling and word errors takes away from her ideas, is distracting, and definitely influences the way the graders look at her paper.

2 — 2 little 2 late: Steer clear of coming in second

I don't agree with the teachers and parents who think we should have a dress code. Our style of dress is what makes us individuals and sets us apart form each other.

At my school students who dress in certain ways find others who are like them. You always know who is interested in the same stuff as you by what they wear. Imposing a dress code doesn't allow us to make friendships with people you are like ourselves.

Uniforms would make people mad. Teachers would find it hard to control all their students because students would want to rebel. Kids wouldn't be able to find friends who are like them and this would cause them to rebel.

These are just a few reasons why we should not have a dress code at school. There are many more reasons then just these but these are the most important.

To ACT graders, a 2 means you show *weak* skill in writing the essay. At least they're saying you have some sort of skill, but it can be improved. This writer answers the question and shows that he can support his point of view, but his lack of organization leaves readers' heads spinning. The writer has paragraph structure in this essay, with clear indentations, an introductory paragraph and conclusion, but transitioning between the two paragraphs is missing. His simple sentence structures let everyone know that his writing skill may not be as high as it should be. A 2 may be better than a 1, but it isn't a score for which you should strive.

3 — Still on the wrong side of the tracks

In my opinion, kids should not have a dress code because it takes away freedoms that they should have. There are some clothing styles that teenagers wear that are not appropriate like tight revealing clothes. But to make students buy certain clothes like blue pants and white shirt infringes on their rights.

In America freedom of expression is very important and by forcing us to wear certain things schools are taking away one of our rights. If they start taking away this right, they might start taking away other ones too.

Dress codes are unfair because some families cannot afford them. Many kids would need a whole new wardrobe and their families would have a hard time buying this for them. Not only would they need clothes, but they also need clothes for outside of school. For poorer families this would be hard.

A dress code would take away some of our freedom of expression and it would be a financial strain for poorer families. I think that there should be no dress code.

A 3 is almost a reason for celebration. Almost. This writer answers the question, gives reasons to support the ideas, and then gives even further reasoning to help with the argument. She has structure, maintains focus in her paragraphs, and has sentences that are longer than the ones written by eighth-graders. However, she's still hanging around on the wrong side of the tracks. The ACT folks are starting to recognize her developing skill, but she's still growing. They want her to include some counterarguments and fully develop her ideas. Her paragraphs are not complete, and she does not include the transitions that she needs to help her essay flow. Ideas are logically grouped, but not logically displayed. With a little work, this essay can make it to the right side of the tracks.

4 — The grass is greener on this side

I believe that it would be a good idea for our schools to adopt dress codes. Some people argue that it would restrict student's freedom of expression, but I do not agree with this position. It is important that we have a right to express ourselves, but our society does not allow us to have unrestricted freedoms like this all the time. It is important to learn discipline, show respect for other's feelings and learn how to be successful operating in the real world. Dress codes create a better learning environment and also helps students prepare for their futures.

Chapter 7: ACT Write: The First Words on Essay Writing

The most important benefit of imposing dress codes would be creating a better school environment. Students who are trying to concentrate and learn would be unfocused because of inappropriate clothing. Small clothing, tight tops, and sagging pants might be okay for after school but not appropriate for the classroom. Certain types of people might find profanity and obscene images offensive. Art and creative writing are better ways to express your creativity rather than on your clothing. Less distractions in the classroom would help a student to get a better education.

Another important benefit of having a dress code would teach students how to dress properly for different occasions. Clothes that you would wear to a party would not appropriate for a dinner with your boyfriends parents. Likewise, you wouldn't wear your work clothes on a date. Some jobs in society require people to wear uniforms. Dress codes in schools help students to realize what the world is like and get ready to enter it.

Another important concern for students is trying to fit in. Dress codes take the emphasis off what you look like and put more emphasis on learning.

In conclusion, it is important for schools to adopt dress codes. Getting an education is the most important thing about school and dress codes take away distractions. Learning how to dress for the real world is also important. And it helps with the pressures of trying to fit in.

A score of 4 would make anyone want to run and frolic through green pastures, because the ACT folks think you have *adequate* writing skills. You may not be the best, but at least you're average and your score is respectable. This writer takes a stance and acknowledges counter-arguments. Focus is maintained throughout the essay, and each idea in the better defined paragraphs is developed enough to make the graders happy. This writer demonstrates a simple organizational structure that works with an introduction and a conclusion that balance out the essay. ACT graders like the appropriate word choice and the ability of the writer to demonstrate language control. This score shows that the writer learned his skills in school, even though he may not become the next Shakespeare.

5 — Star material: Five-star winners

There is a debate now amongst parents and teachers about whether or not a dress code should be used in schools. I agree with the position that believes that it will improve the learning environment in our schools. I think a dress code would significantly improve the excellence of our education. First, students would be able to focus on academics rather than the social facet of school. Second, the appearance of the school would improve and third, students would be better prepared for the working world.

The most crucial benefit of implementing a dress code would be to significantly reduce the distractions in the classroom. For students to be successful in the future it is important that we concentrate on the material being taught in the classroom. It is difficult to do this when you overhear students whispering about their newest Gucci purse or admiring their best friend's Prada shoes. Young people place such an emphasis on style and image rather than substance. In addition, students see school as a social venue rather than a learning environment.

Secondly, if the students and faculty are well groomed I believe that it improves the aesthetic appeal of the school. Formal attire is not necessary to achieve this. For example, requiring long pants and a collared shirt would be sufficient. Not only would the school look more professional, it would change the character of the school. Holding students to a higher standard would require them to do it for themselves. It would improve their maturity level as well.

Finally, supporting a dress code would prepare today's youth for the work of their future. A plethora of jobs require uniforms or a standard dress code. I think it is important for schools to not only prepare students academically for their future, but also in proper conduct and grooming. Just because someone has impressive qualifications doesn't mean they'll be hired if they look like they just rolled in from the beach. Allowing students to dress however they choose might eventually be harmful to their future success.

The opposing view feels that a dress code would hinder a student's freedom of expression, but I still think a dress code is a good idea. A dress code addresses the important issues at hand while at the same time allowing the student to find more appropriate ways of expression. It would be different if you could not paint or write creativity the way you chose in school because that would affect your freedom of expression.

In conclusion, I strongly support the idea of a dress code. Not only does it improve our learning environment but it also improves the character of the school and readies the student for a successful future.

A score of 5 gets you a gold star on the blackboard! It isn't ACT perfection, but it's pretty darn close. This writer was able to effectively address the issue by clearly answering the question and by addressing the counterargument. This essay is organized and fluid and contains a variety of specific examples. The ideas in each paragraph are developed and support the argument. This writer explores a cultural component that shows advanced critical thinking skills and displays a mastery of vocabulary and precise word choice.

6 — You unlocked the code: A perfect score

The trend of inappropriate dress in our schools is causing alarm in our parents and educators. This population argues that inappropriate clothes is distracting in the classroom and interferes in the learning environment. They also believe that adopting a dress code would establish guidelines and frameworks for what students should and should not wear on campus. The opposing view believes that a dress code would hinder the student's freedom of expression.

When freedom of expression begins to interfere with appropriate and clear education in the classroom, we have a serious dilemma and the issue needs to be addressed. Obviously in our schools, the lack of a dress code is not working. We are not breaking new ground when we suggest that the fashion that is spewed upon our youth in the mass media is riddled with sexual undertones. Examples of this can be seen in every teen magazine, every youth oriented television program and on the most popular of music videos. Further, what advertisers would consider benign, stimulates and raises the hormone levels of every young male. In our classrooms this can be very distracting. The only solution to help create an environment where learning takes precedence is to adopt school uniforms. Obviously, a uniform policy would be easier to enforce then a dress code, and would bring many advantages to the entire academic population.

First and foremost, uniforms would help students to fight the materialistic world's values. Our society feels that designer labels, such as Gucci, Louis Vuitton, and Hilfinger create self worth and that without these, a person is open to cruel comments and non-acceptance. Many students cannot afford to "buy" their self worth and are required to rise above the standards our society and media feeds them. As a teenager, acceptance is the most crucial aspect of their daily lives, and school uniforms take away the financial burden that our society imposes upon them. Although uniforms need purchasing, it carries with it a minimal financial burden compared to overly high-priced current designer wear that students will ask for.

Chapter 7: ACT Write: The First Words on Essay Writing

Uniforms could also help curb gang related violence that occurs in many of our nation's schools. Specific colors, logos and signs have all been adopted into the lifestyle of gang members and each carry their own significance. What was once an ordinary red shirt, could now be considered an intentional bullet fired in a gang battle. Uniforms decrease the division lines between gangs, as well as protect students who are ignorant to the unwritten laws that govern gangs.

For myself, uniforms would dramatically decrease the amount of time I spent preparing for my day. No longer would I need to delve into the bottom of my closet to find an outfit that I haven't worn this week. I do not need to worry that I my best friend might come to school in the same outfit as me, because uniforms ensure that they will! Uniforms give me extra time to finish the homework I haven't done, rather than spend it worrying about my wardrobe.

Certainly no one is proclaiming that uniforms are the solution to all school-wide problems. There are still wide spread school related issues that could never be fixed with clothes. Safety concerns, educational standards, bullying, and health related issues are areas that need further research. However, uniforms do help to ensure a learning environment that is free from distractions and fosters creative expression in areas of importance.

So, in conclusion, I highly value the worth of uniforms and feel they should be enforced throughout the entire school district. Solving problems in the entire district would help ensure a safer community, save us all money, and give us all some well needed extra time in the morning.

The secret to your success on the ACT is a 6, and with an essay like this, you can earn it. The ACT graders are practically drooling over this writer's style, because it recognizes the complexity of the issue, creates a stunning thesis, and then supports it with well-thought-out and varied examples. She argues her side well, and includes arguments from opposing points of view. Her structure and organization is logical, and she includes transitions between all of her paragraphs. Her writing displays her own unique wit and personality, which she masterfully executes in her essay. The ACT graders practically fell over in their seats when they stumbled upon her words and her ability to use them. In 30 minutes, this writer glided through the essay with eloquence and thoroughness that left the ACT graders stunned. She deserved the 6.

Chapter 8

Write Right: The Writing Test Review

In This Chapter
▶ Finding out what the ACT is looking for in your essay
▶ Breaking down the essay into manageable parts
▶ Exploring the top five editing techniques

Writing a great essay is totally different from writing a really great ACT essay. A great essay is one you plan, think about for days, edit for more days, and the process usually takes a considerable amount of time. My friend, you have only 30 minutes, and that isn't enough time to write something that wins a literary award. But don't fret! All you need to do is figure out the ACT system.

For the sake of your time and interest, we're just going to tell you exactly what they want from you in your essay.

Did you:

- **Make judgments?** Doing so requires you to evaluate the question, decide your position, and clearly articulate your position.
- **Develop a position?** Establishing a position requires you to explain your thoughts using examples, reasons, and details.
- **Maintain focus?** Staying focused requires you to stay on your topic, not drift around, and make sure you don't add thoughts outside of the prompt question.
- **Organize ideas?** Organizing your thoughts and ideas requires you to present your ideas in a logical way, using transitional words and sequencing your ideas so that they build from each other.
- **Communicate clearly?** Communicating clearly requires you to use variety in sentence structure and word choice, and it requires you to spell correctly and make sure your grammar and punctuation are right.

Now that you know what is required of you when answering the essay question, we will break down the essay step by step into manageable chunks. If you use the steps outlined in this chapter, the essay is much easier than you think. You'll be writing 30-minute essays in less time than it takes to read this chapter! Breaking down the question and making a judgment is the first step to success.

Keeping It Simple: Making a Judgment

Think of the ACT prompt as a courtroom. You're the judge, and two lawyers are going to present opposing sides to you. They will give you their long drawn-out narratives, practically putting you to sleep, before they finally present the question to you. Your job is to rule on the question, regardless of whether you know which lawyer is right. It's your courtroom. You must make a decision.

66   Part III: Writing the Writing Test Rightly: You Have a Choice

The writing prompt presents you with each side in a long statement that addresses common high school ideas such as curfews, dress codes, magazines in libraries, competition, or compromising your beliefs.

> The prompt is written to overwhelm you, bore you, and often includes unnecessary information. The very end of the prompt will finally get to the point, but you have to make it there. The first step is to decide what side to write about. Remember, we told you that you don't really have to believe it yourself, you just need to write about it with confidence. The ACT people don't know you and aren't coming to your house to ask you to explain yourself further. The key to starting a strong essay is taking a strong position right away.

1. **Read the question.** Here is the same sample prompt from Chapter 7:

   > Example Prompt
   >
   > In some high schools, many teachers and parents encourage the school to adopt a dress code that sets guidelines for what students can wear in the school building. Some teachers and parents support a dress code because they think it will improve the learning environment in the school. Other teachers and parents do not support a dress code because they think it restricts the individual student's freedom of expression. In your opinion, should high schools adopt dress codes for students?
   >
   > In your essay, take a position on this question. You may write about either one of the two points of view given, or you may present a different point of view on this question. Use specific reasons and examples to support your position.

2. **Pay attention to the last two sentences of each paragraph.** Typically, the last two sentences in each paragraph of the prompt identify what you need to write about. Can you identify the exact question in the above prompt? The very last sentence in the first paragraph is asking you a specific question and telling you what to do.

   - In your opinion, should high schools adopt dress codes for students?
   - Use specific reasons and examples to support your position.

   The last two sentences of each paragraph in the ACT Writing prompt are where you find the direct question that you need to answer. Make sure to carefully read those last two sentences.

3. **Make a judgment regarding dress codes.** Do you think schools need to have dress codes? Or, do you think students should come to school naked (just needed to wake you up here — did it work)? Do not just start writing before you decide what your position is.

Fightin' with Their Words: Incorporating the Question

Okay, so you've read the question and you've decided your position, now it's time to write your first sentence. You can go the hard way and spend precious time trying to impress and sound really witty in the first sentence, or you can take our advice and *use their words*. Using their words is the best route to go here, because it saves you time and guarantees that you answered their question. The two ways you can do it are to rephrase the test-makers' prompt, and fill in your position.

Rephrase the test prompt in your own words, and make it more specific. Taking the test-makers' prompt:

> Should high schools adopt dress codes for students?

You can write something like this:

> High schools should adopt dress codes for students.

Looking closely, you'll notice that we didn't come up with a single new word! We just moved one word, "Should." It's now the third word in the sentence, not the first. No brainpower needed here. No time wasted. Easy as pie. Keep in mind, however, that this is the most basic way of writing your first sentence. It may not get you a 6, but it definitely gets you started.

Or, you can write this:

> I believe that high schools should adopt dress codes for students.

Check that out! All we did was add to their sentence. We deleted the "Should" in their sentence and replaced it with "I believe that . . . " Then, we took the "should" and stuck it in right after "schools."

Or, you can be a bit more dramatic:

> A debate is being waged among teachers and parents regarding dress codes, and I believe that dress codes should be mandatory for all schools.

TIP: Taking the test-makers' question and turning it around to use it in your first sentence guarantees that you answered the question. Now you can write more confidently because you know that you already answered the question.

Putting Up Your Dukes: Deciding Your Position and Writing About It

Agree or disagree, it's that simple. Don't spend time debating with yourself and thinking, "Well, I kinda agree with the agree side but not really because . . . " You have no time for this. Stop thinking so much! Don't you love teachers that tell you not to think? We love that too. Remember, the ACT folks do not care what you really feel, they just want an essay, and they want one in 30 minutes! After you've rephrased the question, just agree or not.

Here are two "Nevers" to remember: Never tell the ACT folks the reasons why you agree or disagree in the first sentence, and never straddle both sides of an issue.

Throwing a Good First Punch: The Hook

Now that you've taken a stand and answered the question, you need to expand your first paragraph. Getting the reader's attention is key to keeping it. You must *hook* (grab the attention of) your reader right from the beginning. Think of the first paragraph as a funnel going from large thoughts to smaller ones. The first sentence needs to capture the overall debate of the prompt. For example, if your prompt is about dress codes, you may want to write something like:

> The appropriateness of dress codes is the subject of widespread debate.

Although you haven't yet stated your position, you've let the reader know that the essay is going to be about dress codes. You haven't given up or tipped your hand yet, which makes the reader want to continue reading your essay. Good job!

Following the funnel down, you need to express both sides of the argument. Doing that is easier than you think, because the original prompt gives you both sides of the debate. Reread the second and third sentences in your prompt. Reword them in your own voice and stick those thoughts right after your first sentence.

> Example Prompt
>
> In some high schools, many teachers and parents have encouraged their schools to adopt dress codes that set guidelines for what students can wear in the school building. **Some teachers and parents support dress codes because they think they will improve the learning environment in the schools. Other teachers and parents do not support dress codes because they think they restrict the freedom of expression of individual students.** In your opinion, should high schools adopt dress codes for students?

You may write:

> Although some people believe a dress code will improve the learning environment, others argue that dress codes may restrict individual freedom of expression.

Every prompt gives you both sides. You need to include the information it provides to show that you recognize both arguments. The ACT people are sticklers for this. Your score will be low whenever you fail to show counterarguments.

The next sentence in your first paragraph is important. It comes before you hit the graders with your position, and it expands your position on the side that you've chosen. To establish your position, you merely have to state three points that you will cover in your essay that support your side. These points eventually turn into your three essay body paragraphs, which we discuss in more depth later in "The Proof Is in the Pudding: Proving Yourself."

You can write:

> It's apparent to me that certain types of clothing can be **distracting, lead to school violence, and interfere with a student's ability to fit in.**

Now that you've brought the reader closer to home after dancing around the issue, deliver a knockout punch. Be clear, be concise, and let the reader have your opinion. You already wrote it, remember? You even used the test-makers' words.

> I believe that high schools should adopt dress codes for students.

You've hit the bottom of your funnel, and you've hit the reader with one heck of a strong punch.

Your first paragraph is now complete:

> The appropriateness of dress codes is the subject of widespread debate. Although some people believe a dress code will improve the learning environment, others argue that dress codes may restrict individual freedom of expression. It's apparent to me that certain types of clothing can be distracting, lead to school violence, and interfere with student's ability to fit in. I believe that high schools should adopt dress codes for students.

TIP: When writing the proper hook paragraph, the thesis is the last sentence in that first paragraph. Don't give up your hand too early, and don't neglect building the suspense.

The Proof Is in the Pudding: Proving Yourself

To create the great ACT essay, you must use specific examples, reasons, and details that prove your topic. The ACT folks are looking for two things here:

- Specific examples
- Variety of examples

Specific examples

We remember back in high school when our parents were always asking for specific details about how we spent our evenings: Where did you go? Who was there? Why are you home so late? Who drove? How long has he had his license? The list was endless, and vague answers never cut it. This skill you've been practicing for years is going to come in handy when you take your ACT Writing Test, because you're already great at giving the specifics (or making them up). Really good examples discuss extremely specific details, events, dates, and occurrences. Your goal is to write in detail and try not to be too broad and loose. For example, let's say that you're trying to find examples to support dress codes. Perhaps you can come up with an example how allowing students to wear whatever they want leads to distraction among the students. Great, but you need to be more specific. You need to give an example from your life when you witnessed this occurring, or you need to site an article you read, or give the reader a scenario supporting your position. In other words, give dates, mention people, rat on your friends! Just choose examples that you know a lot about so that you can get down to the nitty gritty and be extremely specific.

Variety of examples

Together with specific examples, we often had to come up with a variety of excuses for breaking curfew — the car broke down, traffic was horrendous, the movie ran late, you forgot the time, you fell asleep . . . you know the routine. Again, thank your parents for helping you with yet another skill you can apply to the ACT Writing Test. When you're writing, you need to use a variety of examples. Coming up with three specific examples about how you feel about dress codes just from your personal life is easy, but it also would be boring. Don't take this the wrong way, but the only person who wants to read three pages about you is you.

Use a broad range of examples from different areas such as literature, cultural experience, your personal life, current events, business, and history. If you spend just a few moments thinking about it, you can come up with three great examples all taken from varied areas.

So, to answer the question, "Should schools require students to have dress codes?" you may come up with three examples like these:

- **Personal life:** A scenario where you saw a girl wearing a short skirt and teeny top and how it interfered with other students' ability to concentrate.
- **Literature:** An example from a magazine article you read about Columbine and how the boys who fired guns in their school were trying to hurt the kids who looked and dressed like jocks.
- **Cultural experience:** The concern regarding wearing gang-related colors and logos, and the potential implications doing so may have regarding violence in the schools.

A nice variety of examples like these definitely gets the attention of the ACT folks and helps you sound like the smart writer that you are.

Hamburger Writing: The Organization of the Essay

Ever take apart a Big Mac? Well, okay, we don't blame you for not wanting to really see what's lurking in there (even though they taste darn good). If you ever decided to do it, you would find that every single Big Mac is built the same exact way. They don't ever deviate! "Two-all-beef-patties-special-sauce-lettuce-cheese-pickles-onion-on-a-sesame-seed-bun." Every time, our dear fast-food friends! And boy, did that company know what they were doing! What we are teaching you is that every great essay is organized like a Big Mac. (See Figure 8-1.) No matter what your prompt is, the ACT wants to see a specific format to your writing and doesn't want all the ingredients thrown in any old way. The organization that we are about to explain to you makes sure that you give those ACT people a supersized essay.

Figure 8-1: This burger picture represents the typical five-paragraph essay that you'll use no matter what your topic is.

Paragraph 1: Introduction (The Top Bun)
Paragraph 2: Example 1 (The Meat)
Paragraph 3: Example 2 (The Meat)
Paragraph 4: Example 3 (The Meat)
Paragraph 5: Conclusion (The Bottom Bun)

Top Bun: The introduction

The top bun includes the funnel of information that leads to your thesis. We just taught you how to write it in the previous section. Done.

The Three Meats: Example paragraphs

For your supporting arguments think in terms of three different kinds of meat. Each meat represents a separate paragraph in your essay, the purpose of which is to add specific examples that help prove the position that you stated in your top bun (are you getting hungry yet?). Each paragraph needs to include:

- About four to five sentences.
- A solid topic sentence that relates directly to your position. Remember, you already wrote your three ideas in your top bun (the third sentence of your introduction).
- Variety of reasons, details, and examples that illustrate that specific topic.

In your top bun, you wrote that clothing can be distracting, remember? We are going to use that thought as the topic sentence for this first meat paragraph. You may write:

> One of the reasons that a dress code should be mandated is because some clothing choices can be very distracting in the learning environment.

Now you have to write four or five sentences that prove that clothing can be distracting. Make sure that you use specific and clear examples and details taken from a variety of areas, including personal experience, history, culture, and literature. Do not stray off topic, or in this case, begin writing about anything else other than clothing being distracting. In other words, don't get distracted when writing about distraction.

Sink your teeth into this meat paragraph:

> One of the reasons that a dress code needs to be mandated is because a variety of clothing choices can be very distracting in the learning environment. MTV and pop stars flash images of young girls wearing practically nothing, for example, a fashion that most teenagers try to emulate (culture reference). However, wearing skimpy clothes and showing body parts can make some people look, perhaps react, and maybe even interrupt an important part of class and that can be quite distracting when you're trying to learn the Pythagorean theorem (personal experience reference). Furthermore, paying attention to the teacher is difficult when you hear people discussing another student's $150 Dolce and Gabana jeans (cultural reference). A dress code does away with these distractions by enforcing a more conservative style of clothing, allowing the focus in the classroom to remain on education rather than fashion.

Your essay cannot be full, however, even after a meaty paragraph like the last one. Although you still have two more to gobble down, don't despair, you have time! The topics of the next two examples (meats) already have been decided in your introduction, remember? You mentioned distractions, school violence, and fitting in. You already wrote about distractions; your second meat is about school violence, and your third is about fitting in.

Make it easy on yourself. Structure the second and third examples exactly like you did in the first one by including:

- A solid topic sentence that defends your position.
- Four to five sentences where you give reasons, details, and examples that support your topic in this paragraph.
- A variety of examples taken from different areas such as literature, culture, personal experience, and history.

Transitions

Like the sandwich we're comparing it to, your essay needs to taste good, or read well, as a whole. Transitions serve as the special sauce, smoothing out the differences between your paragraphs. Your second and third meat paragraphs require transitions. The best way to do this is by using transitional words such as secondly, finally, another idea, another example, furthermore, and in addition, to name a few.

The Bottom Bun: Conclusion

No matter how full of this essay you are, you need to eat the bottom bun. Look on the bright side; it's the end. You can throw up in a little while. The bottom bun or conclusion of your essay needs to include:

- A restatement of your position.
- An expansion of your position that looks to the future.

You can do this in three to four sentences. Make sure that you include your position, references to your meat topics, and one sentence that pulls it all together. Here's an example:

> Implementing a dress code policy would be a beneficial school policy (restatement of your position). Implementing a dress code has the potential to limit distractions in the classroom, reduce school-related violence, and help students find more creative ways to fit in (references to your meat topics). A dress code would direct the appropriate school focus back on education rather than on its being a fashion show (looking toward the future).

Wielding the Red Pen: Editing and Proofing

Okay, with the finish line directly in front of you, all you have left to do is a quick sprint to the end of your essay. If you're like us, at this point, you either think that your writing is perfect and doesn't need correcting (ha!) or that you're finished, done, over it, goodbye and see you later, essay, I'm handing you in!

However, our editors don't put our writing on the same pedestal that we do, and your essay score will reflect your hasty goodbye. It isn't over until you've checked your writing. This section gives you five quick editing and proofreading techniques to keep you from tripping before you hit the finish line. You need to double-check what you wrote, correct it, and give it a champion's finish.

Relax, you've already learned it

Chapter 4 of this book reviews the basic rules of grammar and sentence structure and reminds you of simple things to watch for when you check your sentences. Being the wonderful student that you are, you probably already have studied that chapter and now are ready to launch straight into these Top Five Editing Techniques.

Top four editing techniques

Touch method: Spelling and ghost words

Your brain is smarter than you think it is. When proofreading, your brain sees words that you intended to write, but didn't actually get around to writing. Most of time they are just little words, but without them your sentences and essay fail. Use your pencil to physically touch every single word that you wrote. Doing so helps you find words that you omitted, catch simple spelling errors, and find where you repeated words or thoughts. The smallest errors often are the most costly. The three easiest mistakes to catch are "there," "their," and "they're"; "your" and "you're"; and "it's" and "its." Touching the words as you proofread helps you outsmart your brain and catch these simplest of mistakes.

R and R: Review for repetition

Rest and relaxation come after you've checked for repetition. Reading through your essay to see whether you have repeated yourself is important. Sometimes when examples are lacking, writers have a tendency to say the same things again and again, using different words. If you find that your essay reads like one long sentence, you must spice it up and add some different thoughts.

Active voice: Show, not tell

You can't score a 6 if readers fall asleep in the middle of your essay. Wake them up by forcing them to read caffeine-filled words. In other words, use bold, action verbs rather than mild-mannered wimpy verbs. For example, instead of writing, "He ran to the store quickly," replace "ran" with "bolted," "sprinted," or "flew." These words express more action and give the sentence movement. Ran is boring. Replacing boring verbs with verbs that create vivid pictures definitely improves your essay. Check out the three sentences that follow; each is written two ways (one is boring and tired and the other active and engaging):

1. **Boring:** Holden is a dynamic character.

    Exciting: Holden's character screams personality in the novel.

2. **Boring:** My grandfather taught me a lot.

    Exciting: My grandfather's wisdom inspires me every day.

3. **Boring:** There are three reasons why I believe that this invention is the greatest.

    Exciting: Three reasons prove why this invention transformed the world.

Use words that help the reader visualize what you're saying. Caffeinated verbs activate your reader, giving your essay an added boost of action.

Punk-tu-a-tion

Rebellion against authority may be your motto; it certainly was ours in high school. However, you cannot rebel against grammar rules. They always win. Here are the questions you need to ask yourself and the things you need to look for when editing for punctuation:

- Did I use the correct periods, exclamation points, and question marks?
- Did I capitalize the first words of my sentences and proper nouns?
- Do my subjects agree with my verbs?
- Did I use commas correctly?
- Are any of my sentences run-ons or fragments?
- Are my words spelled correctly?

This Was Not a Prescription: Handwriting

You need to get into med school first before you can write like a doctor. If the ACT graders cannot read your prescription for success, then you can bet your bottom dollar that your score will be low. The brilliant essay you just wrote may just save your entire ACT score, but if nobody can read it, it's a prescription for failure. Illegible writing is an easy error to catch as you proofread your essay. If *you* can't read your writing, you must erase what can't be read and rewrite it. Pencils, with erasers, what a brilliant invention!

Chapter 9

Practicing Promptly with Practice Prompts: Essay Practice Examples

In This Chapter
▶ Writing practice essays
▶ Using prompts to practice writing essays

So far, you've done a really good job reading about writing. But, you'll never get better at writing without actually writing. In this chapter, we give you two sample prompts to practice with, and we suggest that you time yourself so that you get a sense for what 30 minutes of writing feels like. Practicing like this also helps you avoid panicking when you take the real test. Pencils out! Here we go.

Writing Prompt #1

> Many successful people believe that a competitive environment fosters high achievement. In high schools, some parents and teachers think that competition between students encourages them to strive toward higher academic potential. Others think that academic competition negatively affects students' performance by causing undue stress and feelings of failure. In your opinion, should high schools encourage a competitive academic atmosphere?
>
> In your essay, take a position on this question. You may write about either one of the two points of view given, or you may present a different point of view on this question. Use specific reasons and examples to support your position.

_____

_____

_____

_____

_____

_____

Writing Prompt #2

> The prevailing attitude in many countries is that leaders must maintain the highest ethical and moral standards. Some people think that this attitude sets a good example for a country and its citizens. Others argue that leaders who show normal, human flaws connect them with their people and thereby enable progress and growth. In your opinion, should leaders always be accountable for high moral and ethical standards?
>
> In your essay, take a position on this question. You may write about either one of the two points of view given, or you may present a different point of view on this question. Use specific reasons and examples to support your position.

Part IV
Don't Count Yourself Out: The Math Review and Mini-Test

The 5th Wave — By Rich Tennant

"I'm always surprised at the amount of English Usage inspired by the Math Review section of the ACT."

In this part...

You knew it was coming, didn't you? There's no way to get through a test prep book without having a math review. This book gives you three for the price of one: geometry, algebra/trigonometry, and miscellaneous math. I've worked hard to make this stuff as painless as possible by throwing in the odd joke here and there and by using some examples that are a lot more fun than any you'd actually see on the ACT. After all, you're bound to experience a little bit of sensory overload as you cover three years of math in just three chapters.

But I don't waste your time. I don't insult you by starting too far back ("here are the multiplication tables you must know"), and I don't give you material that's not tested (like calculus) just to impress you with *my* abilities. (Hey, if I can't impress you with my jokes, forget it!) Instead, I emphasize what you're most likely to see on the test, reviewing all the formulas and even some of the math vocabulary, like prime and composite numbers.

Note: If you haven't covered some of the material in these reviews, don't worry about it. Maybe you haven't had trig yet (only four of the ACT questions cover the subject, so don't start panicking!) or even geometry. That's okay. You should still be able to follow most of the material. Just do what you can and have fun with it.

This part also features a chapter on how to approach the math questions on the ACT, including what to do when you don't have a clue. You can discover how to recognize and avoid built-in traps, how to use the answer choices to save yourself time and headaches in solving the problems, and which questions are time-wasters that are best to guess at quickly and leave behind in your dust. (***Remember:*** The ACT assesses *no penalty* for guessing, so even random guessing is worthwhile.)

After that chapter is a mini-test, just 12 questions, that allows you to download some of the things you've been learning... and see whether you really can recognize those traps.

Chapter 10

Ogling More Figures than a Beauty Pageant Judge: Geometry Review

In This Chapter
- Getting to the point with angles
- Taming triangles
- Matchmaking similar figures
- Presenting polygons
- Running in circles

Geometry is one of the areas that can mess you up on the ACT. But it's easy when you take the time to memorize some rules. This chapter provides a lightning-fast review of the major points of geometry so you can go into the test equipped to tackle the geometry questions with ease.

You Gotta Have an Angle

Angles are a big part of the ACT geometry problems. Fortunately, understanding angles is easy when you memorize a few basic concepts. And keep in mind the best news: You don't have to do proofs. Finding an angle usually is a matter of simple addition or subtraction. These three rules generally apply to the ACT:

- No *negative angles* exist.
- No *zero angles* exist.
- It is extremely unlikely that you'll see any *fractional angles*. (For example, an angle won't measure 45½ degrees or 32¾ degrees.)

Angles are whole numbers. If you're plugging in a number for an angle, plug in a whole number such as 30, 45, or 90.

1. **Angles greater than 0 but less than 90 degrees are called *acute*.** Think of an acute angle as being a *cute* little angle.

45°
Acute angle

Part IV: Don't Count Yourself Out: The Math Review and Mini-Test

2. **Angles equal to 90 degrees are called *right angles*.** They're formed by perpendicular lines and indicated by a box in the corner of the two intersecting lines.

l_1
l_2
Right angles

TRAPS & TRICKS

Don't automatically assume that angles that look like right angles are right angles. Without calculating the amount or degree of the angle, the only ways you know that an angle is a right angle are if: (A) You're expressly told, "This is a right angle"; (B) you see the perpendicular symbol (⊥) indicating that the lines form a 90-degree angle; or (C) you see the box in the angle. Assume otherwise, and you may be headed for a trap!

a | b
Not necessarily right angles

TIP

3. **Angles that total 90 degrees are called *complementary angles*.** Think of C for corner (the lines form a 90-degree corner angle) and C for complementary.

y
x
Complementary x and y angles

4. **An angle that is greater than 90 degrees but less than 180 degrees is called *obtuse*.** Think of obtuse as obese — an obese (or fat) angle is an obtuse angle.

110°
Obtuse angle

5. **An angle that measures exactly 180 degrees is called a *straight angle*.**

180°
Straight angle

6. **Angles that total 180 degrees are called *supplementary angles*.**

y x
Supplementary angles

TIP

Think of S for supplementary (or straight) angles. Be careful not to confuse complementary angles (C for complementary or corner) with supplementary angles (S for supplementary or straight). If you're likely to get these confused, just think alphabetically. C comes before S in the alphabet; 90 comes before 180 when you count.

Chapter 10: Ogling More Figures than a Beauty Pageant Judge: Geometry Review

7. **An angle that is greater than 180 degrees but less than 360 degrees is called a *reflex angle*.**

   320°
   Reflex angle

   TIP: Reflex angles rarely are tested on the ACT.

8. **Angles around a point total 360 degrees.**

   360 degrees

9. **Angles that are opposite each other have equal measures and are called *vertical angles*.** Just remember that vertical angles are *across* from each other, whether they're up and down (vertical) or side by side (horizontal).

   $a = b$ Vertical angles $c = d$ Vertical angles

10. **Angles in the same position around two parallel lines and a transversal (corresponding angles) have the same measures.**

    $l_1 \parallel l_2$

    TIP: When you see two parallel lines and a *transversal* (that's the line going across the parallel lines), number the angles. Start in the upper-right corner with 1 and go clockwise. For the second batch of angles, start in the upper-right corner with 5 and go clockwise:

    $l_1 \parallel l_2$

    1=3=5=7   2=4=6=8

Note that all odd-numbered angles are equal and all even-numbered angles are equal.

Be careful not to zigzag back and forth when numbering. If you zig when you should have zagged, you can no longer use the tip that all even-numbered angles are equal to one another and all odd-numbered angles are equal to one another.

11. **The exterior angles of any figure are supplementary to the interior angles and total 360 degrees.**

Exterior angles

Exterior angles always total 360 degrees, no matter what type of figure you have.

Triangle Trauma

1. **A triangle with three equal sides and three equal angles is called *equilateral*.**

Equilateral

2. **A triangle with two equal sides and two equal angles is called *isosceles*.**

Isosceles

3. **Angles opposite equal sides in an isosceles triangle are also *equal*.**

Isosceles

Chapter 10: Ogling More Figures than a Beauty Pageant Judge: Geometry Review

4. A triangle with no equal sides and no equal angles is called *scalene*.

Scalene

5. In any triangle, the largest angle is opposite the longest side.

6. In any triangle, the sum of the lengths of two sides must be greater than the length of the third side. This statement is often written as $a + b > c$, where a, b, and c are the sides of the triangle.

3+3>3

3+4>4
4+4>3

3+4>5
4+5>3
5+3>4

7. In any type of triangle, the sum of the interior angles is 180 degrees.

A trap question may want you to assume that different-sized triangles have different angle measures. Wrong! A triangle can be seven stories high and have 180 degrees or be microscopic and have 180 degrees. The size of the triangle is irrelevant; every triangle's internal angles add up to 180 degrees.

8. The measure of an exterior angle of a triangle is equal to the sum of the two remote interior angles.

$a = y + z$

Similar figures

1. **The sides of similar figures are in proportion.** For example, if the heights of two similar triangles are in a ratio of 2:3, then the bases of those triangles also are in a ratio of 2:3.

AB:AC=2:3
BE:CD=2:3

2. **The ratio of the areas of similar figures is equal to the square of the ratio of their sides.** For example, if each side of Figure A is ⅓ the length of each side of similar Figure B, then the area of Figure A is ⅑ or $(⅓)^2$ the area of Figure B.

Figure A: A=6, height 4, base 3
Figure B: A=54, height 12, base 9

Example:

Two similar triangles have bases of 5 and 25. Which of the following expresses the ratio of the areas of the two triangles?

A. 1:5

B. 1:15

C. 1:25

D. 1:30

E. 1:50

The ratio of the sides is ⅕. The ratio of the areas is the square of the ratio of the sides: ⅕ × ⅕ = ¹⁄₂₅. *Correct answer:* **C.**

Bonus: What do you suppose the ratio of the *volumes* of two similar figures is? Because volume is found in cubic units, the ratio of the volumes of two similar figures is the *cube* of the ratio of their sides. If figure A has a base of 5 and similar figure B has a base of 10, then the ratio of their volumes is 1:8 (1:2^3, which is ½ × ½ × ½ = ⅛).

Don't assume that figures are similar; you must be told that they are.

Chapter 10: Ogling More Figures than a Beauty Pageant Judge: Geometry Review 85

Area

1. **The area of a triangle is ½ *base* × *height*.** The height always is a line perpendicular to the base. The height may be a side of the triangle, as in a right triangle.

The height may be inside the triangle. It often is represented by a dashed line and a small 90-degree box.

The height may be outside the triangle. *Remember:* You can always drop an altitude. That is, put your pencil on the tallest point of the triangle and draw a line straight from that point to where the base would be if it were extended.

2. **The perimeter of a triangle is the sum of the lengths of its sides.**

Pythagorean theorem

You probably have studied the Pythagorean theorem. Keep in mind that it works only on right triangles. If a triangle doesn't have a right — or 90-degree-angle, you can't use any of the following information.

In any right triangle, you can find the lengths of the sides with the formula

$a^2 + b^2 = c^2$

where *a* and *b* are the sides of the triangle and *c* is the hypotenuse. The *hypotenuse* always is opposite the 90-degree angle and always is the longest side of the triangle.

Pythagorean triples

Having to work the whole Pythagorean Theorem formula every time you want to find the length of a side is a pain in the posterior. You'll find five very common ratios in right triangles.

1. **Ratio 3:4:5.** If one side of the triangle is 3 in this ratio, the other side is 4 and the hypotenuse is 5.

Because Ratio 3:4:5 exists, the sides can be in any multiple of these numbers, such as 6:8:10 (twice 3:4:5), 9:12:15 (three times 3:4:5), or 27:36:45 (nine times 3:4:5).

2. **Ratio 5:12:13.** If one side of the right triangle is 5 in this ratio, the other side is 12 and the hypotenuse is 13.

Because this is a ratio, the sides can be in any multiple of these numbers, such as 10:24:26 (twice 5:12:13), 15:36:39 (three times 5:12:13), or 50:120:130 (ten times 5:12:13).

3. **Ratio s: s: $s\sqrt{2}$, where s stands for the side of the figure.** Because two s's are alike or two sides are the same, this formula applies to an isosceles right triangle, also known as a 45:45:90 triangle. If one side is 2, then the other side also is 2 and the hypotenuse is $2\sqrt{2}$.

This formula is great to know for squares. If a question tells you that the side of a square is 5 and wants to know the diagonal of the square, you know immediately that it is $5\sqrt{2}$. Why? A square's diagonal cuts the square into two isosceles right triangles (*isosceles* because all sides of the square are equal; right because all angles in a square are right angles). What is the diagonal of a square of side 64? $64\sqrt{2}$. What is the diagonal of a square of side 12,984? $12,984\sqrt{2}$.

There's another way to write this ratio. Instead of s: s: $s\sqrt{2}$, you can write it as $\frac{s}{\sqrt{2}}:\frac{s}{\sqrt{2}}:s$ in which s still stands for the side of the triangle, but now you've divided everything through by $s\sqrt{2}$. Why do you need this complicated formula? Suppose you're told that the diagonal of a square is 5. What is the area of the square? What is the perimeter of the square?

If you know the formula $\frac{s}{\sqrt{2}}:\frac{s}{\sqrt{2}}: s$, you know that s stands for the hypotenuse of the triangle, the same as the diagonal of the square. If s = 5, then the side of the square is $\frac{5}{\sqrt{2}}$ and you can figure out the area or the perimeter. After you know the side of a square, you can figure out just about anything.

4. **Ratio $s:s:\sqrt{3}:2s$.** This special formula is for the sides of a 30:60:90 triangle.

This type of triangle is a favorite of test-makers. The important thing to keep in mind here is that the hypotenuse is twice the length of the side opposite the 30-degree angle. If you get a word problem saying, "Given a 30:60:90 triangle of hypotenuse 20, find the area" or "Given a 30:60:90 triangle of hypotenuse 100, find the perimeter," you can do so because you can find the lengths of the other sides.

Thanks 4 Nothing: Quadrilaterals

1. **Any four-sided figure is called a *quadrilateral*.**

Quadrilateral

The interior angles of any quadrilateral total 360 degrees. Any quadrilateral can be cut into two 180-degree triangles.

2. **A *square* is a quadrilateral with four equal sides and four right angles.**

$A = S^2$
$A = 1/2 d^2$

Square

The area of a square is side² (also called *base × height*), or ½ d², where *d* stands for *diagonal*.

3. **A *rhombus* is a quadrilateral with four equal sides and four angles that are not necessarily right angles.** A rhombus often looks like a drunken square, tipsy on its side and wobbly.

   The area of a rhombus is ½ d_1d_2 (or ½ diagonal$_1$ × diagonal$_2$).

   Rhombus

   Any square is a rhombus, but not all rhombuses are squares.

4. **A *rectangle* is a quadrilateral with two opposite and equal pairs of sides.** That is, the top and bottom sides are equal, and the right and left sides are equal. All angles in a rectangle are right angles.

   The area of a rectangle is *length × width* (which is the same as *base × height*).

   Rectangle

5. **A *parallelogram* is a quadrilateral with two opposite and equal pairs of sides.** The top and bottom sides are equal, and the right and left sides are equal. Opposite angles are equal but not necessarily right (or 90 degrees).

   The area of a parallelogram is base × height. Remember that the height always is a perpendicular line from the tallest point of the figure down to the base. Diagonals of a parallelogram bisect each other.

   Parallelogram

   All rectangles are parallelograms, but not all parallelograms are rectangles.

6. **A *trapezoid* is a quadrilateral with two parallel sides and two nonparallel sides.**

   The area of a trapezoid is ½ (*base$_1$* + *base$_2$*) × *height*. It makes no difference which base you label base 1 and which you label base 2, because you're adding them together. Just be sure to add them *before* you multiply by ½.

Chapter 10: Ogling More Figures than a Beauty Pageant Judge: Geometry Review

$A = 1/2 \, (b_1+b_2) h$

Trapezoid

Quaint quads: Bizarre quadrilaterals

Some quadrilaterals don't have nice, neat shapes or special names.

If you see a strange shape, don't immediately say that you have no way of finding its area. You may be able to divide the quadrilateral into two triangles and find the area of each triangle and add them together. You may also see a strange quadrilateral in a shaded-area problem.

Leftovers again: Shaded-area problems

Think of a shaded area as a *leftover*. It is "left over" after you subtract the unshaded area from the total area.

Shaded areas often are very unusual shapes. Your first reaction may be that you can't possibly find the area of that shape. Generally, you're right, but you don't have to find the area directly. Instead, be sly, devious, and sneaky; in other words, think the ACT way! Find the area of the total figure, find the area of the unshaded portion, and subtract.

1. $s = 8$
   Area of square = 64
2. $r = 4$
   Area of circle = 16π
3. Shaded area = $64 - 16\pi$

Missing Parrots and Other Polly-Gones

Triangles and quadrilaterals probably are the most common polygons tested on this exam. A polygon is a closed plane figure bounded by straight sides. Table 10-1 explains a few other polygons you may see:

1. **A polygon with all equal sides and all equal angles is called** *regular*. For example, an equilateral triangle is a regular triangle and a square is a regular quadrilateral.

   You are rarely asked to find the areas of any polygons with more than four sides.

2. **The** *perimeter* **of a polygon is the sum of the lengths of all the sides.**

3. **The** *exterior angle measure* **of any polygon is 360°.**

Now, to find the interior angle measure, use the formula $(n - 2)\,180°$, where n stands for the number of sides.

Table 10-1	Pondering the parameters of polygons	
Number of Sides	**Name**	**Interior angle calculation**
3	Triangle	$(3 - 2)\,180 = 1 \times 180 = 180°$
4	Quadrilateral	$(4 - 2)\,180 = 2 \times 180 = 360°$
5	Pentagon	$(5 - 2)\,180 = 3 \times 180 = 540°$
6	Hexagon (think of x in six and x in hex)	$(6 - 2)\,180 = 4 \times 180 = 720°$
7	Heptagon	$(7 - 2)\,180 = 5 \times 180 = 900°$
8	Octagon	$(8 - 2)\,180 = 6 \times 180 = 1080°$
9	Nonagon	$(9 - 2)\,180 = 7 \times 180 = 1260°$
10	Decagon	$(10 - 2)\,180 = 8 \times 180 = 1440°$

One interior angle

1. **To find the average measure of one angle in a figure, use the formula**

   $$\frac{(n-2)\,180}{n}$$

   where n stands for the number of sides (which is the same as the number of angles).

   Pentagon: $\dfrac{(5-2) \times 180}{5} = \dfrac{3 \times 180}{5} = \dfrac{540}{5} = 108$

   Because all angles are equal in a regular polygon, the same formula applies to one angle in a regular polygon.

2. **If you are given a polygon and are** *not* **told that it's regular, you can't solve for just one angle.**

Chapter 10: Ogling More Figures than a Beauty Pageant Judge: Geometry Review

What's the measure of angle *x*? It cannot be determined. You cannot assume that it is

$$\frac{(7-2)180}{7} = \frac{900}{7} = 128.57$$

Be sure to divide through by *n*, the number of sides (angles), not by (*n* – 2). If you divide through by (*n* – 2), you always get

$$\left(\frac{900}{5}\right) = 180$$

Knowing this, triple-check your work if you come up with 180 for an answer to this type of problem; you may have made this (very typical) careless error.

Volume

The volume of any polygon is *(area of the base)* × *height*. If you remember this formula, you don't have to memorize any of the following more specific formulas.

1. **Volume of a cube:** e^3

    $V = e^3$

    Cube

    A cube is a three-dimensional square. Think of a die (one of a pair of dice). All of a cube's dimensions are the same; that is, *length* = *width* = *height*. In a cube, these dimensions are called *edges*. The volume of a cube is *edge* × *edge* × *edge* = *edge*³ = e^3.

2. **Volume of a rectangular solid:** $l \times w \times h$

    $V = lwh$

    Rectangular solid

    A rectangular solid is a box. The base of a box is a rectangle, which has an area of *length* × *width*. Multiply that by height to fit the original formula: Volume = *(area of base)* × *height*, or $V = l \times w \times h$.

3. **Volume of a cylinder:** $(\pi r^2)height$

    $V = \pi r^2 h$

    Cylinder

    Think of a cylinder as a can of soup. The base of a cylinder is a circle. The area of a circle is πr^2. Multiply that by the height of the cylinder to get *(area of base)* × *height*

= $(\pi r^2) \times height$. Note that the top and bottom of a cylinder are identical circles. If you know the radius of either the top base or the bottom base, you can find the area of the circle.

Total surface area (TSA)

The total surface area, logically enough, is the sum of the areas of all the surfaces of the figure.

1. **TSA of a cube: $6e^2$**

   Cube

   A cube has six identical faces, and each face is a square. The area of a square is $side^2$. Here, that is called $edge^2$. If one face is $edge^2$, then the total surface area is $6 \times edge^2$, or $6e^2$.

2. **TSA of a rectangular solid: $2(lw) + 2(wh) + 2(hl)$**

   Rectangular solid

   A rectangular solid is a box. You need to find the area of each of the six surfaces. The bottom and top have the area of $length \times width$. The left side and right side have the area of $width \times height$. The front side and the back side have the area of $height \times length$. Together, they total $2(lw) + 2(wh) + 2(hl)$ or $2(lw + wh + hl)$.

3. **TSA of a cylinder: $(circumference \times height) + 2(\pi r^2)$**

   Cylinder

   This TSA definitely is the most difficult to figure out. Think of it as pulling the label off the can, flattening it out, finding its area, and then adding that to the area of the top and bottom lids. The *label* is a rectangle. Its *length* is the length of the circumference of the circle.

   $l=c$

Chapter 10: Ogling More Figures than a Beauty Pageant Judge: Geometry Review

Its *height* is the height of the cylinder. Multiply *length* × *height* to find the area of the label.

You also need to find the area of the top and bottom of the cylinder. Because each is a circle, the TSA of the top and bottom is $2(\pi r^2)$. Add everything together.

I'm Too Much of a Klutz for Coordinate Geometry

1. The horizontal axis is the *x*-axis. The vertical axis is the *y*-axis.

2. Points are labeled *(x,y)*, with the first number in the parentheses being how far to the right or left of the vertical line the point is and the second number being how far above or below the horizontal line the point is.

3. The intersection of the *x*- and *y*-axes is called the *point of origin*, and its coordinates are (0,0).

4. A line connecting points whose *x*- and *y*-coordinates are the same forms a 45-degree angle.

5. To find the distance between two points, you can use the distance formula:

$$\sqrt{(x_2-x_1)^2 + (y_2-y_1)^2}$$

Find the distance from (9,4) to (8,6).

$9 = x_1$

$8 = x_2$

$4 = y_1$

$6 = y_2$

$(8-9)^2 = -1^2 = 1$

$(6-4)^2 = 2^2 = 4$

$\sqrt{1+4} = \sqrt{5}$

The distance between the two points is $\sqrt{5}$.

Running Around in Circles

Did you hear about the rube who pulled his son out of college, claiming that the school was filling his head with nonsense? As the rube said, "Joe Bob told me that he learned πr^2. But any fool knows that pie are round; *cornbread* are square!"

Circles are among the less complicated geometry concepts. The most important things are to remember the vocabulary and to be able to distinguish an arc from a sector and an inscribed angle from a central angle. Here's a quick review of the basics.

1. A *radius* goes from the center of a circle to its *circumference* (perimeter).

   Radius

2. A *circle* is named by its *center* (midpoint).

   circle M

   Midpoint

3. A *diameter* connects two points on the circumference of the circle, going through the center, and is equal to two radii.

   Diameter

4. A *chord* connects any two points on a circle.

   Chords

5. **The longest chord in a circle is the diameter.**

   Here's a lovely question you may see on the test. What is the area of a circle of longest chord 12?

   F. 144π

   G. 72π

   H. 36π

   J. 12π

   K. Cannot be determined from the information given

The diameter of this circle is 12, which means its radius is 6, because a diameter is twice the radius. The area of a circle is πr^2. Here, $\pi 6^2 = 36\pi$. *Correct answer:* **H.**

Choice K is the trap answer. If you know only that *a chord* of the circle is 12, you can't solve the problem. A circle has many different chords. You need to know the length of *the longest chord*, or the diameter.

Bonus: You may encounter a wheel question in which you're asked how much distance a wheel covers or how many times a wheel revolves. The key to solving this type of question is knowing that one rotation of a wheel equals one circumference of that wheel.

A child's wagon has a wheel of radius 6 inches. If the wagon wheel travels 100 revolutions, approximately how many feet has the wagon rolled?

A. 325

B. 314

C. 255

D. 201

E. 200

One revolution is equal to one circumference: $C = 2\pi r = 2\pi 6 = 12\pi$ = approximately 37.68 inches. Multiply that by 100 = 3,768 inches = 314 feet. *Correct answer:* **B.**

6. **The area of a circle is $\pi \times$ radius².**

$$4 \quad A = 16\pi$$

7. **A *central angle* has its endpoints on the circumference of the circle and its center at the center of the circle. The degree measure of a central angle is the same as the degree measure of its intercepted arc.**

$$\overarc{AC} = 90°$$

8. **An *inscribed angle* has both its endpoints and its center on the circumference of the circle. The degree measure of an inscribed angle is half the degree measure of its intercepted arc.**

$$40° \quad \overarc{XZ} = 80°$$

Part IV: Don't Count Yourself Out: The Math Review and Mini-Test

> **EXAMPLE**
>
> You may see a figure that looks like a string picture you made at summer camp, with all sorts of lines running every which way. Take the time to identify the endpoints of the angles and the center point. You may be surprised at how easy the question suddenly becomes. In this figure, for example, find the sum of $a + b + c + d + e$.
>
> $\overset{\frown}{XY} = 20°$
>
> Note: Figure not drawn to scale.
>
> **F.** 65°
> **G.** 60°
> **H.** 55°
> **J.** 50°
> **K.** 45°
>
> Each angle is an inscribed angle; it has half the degree measure of the central angle, or half the degree measure of its intercepted arc. If you look carefully at the endpoints of these angles, they're all the same. They are along arc XY, which has a measure of 20 degrees. Therefore, each angle is 10 degrees, for a total of 50. *Correct answer:* **J**.

9. **When a central angle and an inscribed angle have the same endpoints, the degree measure of the central angle is twice that of the inscribed angle.**

10. **The degree measure of a circle is 360.**

11. **An *arc* is a portion of the circumference of a circle.** The degree measure of an arc is the same as its central angle and twice its inscribed angle.

$\overset{\frown}{AC} = 90°$ $\overset{\frown}{AC} = 90°$

To find the length of an arc, follow these steps:

1. **Find the circumference of the entire circle.**

2. **Put the degree measure of the arc over 360 and then reduce the fraction.**

3. **Multiply the circumference by the fraction.**

           Chapter 10: Ogling More Figures than a Beauty Pageant Judge: Geometry Review   **97**

Find the length of arc *AC*.

[Circle with center B, angle ABC = 60°, r=18]

- **A.** 36π
- **B.** 27π
- **C.** 18π
- **D.** 12π
- **E.** 6π

Take the steps one at a time. First, find the circumference of the entire circle. C = 2πr = 36π. Don't multiply π out; problems usually leave it in that form. Next, put the degree measure of the arc over 360. The degree measure of the arc is the same as its central angle, 60 degrees.

$$\frac{60}{360} = \frac{1}{6}$$

The arc is ⅙ of the circumference of the circle. Multiply the circumference by the fraction: 36π × ⅙ = 6π. *Correct answer:* **E.**

After you get the hang of these, they're kinda fun. Try another one.

Find the length of arc *RS*.

[Circle with center O, points R and S on circle, r=5, Angle ROS = 6°]

- **F.** ⅙π
- **G.** π
- **H.** 3π
- **J.** 4π
- **K.** 12

First, find the circumference of the entire circle. C = 2πr = 10π. Second, put the degree measure of the arc over 360. Here, the inscribed angle is 6°. Because an inscribed angle is ½ of the central angle and ½ of its intercepted arc, the arc is 12°. 12⁄360 = 1⁄30. The arc is 1⁄30 of the circle. Finally, multiply the circumference by the fraction: 10π × 1⁄30 = 10⁄30π = ⅓π. The length of the arc is ⅓π. *Correct answer:* **F.**

Be very careful not to confuse the *degree measure* of the arc with the *length* of the arc. The length always is a portion of the circumference, always has a π in it and always is in linear units. If you chose K in this example, you found the degree measure of the arc rather than its length.

12. **A *sector* is a portion of the area of a circle.** The degree measure of a sector is the same as its central angle and twice its inscribed angle.

    To find the area of a sector, do the following:

    1. **Find the area of the entire circle.**
    2. **Put the degree measure of the sector over 360 and then reduce the fraction.**
    3. **Multiply the area by the fraction.**

    Finding the area of a sector is very similar to finding the length of an arc. The only difference is in the first step. Whereas an arc is a part of the *circumference* of a circle, a sector is a part of the *area* of a circle. Try a few examples for sectors.

    Find the area of sector *ABC*.

    r=8

    Angle *ABC* = 90°

    A. 64π

    B. 36π

    C. 16π

    D. 12π

    E. 6π

    First, find the area of the entire circle. $A = \pi r^2 = 64\pi$. Second, put the degree measure of the sector over 360. The sector is 90°, the same as its central angle. $90/360 = 1/4$. Third, multiply the area by the fraction: $64\pi \times 1/4 = 16\pi$. *Correct answer: C.*

    Find the area of sector *XYZ*.

    Circle Y

    r=9

    F. 9.7π

    G. 8.1π

    H. 7.2π

    J. 6.3π

    K. 6π

    First, find the area of the entire circle. $A = \pi r^2 = 81\pi$. Second, put the degree measure of the sector over 360. A sector has the same degree measure as its intercepted arc, here 36°: $36/360 = 1/10$. Third, multiply the area by the fraction: $81\pi \times 1/10 = 8.1\pi$. *Correct answer: G.*

Chapter 11

Catching Some (*X*'s, *Y*'s, and) *Z*'s: Algebra and Other Sleeping Aids

In This Chapter
▶ Relating to each other: ratios
▶ Making life mysterious: symbolism
▶ Lining up: algebra, FOIL, roots, and radicals
▶ Taking your chances: probability
▶ Becoming a statistic: mean, mode, and median
▶ Triggering a response: SOH CAH TOA and other trigonometry

Trivia Question: Where was algebra supposedly invented? *Answer:* Muslim scholars invented Algebra in Zabid, Yemen. See? You can't blame the Greeks for everything!

The Powers That Be: Bases and Exponents

Many ACT questions require you to know how to work with bases and exponents. The following sections explain some of the most important concepts.

1. **The base is the big number (or letter) on the bottom. The exponent is the little number (or letter) in the upper-right corner.**

   In x^5, x is the base and 5 is the exponent.

   In 3^y, 3 is the base and y is the exponent.

2. **A base to the zero power equals one.**

   $x^0 = 1$

   $5^0 = 1$

   $129^0 = 1$

3. **The exponent tells how many times to multiply the base times itself.**

   This is pretty familiar stuff, right?

   $x^2 = x \times x$

   $5^2 = 5 \times 5$

   $129^4 = 129 \times 129 \times 129 \times 129$

   $5^6 = 5 \times 5 \times 5 \times 5 \times 5 \times 5$

When you take a base of ten to some power, the number of the power (or exponent) equals the number of zeroes in the number.

$10^1 = 10$ (one zero)

$10^4 = 10{,}000$ (four zeroes)

$10^0 = 1$ (zero zeroes)

4. A base to a negative exponent is the reciprocal of itself.

This one is a little more confusing. A *reciprocal* is the upside-down version of something. When you have a negative exponent, just put the base and exponent under a 1 and make the exponent positive again.

$x^{-4} = 1/(x^4)$

$5^{-3} = 1/(5^3)$

$129^{-1} = 1/(129^1)$

The resulting number is *not negative*. When you flip it, you get the reciprocal, and the negative just sort of fades away. *Don't* fall for the trap of saying that $5^{-3} = -(1/5)^3$, or $-1/125$.

5. To multiply like bases, add the exponents.

You can multiply two bases that are the same; just add the exponents.

$x^3 \times x^2 = x^{(3+2)} = x^5$

$5^4 \times 5^9 = 5^{(4+9)} = 5^{13}$

$129^3 \times 129^0 = 129^{(3+0)} = 129^3$

You cannot multiply *unlike* bases. Think of it as trying to make dogs and cats multiply — it doesn't work. All you end up with is a miffed meower and a damaged dog.

$x^2 \times y^3 = x^2 \times y^3$ (no shortcuts)

$5^2 \times 129^3 = 5^2 \times 129^3$ (you actually have to work it out)

6. To divide like bases, subtract the exponents.

You can divide two bases that are the same by subtracting the exponents.

$x^5 \div x^2 = x^{(5-2)} = x^3$

$5^9 \div 5^3 = 5^{(9-3)} = 5^6$

$129^4 \div 129^0 = 129^{(4-0)} = 129^4$

(Did I getcha on that last one? It should make sense. Any base to the 0 power is 1. Any number divided by 1 is itself.)

Did you look at the second example, $5^9 \div 5^3$, and think that the answer was 5^3? It's easy to fall into the trap of dividing rather than subtracting, especially when you see numbers that just beg to be divided, like 9 and 3. Keep your guard up.

7. Multiply the exponents of a base inside and outside the parentheses.

That's quite a mouthful. Here's what it means:

$\left(x^2\right)^3 = x^{(2 \times 3)} = x^6$

$\left(5^3\right)^3 = 5^{(3 \times 3)} = 5^9$

$\left(129^0\right)^3 = 129^{(0 \times 3)} = 129^0$

Chapter 11: Catching Some (X's, Y's, and) Z's: Algebra and Other Sleeping Aids

8. To add or subtract like bases, add or subtract the numerical coefficient of the bases.

The *numerical coefficient* (a great name for a rock band, don't you think?) is simply the number *in front* of the base. Notice that it is *not* the little exponent in the right-hand corner but the full-sized number to the left of the base.

$31x^3$: 31 is the numerical coefficient.

$-8y^2$: -8 is the numerical coefficient.

x^3: What is the numerical coefficient? One, because any number is itself times 1; the 1 is not always written out. Good trap.

$37x^3 + 10x^3 = 47x^3$: Just add the numerical coefficients: $37 + 10 = 47$.

$15y^2 - 10y^2 = 5y^2$: Just subtract the numerical coefficients: $15 - 10 = 5$.

You cannot add or subtract like bases with *different* exponents.

$13x^3 - 9x^2$ is *not* equal to $4x^3$ or $4x^2$ or $4x$. All it is equal to is $13x^3 - 9x^2$. The bases *and* exponents must be the same for you to add or subtract the terms.

Keep It in Proportion: Ratios

After you know the tricks, ratios are some of the easiest problems to answer quickly. I call them "heartbeat" problems because you can solve them in a heartbeat. Of course, if someone drop-dead gorgeous sits next to you and makes your heart beat faster, it may take you two heartbeats to solve a ratio problem. So sue me.

1. A *ratio* is written as $\frac{of}{to}$ or of:to.

The ratio *of* sunflowers *to* roses = $\frac{sunflowers}{roses}$.

The ratio *of* umbrellas *to* heads = umbrellas:heads.

2. A possible total is a multiple of the sum of the numbers in the ratio.

You may be given a problem like this: At a party, the ratio of blondes to redheads is 4:5. Which of the following could be the total number of blondes and redheads at the party?

Megaeasy. Add the numbers in the ratio: $4 + 5 = 9$. The total number of blondes must be a multiple of 9, such as 9, 18, 27, 36, and so on.

After a rough hockey game, Bernie checks his body and finds that he has three bruises for every five cuts. Which of the following could be the total number of bruises and cuts on poor ol' Bernie's body?

A. 53

B. 45

C. 35

D. 33

E. 32

Add the numbers in the ratio: $3 + 5 = 8$. The total must be a multiple of 8 (or, looking at it another way, the total must be evenly divisible by 8). Only choice E is a multiple of 8. *Correct answer:* **E.**

One more, because you should always get this type of problem correct.

Trying to get Willie to turn down his stereo, his mother pounds on the ceiling and shouts up to his bedroom. If she pounds seven times for every five times she shouts, which of the following could be the total number of poundings and shouts?

   F. 75
   G. 57
   H. 48
   J. 35
   K. 30

Add the numbers in the ratio: 7 + 5 = 12. The total must be a multiple of 12 (it must be evenly divisible by 12). Here, only 48 is evenly divisible by 12. *Correct answer:* **H.**

3. **When given a ratio and a total and asked to find a specific term, do the following, in order:**

   1. **Add the numbers in the ratio.**
   2. **Divide that sum into the total.**
   3. **Multiply that quotient by each term in the ratio.**
   4. **Add the answers to double-check that they sum to the total.**

Pretty confusing stuff, right? Just take it one step at a time.

Yelling at the members of his team, which had just lost 21–0, the irate coach pointed his finger at each member of the squad, calling everyone either a wimp or a slacker. If there were 3 wimps for every 4 slackers, and every member of the 28-person squad was either a wimp or a slacker, how many wimps were there?

   1. **Add the numbers in the ratio:** 3 + 4 = 7.
   2. **Divide that sum into the total:** 28 ÷ 7 = 4.
   3. **Multiply that quotient by each term in the ratio:** 4 × 3 = 12; 4 × 4 = 16.
   4. **Double-check that the numbers add up to the total:** 12 + 16 = 28.

Now you have all the information you need to answer a variety of questions: How many wimps were there? Twelve. How many slackers were there? Sixteen. How many more slackers than wimps were there? Four. How many slackers would have to be kicked off the team for the number of wimps and slackers to be equal? Four. The ACT's Math Moguls can ask all sorts of things, but if you have this information, you're ready for anything they throw at you.

Be sure that you actually do Step 4, adding the terms to double-check that they add up to the total. Doing so catches any careless mistakes that you may have made.

Things Aren't What They Seem: Symbolism

You may encounter two basic types of symbolism problems. If so, do one of the following:

- Substitute the number given for the variable in the explanation.
- Talk through the explanation to see which constraint fits and then do the indicated operations.

Chapter 11: Catching Some (X's, Y's, and) Z's: Algebra and Other Sleeping Aids

1. Substitute for the variable in the explanation.

You see a problem with a strange symbol. It may be a variable inside a circle, a triangle, a star, or a tic-tac-toe sign. That symbol has no connection to the real world at all. Don't panic, thinking that your teachers forgot to teach you something. Symbols are made up for each problem.

The symbol is included in a short explanation. It may look like this:

$$a \# b \# c = a \# b \# c = \frac{(a+b)^c}{b+c}$$

$$x * y * z = x * y * z = \left(\frac{z}{x}\right) + \left(\frac{y}{z}\right)^x$$

$$m @ n @ o = mn + no - om$$

Again, the symbols don't have any meaning in the outside world; they mean only what the problem tells you they mean, and that meaning holds true only for this problem.

Below the explanation is the question itself:

$$3 \# 2 \# 1 =$$

$$4 * 6 * 8 =$$

$$2 @ 5 @ 10 =$$

Your job is one of substitution. Plug in a number for the variable in the equation. Which number do you plug in? The one that's in the same position as that variable. For example:

$$a \# b \# c = a \# b \# c = \frac{(a+b)^c}{b+c}$$

$$3 \# 2 \# 1 = 3 \# 2 \# 1 = \frac{(3+2)^1}{(2+1)}$$

Because *a* was in the first position and 3 was in the first position, substitute 3 for *a* throughout the equation. Because *b* was in the second position and 2 was in the second position, substitute 2 for *b* throughout the equation. Because *c* was in the third position and 1 was in the third position, substitute 1 for *c* throughout the equation.

Do the same for the other problems.

$$x * y * z = x * y * z = \left(\frac{z}{x}\right) + \left(\frac{y}{z}\right)^x$$

$$4 * 6 * 8 = (8/4) + (6/8)^4 = 2 + 0.316 = 2.316$$

$$m @ n @ o = mn + no - om$$

$$2 @ 5 @ 10 = (2 \times 5) + (5 \times 10) - (10 \times 2) = 10 + 50 - 20 = 40$$

This is the simpler of the two types of symbolism problems. Just substitute the number for the variable and work through the equation.

2. Talk through the explanation and do the operations.

This type of symbolism problem may seem more confusing until you've done a few. Then they become so easy that you wonder why you didn't see it before. Following are two possibilities:

⓪ = 3x if x is odd

ⓧ = ½ if x is even

Solve for ⑤ + ⑧

First, talk through the explanation. You have something in a circle. If that something in the circle is odd, you multiply it by 3. If that something in the circle is even, you divide it by 2.

In the question, there's a 5 in the circle. Because 5 is odd, you multiply it by 3 to get $5 \times 3 = 15$. In the second half of the question, there's an 8 in a circle. Because 8 is even, you divide it by 2. $8 \div 2 = 4$. Now add: $15 + 4 = 19$.

You still may think of this second type of problem as a plug-in or substitution problem because you are plugging the number into the equation for x and working it through. However, you first have to figure out which equation to plug it into. That requires talking things through. You have to understand what you're doing in this type of problem. Try another.

△x = $3x + ⅓x$ if x is prime

△x = $x^2 + \sqrt{2}$

△16 + △3 =

Aha! Now you have to know some math vocabulary. Prime numbers are not the numbers that have stars next to them in your little black book. Prime numbers are numbers that cannot be divided other than by 1 and themselves, such as 2, 3, 5, 7, 11, and 13. Composite numbers are numbers that *can* be divided other than by just 1 and themselves, such as 4, 6, 8, 9, 10, and 12. The first thing you do is decide whether the term in the triangle is a composite number or a prime number.

△16: Because 16 is a composite number, use the second equation. Square 16: $16 \times 16 = 256$. Take the square root of 16: $\sqrt{16} = 4$. Add them together: $256 + 4 = 260$.

△3: Because 3 is a prime number, use the first equation. $3(3) + ⅓(3) = 9 + 1 = 10$. Add the two solutions: $260 + 10 = 270$.

Sometimes, the solutions have symbols in them as well. Here's an example:

ⓧ = ½x if x is composite

ⓧ = 2x if x is prime

Solve for ⑤ × ⑩

A. ⑮

B. ㉕

C. ㊿

D. ⑩⓪

E. ②⓪⓪

Because 5 is prime, you multiply it by 2: Therefore, $5 \times 2 = 10$. Because 10 is composite, you multiply it by ½: $10 \times ½ = 5$. Multiply: $10 \times 5 = 50$.

Chapter 11: Catching Some (X's, Y's, and) Z's: Algebra and Other Sleeping Aids

Noooo! Don't choose answer C; that's the trap answer. Choice C doesn't say 50; it says ㊿. The 50 is in a circle. That means that you have to solve the answer choice to see what *circle* 50 is. Because 50 is composite, you take half of it: 50 ÷ 2 = 25. That isn't the answer you want. Now go through the rest of the choices:

⑮: Because 15 is composite, multiply it by ½: 15 × ½ = 7.5.

㉕: Because 25 is composite, multiply it by ½: 25 × ½ = 12.5.

⑩⓪: Because 100 is composite, multiply it by ½: 100 × ½ = 50. You have a winner! *Correct answer:* **D.**

Have you studied functions yet? Maybe not in school, but if you read the preceding material on symbolism, you have studied functions. A function is very much like the symbolism you've just read about. You may see a problem like this:

$f(x) = (2x)^3$. Solve for $f(2)$.

The *f* stands for function. You do the same thing you did before: Talk through the problem. You say, "I have something in parentheses. My job is to multiply that something by 2 and then cube the whole disgusting mess." In other words, just plug in the 2 where you see an *x* in the explanation.

$f(2) = (2 \times 2)^3 = 4^3 = 64$

Try another one.

$f(x) = x + x^2 + x^3$. Solve for $f(10)$.

Just plug the 10 in for the *x*: $f(10) = 10 + 10^2 + 10^3 = 10 + 100 + 1{,}000 = 1{,}110$.

Now that you've acquired this skill, you can call yourself "fully functional."

Abracadabra: Algebra

You must be able to do three basic algebra concepts for the ACT.

Solve for x in an equation

The first concept to understand is how to solve for *x* in an equation. To solve for *x*, follow these steps:

1. **Isolate the variable, which means get all the *x*'s on one side and all the non-*x*'s on the other side.**
2. **Add all the *x*'s on one side; add all the non-*x*'s on the other side.**
3. **Divide both sides of the equation by the number in front of the *x*.**

Now you try it: $3x + 7 = 9x - 5$.

1. **Isolate the variable. Move the 3x to the right,** *changing the sign* **to make it –3x.**

    Forgetting to change the sign is one of the most common careless mistakes that students make. Test-makers realize that and often include trap answer choices to catch this mistake.

    Move the –5 to the left, *changing the sign* to make it +5. You now have $7 + 5 = 9x - 3x$.

2. **Add the x's on one side; add the non-x's on the other side.**

    $12 = 6x$

3. **Divide both sides through by what is next to the x.**

    $\frac{12}{6} = \frac{6x}{6}$

    $2 = x$

If you're weak in algebra or know that you often make careless mistakes, plug the 2 back into the equation to make sure that it works.

$$3(2) + 7 = 9(2) - 5$$
$$6 + 7 = 18 - 5$$
$$13 = 13$$

If you absolutely hate algebra, see whether you can simply plug in the answer choices. If this were a problem-solving question with multiple-choice answers, you could plug 'n' chug.

$3x + 7 = 9x - 5$. Solve for x.

A. 7

B. 5½

C. 5

D. 3½

E. 2

Don't ask for trouble. Keep life simple by starting with the simple answers first, and begin in the middle, with answer C, as suggested in the lecture. That is, try plugging in 5. When it doesn't work, don't bother plugging in 3½. That's too much work. Go right down to 2. If all the easy answers don't work, then you can go back to the hard answer of 3½, but why fuss with it unless you absolutely have to? Test-makers often put mind-boggling choices at the beginning of the answers (or at the bottom, if you like to work upside down); skip them. *Correct answer:* **E.**

Curses! FOILed again

The second thing you need to know to do algebra is how to use the FOIL method. FOIL stands for *First, Outer, Inner, Last* and refers to the order in which you multiply the variables in parentheses. You can practice by using this equation: $(a + b)(a - b) =$

1. **Multiply the *First* variables:** $a \times a = a^2$.

2. **Multiply the *Outer* variables:** $a \times -b = -ab$.

3. **Multiply the *Inner* variables:** $b \times a = ba$ (which is the same as ab).

4. **Multiply the *Last* variables:** $b \times -b = -b^2$.

Add like terms: $-ab + ab = 0ab$. (Remember that you can multiply numbers forward or backward, such that $ab = ba$.) The positive and negative ab cancel each other out. You're left with only $a^2 - b^2$.

Try another one: $(3a + b)(a - 2b) =$

1. **Multiply the *First* terms:** $3a \times a = 3a^2$.
2. **Multiply the *Outer* terms:** $3a \times -2b = -6ab$.
3. **Multiply the *Inner* terms:** $b \times a = ba$ (which is the same as ab).
4. **Multiply the *Last* terms:** $b \times -2b = -2b^2$.
5. **Combine like terms:** $-6ab + ab = -5ab$.

The final answer is $3a^2 - 5ab - 2b^2$.

You need to out-and-out *memorize* the following three FOIL problems. Don't bother to work them out every time; know them by heart.

$(a + b)^2 = a^2 + 2ab + b^2$

You can prove this equation by using FOIL: $(a + b)(a + b)$

1. **Multiply the *First* terms:** $a \times a = a^2$.
2. **Multiply the *Outer* terms:** $a \times b = ab$.
3. **Multiply the *Inner* terms:** $b \times a = ba$ (which is the same as ab).
4. **Multiply the *Last* terms:** $b \times b = b^2$.
5. **Combine like terms:** $ab + ab = 2ab$.

The final solution is $a^2 + 2ab + b^2$.

$(a - b)^2 = a^2 - 2ab + b^2$

You can prove this equation by using FOIL: $(a - b)(a - b)$

1. **Multiply the *First* terms:** $a \times a = a^2$.
2. **Multiply the *Outer* terms:** $a \times -b = -ab$.
3. **Multiply the *Inner* terms:** $-b \times a = -ba$ (which is the same as $-ab$).
4. **Multiply the *Last* terms:** $-b \times -b = +b^2$.
5. **Combine like terms:** $-ab + -ab = -2ab$.

The final solution is $a^2 - 2ab + b^2$.

Be careful to note that the b^2 at the end is *positive*, not negative, because multiplying a negative times a negative gives a positive.

$(a - b)(a + b) = a^2 - b^2$

You can prove this equation by using FOIL: $(a - b)(a + b)$

1. **Multiply the *First* terms:** $a \times a = a^2$.
2. **Multiply the *Outer* terms:** $a \times b = ab$.

3. Multiply the *Inner* terms: $-b \times a = -ba$ (which is the same as $-ab$).
4. Multiply the *Last* terms: $-b \times b = -b^2$.
5. Combine like terms: $ab + -ab = 0ab$.

The final solution is $a^2 - b^2$. Note that the middle term drops out because $+ab$ cancels out $-ab$.

Again, *memorize* these three equations:

$$(a + b)^2 = a^2 + 2ab + b^2$$
$$(a - b)^2 = a^2 - 2ab + b^2$$
$$(a - b)(a + b) = a^2 - b^2$$

Doing so saves you time, careless mistakes, and acute misery on the actual exam.

Fact-or Fiction: Factoring

Now you know how to do algebra forward; are you ready to do it backward? You need to be able to factor down a quadratic equation (an equation with a variable to the second power) and take an algebraic expression from its final form back to its original form of two sets of parentheses.

Given $x^2 + 13x + 42 = 0$, solve for x. Take this problem one step at a time.

1. **Draw two sets of parentheses.**

   $(\ )(\ ) = 0$

2. **You know that to get x^2, the *First* terms have to be x and x. Fill those in.**

   $(x\ )(x\ ) = 0$

3. **Look now at the *Outer* terms.**

   You need two numbers that multiply together to be $+42$. Well, there are several possibilities: 42×1, 21×2, or 6×7. You can even have two negative numbers: -42×-1, -21×-2, or -6×-7. You aren't sure which numbers to choose yet. Go on to the next step.

4. **Look at the *Inner* terms.**

   You have to add two values to get $+13$. What's the first thing that springs to mind? $6 + 7$, probably. Hey, that's one of the possibilities in the preceding step! Plug it in and try it.

   $(x + 6)(x + 7) = x^2 + 7x + 6x + 42 = x^2 + 13x + 42$

5. **Great, but you're not done yet. If the whole equation equals 0, then either $(x + 6) = 0$ or $(x + 7) = 0$.**

   That's because any number times 0 equals 0. Therefore, x can equal -6 or -7.

Too Hip to Be Square: Roots and Radicals

To simplify working with square roots (or cube roots or any roots), think of them as variables. You work the same way with $\sqrt{7}$ as you do with x, y, or z.

Addition and subtraction

1. To add or subtract like radicals (for the purpose of this exam, think of "radicals" as "roots"), add or subtract the number in front of the radical.

   $2\sqrt{7} + 5\sqrt{7} = 7\sqrt{7}$ $2x + 5x = 7x$

   $9\sqrt{13} - 4\sqrt{13} = 5\sqrt{13}$ $9x - 4x = 5x$

2. You *cannot* add or subtract unlike radicals (just as you cannot add or subtract unlike variables).

   $6\sqrt{5} + 4\sqrt{3} = 6\sqrt{5} + 4\sqrt{3}$. You cannot add the two and get $10\sqrt{8}$.

   $6x + 4y = 6x + 4y$. You cannot add the two and get $10xy$.

Don't glance at a problem, see that the radicals are not the same, and immediately assume that you cannot add the two terms. You may be able to simplify one radical to make it match the radical in the other term.

$\sqrt{52} + \sqrt{13} = 2\sqrt{13} + \sqrt{13} = 3\sqrt{13}$

1. **Begin by simplifying. Take out a perfect square from the term.**

   $\sqrt{52} = \sqrt{4} \times \sqrt{13}$

2. **Because $\sqrt{4} = 2$, then $\sqrt{52} = 2\sqrt{13}$.**

Look at this one:

$\sqrt{20} + \sqrt{45} = (\sqrt{4} \times \sqrt{5}) + (\sqrt{9} \times \sqrt{5}) = 2\sqrt{5} + 3\sqrt{5} = 5\sqrt{5}$

You must simplify *first*. You can't say that $\sqrt{20} + \sqrt{45} = \sqrt{65} = 8.06$. When you work out the correct answer, $5\sqrt{5}$, you see that it isn't 8.06 but rather 11.18.

Multiplication and division

Just do it. When you multiply or divide radicals, you just multiply or divide the numbers and then pop the radical sign back onto the finished product.

$\sqrt{5} \times \sqrt{6} = \sqrt{30}$

$\sqrt{15} \div \sqrt{5} = \sqrt{3}$

If you have a number in front of the radical, multiply it as well. Let everyone in on the fun.

$6\sqrt{3} \times 4\sqrt{2} =$

$6 \times 4 = 24$

$\sqrt{3} \times \sqrt{2} = \sqrt{6}$

$24\sqrt{6}$

Here's a pretty typical problem: $37\sqrt{5} \times 3\sqrt{6}$

F. $40\sqrt{11}$

G. $40\sqrt{30}$

H. $111\sqrt{11}$

J. $111\sqrt{30}$

K. 1,221

This problem takes straightforward multiplication: $37 \times 3 = 111$ and $\sqrt{5} \times \sqrt{6} = \sqrt{30}$, so $111\sqrt{30}$. *Correct answer:* **J.**

Inside out

When there is an operation under the radical, do it first and then take the square root.

$$\sqrt{\frac{x^2}{40} + \frac{x^2}{9}}$$

First, solve for $x^2/40 + x^2/9$. You get the common denominator of 360 (40×9) and then find the numerators: $9x^2 + 40x^2 = 49x^2/360$. *Now* take the square roots: $\sqrt{49x^2} = 7x$ (because $7x \times 7x = 49x^2$). $\sqrt{360} = 18.97$. Gotcha, I bet! Did you say that $\sqrt{360} = 6$? Wrong! $\sqrt{36} = 6$, but $\sqrt{360}$ = approximately 18.97. Beware of assuming too much; you can be led down the path to temptation.

Your final answer is $7x/18.97$. Of course, you can bet that the answer choices will include $7x/6$.

Probably Probability

Probability questions usually are word problems. They may look intimidating, with so many words that make you lose sight of where to begin. Two simple rules can solve nearly every probability problem that the ACT tosses at you.

Rule 1: Create a fraction

To find a probability, use this formula:

$$P = \frac{\text{Number of possible desired outcomes}}{\text{Number of total possible outcomes}}$$

Make a probability into a fraction. The denominator is the easier of the two parts to begin with. The *denominator* is the total possible number of outcomes. For example, when you're flipping a coin, there are two possible outcomes, giving you a denominator of 2. When you're tossing a die (one of a pair of dice), there are six possible outcomes, giving you a denominator of 6. When you're pulling a card out of a deck of cards, there are 52 possible outcomes (52 cards in a deck), giving you a denominator of 52. When 25 marbles are in a jar and you're going to pull out one of them, there are 25 possibilities, giving you a denominator of 25. Very simply, the denominator is the whole shebang — everything possible.

The *numerator* is the total number of the things you want. If you want a head when you toss a coin, there is exactly one head, giving you a numerator of 1. Your chances of tossing a head, therefore, are ½, one possible head, two possible outcomes altogether. If you want to get a 5 when you toss a die, there is exactly one 5 on the die, giving you a numerator of 1. The probability of tossing a 5 is ⅙. There are one 5 and six possible outcomes altogether.

If you want to draw a jack from a deck of cards, there are four jacks: hearts, diamonds, clubs, and spades. Therefore, the numerator is 4. The probability of drawing a jack out of a deck of cards is 4/52 (which reduces to 1/13). If you want to draw a jack of hearts, the probability is 1/52 because there is only one jack of hearts.

A jar of marbles has 8 yellow marbles, 6 black marbles, and 12 white marbles. What is the probability of drawing out a black marble?

Use the formula. Begin with the denominator, which is all the possible outcomes: 8 + 6 + 12 = 26. The numerator is how many there are of what you want: six black marbles. The probability is 6/26, which can be reduced or (as is more customary) changed to a percentage. The correct answer is 6/26, or 3/13, or 23 percent. What's the probability of drawing out a yellow marble? 8/26, or 4/13. A white marble? 12/26, or 6/13.

A drawer contains 5 pairs of white socks, 8 pairs of black socks, and 12 pairs of brown socks. In a hurry to get to school, Austin pulls out a pair at a time and tosses them on the floor if they are not the color he wants. Looking for a brown pair, Austin pulls out and discards a white pair, a black pair, a black pair, and a white pair. What is the probability that on his next reach into the drawer he will pull out a brown pair of socks?

This problem is slightly more complicated than the preceding one, although it uses the same formula. You began with 25 pairs of socks. However, Austin, that slob, has thrown four pairs on the floor. That means only 21 pairs are left. The probability of his pulling out a brown pair is 12/21, or 4/7, or about 57 percent.

A cookie jar contains chocolate, vanilla, and strawberry wafer cookies. There are 30 of each type. Bess reaches in, pulls out a chocolate and eats it, and then in quick succession, she pulls out and eats a vanilla, a chocolate, a strawberry, a strawberry, a chocolate, and a vanilla. Assuming that she doesn't get sick or get caught, what is the probability that the next cookie she pulls out will be a chocolate one?

Originally, there were 90 cookies. Bess has scarfed down 7 of them, leaving 83. Careful! If you're about to put 30/83, you're headed for a trap. There are no longer 30 chocolate cookies; there are only 27, because Bess has eaten 3. The probability is now 27/83, or about 33 percent.

TIP

Probability must always be between 0 and 1. You cannot have a negative probability, and you cannot have a probability greater than 1, or 100 percent.

Rule 2: Multiply consecutive probabilities

What is the probability that you'll get two heads when you toss a coin twice? You find each probability separately and then *multiply* the two. The chance of tossing a coin the first time and getting a head is ½. The chance of tossing a coin the second time and getting a head is ½. Multiply those consecutive probabilities: ½ × ½ = ¼. The chance of getting two heads is 1 out of 4.

What is the probability of tossing a die twice and getting a 5 on the first toss and a 6 on the second toss? Treat each toss separately. The probability of getting a 5 is ⅙. The probability of getting a 6 is ⅙. Multiply consecutive probabilities: ⅙ × ⅙ = 1/36.

The Stats Don't Lie: Statistics

Don't panic; the ACT tests your skill with statistics in only the most rudimentary way. If you can master three basic concepts, you can do any statistics on this exam. Those concepts are median, mode, and range.

Median

Simply put, the median is the middle number when all the terms are arranged in order. Think of the median strip, which is the middle of the road. Median = middle. Be sure that you arrange the numbers in order (increasing or decreasing, it makes no difference) before you find the median.

Find the median of –3, 18, –4, ½, 11.

  A. –3
  B. 18
  C. –4
  D. ½
  E. 11

Put the numbers in order: –4, –3, ½, 11, 18. The one in the middle, ½, is the median. It's as simple as that. *Correct answer:* **D.**

Mode

The mode is the most frequent number. I suggest that you put the numbers in order again. Then look for the one that shows up the most often. It's the mode.

Find the mode of 11, 18, 29, 17, 18, –4, 0, 11, 18.

  F. 11
  G. 17
  H. 18
  J. 19
  K. 29

The question has three 18s but no more than two of any other number. *Correct answer:* **H.**

Range

The range is the distance from the greatest to the smallest. In other words, you subtract the smallest term from the largest term, and you have the range.

Find the range of the numbers 11, 18, 29, 17, 18, –4, 0, 11, 18.

  A. 33
  B. 29
  C. 19
  D. 0
  E. –4

Ah, did this one getcha? True, 33 is not one of the numbers in the set. But to find the range, subtract the smallest from the largest number: 29 – (–4) = 29 + 4 = 33. *Correct answer:* **A.**

Chapter 11: Catching Some (X's, Y's, and) Z's: Algebra and Other Sleeping Aids

Trig-o-trivia: A few soothing words

Don't know a sine from a sign? Don't worry about it. The ACT has only four trigonometry questions. If you guess wildly at all four, you'll probably get at least one correct. (You should always guess, because the ACT has no penalty for wrong answers.) And that means that a total lack of trig is likely to cost you only three questions, which translates to only one or two points on the mathematics scale and half a point or less on the composite score scale. In other words, you still can get a great ACT score, get into a good college, have an excellent career, win a Nobel prize or two, marry a movie star, and rear children who find the cure for cancer, all without knowing the first thing about trigonometry. Feel better now?

The only trap you're likely to see in the statistics questions is in the answer choices. The questions themselves are quite straightforward, but the answer choices may assume that some people don't know one term from another. For example, one answer choice to a median question may be the mean (the average). One answer choice to a range question may be the mode. In each question, circle the word that tells you what you're looking for to keep from falling for this trap.

Don't Soak Your Head: SOH CAH TOA

You can go a long way in trigonometry with just a few basic points. Just remember SOH CAH TOA.

SOH CAH TOA stands for

> **S**ine = **O**pposite/**H**ypotenuse
>
> **C**osine = **A**djacent/**H**ypotenuse
>
> **T**angent = **O**pposite/**A**djacent

Are you scratching your head now and saying, "Opposite? Opposite *what*?" Take a look at the following right triangle:

1. **Side AB is the hypotenuse.**

    It is the longest side of the right triangle, and the side opposite the right angle.

2. **To find sin A (*sine* usually is abbreviated as *sin*; the terms mean the same thing), all you need to do is find the length of side BC and divide it by the length of the hypotenuse.**

    This is because $\sin A = \frac{\text{opposite } A}{\text{hypotenuse}}$ and side BC is the side opposite A. Therefore, $\sin A = \frac{\text{length of BC}}{\text{length of AB}}$.

3. To find cos A (*cosine* usually is abbreviated as *cos*; the terms mean the same thing), find the length of side AC and use the CAH part of SOH CAH TOA.

   Cos A = $\frac{\text{adjacent A}}{\text{hypotenuse}}$, which in turn equals $\frac{\text{length of BC}}{\text{length of AB}}$.

4. To find tan A (yes, *tangent* usually is abbreviated as *tan*; they mean the same thing), use the TOA part of SOH CAH TOA:

   Tan A = $\frac{\text{opposite A}}{\text{adjacent A}}$, which in turn is equal $\frac{\text{length of BC}}{\text{length of AC}}$.

Here's an example of just how far you can go when you SOH CAH TOA. What is sin A if tan A = $\frac{9}{40}$?

   F. $\frac{9}{41}$

   G. $\frac{40}{41}$

   H. $\frac{41}{40}$

   J. $\frac{40}{9}$

   K. $\frac{41}{9}$

Because tan A = $\frac{9}{40}$, you can draw a picture with opposite A = 9 and adjacent A = 40.

Use the Pythagorean Theorem to determine the length of hypotenuse AB:

$9^2 + 40^2 = (AB)^2$

$1681 = (AB)^2$

$41 = AB$

Sin A = $\frac{\text{opposite A}}{\text{hypotenuse}}$, so sin A = $\frac{9}{41}$.

You could have eliminated choices H, J, and K immediately if you realized that the sin cannot be greater than 1. *Correct answer:* **F.**

5. Sin = $\frac{\text{opposite}}{\text{hypotenuse}}$. **No side in a triangle can be greater than the hypotenuse, so that makes it impossible to have a sin greater than 1.**

6. Cos = $\frac{\text{adjacent}}{\text{hypotenuse}}$. **The side adjacent cannot be greater than the hypotenuse, so cos cannot be greater than 1.**

Chapter 11: Catching Some (*X*'s, *Y*'s, and) *Z*'s: Algebra and Other Sleeping Aids

TIP

That's so important that I'm repeating it here as a tip for you to burn into your brain: Neither a sin nor a cos can be greater than 1.

Making things a little more interesting, what if you were asked for secant A (also called sec A), cosecant A (also called csc A), or cotangent A (known to his friends as cot A) in the preceding example? Just remember the following:

$$\sec A = \frac{1}{\cos A}$$

$$\csc A = \frac{1}{\sin A}$$

$$\cot A = \frac{1}{\tan A}$$

So *if* $\cos A = \frac{40}{41}$, then $\sec A = \frac{41}{40}$ or if $\sin A = \frac{9}{41}$, *then* $\csc A = \frac{41}{9}$.

How to Use All This Junk: Trigonometric Ratios of Angles

You can combine SOH CAH TOA with some basic geometry knowledge to figure out the trigonometric ratios of some key angles.

What is cos 30°? (***Note:*** On the real exam, you have multiple-choice answers. Here, I'm going to let you figure this out from scratch.)

Draw a 30:60:90 triangle. (Remember that the ratio is $s : s\sqrt{3} : 2s$. I discuss this ratio in detail in the triangles section of Chapter 7.)

$$\cos 30° = \frac{\text{adjacent } 30°}{\text{hypotenuse}}, \text{ which equals } \frac{\sqrt{3}}{2}.$$

What is tan 45°? (Again, remember the actual ACT has multiple-choice answer responses, but I want you to do this one all on your own.)

Draw a 45:45:90 triangle. Remember, the ratio of the sides of this triangle is $s : s : s\sqrt{2}$, where *s* stands for the length of the side. (I discuss this ratio in the triangles portion of Chapter 7.)

$$\tan 45° = \frac{\text{opposite } 45°}{\text{adjacent } 45°} = 1/1 = 1$$

The ACT doesn't usually accept a square root in the denominator, so you have to rationalize your answer. ("To rationalize your answer" doesn't mean to justify to the teacher how on earth you came up with that answer, but rather to get rid of the root in the denominator.) Do so by multiplying both top and bottom by the square root:

$$\frac{1}{\sqrt{2}} \times \frac{\sqrt{2}}{\sqrt{2}} = \frac{\sqrt{2}}{2}$$

No Nervous Breakdowns, Please

Let us end this section on trig the way we began it, with a few words of reassurance. With a little practice, you should be able to handle just about anything the ACT test-makers throw at you regarding the preceding material. (And remember, the answer explanations to the trig problems in the practice exams repeat all this info and take you through everything step by step.) If you're still confused after those exams or you're concerned about some of the more advanced trigonometry that has only a very slight chance of appearing on the test, don't worry. Keep chanting to yourself, "Only four, no more; only four, no more." The entire ACT has only four trig problems. Trigonometry won't make or break your ACT score.

Chapter 12

Reviewing Miscellaneous Math You Probably Already Know

In This Chapter
- Running in place: time, rate, and distance problems
- Averaging out
- Playing with percentages
- Identifying the players: number sets and prime and composite numbers
- Formulating a plan: additional formulas and terms you need to know

*E*ven though you may already know most or all of the math discussed in this chapter, it never hurts to refresh your memory. These questions tend to be the easiest, so they offer you the best chance for getting correct answers. Brush up on your miscellaneous math, and you're sure to improve your score on the math section of the ACT.

DIRTy Math: Time, Rate, and Distance

Let's dish the dirt here, okay? D.I.R.T. Distance Is Rate × Time. $D = RT$. When you have a time, rate, and distance problem, use this formula. Make a chart with the formula across the top and fill in the spaces on the chart.

Jennifer drives 40 mph for 2½ hours. Her friend Ashley goes the same distance but drives at 1½ times Jennifer's speed. How many minutes longer does Jennifer drive than Ashley?

Do *not* start making big, hairy formulas with *x*'s and *y*'s. Make the DIRT chart.

	Distance	=	*Rate*	×	*Time*
Jennifer	100		40 mph		2½ hours
Ashley	100		60 mph		100 minutes

When you fill in the 40 mph and 2½ hours for Jennifer, you can calculate that she went 100 miles. Because Ashley drives the same distance, fill in 100 under distance for her. She goes 1½ times as fast. Ashley drives 60 mph. Now this gets really easy. If she drives at 60 mph, she drives one mile a minute. (60 minutes in an hour, 60 miles in an hour. You figure it out, Einstein.) Therefore, to go 100 miles takes her 100 minutes. Because the question asks for your final answer in minutes, don't bother converting this to hours; leave it the way it is.

Last step. Jennifer drives 2½ hours. How many minutes is that? Do it the easy way, in your brain. One hour is 60 minutes. A second hour is another 60 minutes. A half hour is 30 minutes. Add them together: 60 + 60 + 30 = 150 minutes. If Jennifer drives for 150 minutes and Ashley drives for 100 minutes, Jennifer drives 50 minutes more than Ashley.

Be careful to note whether the people are traveling in the *same* direction or in *opposite* directions. Suppose that you're asked how far apart drivers are at the end of their trip. If you're told that Jordan travels 40 mph east for 2 hours and Connor travels 60 mph west for 3 hours, they are going in opposite directions. If they start from the same point at the same time, Jordan has gone 80 miles one way, and Connor has gone 180 miles the opposite way. They are 260 miles apart. The trap answer is 100, because careless people (not *you!*) simply subtract 180 – 80.

It All Averages Out: Averages

You can always do averages the way Ms. Jones taught you when you were in third grade: Add all the terms and then divide by the number of terms. Or you can save wear-and-tear on the brain cells and know the following rules:

1. **The average of evenly spaced terms is the middle term.**

    5 + 11 + 17 + 23 + 29 = 85

    $85/5 = 17$

    First, check that the terms are evenly spaced. That means that there is an equal number of units between each term. Here, the terms are six apart. Second, circle the middle term, which here is 17. Third, go home, make popcorn, and watch the late-night movie with all the time you've saved.

    Try another one. Find the average of 32, 41, 50, 59, 68, 77, 86, 95, and 104.

    You look and see that the terms are all nine units apart. Because they are evenly spaced, the middle term is the average: 68.

    This trick is an easy one to love, but don't march down the aisle with it yet. The tip works only for evenly spaced terms. If you have just any old batch of numbers, such as 4, 21, 97, 98, and 199, you can't look at the middle term for the average. You have to find the average of those numbers the old-fashioned way.

    Find the average of these numbers: 3, 10, 17, 24, 31, 38, 45, and 52.

    First, double-check that they are evenly spaced. Here, the numbers are spaced by sevens. Next you look for the middle number . . . and there isn't one. You can, of course, find the two central terms, 24 and 31, and then find the middle between them. That works, but what a pain. Not only that, but suppose that you have 38 numbers. Making a mistake as to which term is the central one is easy to do. If you're off just a little bit, you miss the question. Instead, use rule number two.

2. **The average of evenly spaced terms is (first + last)/2.**

    Just add the first and the last terms, which are obvious at a glance, and divide that sum by 2.

    3 + 52 = 55

    $55/2 = 27.5$

Note: Double-check by using your common sense. Suppose that you made a silly mistake and got 45 for your answer. A glance at the numbers tells you that 45 is not in the middle and therefore cannot be the average.

This tip works for *all* evenly spaced terms. It doesn't matter whether there is a middle number, as in the first example, or no middle number, as in the second example. Go back to the earlier example.

32, 41, 50, 59, 68, 77, 86, 95, 104

Instead of finding the middle term, add the first and last terms and divide by 2, like this:

32 + 104 = 136

136/2 = 68

Either way works.

Missing term average problem

You are likely to find a problem like this:

Jeanette takes seven exams. Her scores on the first six are 91, 89, 85, 92, 90, and 88. If her average on all *seven* exams is 90, what did she get on the seventh exam?

This problem is called a missing term average problem because you are given an average and asked to find a missing term. Duh.

1. **You can do this the basic algebraic way: Average = Sum/Number of terms**

   90 = Sum/7

Because you don't know the seventh term, call it *x*. Add the first six terms (and get 535) and *x*.

90 = (535 + x)/7

Cross-multiply: 90 × 7 = 535 + x

630 = 535 + x

95 = x

The seventh exam score was 95.

Weighted averages

In a *weighted average,* some scores count more than others.

Number of Students	Score
12	80
13	75
10	70

If you're asked to find the average score for the students in this class, you know that you cannot simply add 80, 75, and 70 and divide by 3, because the scores weren't evenly distributed among the students. Because 12 students got an 80, multiply 12 × 80 = 960. Do the same with the other scores:

$13 \times 75 = 975$

$10 \times 70 = 700$

$960 + 975 + 700 = 2635$

Divide *not by 3* but by the total number of students: 35 (12 + 13 + 10)

$2635/35 = 75.29$

Percentage Panic

The mere mention of the word *percentage* may strike terror in your heart. There's no reason to panic over percentages; there are ways of getting around them.

1. **The first way is to ignore their very existence.** You can express a percentage as a decimal, which is a lot less intimidating. You do so by putting a decimal point two places to the left of the percentage and dropping the percent sign.

   - 35% = .35
   - 83% = .83
   - 50% = .50
   - 33.3% = .333
   - 66.6% = .666

   If you have a choice of working with percentages or decimals, it's better to choose decimals (in my humble opinion).

2. **Another way to ignore a percentage is to convert it to a fraction.** The word *percent* means *per cent*, or *per hundred*. Every percentage is that number over 100.

   - 50% = 50/100
   - 33% = 33/100
   - 75% = 75/100

   If you can't ignore the percentage, remember that a percent is $\text{part}/\text{whole} \times 100$, or $\text{is}/\text{of} \times 100$.

   What percent of 90 is 45? Put the *part*, 45, over the *whole*, 90. Or put the *is*, 45, over the *of*, 90:

   $45/90 = 1/2 \times 100 = 100/2 = 50\%$

   42 *is* what percent of 126? Put the *part*, 42, over the *whole*, 126. Or put the *is*, 42, over the *of*, 126.

   $42/126 = 1/3 \times 100 = 100/3 = 33\frac{1}{3}\%$

   Here's a slightly harder one: What is 40% of 80? You may be tempted to put the *is*, 40, over the *of*, 80, and get $40/80 = 1/2 \times 100 = 100/2 = 50\%$. However, when the problem is worded this way ("what is *x*% of *y*?" rather than "what % is *x* of *y*?"), you don't know the *is*. Your equation must be: $x/80 = 40/100$. Cross-multiply: $3200 = 100x$. $x = 32$. There's an easier way to do it: *of* means times, or multiply. Because 40% = .40, multiply that by 80 to get 32.

Chapter 12: Reviewing Miscellaneous Math You Probably Already Know

You may see a problem asking you what percent increase or decrease occurred in the number of games a team won or the amount of commission a person earned. To find a percent increase or decrease, use this formula:

$$\text{percent increase or decrease} = \frac{\text{number increase or decrease}}{\text{original whole}}$$

In basic English, to find the percent by which something has increased or decreased, you take two simple steps:

1. **Find the number (amount) by which the thing has increased or decreased.**

   For example, if a team won 25 games last year and 30 games this year, the number increase was 5. If a salesperson earned $10,000 last year and $8,000 this year, the number decrease was $2,000. Make that the *numerator* (top or left) of the fraction.

2. **Find the original whole.**

   This figure is what you started out with before you increased or decreased. If a team won 25 games last year and won 30 games this year, the original number was 25. If the salesperson earned $10,000 last year and $8,000 this year, the original number was 10,000. Make the number you started out with the *denominator* (bottom or right).

You now have a fraction. Divide the fraction to convert to a decimal and multiply by 100 to make it a percentage.

In 1992, Coach Denges won 30 prizes at the county fair by tossing a basketball into a bushel basket. In 1993, he won 35 prizes. What was his percent increase?

A. 100

B. 30

C. 16⅔

D. 14.28

E. .166

The number by which his prizes increased, from 30 to 35, is 5. That is the numerator. The original whole, or what he began with, is 30. That is the denominator. 5/30 = 1/6 = 16⅔%. *Correct answer:* **C.**

If you chose E, I fooled you. The question asks what *percent* increase there was. If you say E, you're saying that the increase was .166%. Not so. The increase *as a percentage* is 16⅔%. If you chose D, you fell for another trap. You put the 5 increase over the 35 instead of over the 30.

Two years ago, Haylie scored 22 goals at soccer. This year, she scored 16 goals. What was her approximate percentage decrease?

F. 72

G. 37.5

H. 27

J. 16

K. .27

Find the number of the decrease: 22 − 16 = 6. That is the numerator. Find the original whole from which she is decreasing: 22. That is the denominator. 6/22 = approximately .27, or approximately 27 percent. *Correct answer:* **H.**

If you chose F, you put 16 over 22 instead of putting the decrease over the original whole. If you chose K, you forgot the difference between .27 and .27 *percent*. If you chose G, you put the decrease of 6 over the new amount, 16, rather than over the original whole. Note how easy these traps are to fall for. My suggestion: Write down the actual formula and then plug in the numbers. Writing down the formula may be boring, but doing so takes only a few seconds and may save you points.

Here's a tricky question that many people do in their heads (instead of writing down the formula and plugging in numbers) and blow big-time. Carissa has three quarters. Her father gives her three more. Carissa's wealth has increased by what percent?

A. 50

B. 100

C. 200

D. 300

E. 500

Did you fall for the trap answer, C? Her wealth has doubled, to be sure, but the percent increase is only 100. You can prove that with the formula: The number increase is 75 (she has three more quarters, or 75 cents). Her original whole was 75. $75/75$ = 1 = 100%. *Correct answer:* **B**.

Do not fall into the trap of assuming that a 200 percent increase means that something doubled. When you double something, you increase it by 100 percent because you have to subtract the original "one" you began with. When you triple something, you increase by 200 percent because you have to subtract the original you began with. If you had three dollars and you now have nine dollars, for example, you have tripled your money but increased it by only 200 percent. Do the formula:

number increase = 6 dollars

original whole = 3 dollars

$6/3$ = 2 = 200 percent

Take a wild guess at what percent you increase when you quadruple your money? That's right, 300 percent. Just subtract the original 100 percent.

Ready, Sets, Go: Number Sets

How can you solve a problem that asks you to "state your answer in integral values only" if you don't know what integral values are? Here are the number sets with which you'll be working. (I once got a call from a *very* irate parent, who misunderstood her child to say that I was teaching "number sex." Life as an ACT tutor is never dull.)

- **Counting numbers:** 1, 2, 3 . . . Note that 0 is *not* a counting number.

- **Whole numbers:** 0, 1, 2, 3 . . . Note that 0 *is* a whole number.

- **Integers:** . . . –3, –2, –1, 0, 1, 2, 3 . . . When a question asks for integral values, make sure that the answer is in integers only. For example, you can't give an answer like 4.3 because that's not an integer. You need to round down to 4.

- **Rational numbers:** Rational numbers can be expressed as *a/b*, where *a* and *b* are integers.

    Examples: 1 (because 1 = $1/1$ and 1 is an integer), $1/2$ (because 1 and 2 are integers), $9/2$ (because 9 and 2 are integers), and $-4/2$ (because –4 and 2 are integers).

Notice that every number set so far has included the previous number sets. Whole numbers include counting numbers, integers include counting numbers and whole numbers, and rational numbers include counting numbers, whole numbers, and integers.

- **Irrational numbers:** The highly technical definition here is "anything not rational." That is, an irrational number cannot be written as a/b, where a and b are integers. Numbers that do not terminate and do not repeat cannot be written as fractions and therefore are irrational.

  Examples: π cannot be written exactly as 3.14; it is nonterminating and nonrepeating. $\sqrt{2}$ is approximately 1.4142 but is nonterminating and nonrepeating.

  Irrational numbers do not include the previous numbers sets. That is, irrational numbers *don't* include counting numbers, whole numbers, integers, and rational numbers.

- **Real numbers:** Briefly put, all of the above. Real numbers include counting numbers, whole numbers, integers, rationals, and irrationals. For all practical purposes, real numbers are everything you think of as numbers. When a question tells you to "express your answer in real numbers," don't sweat it. That's almost no constraint at all, because nearly every number you see is a real number.

Prime and Composite Numbers

1. **Prime numbers have exactly two factors; they cannot be divided by numbers other than 1 and themselves.** Examples include 2, 3, 5, 7, and 11.

   There are a few lovely tricks to prime numbers:

   - Zero is *not* a prime number. Why? Because it is divisible by more than two factors. Zero can be divided by 1, 2, 3, and on to infinity. Although division *by zero* is undefined (and isn't tested on the ACT), you *can* divide zero by other numbers; the answer, of course, is always zero. $0 \div 1 = 0$; $0 \div 2 = 0$; $0 \div 412 = 0$.

   - One is *not* a prime number. There are not two factors of 1. It cannot be divided only by 1 *and* itself. Confused? Don't worry about it. Just memorize that 1 is not a prime number.

   - Two is the *only* even prime. People tend to think that all prime numbers are odd. Well, almost. Two is prime because it has only two factors; it can be divided only by 1 and itself.

   - Not all odd numbers are prime. Think of 9 or 15; those numbers are odd but not prime, because they have more than two factors and can be divided by more than just 1 and themselves. $9 = (1 \times 9)$ and (3×3). $15 = (1 \times 15)$ and (3×5).

2. **Composite numbers have more than two factors and can be divided by more than just 1 and themselves.** Examples include 4, 6, 8, 9, 12, 14, and 15.

   Note that composite numbers (called that because they are *composed of* more than two factors) can be even or odd.

124 Part IV: Don't Count Yourself Out: The Math Review and Mini-Test

Don't confuse *even* and *odd* with *prime* and *composite*. That's an easy mistake to make in the confusion of the exam. If a problem that you know should be easy is flustering you, stop and ask yourself whether you're making this common mistake.

I said that 0 and 1 are not prime. They are also not composite. What are they? Neither. You express this as, "0 and 1 are neither prime nor composite."

I'm All Mixed Up: Mixture Problems

A mixture problem is a word problem that looks much more confusing than it actually is. There are two types of mixtures: those in which the items remain separate (when you mix peanuts and raisins, you still have peanuts and raisins, not pearains or raispeans) and those in which the two elements blend (these are usually chemicals, like water and alcohol). Check out the separate mixture type first.

> Marshall wants to mix 40 pounds of beads selling for 30 cents a pound with a quantity of sequins selling for 80 cents a pound. He wants to pay 40 cents per pound for the final mix. How many pounds of sequins should he use?

The hardest part for most students is knowing where to begin. Make a chart.

	Pounds	Price	Total
Beads	40	.30	$12.00
Sequins	x	.80	.80x
Mixture	40 + x	.40	.40 (40 + x)

Reason it out. The cost of the beads (1200) plus the cost of the sequins (80x) must equal the cost of the mixture (1600 + 40x). Note that you dump the decimal point (officially, you multiply by 100 to get rid of the decimal point, but really you dump it). Now you have a workable equation:

$1200 + 80x = 1600 + 40x$

$80x - 40x = 1600 - 1200$

$40x = 400$

$x = 10$

Careful! Keep in mind what x stands for. It represents the number of pounds of sequins, what the question asks for.

Go back and double-check by plugging this value into the equation. With a multiple-choice question, it may be easier to plug in the answer choices and work backward through the problem. Don't forget that you have that option.

Greed Is Great: Interest Problems

A problem usually asks you how much interest someone earned on an investment. This problem is pretty: PRTI, to be exact.

- P = Principal, the amount of money you begin with, or the amount you invest
- R = Rate, the interest rate you're earning on the money (stated as a decimal)

- T = Time, the amount of time you leave the money in the interest-bearing account
- I = Interest, the amount of interest you earn on the investment

The formula is PRT = I, or Principal × Rate × Time = Interest

> Janet invested $1,000 at 5 percent annual interest for one year. How much interest did she earn?

This is the simplest type of problem. Plug the numbers into the formula.

PRT = I

1000 × .05 × 1 = 50. She earned $50 interest.

The answer choices may try to trap you with variations on a decimal place, making the answers 5, 50, 500, and so on. You know that 5% = 5/100 = .05; be careful how you multiply.

These problems are not intentionally vicious. You won't see something that gets crazy on interest rates, like "5 percent annual interest compounded quarterly for 3 months and 6 percent quarterly interest compounded daily," blah, blah, blah.

(Useless but fascinating trivia I learned on a trip a few years ago: In Bulgarian, the word for *thank you* is pronounced *blah-go-dah-ree-uh*. But a shortened form, like *thanks*, is simply *blah*. If your mother takes you to task for being a smart aleck and going "blah, blah, blah" when she talks, you can innocently claim that you're practicing your Bulgarian and you're just thanking her for her wisdom.)

All Work and No Play: Work Problems

The formula most commonly used in a work problem is

$$\frac{\text{Time put in}}{\text{Capacity(or time to do the whole job)}}$$

Find each person's contribution. The denominator is the easy part; it represents how many hours (minutes, days, weeks, and so on) it takes the person to do the whole job, working alone. The numerator is how long the person already has worked. For example, if Janie can paint a house in six days and has been working for one day, she has done 1/6 of the work. If Evelyn can paint a house in eight days and has been working for five, she has done 5/8 of the project.

So far, so good. The problem comes when more than one person works at a task. What happens when Janie and Evelyn work together? Janie working alone can paint a house in six days. Evelyn working alone can paint it in eight days. Working together, how long will it take them to paint the house?

Find Janie's capacity: $x/6$. Find Evelyn's capacity: $x/8$. Together, the two fractions must add up to 1, the entire job.

$x/6 + x/8 = 1$

Multiply by the common denominator, 48, to eliminate the fractions:

$48x/6 + 48x/8 = 48$

$8x + 6x = 48$

$14x = 48$

x = approximately 3.43. It would take the two women working together about 3.43 days to paint the house.

Double-check by using your common sense. If you get an answer of 10, for example, you know that you must have made a mistake, because the two women working together should be able to do the job *more quickly* than either one working alone.

Smooth Operator: Order of Operations

When you have several operations (addition, subtraction, multiplication, division, squaring, and so on) in one problem, you must perform the operations in a definite order:

1. **Parentheses.**

   Do what's inside the parentheses first.

2. **Power.**

   Do the squaring or the cubing, whatever the exponent is.

3. **Multiply or divide.**

   Do multiplication and division left to right. If multiplication is to the left of division, multiply first. If division is to the left of multiplication, divide first.

4. **Add or subtract.**

   Do addition and subtraction left to right. If addition is to the left of subtraction, add first. If subtraction is to the left of addition, subtract first.

An easy mnemonic (memory device) for remembering these is *Please Praise My Daughter And Son (PPMDAS)*: Parentheses, Power, Multiply, Divide, Add, Subtract.

$$10(3-5)^2 + (30/5)^0 =$$

First, do what's inside the parentheses: $3 - 5 = -2$. $30/5 = 6$. Next, do the power: $-2^2 = 4$ and $6^0 = 1$. (Did you remember that any number to the 0 power equals 1?) Next, multiply: $10 \times 4 = 40$. Finally, add: $40 + 1 = 41$. *Correct Answer:* 41.

Try another:

$$3 + (9-6)^2 - 5(8/2)^{-2} =$$

First, do what's inside the parentheses: $9 - 6 = 3$ and $8/2 = 4$. Second, do the powers: $3^2 = 9$ and $4^{-2} = 1/4^2 = 1/16$. Multiply: $5 \times 1/16 = 5/16$. Finally, add and subtract left to right. $3 + 9 = 12$. Then, $12 - 5/16 = 11\,11/16$. *Correct answer:* $11\,11/16$.

Bonus: Speaking of mnemonics, here's my favorite. Can you tell me what it stands for?

My Very Educated Mother Just Served Us Nine Pickles.

Give up? It's the mnemonic of the planets in our solar system: Mercury, Venus, Earth, Mars, Jupiter, Saturn, Uranus, Neptune, and Pluto.

Measuring Up: Units of Measurement

Occasionally, you may be expected to know a unit of measurement that the test-makers deem obvious but that you have forgotten. Take a few minutes to review this brief list.

Chapter 12: Reviewing Miscellaneous Math You Probably Already Know

Because the units of measurement in your native land may be different from these (especially pints and quarts and gallons), it's especially important that you memorize these units. I'd really hate to see you work through an entire question beautifully and then miss it because of an unfamiliarity with the units of measurement.

1. **Time**
   - 60 seconds = 1 minute
   - 60 minutes = 1 hour
   - 24 hours = 1 day
   - 7 days = 1 week
   - 52 weeks = 1 year
   - 365 days = 1 year
   - 366 days = 1 leap year

Leap year is an interesting concept in terms of math problems. It comes around every four years. The extra day, February 29, makes 366 days in the year. Why do you need to know this? Suppose that you see this problem:

> Mr. Pellaton's neon sign flashes four hours a day, every day all year, for four years. If it costs him three cents a day for electricity, how much will he owe for electricity at the end of the fourth year?

You may be tempted to say that this problem is supereasy — multiply 365 × 4 to find the number of days and then multiply that number by .03. Wrong-o! You forgot that extra day for leap year, and your answer is off by three cents. You *know* that the test-makers will have that wrong answer lurking among the answer choices just to trap you. Whenever there is a four-year period, look out for the leap year with an extra day.

2. **Quantities**
   - 16 ounces = 1 pound
   - 2,000 pounds = 1 standard ton
   - 2 cups = 1 pint
   - 2 pints = 1 quart
   - 4 quarts = 1 gallon

You can calculate that a gallon has 16 cups, or 8 pints. To help you remember, think of borrowing a cup of sugar, sugar is sweet, and you have a Sweet 16 birthday party: 16 sweet cups of sugar in a gallon. It may be silly, but the best memory aids usually are.

3. **Length**
   - 12 inches = 1 foot
   - 3 feet (36 inches) = 1 yard
   - 5,280 feet (1,760 yards) = 1 mile

Everyone knows that there are 12 inches in a foot. How many square inches are there in a square foot? If you say 12, you've fallen for the trap. 12 × 12 = 144 square inches in a square foot.

Bonus: How many cubic inches are there in a cubic foot? Not 12, and not even 144. A cubic foot is 12 × 12 × 12 = 1,728 cubic inches.

Broken Hearts, Broken Numbers: Fractions

Did you hear about the town so small that its population was a fraction?

Adding or subtracting fractions

1. **You can add or subtract fractions only if they have the same denominator.**

    $1/8 + 2/8 = 3/8$

    $3/8 - 2/8 = 1/8$

2. **When fractions have the same denominator, add or subtract the numerators only.**

3. **When fractions don't have the same denominator, you have to find a common denominator.**

    You can, of course, multiply all the denominators, but that often doesn't give you the lowest common denominator. You end up with some humongous, overwhelming number that you'd rather not work with.

4. **To find the lowest (least) common denominator, identify the highest denominator and count by it.**

    Here's an example: Find the lowest common denominator of 15 and 6. Sure, you can multiply $15 \times 6 = 90$, but that's not the lowest common denominator. Instead, count by fifteens, because it's the larger of the two. 15? No, 6 doesn't go into that. 30? Yes, both 15 and 6 go into 30. That's the lowest common denominator.

    Try another problem. Find the lowest common denominator for 2, 4, and 5. Count by fives: 5? No, 2 and 4 don't go into it. 10? No, 4 doesn't go into it. 15? No, 2 and 4 don't go into it. 20? Yes, all the numbers divide evenly into 20.

    In many problems, you don't even have to find the lowest common denominator. You can find any common denominator by multiplying the denominators.

    $4/15 + 1/6 =$

    The common denominator is $15 \times 6 = 90$. Cross-multiply: $4 \times 6 = 24$. The first fraction becomes $24/90$. Cross-multiply: $1 \times 15 = 15$. The second fraction becomes $15/90$. Now add the numerators: $24 + 15 = 39$. Put the sum over the common denominator: $39/90$. Can you reduce? Yes, by 3: $13/30$.

    Do the same thing when working with variables instead of numbers.

    $a/b - c/d =$

    Find the common denominator by multiplying the two denominators: $b \times d = bd$. Cross-multiply: $a \times d = ad$. Cross-multiply: $c \times b = cb$. Put the difference of the results of the cross-multiplication over the common denominator: $(ad - cb)/bd$.

Multiplying fractions

This is the easy one. Just do it. Multiply horizontally: Multiply the numerators and then multiply the denominators.

$$\frac{3}{4} \times \frac{2}{5} = \frac{(3 \times 2)}{(4 \times 5)} = \frac{6}{20} = \frac{3}{10}$$

Always check whether you can cancel before you begin working to avoid having to deal with big, awkward numbers and having to reduce at the end. In the preceding example, you can cancel the 4 and the 2, leaving you with

$$\frac{3}{\cancel{4}_2} \times \frac{\cancel{2}^1}{5} = \frac{(3 \times 1)}{(2 \times 5)} = \frac{3}{10}$$

You get to the right solution either way; canceling in advance just makes the numbers smaller and easier to work with.

Dividing fractions

To divide by a fraction, invert it (turn it upside down) and multiply.

$$\frac{1}{3} \div \frac{2}{5} = \frac{1}{3} \times \frac{5}{2} = \frac{5}{6}$$

Working with mixed numbers

A *mixed number* is a whole number with a fraction tagging along behind it, such as $2\frac{1}{3}$, $4\frac{2}{5}$, or $9\frac{1}{2}$. Multiply the whole number by the denominator and add that to the numerator. Put the sum over the denominator.

$2\frac{1}{3} = (2 \times 3) + 1 = 7 \rightarrow \frac{7}{3}$

$4\frac{2}{5} = (4 \times 5) + 2 = 22 \rightarrow \frac{22}{5}$

$9\frac{1}{2} = (9 \times 2) + 1 = 19 \rightarrow \frac{19}{2}$

Chapter 13

Numb and Number: Acing the Mathematics Test

In This Chapter
- How you're expected to perform: amateur "mathletics"
- Grinding it out: a common-sense approach
- Time flies when you're having fun: timing tips
- The details that make the difference: do's, don'ts, and darns

Okay, you math whiz, here's a question for you. Quick, without your calculator, tell us:

Question: How many seconds are there in a year?

Answer: Exactly 12. January 2nd, February 2nd, March 2nd . . .

Your number's up. You cannot escape the ACT Mathematics Test, no matter how hard you try. One of the four tests of the ACT is the one-hour Mathematics Test, whose questions, alas, are not quite as much fun as the one above. This chapter tells you what the test contains.

What You See Is What You Get: The Format and Breakdown

No, the "breakdown" in the preceding heading doesn't refer to *your* (nervous) breakdown, but rather to the breakdown of the number and types of problems in the Mathematics Test. This 60-minute test features 60 questions (which makes figuring out your time per problem convenient, no?). The questions fall into pretty standard categories.

In the ACT bulletin and in many ACT study books, you have to slog through incredibly detailed analyses of the exact number of each question type on the test: 14 plane geometry questions, 4 trigonometry questions, blah blah blah. We refuse to put either of us to sleep with that sort of detail. We mean, it's not as if you have any control over the distribution of questions, right? (We can just see the letter: "Dear ACT: Please be sure that I have more geometry and fewer algebra problems — thanks . . . ") The following is the short 'n' sweet version of the kinds of math questions that you'll encounter in the dark alleyways of the ACT.

- **Pre-algebra:** (Normal people refer to this as "arithmetic.") About 20 percent, or one-fifth, of the questions cover basic arithmetic, including such concepts as fractions and decimals and the dreaded word problems.
- **Elementary algebra:** This is the type of material that you learn in your first semester or two of algebra. These questions test your ability to work with positive and negative

integers, set up algebraic formulas, solve linear equations, and do the occasional FOIL problem. About 20 percent, or one-fifth, of the questions cover elementary algebra.

If you don't know what a FOIL problem is, don't despair. We discuss FOIL in excruciating detail in Chapter 8.

- **Intermediate algebra/coordinate geometry:** About 30 percent of the questions cover more difficult quadratic problems, as well as inequalities, bases, exponents, radicals, and basic graphing (finding points on an *x, y*–coordinate graph).

- **Plane geometry and trigonometry:** About 23 percent of the questions cover plane figures (what you think of as "just plain figures," like triangles, circles, quadrilaterals, and so on). The trig questions make up only 7 percent of the test, so if you haven't had trig yet, don't freak out. Trig questions are very basic, covering trig ratios and basic trigonometric identities.

Confused? Don't worry about the exact number of questions. Just remember two basic points:

- You have 60 minutes to do 60 questions.
- One-third of the questions are arithmetic, one-third are algebra, and one-third are geometry.

Absence Makes the Heart Grow Fonder: What Isn't on the Mathematics Test

Instead of obsessing over how awful the ACT Mathematics Test is, focus on a few of its good points.

- **Calculus:** The ACT does not — We repeat, *does not* — test calculus. You don't even have to know how to pronounce "calculus" to get a good ACT Mathematics Test score. You also don't have to know trigonometry. Yes, 7 percent of the test (approximately four questions) covers trig concepts, but if you miss only four questions, *we're* happy, *you're* ecstatic, and Harvard is calling.

- **Quantitative Comparisons, grid-ins, and so on:** The bizarre math questions found in other standardized exams are also missing from the ACT. If you've taken the SAT I, for example, you've seen the Quantitative Comparison (or QC) question, which has no multiple-choice answers. (For more information about preparing for the SAT I, read *The SAT I For Dummies,* published by Wiley Publishing, Inc.) Some exams have a grid-in style question, in which no answer choices are given. You don't have to worry about those weird formats here. All the math questions on the ACT are in straightforward multiple-choice format.

  All the math questions have *five* answer choices. The rest of the questions on the ACT have only four answer choices. Be sure to look at all the possible choices in this section. We're always amazed by how many students, used to looking at answers A, B, C, and D in other sections, totally don't see the E answer choices in the math section.

- **Traps:** Most math exams are full of nasty old traps. The ACT is not. It's not out to getcha, like other tests. Here, the questions really test your math knowledge, not your patience. You don't have to be quite as paranoid on the ACT as you do on other exams.

Getting into the Grind: The Approach

You've done multiple-choice math problems all your life. You don't have much more to learn about doing multiple-choice math questions. However, the following common-sense steps can help you stay focused.

1. **Identify the point of the question.**

    Yes, even the stupid word problems have a point. Each question is trying to get you to supply one specific piece of information. Does the question ask you to solve for a circumference, or for an area? Do you have to state the value of x or of $2x$? Circle precisely what the question asks for. After you finish the problem, go back and double-check that your answer provides the circled information.

    We just said that the ACT is not out to trap you — but that doesn't mean you can't trap yourself. Among the answer choices are answers that you get by making careless errors. Suppose, for example, that the problem asks for the *product* of numbers, and you find the *sum*. That answer will be there. If the question asks for one-half of a quantity and you solve for twice the quantity, that answer will be there. Because these types of answer choices are available to you, it's especially important that you identify *exactly* what the problem asks for and supply only that.

2. **Budget your time and brain strain: Decide whether the problem is worth your time and effort.**

    You don't have to do every math problem in order, you know. Read the question and then predict how time-consuming it will be to solve. If you know that you have to take several steps to answer the question, you may want to skip the problem and go back to it later. If you're not even sure where to start the problem, don't sit there gnawing at your pencil as if it were an ear of corn (unless you're Pinocchio, wood really isn't brain food). Guess and go.

    Guess, guess, guess! The ACT has no penalty for wrong answers. You're going to (or already have) read that statement hundreds of times throughout this book. We say it every chance we get to remind you that you can guess without fear of reprisal. Whenever you skip a problem, choose an answer, any answer, and hope that you'll get lucky. Put a big arrow in the margin of the test booklet next to the question (not on the answer grid, because it may mess up the computer grading) to remind yourself that you made a wild guess. But if you run out of time and don't get back to the question, at least you have a chance of getting the answer right.

3. **Look before you leap: Preview the answer choices.**

    We'd be wealthy women if we had a nickel for every student who groaned and complained as he or she looked at the answer choices, "Man, I didn't really have to work that whole problem out. I could've just estimated from the answer choices." Absolutely true.

    Look at the answer choices before you begin doing any pencil-pushing. Often, the choices are variations on a theme, like .5, 5, 50, 500, 5,000. If you see those answers, you know that you don't have to worry about the digit, only the decimal. Maybe the answers are very far apart, like 1, 38, 99, 275, and 495. You probably can make a wild estimate and get that answer correct. But if you see that the answers are close together (like 8, 9, 10, 11, and 12), you know that you have to invest a little more time and effort into being extra careful when solving the problem.

4. **Give yourself a second chance: Use your answer to check the question.**

    Think of this as working forward and backward. First, work forward to come up with the answer to the question. Then plug the answer into the question and work backward to check it. For example, if the question asks you to solve for x, work through the equation until you get the answer. Then plug that answer back into the equation and make sure that it works out. This last step takes less time than you may think and can save you a lot of points.

Time Flies When You're Having Fun: Timing Tips

The most common complaint we hear from students about the Mathematics Test is, "There's just not enough time. If I had more time, I could probably do every single question, but I always run out of time." True enough. Although having one minute per question (60 math questions, 60-minute section) sounds good, you'd be surprised at how fast time goes by. We have a few suggestions to make the best use of your time.

Skim for your favorite questions

We think of this technique as eating dessert first (something we always do). Go for the chocolate cake first (the easy questions) to make sure that time doesn't run out before you get to the good stuff. Leave the green beans (the harder problems) for the end. If you run out of time (which happens to most test-takers), at least you will have finished those questions that you had the best chance of answering correctly.

Start in the middle when plugging in the answer choices

On many problems, you'll be able to plug in the answer choices and see which one fits. For example, suppose that the question is something like:

$x + \frac{1}{2}x + \frac{1}{3}x = 110$. What is the value of x?

A. 95

B. 90

C. 72

D. 60

E. 30

Yes, you can use a common denominator and actually work through the problem forward to find x directly. But it may be just as quick and easy to plug in the answer choices. Start with the middle choice, choice C. If $x = 72$, then $\frac{1}{2}x = 36$, and $\frac{1}{3}x = 24$. But $72 + 36 + 24 = 132$, not 110. Because the sum is too big, you know the number you plugged in is too big as well. Go down the list, plugging in the smaller numbers. Try choice D. Let $x = 60$. Then $x(60) + \frac{1}{2}x (30) + \frac{1}{3}x (20) = 110$. Voilà!

Kindly refrain from showing off everything you know

Some of the ACT problems have extraneous information. For example, a geometry problem may list all sorts of numbers, including lengths of sides and measures of interior angles. If the question asks you to find the area of a trapezoid, you need just the numbers for base and height. (Remember the formula? The area of a trapezoid is ½[base 1 + base 2] × height.) Extra red-herring info can make you waste a lot of time. We already know that you're brilliant (you bought this book, didn't you?); you don't need to prove it by doing more than you're asked during the test. If you convert every problem into two or three new problems, you'll never finish this section on time.

Put aside two minutes to fill in the remaining ovals

The ACT assesses no penalty for guessing. We like to say that over and over and over again until you're so exasperated that you want to cut off our air supply. It's critical to remember that you don't lose points for wrong answers; always keep in mind that wild guesses are worth making. Nothing is worse than that sinking feeling you get when the proctor calls time, and you still have ten problems you haven't even looked at. If you save a few minutes at the end, you can fill in some answers wildly for those last ten problems. You have a good chance of getting at least a few of them correct.

The proctor is *supposed* to tell you when you have only five minutes left in the test. Before the test actually begins, you may want to remind your proctor to do so.

Do's, Don'ts, and Darns: What to Do and Not Do in the Math Test

Although the math questions are pretty straightforward, a few basic do's and don'ts are worth noting here.

Do get the lead out

Give your pencil a workout. If you have to solve a geometry problem, jot down the formula first and then just fill in the numbers. If you have the formula staring at you, you're not as likely to make a careless mistake as you would if you tried to keep everything in your head. If the geometry problem has words, words, words but no picture, draw the picture yourself. When you plug in the answer choices or make up your own numbers to substitute for variables, write down what you plugged in and tried. We see students redoing the same things over and over because they forgot what they plugged in. Doodle away. You get no scratch paper for the ACT, but the test booklet has plenty of white space.

The ACT provides very few formulas. None are given in the directions, and only rarely is a formula given in an individual problem. The test-makers actually expect you to know what you're doing and to have the formulas memorized. Heaven forbid that you disappoint them. Take the time to go through the math reviews in Chapters 10, 11, and 12 (one for geometry, one for algebra, and one for miscellaneous math) and memorize every formula possible. Pay special attention to the ones you rarely use, like the formula for determining the interior angles of a figure. Based on Murphy's Law ("Whatever *can* go wrong *will* go wrong"), the exam is likely to require the use of those formulas.

Don't start working until you've read the entire problem

So you read the first part of a problem and start trying to solve for the area of the triangle or the circumference of the circle. But if you read further, you may find that the question asks only for a *ratio* of the areas of two figures, which you can figure out without actually finding the precise areas. Or you may solve a whole algebraic equation, only to realize that the question didn't ask for the variable you found, but for something else entirely. As we say in the "Getting into the Grind: The Approach" section, earlier in this chapter, circle the part of the problem that specifies exactly what is asked for.

Just because the answer you got is staring up at you from the test booklet, that does not, in the least, mean that it's the right answer. (That's as bad as thinking that someone is Mr. Right just because he's gawking at you in the lunchroom.) The answer may be an interim answer, like what x is when you're asked to find the square root of x. The answer may be a careless-mistake answer, like what you get if you don't keep your decimal point straight. Or the answer may be a write-your-own-question answer, in which you give the test-makers something they weren't asking for, like finding the perimeter when the question wants the area. (Creativity is rewarded in the Real World, but it's punished on the ACT. Much as you'd like to, you can't create your own new problems.)

Do reread the problem with your answer inserted

Very few students take this last critical step. Most test-takers are so concerned with finishing on time that they solve the problem and zoom on to the next question. Big tactical error. Rereading the question in light of your answer can show you some pretty dumb mistakes. For example, if the question asks you for the average of 5, 9, 12, 17, and 32, and your answer is 75, you can immediately realize that you found the sum but forgot to divide by the number of terms. (And of course, 75 is one of the answer choices.) Maybe the question asks you to find one interior angle of a figure, and your answer is 190. If you look at the angle and see that it is acute (less than 90 degrees), you've made a mistake somewhere.

The ACT very carefully says, "figures are NOT necessarily drawn to scale." However, in the majority of cases, the figures are pretty darn close, and eyeballing them can help you at least eliminate some wrong answers.

Don't strike out over a difficult question early on

Most standardized exams put their questions in order of difficulty, presenting the easy ones first, then the medium ones, and finally the hard ones. Things aren't as cut and dried on the ACT Mathematics Test. You may find a question that you consider really tough very early in the exam. Although "easy" and "hard" are subjective, many of my students over the years have been furious with themselves because they never looked at the last several questions — reasoning that if they couldn't get the earlier ones right, they obviously couldn't get the later ones at all. Wrong. We've seen some relatively simple questions, especially basic geometry questions, close to the end of the exam.

"Easy" and "difficult" for international students often have more to do with the language than with the math. Many students for whom English is a second language do better on the basic equations than on the word problems. We suggest that you leaf through each exam as soon as you begin it, marking which problems you want to do, and then be sure to get to them. If you have time, you can go back to the others. And don't forget to fill in an answer for every question. The ACT does not penalize you for wrong answers.

Chapter 14

More Fun Than a Root Canal: Mathematics Practice Questions

In This Chapter
▶ Making your brain earn its keep with practice questions
▶ Destroying your self-esteem with trick questions
▶ Testing your patience with the dreaded word problems

*E*ither you paid close attention in school or you've memorized all the formulas and concepts in Chapters 10, 11, and 12 and reviewed the tricks and traps in Chapter 13, right? Now you're frothing at the bit, eager to show off what you know. Don't let us hold you back. Here are a dozen practice questions — give 'em your best shot!

DIRECTIONS: Each of the following questions has five answer choices. Select the best choice.

1. $\dfrac{\left(a^4 \times a^3\right)^2}{a^4} =$

   A. a^{36}
   B. a^{10}
   C. a^9
   D. a^6
   E. a^4

First, do the operation inside the parentheses. When you multiply like bases, you add the exponents: $a^4 \times a^3 = a^7$. When you have a power outside the parentheses, you multiply the exponents: $\left(a^7\right)^2 = a^{14}$. Finally, when you divide by like bases, you subtract the exponents: $a^{14} \div a^4 = a^{14-4} = a^{10}$. Correct answer: **B**.

If you chose D, you fell for a trap answer. If you said $a^4 \times a^3 = a^{12}$ and $a^{12 \times 2} = a^{24}$, you may have divided a^{24} by a^4 and gotten a^6.

If you chose A, you fell for another trap. You may have reasoned that $a^4 \times a^3$ is a^{12}. Because 12 squared is 144, you may have thought that $\left(a^{12}\right)^2 = a^{144}$ and that $a^{144} \div a^4 = a^{36}$.

All these trap answers are intentional; the ACT-makers realize that you're likely to do simple multiplication and division rather than use the exponents correctly. If you're still confused about how to multiply and divide like bases, see the exponents section in Chapter 11.

2. The ratio of knives to forks to spoons in a silverware drawer is 3:4:5. Which of the following could be the total number of knives, forks, and spoons in the drawer?

   F. 60

   G. 62

   H. 64

   J. 65

   K. 66

A total must be a multiple of the sum of the numbers of the ratios. In other words, add 3 + 4 + 5 = 12. The total must be a multiple of 12. Only one answer choice divides evenly by 12. If you're confused about ratios (supposedly one of the easiest portions of the exam), see the ratio section of Chapter 11. *Correct answer:* **F.**

3. An usher passes out 60 percent of his programs before the intermission and 40 percent of the remainder after the intermission. At the end of the evening, what percent of the original number of programs does the usher have left?

   A. 60

   B. 40

   C. 24

   D. 16

   E. 0

Whenever you have a percentage problem, plug in 100 for the original total. Assume that the usher begins with 100 programs. If he passes out 60 percent of them, he has passed out 60, leaving him with 40. Now comes the tricky part. After the intermission, the usher passes out 40 percent of the *remainder:* 40 percent of 40 is 16 (.40 × 40 = 16) and 40 – 16 = 24. Correct answer: **C.**

Did you fall for the trap answer of choice E? If you thought the usher first passed out 60 programs and then the remaining 40, you believed that he had no programs left at the end of the evening. The word *remainder* is the key to this problem. The usher did not pass out 40 percent of his original total, but 40 percent of the *remainder.*

If you chose D, you made a careless mistake. The number 16 represents the percentage of programs the usher passed out after the intermission. The question asks for the percent of programs the usher had left. We suggest that you circle the portion of the question that tells you what you're looking for. When you are double-checking your work, this circled portion is the first thing to review.

4. A salesman makes a commission of $1.50 per shirt sold and $2.50 per pair of pants sold. In one pay period, he sold 10 more shirts than pairs of pants. If his total commission for the pay period was $215, what was the total number of shirts and pairs of pants he sold?

   A. 40

   B. 50

   C. 60

   D. 110

   E. 150

Let x be the number of pairs of pants the salesman sold. Then the number of shirts is $x + 10$ (because the problem tells you that the salesman sold 10 more shirts than pairs of pants).

Make the equation $1.50(x + 10) + 2.50(x) = $215.

Multiply: $1.50x + 15 + 2.50x = 215$.

Chapter 14: More Fun Than a Root Canal: Mathematics Practice Questions

Combine like terms: 4.00x + 15 = 215.

Isolate the x on one side: 4.00x = 215 − 15.

Subtract: 4.00x = 200.

Divide: $x = {}^{200}\!/\!_4$, or $x = 50$.

TRAPS & TRICKS

If you chose answer B, you fell for the trap answer (after all that hard work)! Remember to go back and reread what the question is asking for. In this case, it wants to know the total number of pants and shirts sold. You're not done working yet. If x (50) is the number of pairs of pants, then x + 10 (60) is the number of shirts sold. (Note that 60 is a trap answer as well.) Combine 50 + 60 to get the right answer, 110. *Correct answer:* **D**.

5. Kim and Scott work together stuffing envelops. Kim works twice as fast as Scott. Together they stuff 2,100 envelopes in four hours. How long would Kim working alone take to stuff 175 envelopes?

   A. 20 minutes

   B. 30 minutes

   C. 1 hour

   D. 3 hours

   E. 6 hours

The ratio of Kim's work to Scott's work is 2:1. In other words, she does two out of every three envelopes. Scott does one out of every three envelopes, or 2,100 ÷ 3 = 700. Scott does 700 in four hours, and Kim does 1,400 in four hours. Divide 1,400 by 4 to find that Kim does 350 per hour. That means 175 is ½ of 350. Therefore, in one half-hour (or 30 minutes), Kim can stuff 175 envelopes. *Correct answer:* **B**.

When you encounter a word problem like this, don't start thinking equations immediately. Power math won't help you on this problem as much as simply talking the problem through.

6. If DC = 6, what is the shaded area in the figure?

   F. 72 − 18π

   G. 72 − 36π

   H. 9π

   J. 36 − 18π

   K. 36 − 36π

A shaded area is a leftover. To find a shaded area, you usually find a total, find a subtotal, and then subtract. If the side DC is 6, that is the same as the radius of the circle.

Part IV: Don't Count Yourself Out: The Math Review and Mini-Test

The area of a circle is πr^2; therefore, $\pi 6^2 = 36\pi$. Be careful to remember that you're working only with a semicircle. The shaded area subtracts only half the area of the circle, so you subtract 18π. That immediately narrows the answers down to F and J.

Next, find the area of the rectangle. (The area of a rectangle equals length × width.) The width of DC is 6. Because the radius of the circle is 6, the diameter of the circle is 12. BC, the diameter of the circle, is the same as the length of the rectangle. $6 \times 12 = 72$. Finally, subtract: $72 - 18\pi$. *Correct answer:* **F.**

Shaded-area questions should be one of the easiest types of questions to get correct. If you got confused on this problem, flip to the shaded-area portion of Chapter 10.

7. $5a^2 + (5a)^2 = 120$. Solve for *a*.

   A. 2

   B. 3

   C. 4

   D. 5

   E. 6

$(5a)^2$ is $5a \times 5a$, which is $25a^2$.

$25a^2 + 5a^2 = 30a^2$

$30a^2 = 120$

$a^2 = 120 \div 30$

$a^2 = 4$

$a = 2$

Correct answer: **A.** Choice C is the trap answer. If you divided 120 by 30 and got 4, you may have chosen C, forgetting that 4 represented a^2, not *a*.

Of course, you also could simply plug in each answer choice and work backward. Here, if $a = 2$, then

$5(2)^2 + (5 \times 2)^2 = 120$

$(5 \times 4) + 10^2 = 120$

$20 + 100 = 120$

$120 = 120$

8. Three times as much as ⅓ less than $3x$ is how much in terms of *x*?

   F. $9x$

   G. $8x$

   H. $6x$

   J. x

   K. $\frac{1}{3x}$

Working backward in this type of problem usually is easier. One-third less than $3x$ is $2x$. You can calculate it this way: $3x - \frac{1}{3}(3x) = 3x - x = 2x$. Then $3 \times 2x$ is $6x$. *Correct answer:* **H.**

If English is your second (or third or fourth) language, a problem like this can be extremely difficult to understand. The math is easy to do, but the English is hard to translate. This type of problem is a good one for you to guess at quickly and just go on.

Chapter 14: More Fun Than a Root Canal: Mathematics Practice Questions

9. The following chart shows the weights of junior high school students. What is the sum of the mode and the median weights?

Weight in Pounds	Number of Students
110	4
120	2
130	3
140	2

- **A.** 230 pounds
- **B.** 235 pounds
- **C.** 250 pounds
- **D.** 255 pounds
- **E.** 258 pounds

This question tests vocabulary as much as it tests math. The *mode* is the most frequently repeated number. In this case, 110 is repeated more often than any other term. The *median* is the middle term when the numbers are arranged in order. Here you would have 110, 110, 110, 110, 120, 120, 130, 130, 130, 140, 140. Of these 11 numbers, the sixth one, 120, is the median. 110 + 120 = 230. *Correct answer:* **A.**

Don't confuse *median* with *mean*. The *mean* is the average. You get the mean by adding all the terms and then dividing by the number of terms. If you chose B, you fell into a different trap. You thought that 125 was the *median*, because you added the first and last terms and divided by 2. Sorry. To find the median, you have to write out all the terms (all four 110s, both 120s, and so on) and then locate the middle term.

10. The ratio of the area of triangle EBD to triangle ABE is

AE=ED=DC

- **F.** 3:2
- **G.** 3:1
- **H.** 2:1
- **J.** 1:1
- **K.** 1:2

The area of a triangle is ½ base × height. The base of EBD is ED. That is equal to AE, which is the base of triangle ABE. The bases of the two triangles are equal. The heights are equal, as well. By definition, a height of a triangle is a line from the tallest point perpendicular to the base. If the triangles have the same base and the same height, the ratio of their areas is 1:1. *Correct answer:* **J.**

11. $\begin{array}{r} 95c5 \\ + \ 3cbc \\ \hline ab3a2 \end{array}$

   Solve for the sum of $a + b + c$.

   A. 15

   B. 14

   C. 13

   D. 12

   E. 11

If you're rushed for time, this problem is a good one to guess at quickly. (**Remember:** The ACT does not assess a penalty for wrong answers. Never leave an answer blank. Even a wild guess is worthwhile.) However, if you do a few of these practice problems, you'll be surprised at how quickly you can get them right.

Don't panic. This problem is much easier than it appears. Start with the right-hand column, the ones or units column: $5 + c = 2$. You know that it must be a 12 instead of a 2, making $c = 7$. Jot $c = 7$ to the side.

Carry the 1 to the tens column: $1 + 7$, which is 8, and $8 + b = a$. You don't know a yet ... or do you? Go to the far-left column (the thousands column). If the answer is $ab3a2$, the variable a must equal 1. You cannot add two four-digit numbers and get 20,000-something. The most you can get would be 10-000-something (for example, $9,999 + 9,999 = 19,998$). Now you know that a is 1. Jot down $a = 1$ on the side.

Go back to the tens column. $1 + 7$; $8 + b = 11$ (it can't be 1; it must be 11). Therefore, $b = 3$. Carry the 1 to the hundreds column. $1 + 5$ is 6. $6 + c$ (which is 7) = 13. Yes, this is true — a good check. Carry the 1 to the next column. $1 + 9$ is 10. $10 + 3$ is 13, which is what I said ab was in the first place. Therefore, $c = 7$, $b = 3$, $a = 1$ and $7 + 3 + 1 = 11$. *Correct answer:* **E.**

The most common mistake that students make on this type of problem is forgetting to carry the 1 to the next column. Double-check that you have done so.

12. $3 * 4 = \frac{1}{3} + \frac{1}{4}$. Solve for $\frac{2}{15} * \frac{2}{18}$.

   F. 14

   G. 14.5

   H. 15

   J. 16

   K. 16.5

This problem is a *symbolism*, one that you should think through in words instead of heading for an equation. When you have an asterisk between two numbers as in this problem, you add the reciprocals of those two numbers. For example, the reciprocal of 3 is $\frac{1}{3}$, and the reciprocal of 4 is $\frac{1}{4}$. Therefore, add the reciprocals of $\frac{2}{15}$ and $\frac{2}{18}$. Then $\frac{15}{2} + \frac{18}{2} = \frac{33}{2} = 16½ = 16.5$ *Correct answer:* **K.**

The * has this meaning *for this problem only*. The meanings of symbols vary from problem to problem; always read the directions.

Part V
Time to Read the Riot ACT: The Reading Test

The 5th Wave — By Rich Tennant

"IT SAYS, 'BREAK GLASS,' BUT IT DOESN'T SAY WHAT GLASS!"

"TRY THE DOOR AGAIN!"

"MAYBE THE WHOLE THING IS SUPPOSED TO COME OFF THE WALL."

"AIM THE HOSE?" AIM IT AT WHAT?!"

"LET'S GO OVER IT ONCE MORE—SLOWLY!"

"I COULD BREAK A WINDOW! THAT'S GLASS!"

ROOM 101 — ACT Reading Comprehension

In this part...

How long have you been reading now: 10 years? 12 years? The purpose of this part is not to teach you how to read. I assume that you can sound out the words and make at least a little sense of the passages (although with some of *these* passages . . .). Instead, most of the material in this part discusses the types of questions you're going to encounter on the test and the traps built into them. After you understand the techniques of handling each question type, you get to put the techniques into action with a mini-reading test based on two abbreviated passages and eight questions.

Keep in mind that the reading passages in the ACT have little connection to the reading passages in the Real World, so don't try to use the information I give you here on your reading assignments at school. Learn the techniques, use them on the ACT, and then file them away under "Been there, done that."

Chapter 15

This, Too, Shall Pass(age): Sailing through the Reading Test

In This Chapter
▶ Enlightening yourself with 3,000 words of wisdom: the Reading Test passages
▶ Questioning your sanity: The Reading Test questions
▶ Experiencing illusion, delusion, and confusion: tips and traps

I once had a student tell me, "If I'd known it would end up like this, I never would have let my first-grade teacher show me how to read!" Ah, we never know what consequences our actions will have someday. The first day with your ABCs led you straight to this chapter, which explains to you the Reading Test portion of the ACT.

In this chapter, you find out what types of passages to expect and what the questions look like that pertain to each type of passage. It's too late now to pretend you can't read, so just get ready to enjoy the ride.

Facing Forty (Questions): The Reading Test

The Reading Test consists of four passages. Each passage is supposed to be similar in difficulty to materials you encounter during your freshman year of college. The test contains one passage on each of the following topics:

- **Humanities:** This passage can be about music, dance, theater, art, architecture, language, ethics, literary criticism, and even philosophy. Most students tend to like these passages because (believe it or not) they are actually interesting.

- **Social studies:** The social studies passage covers sociology, anthropology, history, geography, psychology, political science, and economics. That's an incredibly wide range of topics when you think about it. The history passages usually are pretty good; some of the psychology ones can be intense.

- **Natural sciences:** This passage is what most people think about when they say "science." The natural science passage can cover chemistry, biology, physics, and other physical sciences.

  Are you panicking right now, screaming, "I haven't taken physics! No fair!" Not to worry. The questions don't require you to know any particular subjects. Everything you'll need to answer the questions is right there in the passages, and you can go back to the passages as often as you like.

- **Prose fiction:** The fiction passage can be taken from a novel or can be a short story. Some of these are very fun to read. But don't expect that you'll have read them before.

In all the years I've been teaching, I've had only one student tell me she remembers having read the passage before in a novel. The ACT test-makers obviously don't want to test you on what you are familiar with (and maybe have even discussed in class), but on how well you evaluate a passage that is new to you.

Each passage has 10 questions, for a grand total of 40 questions.

Timing

The Reading Test is 35 minutes long. Assuming you live to an average age of 72, the Reading Test, therefore, is only about 1/1,081,975th of your life. Now that doesn't seem so bad, does it?

Scoring

You get three reading scores. One is the total score, based on all 40 questions. Then you get two subscores: one in natural sciences/social studies (based, obviously, on those two passages) and one on arts/literature (based on those two passages).

Reading strategies

You've been reading since you were about 5 years old. It's a little late for me to teach you the basics. What I can do, however, is teach you how to make the best use of your time in this test. (After all, 35 minutes for four passages and 40 questions means you have only about 8 or 9 minutes per passage. That's not a great deal of time for most people.)

1. **Preview.**

    You are naturally going to like one type of passage more than the others. Look for it and do it first, being extremely careful to shade in the correct bubbles on your answer grid. (When you skip around, it's easy to mess up the grid.)

    What happens if your brain takes a little vacation and you suddenly find you've filled in the bubbles all wrong? Maybe you started off by reading passage 2, with questions 11–20, but you filled in the bubbles for questions 1–10? Hey, you laugh now, but that's easy to do. The first reaction usually is panic; first you erase all your answers, and then you try to remember what they were. Bad move. Here's how to handle this problem: As you answer a question, first circle the correct response in your booklet, and then fill in the bubble for that response on the answer grid. This way, if you mess up and have to erase your answer grid, you can just glance at your answer booklet and find the right answers again.

2. **Decide on a strategy.**

    Some students do well under time pressures and can finish all four passages and the questions. These are students who don't have to read slowly and carefully, getting every little morsel the passages have to offer, but can get the overall idea. Other students get so totally nervous if they have to rush, they'll mess up completely. If you're one of these students, it may be better to concentrate on reading three of the passages carefully and answering all the questions correctly on them.

    If you decide to do only three passages, be sure to fill in answers for the last passage. Remember, the ACT has no penalty for wrong answers, meaning that you should guess your brains out. Never, ever leave an answer blank.

Chapter 15: This, Too, Shall Pass(age): Sailing through the Reading Test

3. Pay special attention to the first and last paragraphs and to the first and last lines of each paragraph.

Most writers (except writers of literature) pay attention to the maxim, "Tell 'em what you're gonna tell 'em; tell 'em; and tell 'em what you told 'em." That means that the first sentence of a paragraph or the first paragraph of a passage usually gives the main idea and sets up the paragraph or the passage. The last sentence or paragraph summarizes what's been said. If you are absolutely short on time, you can often get away with focusing on these parts of the passage. Even if you are reading carefully and have plenty of time, think about these parts carefully.

This tip works best if the passage is a complete essay or short story. It doesn't work as well if the passage is an excerpt from a longer work. Occasionally, an excerpt seems to begin in the middle and end just as abruptly. However, most passages have some coherent format on which you can concentrate.

4. Don't memorize!

I see some students stop reading, gaze out into the distance, and mutter to themselves, counting off on their fingers. It's apparent that these students are trying to memorize facts from the passage: "Let's see, the three basic elements that make up Kleinschwab's Elixir are . . . ." You do not have to memorize anything; in fact, doing so can be counterproductive. Although you naturally want to remember some of what you've read, you can always go back to the passage as often as you'd like.

5. Summarize.

As you're reading, think about what you've learned, and maybe summarize it in your own words. Don't make things complicated. A simple "This passage is about the differences in the way the Greeks looked at nature and the way the Romans looked at nature" helps to focus your thoughts.

Question: Should I underline or outline as I go?

Answer: If doing so is your normal method of reading, yes. If you rarely outline or underline, doing so now may tend to confuse you. I see students who have been told to underline or outline spending more time worrying about what to underline than thinking about what's in the passage. I personally like to circle key words (especially unusual vocabulary that I think may be important) and occasionally jot a note in the margin, summarizing a paragraph. For example, next to paragraph 1, I may write, "Need for elixir." Next to paragraph 2, I write, "Failed experiments." By paragraph 3, I write, "Success; uses of elixir." You get the idea. You are allowed to refer to the passages as often as you want; having an idea of what is where in the passage can save you precious seconds.

6. Look for relationships and connections.

Maybe the concepts are given in a contrasting form: what makes one idea different from another? Perhaps you are given thoughts in sequence, like what came first, next, last. Some passages talk about the cause and effect, how one thing impacts another.

Question: Should I read the questions before the passages?

Answer: Probably not. I would not suggest starting off by reading the questions before even glancing at the passages, as the questions make no sense out of context. You'll just confuse yourself. Some students use a worthwhile technique of looking at the first few sentences of the passage to get an overview, then reading the questions, and then going back and reading the passage, keeping the ideas in the back of their brains. And of course, some of us just read the passage and then go back and forth looking at the questions. There's no one right or wrong way. When you're doing the passages in the practice exams, try each technique and see which one works best for you individually.

I've Been Meaning to Ask You Something: The Questions

Although you may encounter many different types of questions on the ACT, the following are some that have shown up frequently in the past. Make like a Boy Scout and Be Prepared.

Main idea

A question may ask, "Which of the following is the main idea of the passage?" or "The theme of paragraph 3 is which of these?" You've likely done "main-idea" questions on other exams before. Keep in mind three things:

- A *main idea* is broad and general. It covers the entire passage (or, if the question is asking about a paragraph, the entire paragraph). Be sure not to choose a "little" answer. The mere fact that a statement is true does not mean it is the main idea. Suppose you have a passage about high school education, and a question asks for the main idea. One answer choice says, "The ACT gives students the heebie-jeebies." No one can argue with that statement, but it isn't the main idea of the passage.

- The right answer often repeats the topic sentence or key words. If the passage is about Asian philosophy, the correct answer will most likely have the words Asian philosophy in it. Don't immediately choose any answer just because it has those words, but if you're debating between two answers, the one with the key words may be a better choice.

- Keep in mind the tone of the passage and the attitude of the author. If the passage is positive and the author is impressed by the philosophy, the main idea will be positive, not negative or neutral. If the author is criticizing something, the main idea will be negative. The main idea should always reflect the attitude of the author or the tone of the passage.

Details

The detail question is the opposite of the main idea. It covers one particular point, not the passage as a whole. This question is one of the easiest to get correct; you need only go back to the passage and find the specific answer. Some examples include, "According to the passage, James confronted Gary about the business when which of the following occurred?" or "The results of the experiments were considered unacceptable because . . . ."

If you're running short of time or your brain cells are about ready to surrender, look for this type of question and answer it first. You can often answer this detail question correctly even if you haven't read the entire passage. Find the key word in the question (such as "elixir") and skim for that word in the passage.

Tone, attitude, and inference

This question is more of a read-between-the-lines question. You can't go back to one specific line of the passage to find the answer. Nowhere in the passage will it say, for example, "My belief is that physical violence rarely solves problems." You have to infer from the passage as a whole that the author prefers negotiation to confrontation. You have to infer that the author is contemptuous of violence and those who practice it, that his or her attitude throughout the passage is negative. Examples of this sort of question include, "The author implies that he believes violence is . . . ." and "The fact that the product line included a new model that James insisted upon carrying despite Gary's objections indicates that . . . ."

Vocabulary in context

You may have to determine the meaning of a word by its use in context.

Sometimes, common words are used in an uncommon way. For example, the author may mention that, "Lawrence was unable to cow Michael, despite his frequent threats." Although "cow" usually refers to a four-footed bovine, in this case, the word is used as a verb, meaning to intimidate or frighten (don't let the ACT cow you).

A question may ask you to interpret what the author means by a short phrase, not just a word. Here's an example.

When the author states, "He had done nothing but suffer in silence, which in itself is a type of strength," the author means that

- A. only strong people are able to go without complaining.
- B. the strength required for suffering is greater than that required for inflicting suffering.
- C. the person who can suffer the longest is the strongest.
- D. criticism is a sign of weakness.

Negative or reverse questions

Although this type of question is rare, a question may be phrased in the negative, such as "Which of the following is NOT indicative of dissatisfaction in a relationship?" or "With which one of the following statements would the author disagree?" You may also have a question that is phrased positively but expects you to find an inconsistency or a logical fallacy. You're really pointing out what is wrong, given the reasoning of the passage. For example, if the passage states that all strong people are able to handle adversity, you can't also state that all people who can handle adversity can also handle tragedy. That's going too far in the reasoning.

The ACT features many different types of reading questions. Don't panic if you see some question styles beyond the basic ones covered in this chapter. You may also encounter comparison questions, cause-and-effect questions, and generalization questions, just to mention a few. The ACT always is coming up with new ways to test your reading skills.

Tips and Traps

The ACT is not an exam that is especially tricky (unlike, say, the SAT, if you're taking it). However, some basic tips can prevent you from falling for the few traps that do exist . . . or from creating traps of your own.

> ✔ **Be willing to move around.** I'm often asked, "Should I do the questions in order or skip around?" My answer is that, for the most part, it's best to go in order. However, if you are running short of time, look for the "easier" types of questions. For most people, these are the detail questions, in which you may just go back and skim for a specific

fact. A main idea/primary purpose question is also a pretty good candidate for doing quickly, because you can answer it from your overall impression of the passage, or by looking at just the first paragraph.

Negative questions ("Which of the following is NOT true?" or "The author would reject which of the following conclusions?") can often take a long time to answer because you have to find four statements that are true and then, by process of elimination, choose the one that is not. Roman numeral questions ("Solana Beach is renowned for its athletes because: I. It has an Olympic training center. II. The junior training program is excellent. III. World-class coaches have moved there to retire.") can also take a great deal of time because you have to go through the passage looking for each point.

- **Look for key connecting or changing words.** A simple word such as "but" or "however" or "whereas" can indicate that things are about to change. There you are, reading a passage about how an economic theory has failed to prove valid, when you encounter a "however." That may indicate an entire switch, such that the author is now going to tell you that he or she believes that the policy will be effective in the future. I make a habit of circling "indicator" words like these. Here's a short list of words I look for:

but	although	despite
however	whereas	in spite of
nonetheless	on the other hand	

- **Keep an eye on the time.** You have to make a pretty quick decision about whether to do all the passages or three of the passages more slowly. Whichever you choose (and you should have your strategy firmly in mind before you get into the test room), divide your time appropriately and stick to that schedule. If you get bogged down on one question, fill in something, anything (there's no penalty for wrong answers on the ACT), and go on to the next question. You can always come back to it if you have time left at the end of the section.

- **Don't read more into the passage than is there.** Many questions are based on information that is specifically stated in the passage. Other questions are based on information that is implied by the passage. Don't take matters to extremes or bring in background information that you happen to have. Suppose that the passage talks about the fall of communism in the Soviet Union and its satellite countries. You cannot automatically assume the author also believes that communism will fail in China. Don't take the reasoning that one step too far (and of course, nestled snugly among the answer choices, will be one that does just that).

One final word: Try to enjoy the passages. Yeah, I know that's easy for me to say. But believe it or not, some of this reading material is very interesting. If you approach it with a negative attitude, your mind is already closed to it, making the material much more difficult to comprehend and remember. If you at least pretend that you're going to have a good time getting through it, you're much more likely to put things in perspective and get a better handle on the material.

Chapter 16

Where Are CliffsNotes When You Need Them? Reading Practice Questions

In This Chapter
▶ Celebrating diversity: practicing the various passage types
▶ Distinguishing the time-worthy questions from the time-waster ones

On the actual ACT, you have four full-length (about 750 words each) passages. Each passage is followed by ten questions. You have only 35 minutes to do that whole test. This abbreviated practice exam (I want to ease you into this stuff slowly) has two shorter passages and a total of eight questions. Don't worry about timing now. Think about what type of passage each portion is (humanities, prose fiction, science, or social studies) and identify each of the question types. See Chapters 19 and 21 for the real tests.

DIRECTIONS: Read each passage and then complete the questions that follow.

Passage 1

Social Science

Line　　　Multinational corporations frequently have difficulty explaining to politicians, human rights groups, and (perhaps most important) their consumer base why they do business with, and even seek closer business ties to, countries whose human rights records are considered very bad by United States standards. The CEOs say that in the business trenches, the
(05)　issue of human rights must effectively be detached from the wider spectrum of free trade.
　　　Discussion of the uneasy alliance between trade and human rights has trickled down from the boardrooms of large multinational corporations to the consumer on the street who, given the wide variety of products available to him, is eager to show support for human rights by boycotting the products of a company he feels does not do enough to help its over-
(10)　seas workers.
　　　International human rights organizations also are pressuring the multinationals to push for more humane working conditions in other countries and to, in effect, develop a code of business conduct that must be adhered to if the American company is to continue working with the overseas partner.
(15)　　　The President, in drawing up a plan for what he calls the "economic architecture of our times," wants economists, business leaders, and human rights groups to work together to develop a set of principles that the foreign partners of United States corporations will voluntarily embrace. Human rights activists, angry at the unclear and indefinite plans for implementing such rules, charge that their agenda is being given low priority by the State
(20)　Department. The President strongly denies their charges, arguing that each situation is approached on its merits without prejudice, and hopes that all the groups can work together

to develop principles based on empirical research rather than political fiat, emphasizing that the businesses with experience in the field must initiate the process of developing such guidelines. Business leaders, while paying lip service to the concept of these principles, (25) secretly fight against their formal endorsement as they fear such "voluntary" concepts may someday be given the force of law. Few business leaders have forgotten the Sullivan Principles, in which a set of voluntary rules regarding business conduct with South Africa (giving benefits to workers and banning apartheid in the companies that worked with U.S. partners) became legislation.

1. Which of the following best states the central idea of the passage?

   A. Politicians are quixotic in their assessment of the priorities of the State Department.

   B. Multinational corporations have little, if any, influence on the domestic policies of their overseas partners.

   C. Disagreement exists between the desires of human rights activists to improve the working conditions of overseas workers and the practical approach taken by the corporations.

   D. It is inappropriate to expect foreign corporations to adhere to American standards.

The main idea of the passage is usually stated in the first sentence or two. The first sentence of this passage discusses the difficulties that corporations have in explaining their business ties to certain countries to politicians, human rights groups, and consumers. From this statement, you may infer that those groups disagree with the policies of the corporations. *Correct answer:* **C.**

Did you choose A just because of the hard word, quixotic? It's human nature (we're all so insecure) to think that the hard word we don't know must be the right answer, but it isn't always so. Never choose a word you can't define unless you're sure that all the words you can define are wrong. *Quixotic* means idealistic, impractical (think of the fictional character Don Quixote tilting at windmills). The President's belief is not the main idea of the passage.

Just because a statement is (or may be) true does not necessarily mean that it's the correct answer to a question. The answer choices to a main-idea question in particular often are true or at least look plausible.

To answer a main-idea question, I like to pretend that a friend of mine just came up behind me and said, "Hey, what'cha reading there?" My first response is the main idea: "Oh, I read this passage about how corporations are getting grief from politicians and other groups because they do business with certain countries." Before you look at the answer choices, predict in your own words what the main idea is. You'll be pleasantly surprised how close your prediction is to the correct answer (and you won't be confused by all the other plausible-looking answer choices).

Choice D is a moral value, a judgment call. Who is to say what's appropriate and what's inappropriate? An answer that passes judgment, one that says something is morally right or morally wrong, is almost never the correct answer.

2. The author of the passage would most likely agree with which of the following statements?

   F. Business leaders, human rights groups, and economists will create the guidelines or principles; business leaders will initiate the processes.

   G. Workers will not accept principles drawn up by politicians whom they distrust but may agree to principles created by the corporations that pay them.

   H. Political activist groups have concerns that are too dramatically different from those of the corporations for the groups to be able to work together.

   J. Foreign nations are distrustful of U.S. political intervention and are more likely to accept suggestions from multinational corporations.

Chapter 16: Where Are CliffsNotes When You Need Them? Reading Practice Questions   **153**

The passage gives you the answer quite specifically. In lines 19 and 20, you're told that "... businesses with experience in the field must initiate the process of developing such guidelines." *Correct answer:* **F.**

Choices G, H, and J are all judgment calls. You're assuming facts not in evidence, as lawyers say. Although you personally may believe the statements in these answer choices to be true, they don't answer the specific question. The concerns in G and J aren't even mentioned in the passage, a tip-off that they probably will not be the correct answer to an "according to the passage" question.

3. Which of the following best describes the reason the author mentions the boycott of a corporation's products by its customers?

   A. to ridicule the consumers for believing that their small boycott would significantly affect the sales of a multinational corporation

   B. to predict the inevitability of failure of any plan that does not involve customer input

   C. to disagree with the President's contention that big business is best qualified to draw up the voluntary principles of workplace conduct

   D. to indicate the pressures that are on the multinational corporations

This question is one of those mind-reading questions I warn you about in Chapter 13. You are expected to get into the author's mind and understand why he or she said what he or she did. The concept of the consumer boycott follows closely the main idea of the passage, which is that the corporations have difficulty trying to explain themselves and their actions to all sorts of groups, including their customers. From this, you may infer that the point of the statement is to indicate the pressures placed on the corporations.

Line 10 states that human rights organizations also are pressuring multinational corporations, allowing you to infer that the consumers are applying pressure. Remember to expand your horizons: Read until you find what you think is the right answer ... and then read a little further. *Correct answer:* **D.**

Choices A and C begin with negative words, "ridicule" and "disagree." Negative answer choices are rarely correct. Be careful, however, not to take this tip as a hard-and-fast rule. If you go back to the correct answer to question number one, you can see that you may interpret that answer as negative.

Choice B seems logical; common sense tells you that a company that ignores its customers will probably fail. However, a strong, dramatic word like "inevitably" is rarely correct. Few things in life are inevitable: just death, taxes, and the ACT.

4. Which of the following statements about the Sullivan Principles can best be inferred from the passage?

   F. They had a detrimental effect on the profits of those corporations doing business with South Africa.

   G. They represented an improper alliance between political and business groups.

   H. They placed the needs of the foreign workers over those of the domestic workers whose jobs would therefore be in jeopardy.

   J. They will have a chilling effect on future adoption of voluntary guidelines.

Choice F is the major trap here. Perhaps you assumed that because the companies seem to dislike the Sullivan Principles, they hurt company profits. However, nothing was said in the passage about profits. Maybe the companies still made good profits but objected to the

154 Part V: Time to Read the Riot ACT: The Reading Test

Sullivan Principles on principle. The companies just may not have wanted such governmental intervention even if profits weren't decreased. If you chose F, you read too much into the question and probably didn't read the rest of the answer choices.

In choice J, the words "chilling effect" mean negative effect, discouraging effect. Think of something with a chilling effect as leaving you cold. Because few corporations have forgotten the Sullivan Principles, you may infer that these principles will discourage the companies from agreeing to voluntary principles in the future. *Correct answer:* **J.**

TIP: To get this question correct, you really need to understand the whole passage. If you didn't know what was going on here, you'd be better off to just guess and go. An inference question usually means you have to read between the lines; you can't just go back to one specific portion of the passage and get the answer quickly.

Passage 2

Prose Fiction. This passage is from the Robert Louis Stevenson novel *Kidnapped*, 1886.

Line Meanwhile such of the wounded as could move came clambering out of the fore-scuttle and began to help; while the rest that lay helpless in their bunks harrowed me with screaming and begging to be saved.
    The captain took no part. It seemed he was struck stupid. He stood holding by the
(05) shrouds, talking to himself and groaning out aloud whenever the ship hammered on the rock. His brig was like wife and child to him; he had looked on, day by day, at the mishandling of poor Ransome; but when it came to the brig, he seemed to suffer along with her.
    All the time of our working at the boat, I remember only one other thing; that I asked Alan, looking across at the shore, what country it was; and he answered, it was the worst
(10) possible for him, for it was a land of the Campbells.
    We had one of the wounded men told off to keep a watch upon the seas and cry us warning. Well, we had the boat about ready to be launched, when this man sang out pretty shrill: "For God's sake, hold on!" We knew by his tone that it was something more than ordinary; and sure enough; there followed a sea so huge that it lifted the brig right up and canted
(15) her over on her beam. Whether the cry came too late or my hold was too weak, I know not; but at the sudden tilting of the ship I was cast clean over the bulwarks into the sea.
    I went down, and drank my fill; and then came up, and got a blink of the moon; and then down again. They say a man sinks the third time for good. I cannot be made like other folk, then; for I would not like to write how often I went down or how often I came up again. All the
(20) while, I was being hurled along, and beaten upon and choked, and then swallowed whole, and the thing was so distracting to my wits, that I was neither sorry nor afraid.
    Presently, I found I was holding to a spar, which helped me somewhat. And then all of a sudden I was in quiet water, and began to come to myself.
    It was the spare yard I had got hold of, and I was amazed to see how far I had traveled
(25) from the brig. I hailed her indeed; but it was plain she was already out of cry. She was still holding together; but whether or not they had yet launched the boat, I was too far off and too low down to see.
    While I was hailing the brig, I spied a tract of water lying between us, where no great waves came, but which yet boiled white all over, and bristled in the moon with rings and bubbles. Sometimes the whole tract swung to one side, like the tail of a live serpent; some-
(30) times, for a glimpse, it all would disappear and then boil up again. What it was I had no guess, which for the time increased my fear of it; but I now know it must have been the roost or tide race, which carried me away so fast and tumbled me about so cruelly, and at last, as if tired of that play, had flung me and spare yard upon its landward margin.

Chapter 16: Where Are CliffsNotes When You Need Them? Reading Practice Questions 155

5. The narrator compares the ship to the captain's wife and child to

   A. lament the captain's long separation from his family.

   B. demonstrate the difficulty the captain has keeping focused on his job.

   C. predict the captain's future madness.

   D. show the depth of the connection the captain has to his ship.

The focus of lines 7–9 is on how the captain is upset by the condition of his ship. To compare his ship to his wife and child is to show how much he loves the ship and thus to emphasize the deep attachment he has to the vessel. *Correct answer:* **D.**

6. Which of the following may you infer from the passage?

   F. Alan and the Campbells are enemies.

   G. The ship had been attacked by another ship.

   H. The narrator was on his first sea voyage.

   J. Alan and the author are brothers.

This is a pretty simple question. In lines 8 and 9, you read that Alan felt the land was the worst possible for him because it was a land of the Campbells. From this, you may readily infer that he and the Campbells weren't about to sit down to soup together — that they were enemies. *Correct answer:* **F.**

7. By saying that he "got a blink at the moon," in line 15, the narrator means that

   A. he foresaw his own demise.

   B. he saw the sky as he came up out of the water to get air.

   C. he was hallucinating as he was drowning.

   D. he saw the captain with his pants down.

Line 15 describes the narrator's dunking and near drowning. He was bobbing up and down in the water, going under the sea and then coming up for air, at which point he saw the moon. Make sure you answer the question in the context in which you find the statement; don't use your own common sense. And if you chose D (which, of course, would never be on the actual exam) — man, you're having altogether too much fun for the ACT! *Correct answer:* **B.**

8. The purpose of the passage is

   F. to portray a mood of terror.

   G. to urge others not to go to sea.

   H. to describe an event.

   J. to contrast lifestyles of sailors from different countries.

The passage merely tells of something that happened to the author. (Choices using the words "describe," "discuss," and "explain" are often excellent answers to a "What is the purpose?" question.) Choice F is tempting, but surprisingly, the passage is not all that terrifying. You read in lines 19 and 20 that the narrator was so distracted that he was "neither sorry nor afraid" to describe an event. *Correct answer:* **H.**

Part VI
Proven to Cause Brain Defects in Laboratory Rats: The Science Reasoning Test

The 5th Wave — By Rich Tennant

"There'll be an additional question on the science portion of the test. It has to do with the digestive tract of a dog who has just eaten an entire can of pink Play-Doh."

In this part...

I've had students complain that the ACT Science Reasoning Test made them feel as confused as rats in a maze, but things aren't quite that bad. This part introduces you to the three types of ACT Science Reasoning passages; you can see what they look like, how to approach them, and when to run like heck and leave them alone. You'll also see several of the most common questions that follow the passages and discover what traps are built into them.

The material in this part does not — I repeat, *does not* — lecture on science per se. That is, I'm not about to give you chemistry formulas or physics principles or biology maxims. That's not laziness or stupidity on my part (although you probably do know more about chemistry, physics, and biology than I do), but rather a matter of focus. The ACT Science Reasoning Test doesn't expect you to know those sorts of things. All the information that you need to answer the questions is given to you in the passages themselves.

Chapter 17

Frankenstein to Einstein: Excelling on the Science Reasoning Test

In This Chapter
- Eliminating brain strain by knowing what you don't need to know
- Getting comfortable with the three you'll see: Data Representation, Research Summaries, and Conflicting Viewpoints
- Questioning your sanity: Science Reasoning questions and the traps built into them

*R*eturn your brain to the full upright and locked position. You're not going to need to use it as much as you may fear for this section.

I'm Mad, but I'm No Scientist: What Do I Need to Know?

Relax. Unclench your hands. Take a few deep breaths. You are not, repeat, *not* expected to be able to remember the entire periodic table or to know the difference between the substantia nigra and a Lorentz transformation. This section of the test is called science *reasoning,* which means that you are generally not required to know a lot of science facts. After all, your grades in science classes are there on the transcript for the admissions officers to read if they really want to assess your science knowledge. That's not the point here. The point is to demonstrate that you have an important collegiate skill: the ability to approach novel information, sort it out, and draw conclusions from it. The ACT actually includes bizarre and weird information to give science "dummies" (that's me!) a break. In other words, you don't have to know what a scientist knows, but you should be able to think as a scientist thinks. (***Question:*** Did ya ever stop to think — and forget to start again?)

Too Graphic for Words: The Format

The Science Reasoning Test consists of 40 questions that are based on seven passages (five to seven questions per passage). You have 35 minutes to answer these questions, about an average of 5 minutes per passage.

Each passage should take you about 2 minutes to read and — at least partially — understand. As you go through the following material, and especially as you are held spellbound by the excruciatingly detailed answer explanations to the practice exam questions, you'll find out which types of passages require a lot of upfront work and which you should straight-arm on your way to the questions.

Plan on allotting yourself approximately 30 seconds per question. You may not think that that sounds like a lot, but some of the questions will be so easy that you'll answer them in a heartbeat and build up a reservoir of time for the harder questions. But, of course, some of the questions will be so impossible that you'll want to sue your brain for nonsupport. If you can't answer a question within a half-minute, put down something, anything, and go on.

Remember: The ACT has *no* penalty for wrong answers. Never leave any bubble blank. Fill in something and hope you get lucky.

Chalk Talk: Developing a Game Plan

The ACT features three basic types of science passages. One of the best things you can do for yourself is to have a game plan: Recognize which type of passage the material is, have a strategy for reading or evaluating it, and know which types of questions are likely to follow it. The following is a brief overview of what to expect and how to approach each type of passage.

The Android's Favorite: Data Representation

Not only Mr. Data's favorite, this passage should be your favorite, as well. Most of my students tell me that this is the easiest type of passage . . . not coincidentally because it usually has the least text to read. The ACT has 3 Data Representation passages, 5 questions each, for a total of 15 questions. This passage is the only one in the science section with only 5 questions; all the other sections have at least 6 questions per passage.

The Data Rep questions are based on one or more tables, graphs, or diagrams chock-full of information, preceded or followed by text. Read the text so that you can get an idea about what point the table, graph, or diagram is trying to make, but don't get hung up on any complicated terms or sentences. Here's an example.

Scientists studied the effect that variations in paraloxin had on the rate of samanity in the species *Braisia idioticus*. The results are summarized in Table 1 (an example of a Data Rep table).

Table 1

Paraloxin (microshels)	Samanity Rate (rics/sec)
0	14
1	18
2	23
3	27
4	31
5	89
6	90
7	34
8	29
9	24

Chapter 17: Frankenstein to Einstein: Excelling on the Science Reasoning Test

What? You don't know what paraloxin, samanity, rics, and microshels are? That's not surprising, considering that I've just made them up. I'm babbling here to make the point that you can get an idea of what the passage is discussing *without* having a clue about what all the terms mean. Say to yourself, "When this thing called paraloxin is changed, samanity rate, whatever it is, may also change. I'll take a look at the table and see if this happens. The weird units simply measure paraloxin and samanity rate."

No, no, alas, the actual ACT will not be as much fun as this book is. On the real test, all the science is dull, boring . . . real. But my point is that if you don't know the big hairy terms, they may as well be made up as far as you're concerned. The ACT gives everyone, science geniuses and science morons alike, an equal chance by using unfamiliar science.

International students, this unfamiliar science is a boon for you. Yes, the passages can be difficult to read, but they are just as hard for someone who is a native English speaker as they are for you. The terminology is unfamiliar to everyone, giving you all an equal opportunity . . . and an equal headache.

After the game plan: Executing the play

When you encounter a Data Representation passage, here's a suggested approach.

1. **Read the introductory text.**

   Remember, don't get psyched out about unfamiliar terms. And don't try to understand every little thing. Just get an overview of what the passage is about.

2. **Look at the table, diagram, or graph.**

   Identify what is being displayed (for example, drug dosages, reaction times, kinetic energy, astronomical distances).

3. **Look at what the columns, rows, axes, and so on represent and determine how they are related to one another.**

   An *independent,* or *controlled, variable* is the factor that the experimenter can change to a specific value, such as the amount of water added. The *dependent* variable is the factor that is not under the experimenter's direct control, such as the amount of energy released.

   Here's another way to remember which variable does what: The terms *dependent variable* and *independent variable* mean almost the opposite of what you may think. The independent variable is not really independent; it is the one that the experimenter is changing. The dependent variable is dependent on the independent variable. The most typical relationship is one in which one column, row, axis, and so on, presents values for the independent, or controlled, variable and another shows what happens to the dependent variable.

   The following graph presents a classic relationship.

Here, the amount of growth factor added is the *independent* variable, and the plant height is the *dependent* variable. The experimenter can't directly manipulate plant height. He or she can add a certain amount of growth factor but then has no choice but to wait and see what happens to the plant.

The ability to distinguish the independent from the dependent variable is essential for understanding many passages. You may even get a question directly asking about this distinction.

4. **Note the units of measurement.**

   Don't freak out if the units are unfamiliar to you. Units of measurement (even the bizarre ones) are presented very clearly. The axes on graphs are usually labeled, legends typically accompany diagrams, and graphs and column and row headings usually include the units.

5. **Look for trends in the data, noting any significant shifts.**

   Take another look at the first example. In the paraloxin-samanity table, you see that samanity increases at regular intervals as paraloxin is gradually increased up through 4 microshels. Samanity rate hits a sharp peak when paraloxin rises to 5 and 6 microshels and then falls to levels comparable to those obtained when paraloxin was lower. In the plant growth graph, note that for the range of values shown on the graph, plant height steadily increases with increases in growth factor.

Don't waste time trying to memorize the numbers! If a question requires specific details, you can always go back and look at the table for them. Why destroy any more brain cells than you absolutely have to?

Going for pay dirt: The "data-analysis" question

The most common type of question you will get on Data Representation passages is one that requires some sort of data analysis. This type of question simply tests your ability to read the table or figure and extract information from it.

Use the graph on plant growth shown in the preceding section to answer the following question:

What is the plant height when 5 mg of plant growth factor are used?

Find 5 mg along the horizontal axis, go up to the plotted line, and then go left to the vertical axis to read the value, which is 3 cm. Notice that you don't have to know anything about plants. You have to look only at what's in front of you.

What if a point is not actually plotted (or a value specifically given) on the table? You can still answer the question. You *interpolate* by looking at the two closest values (translated into plain English, that means insert an intermediate term by estimating). For example, you may be asked (from Table 1, shown in "The Android's Favorite: Data Representation" section, earlier in this chapter) for the samanity rate when paraloxin is 1.5. Because the samanity rate is 18 when paraloxin is 1, and 23 when paraloxin is 2, the samanity rate when paraloxin is 1.5 is probably between 18 and 23. Given that the values are going up in a regular fashion in this region of the table, it is reasonable to say that the samanity rate is close to 20.5 when paraloxin is 1.5.

Along with interpolation, you have to worry about *extrapolation*. As the "extra" in its name implies, extrapolation asks you to come up with a value that is beyond the range depicted in the table or figure. In the plant growth passage, it is probably safe to predict that the straight upward line will continue for a while as growth factor moves past 20 mg, the last number presented in the horizontal axis. Therefore, you can make predictions about plant growth when growth factor is 21 mg by extending the line. However, you are *not* justified in predicting what will happen when growth factor is 50 mg. That number is far greater than what is shown on the graph. For all you know, the plants will die from an overdose of growth factor if 50 mg is administered.

That's It in a Nutshell: Research Summaries

The ACT has three Research Summary passages, with six questions each. The Research Summary questions make up 18 of the 40 questions — almost half — that you will encounter on the ACT Science Reasoning. Like Data Representation passages, Research Summaries usually include one or more tables or diagrams. Research Summaries, however, are a little more sophisticated than Data Representation. Here, you must pay attention to what is being tested in the experiments and how the researchers go about performing the studies.

Fortunately, Research Summary passages are predictable. You can expect each passage to tell you three things that you should always note:

- **The purpose of the study** (You may be very familiar with identifying the goal of the project or the purpose of the study, as you have probably done so on every lab write-up you've turned in since kindergarten. Sometimes the ACT is kind enough to do your work for you by stating or implying the purpose in the introductory paragraph.)
- **The experimental design**
- **The results** (which are usually presented in the same table, chart, or graph format that I discuss in "The Android's Favorite: Data Representation" section)

Here's more detail on these three concepts.

Purpose

Identifying the purpose of the experiment takes only a few seconds. Usually, the purpose is to examine what effect x has on y. The ACT expects you to understand some key principles of why the researchers created the experiment in the first place. After you pick up on the purpose, you must analyze how the researchers set up experiments to investigate these possible cause-and-effect relationships.

Experimental design

A proper experiment systematically varies the factor that is the possible cause and holds all other factors constant. For example, if scientists are interested in investigating what effect having the flu has on one's ability to perform multiplication problems, a proper experiment will compare people who have the flu with those who do not, while keeping the groups equal in terms of such factors as age, mathematical ability, and the presence of psychological disorders. If the groups differ on one or more of these other factors, it cannot be certain that any observed difference in multiplication performance was a *result* of the flu. What would you think if the nonflu group did better on multiplication but that nonflu group consisted of 12-year-olds while the flu group children were all 8 years old? You could not be certain whether age or the flu virus accounted for the difference.

Defective designs produce limited results. The experimenters don't always include proper controls. Some studies, by their very nature, cannot adhere to ideal experimental design. For example, if a scientist suspected that 2-year-olds who had been vaccinated for measles got more colds than 2-year-olds who had not been vaccinated, a proper design would be to give one group the vaccine and to withhold it from another group. However, it's not fair to keep one group of kids unvaccinated (mothers tend to get cranky when you make their kids sick "in the best interests of science"). What the experimenters would try to do is collect data on how frequently the children came down with colds before they were immunized (children are not immunized against measles until they are at least 1 year old) and perhaps collect data about the children's parents when the parents themselves were 2 years old. (The measles vaccine was not developed then.)

When an experiment lacks certain controls, take note of how the experiment is limited. You may be asked to come up with a good control. If you have noted the limitation, you can quickly say what "shoulda been done." If you are asked about what conclusions can be made, be very cautious. It's hard to come up with definitive conclusions when the experiments don't have proper controls.

The different studies presented in a Research Summary passage may differ in terms of what factor is being manipulated. For example, a study could look at how flu affects multiplication ability or how multiplication ability varies according to the child's age. Another study may examine what dependent variable is being measured (multiplication drills in one study, word problems involving multiplication in another). Be sure to follow the key way in which the studies differ. You may want to write some very brief notes in the margin to help you keep everything straight: "having the flu" or "kids' ages," for example.

Although the studies may differ somewhat, they are all designed to answer a key question stated in the purpose. Read each study with an eye toward how it fills in the big picture.

Just tell me what you want: Question styles

Some of the Research Summaries' questions are similar to the Data Analysis questions already discussed in Data Representation. The following are a couple of other question styles that are more typical of the Research Summaries:

- **Experiment design:** This question tests your ability to follow the logic of the design itself. Why or how was the experiment designed? What was the purpose of choosing one variable or one control?

- **Conclusions that can be drawn from one or more of the studies:** Be sure to pay attention to the question stem. If a question asks you about what can be concluded in Experiment 1 about the effects of one factor on the dependent variable, you don't want to spend a lot of time searching through the information for Experiments 2 and 3.

   To answer result/conclusion-type questions, you must be careful not to go overboard. Suppose that the study about the flu and multiplication showed that the flu group made substantially more errors on a multiplication drill than did the nonflu group. (And let's assume that this study *did* control for other factors.)

   Here is an example of a *correct* way of thinking about this question.

   Question: Which of the following statements is consistent with the study?

   Answer: The flu impaired the ability of the students studied to perform multiplication drills.

   Notice that this question asked for something probable, not a big, sweeping conclusion. You are not going out on a limb by saying that the flu seemed to have an effect. The study didn't prove that the flu was the definite cause of the multiplication difficulties, but the statement certainly follows from the data presented.

Now for an example of going too far (remember that this answer is *wrong!*):

Question: What can be concluded about the effects of the flu?

Answer: The flu impairs mathematical functioning by interfering with connections in the brain.

Did the study investigate how the flu changed brain functioning? The study investigated multiplication drills. "Mathematical functioning" is much too broad a topic.

✔ **New or additional results:** The results of one study may have an effect on another study. Your job is to determine how these new results fit into what you already learned. Do the new results confirm what the studies showed, or are they in conflict? If they don't invalidate what you concluded earlier, do they limit what you can say? Perhaps the results of the flu and multiplication study investigated only children of elementary-school age. If a question gives you the additional information that there was no difference between the flu and nonflu groups when high school students were studied, you have to limit your conclusion about the flu's impairing-multiplication ability to a group of *younger* children. If the results with high school students were similar to what was found with elementary school children, *then* you may generalize your conclusions to include a wider range of students.

Warring Factions: Conflicting Viewpoints

The ACT has one Conflicting Viewpoints passage, with seven questions. You can recognize the Conflicting Viewpoints passage because it has two major portions of text with headings similar to "Scientist 1" and "Scientist 2" or titles of theories, such as "extinction by meteorites" and "extinction by natural selection." (Research Summaries have headings, too, but the headings on those passages are almost always "Experiment 1, 2, 3" or "Study 1, 2, 3.")

The Conflicting Viewpoints passage, as the title indicates, presents two different explanations about the same scientific situation. The following approach can help you to get started:

1. **Read the introduction.**

   Find out what phenomenon is being debated. Maybe the scientists disagree on whether objects can travel faster than the speed of light or whether other planets in the solar system could support life. (Know why there are no restaurants on the moon? Great food, but no atmosphere!)

2. **Read the first viewpoint and make some kind of brief notation (using your own words) about the author's main idea.**

   This main idea will express the scientist's position on the situation discussed in the passage's introduction. It is important to note this main idea because you want to be able to identify, for example, that Scientist 1 says "pro" while Scientist 2 says "con." You don't want to become engrossed in a question that asks you to support Scientist 1 and forget that he or she took the "pro" side. (And yes, sometimes your notes to yourself *should* be as succinct as "pro" and "con" or "yes" and "no.")

3. **Identify the evidence that the first scientist uses to support his or her main idea.**

   Does the evidence support the main idea, or is the scientist making a leap of faith? This "leap of faith" is called an *assumption*. Questionable assumptions open up the door for the other scientist to dispute the first scientist and come up with an explanation of his or her own.

Assumptions usually are pretty sneaky and can be well disguised. Suppose, for example, that the scientist claims that pandas are carnivores. He or she backs this up by showing that bears are carnivores. Do you see a gap between the main idea and the evidence? There is evidence that *bears* are carnivores, but is this enough to say that *pandas* are carnivores? You can do so only if you assume that pandas are bears, which may or may not be true.

4. **Identify and analyze the second scientist's point of view.** After you finish with the first viewpoint, follow the same procedure to identify and analyze the second viewpoint. Usually the second viewpoint is easier to follow because it is so predictable. The main idea of the second scientist is a statement that is directly opposed to the main idea of the first scientist.

The evidence used *may* be different, but it may also be the same as that which was used by the first scientist. The key difference lies in how the second scientist interprets the evidence. Don't look exclusively for differences between the two viewpoints. The ACT may throw in some similarities.

Your job is to follow the logic of each viewpoint. Do not try to decide which viewpoint is correct. No one cares — not the ACT, not the college admissions office, and certainly not you. In fact, the ACT sometimes presents a viewpoint that is clearly false. For example, one scientist may claim that evolution takes place as a result of inheritance of *acquired* characteristics. You know that this does not happen. Think about it. If you gnaw your fingernails down to the bone worrying about the ACT, it does not follow that someday your children will be born with no fingernails! Again, worry only about the logic of the viewpoint, not whether it is correct or wrong.

Bonus: Are you in fact an onychophagist? Nah, it's not as serious as it sounds. ***Onychophagia*** is merely nail biting. The next time that you want to get out of going to school, tell your mom that you are suffering from onychophagia. She may be too embarrassed to ask what it is, and let you stay home.

Asking for Trouble: Question Styles

Some questions in Conflicting Viewpoints passages ask you to support or weaken a scientist's viewpoint. To do so, you first have to identify any assumption that the scientist made in creating his or her theory. The best way to strengthen a viewpoint is to come up with evidence that confirms that the assumption is valid. The best way to weaken a viewpoint is to present evidence that casts doubt on the assumption. For example, the previous conclusion that pandas are carnivores is strengthened if pandas are bears. The conclusion is weakened if pandas are not bears.

Be careful to keep in mind all the time just which of the two viewpoints you are addressing. Some of the wrong (trap!) answer choices deal with the other viewpoint and, as a consequence, do not answer the question.

The answer choices for a strengthening/supporting question usually follow a predictable pattern. One choice, the correct answer, supports the correct viewpoint. One incorrect choice deals with the correct viewpoint but weakens it rather than strengthens it. Another incorrect choice deals with the other viewpoint. Usually this choice strengthens the other viewpoint, so it is testing your ability to keep the viewpoints straight. Occasionally, this incorrect choice weakens the other viewpoint. Such a choice is tough to eliminate, but you must remember that weakening one viewpoint does not automatically strengthen the other. The third incorrect choice will likely present irrelevant evidence.

Suppose you have a passage about whether smoking cigarettes causes cancer. Scientist 1 says that it does, citing the fact that smokers have a higher incidence of cancer than do nonsmokers. Scientist 2 says that smoking cigarettes does not cause cancer, claiming that there is no proof that smoking causes the uncontrolled growth seen in cancer. Scientist 2 (yes, the ACT does use catchy names like "Scientist 1" and "Scientist 2") explains the association between smoking and cancer as a result of the fact that some people have a certain body chemistry that leads to both a smoking habit and cancer.

The first question asks you to identify evidence to support Scientist 1. Here are some very typical answer choices.

- **A.** Nicotine, a major cigarette ingredient, has been shown to cause cancer in laboratory rats. (This statement supports Scientist 1's theory and is the right answer.)
- **B.** Smokers invariably eat a lot of fatty foods, which have been shown to cause cancer. (This statement weakens Scientist 1's point of view by suggesting that another cause is at work.)
- **C.** Injecting rats with Chemical ABC caused them to seek out tobacco and also produced cancer cells. (This statement goes right along with Scientist 2's suggestion.)
- **D.** Lack of exercise causes heart disease. (This statement is irrelevant. It discusses neither cigarettes nor cancer.)

Remember: You don't care whether the statement is actually true in the Real World or false in the Real World. For example, statement D, claiming that lack of exercise causes heart disease, may very well be true. So what? It has nothing to do with supporting Scientist 1's statement that smoking cigarettes causes cancer.

Parting Is Such Sweet Sorrow: The Conclusion

The ACT follows a pretty dependable format. Therefore, you can develop and stick to a plan of attack.

- ✔ **Identify the type of passage** (three are Data Representation, three are Research Summaries, and one is Conflicting Viewpoints).
- ✔ **For Data Representation,** read the intro, look at the table/graph (paying special attention to the units of measurement), note the relationship between the units, and identify any trends or patterns.
- ✔ **For Research Summaries,** note the purpose of the study, the experimental design, and the results.
- ✔ **For Conflicting Viewpoints,** jot down the viewpoint of each scientist and the evidence used to support his or her main idea.

Chapter 18

Faking Atomic Ache Won't Get You Out of This: Science Practice Questions

In This Chapter
- Getting through science without blowing up your chemistry set
- Sorting through traps and tricks on the Science Reasoning section

Question: What happened to the band director when he stuck his finger into an electrical outlet?

Answer: Nothing. He was a bad conductor!

If your store of science knowledge is so low that you don't even understand my joke, don't worry. You don't need any specific science knowledge to do well in the science section. Everything that you need is stated or implied in the passages or experiments. (If you get the joke but don't laugh, maybe your standards are higher than my comedic ability!)

This chapter gives you a Research Summary with twice the usual number of questions. On the actual ACT, a Research Summary has only 6 questions, not 12, as in this practice test. I give you double the usual number so that you can get an idea of the various ways in which the same basic points are tested. For now, don't worry about the format or the timing. Review the material in Chapter 17, and then apply that material to these questions.

DIRECTIONS: Read the science reasoning passage and the analysis that follows it. Then complete the 12 questions that follow and study the answer explanations.

Passage

By using electrical recording devices, scientists have shown that many cells in the part of the brain involved with processing visual information respond only to lines of a certain orientation. For example, some brain cells fire when vertical lines are present but do not respond to horizontal lines. Animals that rely on vision must have an entire set of cells so that at least some part of their brains responds when lines of a given orientation are present in their environment.

A major question is, how much is brain organization affected by the animal's environment? The following series of studies investigates this possible environmental role in the development of cat vision.

Study 1

Scientists presented lines of various orientations to newborn kittens while recording electrical activity from the visual part of the brain. No matter what the orientation, some cells fired while others did not.

These kittens were able to walk around both vertical and horizontal obstacles without bumping into them.

Study 2

Scientists conducted the same test used in Study 1 on 6-month-old kittens that were raised in a normal environment. Results matched those of Study 1.

Study 3

Scientists raised newborn kittens for six months in a completely dark environment. The scientists recorded very little brain cell activity when the kittens were presented with a wide variety of stimuli.

These kittens had great difficulty navigating around various mazes. They bumped into both vertical and horizontal obstacles.

Study 4

Scientists placed newborn kittens in an environment in which all they saw were vertical lines. At 6 months, none of their brain cells responded to horizontal lines, but their brain cells had more activity than what was found in Studies 1 and 2 when vertical lines were present.

These 6-month-old kittens easily walked around a maze of vertical obstacles but bumped into and could not walk around horizontal obstacles placed in their paths.

Study 5

This study was identical to Study 4 except that the scientists exposed the kittens to only horizontal lines. At 6 months, their brain cells showed no activity in response to vertical lines and, when presented with horizontal lines, showed increased activity as compared to the kittens in Studies 1 and 2.

These kittens negotiated a maze of horizontal obstacles but could not navigate around vertical obstacles.

Study 6

Scientists placed 1-year-old cats that were raised in a normal environment and had normal vision in a dark environment for six months. At the end of this time, these cats displayed a brain-cell firing pattern similar to that of the cats used in Studies 1 and 2.

Study 7

For six months, scientists exposed 1-year-old cats with normal vision and a prior normal environment to only vertical lines. Results were identical to those of Study 6.

Study 8

For six months, scientists exposed 1-year-old cats with normal vision and a prior normal environment to only horizontal lines. No difference was found between these cats and those of Study 7.

Chapter 18: Faking Atomic Ache Won't Get You Out of This: Science Practice Questions

Initial Analysis

Are you complaining that you're not "feline" too well after that, uh, *cat*astrophic passage? Actually, the passage isn't that bad. The language is a bit technical, but it's understandable. First, try to understand the introductory material, the point of the passage. Then determine what each study tells you.

The first paragraph basically says that brain cells controlling vision are specialized. Each cell does a particular job. To cover all possible jobs, a brain needs many different specialized cells.

You can grasp a concept easily if you relate it to something in your own life. Think about how physicians, for example, specialize in their fields. An ophthalmologist treats your eyes. A dermatologist cures your zits. If you have a zit, the ophthalmologist doesn't treat you, just as a vertical-responding cell doesn't fire in response to a horizontal line.

The question in the second paragraph is one you have probably heard applied to many aspects of development: How much of a characteristic is caused by your genes and how much by environment? For example, do you have a Tom Cruise smile because you inherited good teeth from your parents or because you eat the right foods and brush after meals? Can you outrun the Road Runner because your parents are athletic or because you train very hard?

In Study 1, don't sweat the details regarding how the scientists measured the electrical activity. All you have to get from this study is that the scientists came up with a way to determine which cells respond to a certain type of line. The results of Study 1 were entirely expected. Because the visual part of the brain has the whole spectrum of specialized cells, the fact that some, but not all, cells respond makes sense. If no cells respond, the animal has a tough time seeing certain kinds of objects in the world. If all cells respond, the brain cells aren't specialized.

The most significant result of Study 1 is that the cells responded the way they did soon after the kittens were born. This result seems to indicate that the cat brain is wired the way it should be at birth and suggests that genes play a major, if not the only, role in determining how vision is handled by a cat brain.

On to Study 2. Its results make complete sense. If a newborn kitten is well equipped to handle its visual world, six months of normal development does not change that ability.

So far, no evidence implicates an environmental role in the development of cat vision. Ah, but so far, the experiments have been conducted in normal environments. What about abnormal environments?

Study 3 shows that after six months of no stimulation from the environment, the cells in the visual part of the brain do not function properly. Do not, I repeat, *do not* immediately go overboard and say that a normal environment is necessary for normal responses. Remember, newborn kittens had normal responses. Instead, play it safe (think like a scientist and don't jump to conclusions too rapidly) and say that a normal environment *seems* to be necessary to maintain normal response from the visual part of the brain.

In Study 4, the kittens were denied exposure to horizontal lines. You probably shouldn't be too surprised, then, to learn that their brain cells did not respond to horizontal lines or that the brain cells, at least functionally, did not see the horizontal obstacles.

Study 3 shows that, when the cells in the visual part of the brain are not given proper stimulation, they lose their ability to respond. The cells that normally respond to horizontal lines were not stimulated, so they lost their ability to respond to horizontal lines.

Study 4 also indicates that at least some of these horizontal-responding cells convert to vertical-responding cells. This result provides strong support for the argument that favors environment over genetics. Under certain circumstances, the environment can change what the genes set up. (Using the earlier analogy, you can inherit your parents' gorgeous teeth, but if you live on nothing but soda pop and candy bars, those gorgeous teeth are going to turn brown and fall out.)

You can breeze through Study 5. *Vertical* and *horizontal* switch roles and results perfectly. Everything is as expected; zoom on to the next study.

The results of Study 6 may surprise you. As in Study 3, the scientists deprived the cats of visual stimulation for six months. This time, however, everything was normal when the cats were tested. At the very least, you can deduce that being a year old makes a difference. A good scientist would reason that the visual part of the brain is flexible for at least some part of the first year of a cat's life, but thereafter the wiring becomes somewhat permanent.

Study 7 follows from Study 6. The wiring of the visual part of a cat's brain becomes somewhat fixed at about 1 year of age. You can't teach an old cat new tricks.

And finally, Study 8 also follows from Study 6. The environment loses much of its ability to influence the organization of the visual part of a cat's brain when the cat is about 1 year of age.

In general, you want to summarize briefly to yourself, and maybe even write a note in the margin, what each study tested and what the conclusions were. Be sure to note the variables tested, such as the age of the cats and the horizontal or vertical lines.

1. On the basis of Study 1, can newborn kittens see vertical lines?

    A. No, because newborn kittens have brain cells that respond to horizontal lines.

    B. No, because newborn kittens can move around horizontal obstacles.

    C. Yes, because newborn kittens have been exposed to many vertical lines in their environment.

    D. Yes, because newborn kittens have brain cells that respond to vertical lines.

The newborn kittens' brains responded the way that you would expect if the cats were to get around in their environment, so the Yes answers, choices C and D, are the most probable. Besides, choices A and B give pretty weak reasons for the lack of responses. The ability to respond to horizontal lines does not make it impossible to respond to vertical lines.

Choice C is illogical; you can dump that choice by using your common sense alone. If the kittens are newborns, how much exposure could they have had?

Choice D provides a good explanation. The kittens had brain cells that responded to vertical lines; you can logically make the conclusion that the vertical-lines information gets to the kittens' brains. This conclusion in turn makes it likely that the kittens can see the lines. *Correct answer:* **D**.

2. Scientists place a 3-month-old kitten that was raised in a normal environment in a maze of vertical and horizontal obstacles. Which of the following is the most likely result?

    F. The kitten bumps into horizontal obstacles but gets around vertical obstacles.

    G. The kitten bumps into vertical obstacles but gets around horizontal obstacles.

    H. The kitten bumps into both vertical and horizontal obstacles.

    J. The kitten negotiates around both vertical and horizontal obstacles.

Chapter 18: Faking Atomic Ache Won't Get You Out of This: Science Practice Questions 173

If a newborn kitten can get around the maze and a kitten raised in a normal environment for six months can get around the maze, then you logically can conclude that a kitten raised in a normal environment for three months would be able to do so also. Only choice J has a kitten that doesn't need a crash helmet. *Correct answer:* **J.**

Did you have Smart Students' Disease on this question and read more into the question? If you said, "Yeah, but what if . . ." and started imagining all sorts of horrible and unlikely possibilities ("Maybe the kitty OD'd on catnip and staggered around . . ."), you made this problem much harder than it really was. Keep it simple, okay?

3. Scientists place a 1-year-old cat that was raised in a normal environment in a maze of vertical and horizontal obstacles. Which of the following is the most likely result?

    A. The cat makes no attempt to get around the obstacles.

    B. The cat negotiates around both vertical and horizontal obstacles.

    C. The cat bumps into horizontal obstacles but gets around vertical obstacles.

    D. The cat bumps into vertical obstacles but gets around horizontal obstacles.

Did you try to answer this question based on Studies 1 and 2? Doing so worked for the previous question because it spoke of an age, 3 months, that was between newborn (Study 1) and 6 months (Study 2). In this question, the cat is twice as old as the oldest kitten in Studies 1 and 2, meaning that you can't be sure that the present trend continues. (Common sense tells you that the trend probably will continue, but you must be able to distinguish between what will probably happen and what will necessarily happen.)

A more definitive answer comes from looking at Studies 6, 7, and 8. In these studies, scientists gave normal cats that had a normal environment for one year an abnormal environment for six months. The cat in this question still responded normally, the same way that the cats in Studies 6, 7, and 8 responded, but didn't have to endure an abnormal experience. If the vision of the cats exposed to the abnormal environments turned out okay, then the cat that was not placed in such an environment should also be okay. *Correct answer:* **B.**

If you were really lost on this problem, eliminate choice A as much too extreme. You'll do better when you hedge by using words such as "rarely" or "infrequently" than when you use dramatic terms like "no" or "never." Because nothing indicates a favoring of vertical over horizontal lines or vice versa, you can eliminate choices C and D as well.

4. Which of the following was not under the direct control of the experimenters?

    F. The length of time that the cat spent in an abnormal environment

    G. The number of brain cells that responded to horizontal lines

    H. The age at which the cat was tested for visual response

    J. The types of obstacles placed in a maze

When an experimental factor, or *variable,* is under the direct control of the experimenters, the experimenters are able to decide exactly how much (or what type) of that factor to use without having to depend on any intervening process. Choice F is clearly under the control of the experimenters. The experimenters can let the cat out of the bag (the environment) any time they want. Choice J is just as clear. The experimenters can throw in more vertical or horizontal obstacles at will.

Choice H is a little tougher to eliminate. You may think that the cat's age is up to the cat (or at least up to its parents), but the experimenters can decide exactly how old the cats have to be in order to be used in a certain part of the experiment.

By process of elimination, choice G is correct. The experimenters can try to change this factor by changing the environment, but exactly how many cells are going to respond depends on the way the cat's brain is set up and on how the cat's brain interacts with the environment. *Correct answer:* **G.**

TIP

You can use this basic science info in many different passages: *Independent variables* (choices F, H, and J, in this case) are those that can be manipulated independently of any other factor. For example, the experimenter can change the time spent in the dark environment from six months to five months without changing the type of obstacles in the maze. A *dependent variable* (choice G in this case) depends on what else was done in the experiment.

5. Why is Study 6 so important in relation to Study 3?

   A. Study 6 shows that the effects of six months in darkness may depend on the cat's age when scientists place it in such an environment.

   B. Older cats have more reliable brain-cell responses than younger cats.

   C. Study 6 extends the findings of Study 3 by showing that longer periods of darkness also change brain-cell responses.

   D. Study 6 contradicts the findings of Study 3 by showing that, when cats are placed in darkness for a longer period of time, the effect found in Study 3 disappears.

Dump choices C and D immediately. Study 6 used older cats (ones that have been alive for a longer period of time), but these cats, as well as those of Study 3, were in darkness for only six months.

HEADS UP

The ACT tests no expert knowledge. You can answer all questions based on what is stated or implied in the passages. In other words, you are not required to be an expert on cat brain physiology. Because only such experts (and maybe Garfield) know whether choice B is true, you can reject it. Six months in darkness does not have such a devastating effect when the cats are older. *Correct answer:* **A.**

6. Some humans who have suffered brain injuries have been able to recover a lost brain function by having the brain reorganize itself. On the basis of all the cat-vision studies, which of the following humans would be most likely to recover a lost function through brain reorganization?

   F. A 50-year-old man who suffers a stroke (lack of oxygen to a certain region of the brain)

   G. An 80-year-old woman who suffers a stroke

   H. A 30-year-old combat soldier who suffers a bullet wound in the brain

   J. A baby who has had part of the left side of his brain surgically removed along with a tumor

HEADS UP

Calm down, calm down — no one expects you to know exactly how each of these brain traumas affects brain functioning. Everything you need to answer this question is given in the passage. The key is to pick up on the ages. Which cats showed a change from the ordinary response pattern when the environment changed? The young cats. Similarly, a young human's brain is likely to be more flexible than that of an older human (haven't you always yelled at your parents not to be so narrow-minded and set in their ways?). Choice J, which features the youngest human, is the correct answer. *Correct answer:* **J.**

If you're almost having a stroke right now arguing with me, you probably didn't notice how carefully the question was worded: "Which of the following humans would be *most likely* to . . . ?" True, you don't know for sure that the baby would have some lost brain function, but all you are asked is which of the answer choices (no, "a student studying for the ACT" was not among them) is the most likely.

Chapter 18: Faking Atomic Ache Won't Get You Out of This: Science Practice Questions

7. Scientists exposed a 2-year-old cat that was raised in a normal environment and had normal vision to only horizontal lines. Which of the following is the most reasonable prediction?

    A. After three months, the cells in the visual part of the cat's brain fail to respond to vertical lines.

    B. After six months, the cells in the visual part of the cat's brain fail to respond to vertical lines.

    C. After six months, the cells in the visual part of the cat's brain respond to vertical lines.

    D. After 12 months, the cells in the visual part of the cat's brain respond to vertical lines.

Study 8 shows that 1-year-old cats exposed to only horizontal lines for six months still have brain cells capable of responding to vertical lines. This info knocks out choices A and B. After one year, the wiring in the cat's visual part of the brain seems to be fixed, so you can assume that the 2-year-old cat's brain has fixed wiring.

Be careful of choice D. You cannot say for sure what effects an exposure longer than six months will have. Choice C is a much safer choice and is the correct answer. *Correct answer: C.*

TIP: Have you been noticing throughout these answer explanations how often you can narrow the answers down to two choices very quickly? If you're in a hurry or if you're confused, make a quick guess. Remember that the ACT does not penalize you for wrong answers.

8. In considering all the studies, which of the following is true regarding the brain-cell electrical measurements and the maze results?

    F. The measurements and results are consistent with each other.

    G. The measurements and results are consistent with each other only for newborn kittens.

    H. The measurements and results are consistent with each other only for cats more than 1 year old.

    J. The measurements and results are inconsistent with each other.

When the electrical measurements showed reduced response to vertical lines, the cats could negotiate around vertical obstacles. Reduced response to horizontal lines corresponds to failure to negotiate around horizontal obstacles. The electrical measurements and the maze results always provided the same information regarding what type of lines the cats could handle. *Correct answer: F.*

9. Which of the following studies shows that environmental stimulation can lead to a change in the way the cells in the visual part of a cat's brain respond?

    I. Study 1

    II. Study 4

    III. Study 5

    IV. Study 8

    A. II only

    B. II and III only

    C. III and IV only

    D. I, III, and IV only

Study 1 was performed with newborn kittens. With such minimal environmental stimulation, this study can't be used to show that the environment has an effect. This eliminates option I; put a big X through it. You can now dump choice D.

Study 4 looks good. Exposure to only vertical lines caused a loss of cells able to respond to horizontal lines and a gain of those able to respond to vertical lines. Option II is correct. Put a circle around it. Because the correct answer must have II in it, eliminate choice C.

Study 5 is very similar to Study 4, except that the roles of the vertical and horizontal lines are reversed. Study 5 shows a loss of cells able to respond to vertical lines and a gain of those able to respond to horizontal lines. Circle option III. *Correct answer:* **B.**

To check your work, verify that option IV doesn't work. Study 8 shows that the environment has no effect on 1-year-old cats. This study, taken by itself, lends no support to an environmental contribution.

10. If Study 4 is conducted but Studies 3 and 5 are not, can the scientists conclude that all cells in the visual part of a kitten's brain require stimulation in order to function?

    F. Yes, because some brain cells stop responding to horizontal lines.

    G. Yes, because some brain cells respond to vertical lines.

    H. No, because some brain cells respond to vertical lines.

    J. No, because Study 4 does not test whether vertical-responding cells require stimulation.

This question tests whether you understand that experimental results are limited when only certain conditions are tested. The results of Study 4 indicate only that horizontal-responding cells require stimulation early in a kitten's life in order to function. Study 4 does not establish whether vertical-responding cells require such stimulation because the study does not examine what happens to the cells when they are deprived of vertical-line input. A conclusion regarding *all* cells is not justified. Eliminate choices F and G. For all you know, horizontal lines and the cells that respond to them can be special.

Choice H is out because all this study establishes in regard to vertical lines is that the cells continue to respond when given vertical-line input. Perhaps the cells could have responded in the absence of such input.

Choice J pinpoints the limitations of the study and is the correct answer. Studies 3 and 5 did test this factor and allow for a more general conclusion regarding brain cells and environmental input. *Correct answer:* **J.**

11. On the basis of all the studies, which of the following best summarizes the role of the environment in the development of a cat's visual brain-cell responses?

    A. The environment has no effect.

    B. Environmental input early in a cat's life contributes to the continuation of normal responding.

    C. Environmental input can change the pattern of responses throughout a cat's life.

    D. The environment is the only factor that influences the responses.

If choice A is true, the kittens in Studies 3, 4, and 5 would have normal visual responses. Eliminate choice A. If choice C were true, the cats in Studies 6, 7, and 8 would show a change in response patterns. Choice D is at odds with Study 1. If the environment is the only factor, why do newborn cats show responses to all types of stimuli? This reasoning leaves only choice B. *Correct answer:* **B.**

Chapter 18: Faking Atomic Ache Won't Get You Out of This: Science Practice Questions

Are you noticing and using the wording to help you choose and eliminate answers? The conservative language ("contributes to the continuation" rather than "directly determines") reinforces choice B as the answer. It is tough to argue with a choice that doesn't say something so extreme that one example would be enough to contradict it. Notice how easily you can contradict choice A, which has the word "no," choice C, which says "throughout," and choice D, which contains "only."

12. Which of the following studies would probably add the most new information to the work done in this set of experiments?

    F. A study identical to Study 3, except that the kittens are in the dark environment for seven months.

    G. A study identical to Study 6, except that the cats are in the dark environment for five months.

    H. A study identical to Study 6, except that the study uses 2-year-old cats.

    J. A study identical to Studies 4 and 5, except that the cats are exposed only to diagonal lines.

Study 3 shows that six months of darkness almost entirely wipes out the cells' ability to respond. Perhaps seven months would cause a complete cessation of responding, but the point made from Study 3 (namely, that lack of visual stimulation leads to impaired brain-cell responding) is already established. Therefore, the study mentioned in choice F will not add much.

Study 6 strongly suggests that the response patterns in the visual part of a cat's brain are fixed enough at 1 year so that six months of an abnormal environment has no noticeable effect. If six months has no noticeable effect, why would five months be any different? Eliminate choice G. If the brain-cell responses are fixed by the time that a cat is 1 year old, it seems reasonable to expect that a 2-year-old cat would show the same responses. Eliminate choice H.

The study mentioned in choice J would help because it would show what happens to cells that respond to lines that are in between vertical and horizontal. This study would add some information regarding how precise the brain cells are in regard to lines in the environment. For example, is a diagonal line close enough to a vertical line that the exposure only to diagonal lines still allows the cat to respond to vertical lines? The answer to this question would increase understanding of how the environment interacts with the visual part of a cat's brain. *Correct answer:* **J.**

Part VII
I'd Rather Wait for the Movie: Full-Length Practice ACTs

In this part . . .

It's the moment you've been waiting for: a chance to download all that stuff you've been cramming into your brain. This part contains two full-length practice exams. I take these tests seriously, and you should, too. Do them under actual test conditions, sitting in a quiet room and timing yourself. Open books are definitely out. (Sorry!) I have spies everywhere. I'll know if you cheat on these tests — you'll hear a knocking at your door one foggy night . . . .

Unlike the questions, however, the answer explanations don't have to be serious; in fact, they're a lot of fun. Ready? Show me what you can do.

Chapter 19

How to Ruin a Perfectly Good Day, Part I: Practice Exam 1

You are now ready to take a sample ACT. The following exam consists of four tests: a 45-minute English Test, a 60-minute Mathematics Test, a 35-minute Reading Test, and a 35-minute Science Reasoning Test. You probably are familiar with the format of each test by now.

Please take this test under these normal exam conditions. (This is serious stuff!)

1. **Sit where you won't be interrupted (even though you'd probably welcome any distractions).**
2. **Use the answer grid provided.**
3. **Set your alarm clock for the intervals indicated at the beginning of each test.**
4. **Do not go on to the next test until the time allotted for the test you are taking is up.**
5. **Check your work for that test only.**
6. **Do not take a break during any test.**
7. **Give yourself one ten-minute break between tests two and three.**

When you've completed the entire test, check your answers with the answer key at the end of this chapter. A section explaining your score precedes the answer key.

Chapter 20 gives detailed explanations of the answers. Go through the answer explanations to *all* the questions, not just the ones you missed. You will find a plethora of worthwhile information, material that provides a good review of everything you've learned in the other chapters of the book. We even toss in a few good (?) jokes to keep you somewhat sane.

Answer Sheet

Begin with Number 1 for each new section.

Chapter 19: How to Ruin a Perfectly Good Day, Part I: Practice Exam 1

Reading Test	*Science Test*
1. Ⓐ Ⓑ Ⓒ Ⓓ	1. Ⓐ Ⓑ Ⓒ Ⓓ
2. Ⓕ Ⓖ Ⓗ Ⓙ	2. Ⓕ Ⓖ Ⓗ Ⓙ
3. Ⓐ Ⓑ Ⓒ Ⓓ	3. Ⓐ Ⓑ Ⓒ Ⓓ
4. Ⓕ Ⓖ Ⓗ Ⓙ	4. Ⓕ Ⓖ Ⓗ Ⓙ
5. Ⓐ Ⓑ Ⓒ Ⓓ	5. Ⓐ Ⓑ Ⓒ Ⓓ
6. Ⓕ Ⓖ Ⓗ Ⓙ	6. Ⓕ Ⓖ Ⓗ Ⓙ
7. Ⓐ Ⓑ Ⓒ Ⓓ	7. Ⓐ Ⓑ Ⓒ Ⓓ
8. Ⓕ Ⓖ Ⓗ Ⓙ	8. Ⓕ Ⓖ Ⓗ Ⓙ
9. Ⓐ Ⓑ Ⓒ Ⓓ	9. Ⓐ Ⓑ Ⓒ Ⓓ
10. Ⓕ Ⓖ Ⓗ Ⓙ	10. Ⓕ Ⓖ Ⓗ Ⓙ
11. Ⓐ Ⓑ Ⓒ Ⓓ	11. Ⓐ Ⓑ Ⓒ Ⓓ
12. Ⓕ Ⓖ Ⓗ Ⓙ	12. Ⓕ Ⓖ Ⓗ Ⓙ
13. Ⓐ Ⓑ Ⓒ Ⓓ	13. Ⓐ Ⓑ Ⓒ Ⓓ
14. Ⓕ Ⓖ Ⓗ Ⓙ	14. Ⓕ Ⓖ Ⓗ Ⓙ
15. Ⓐ Ⓑ Ⓒ Ⓓ	15. Ⓐ Ⓑ Ⓒ Ⓓ
16. Ⓕ Ⓖ Ⓗ Ⓙ	16. Ⓕ Ⓖ Ⓗ Ⓙ
17. Ⓐ Ⓑ Ⓒ Ⓓ	17. Ⓐ Ⓑ Ⓒ Ⓓ
18. Ⓕ Ⓖ Ⓗ Ⓙ	18. Ⓕ Ⓖ Ⓗ Ⓙ
19. Ⓐ Ⓑ Ⓒ Ⓓ	19. Ⓐ Ⓑ Ⓒ Ⓓ
20. Ⓕ Ⓖ Ⓗ Ⓙ	20. Ⓕ Ⓖ Ⓗ Ⓙ
21. Ⓐ Ⓑ Ⓒ Ⓓ	21. Ⓐ Ⓑ Ⓒ Ⓓ
22. Ⓕ Ⓖ Ⓗ Ⓙ	22. Ⓕ Ⓖ Ⓗ Ⓙ
23. Ⓐ Ⓑ Ⓒ Ⓓ	23. Ⓐ Ⓑ Ⓒ Ⓓ
24. Ⓕ Ⓖ Ⓗ Ⓙ	24. Ⓕ Ⓖ Ⓗ Ⓙ
25. Ⓐ Ⓑ Ⓒ Ⓓ	25. Ⓐ Ⓑ Ⓒ Ⓓ
26. Ⓕ Ⓖ Ⓗ Ⓙ	26. Ⓕ Ⓖ Ⓗ Ⓙ
27. Ⓐ Ⓑ Ⓒ Ⓓ	27. Ⓐ Ⓑ Ⓒ Ⓓ
28. Ⓕ Ⓖ Ⓗ Ⓙ	28. Ⓕ Ⓖ Ⓗ Ⓙ
29. Ⓐ Ⓑ Ⓒ Ⓓ	29. Ⓐ Ⓑ Ⓒ Ⓓ
30. Ⓕ Ⓖ Ⓗ Ⓙ	30. Ⓕ Ⓖ Ⓗ Ⓙ
31. Ⓐ Ⓑ Ⓒ Ⓓ	31. Ⓐ Ⓑ Ⓒ Ⓓ
32. Ⓕ Ⓖ Ⓗ Ⓙ	32. Ⓕ Ⓖ Ⓗ Ⓙ
33. Ⓐ Ⓑ Ⓒ Ⓓ	33. Ⓐ Ⓑ Ⓒ Ⓓ
34. Ⓕ Ⓖ Ⓗ Ⓙ	34. Ⓕ Ⓖ Ⓗ Ⓙ
35. Ⓐ Ⓑ Ⓒ Ⓓ	35. Ⓐ Ⓑ Ⓒ Ⓓ
36. Ⓕ Ⓖ Ⓗ Ⓙ	36. Ⓕ Ⓖ Ⓗ Ⓙ
37. Ⓐ Ⓑ Ⓒ Ⓓ	37. Ⓐ Ⓑ Ⓒ Ⓓ
38. Ⓕ Ⓖ Ⓗ Ⓙ	38. Ⓕ Ⓖ Ⓗ Ⓙ
39. Ⓐ Ⓑ Ⓒ Ⓓ	39. Ⓐ Ⓑ Ⓒ Ⓓ
40. Ⓕ Ⓖ Ⓗ Ⓙ	40. Ⓕ Ⓖ Ⓗ Ⓙ

English Test

45 Minutes — 75 Questions

DIRECTIONS: Following are five passages with underlined portions. Alternate ways of stating the underlined portions are to the right of the passages. Choose the best alternative; if the original is the best way of stating the underlined portion, choose NO CHANGE.

The test also has questions that refer to the passage or ask you to reorder the sentences within the passages. These questions are identified by a number in a box. Choose the best answer and blacken in the corresponding oval on your answer grid.

Passage 1

My Favorite Zoo Animal

Last weekend my mother took <u>my younger brother and I</u> to the zoo. <u>The zoo, it is not far from our house,</u> is my favorite place to visit. <u>My brother, too.</u> My brother asked me which animal I liked <u>best</u>. I told him I had <u>trouble choosing among the giraffe and the zebra,</u> but I finally decided on the <u>latter</u>. We stood and watched the giraffe for an hour. The keeper<u>, noticing our interest, and coming over to us to tell us about the animal.</u> I learned a lot I didn't know before.

1. **A.** NO CHANGE
   B. my younger brother and me
   C. I and my younger brother
   D. me and my younger brother

2. **F.** NO CHANGE
   G. The zoo is not far from our house, it
   H. It is not far from our house (the zoo) and it
   J. The zoo, which is not far from our house,

3. **A.** NO CHANGE
   B. It is my brother's favorite place to visit, too.
   C. The zoo being my brother's favorite place also to visit.
   D. My brother, his favorite place is the zoo, too.

4. **F.** NO CHANGE
   G. trouble to choose among the giraffe and the zebra,
   H. trouble choosing between the giraffe and the zebra,
   J. trouble, to choose between the giraffe and the zebra,

5. **A.** NO CHANGE
   B. last
   C. better
   D. best

6. **F.** NO CHANGE
   G. , noticed our interest, and coming over to tell us about the animal.
   H. noticing our interest by coming over to tell us about the animal.
   J. noticed our interest and came over to tell us about the animal.

Go on to next page

For example, I learned that the word giraffe is thought to be derived from the Arabic word *zirafah,* which means "tallest of all." The name is not inappropriate. Giraffes are the tallest animals on earth, and may reach a height of more than 15 feet. The more detailed scientific name also interesting. Scientists officially call this animal *Giraffa camelopardalis* because it considers the animal to look like a camel with the markings of a leopard.

It appears that no two sets of markings are alike. While most visitors to the zoo consider all giraffes to have the same markings, a trained eye can distinguish subtle differences. The patterns vary from subspecies to subspecies, as does the location of the patterns. Some giraffes, for example, have spots running down their legs, and others do not. The colors can also vary, from a blackish hue to a light yellow. The colors serve the purpose of camouflaging the giraffe, being that it blends in well with the leaves of the trees in which it hides. The long neck of the giraffe is mistaken for a tree branch. [13] The theory that the markings on a giraffe are comparable to the fingerprints of a human has gained ground. [15]

7. A. NO CHANGE
   B. not appropriate
   C. not appropriately
   D. not inappropriately

8. F. NO CHANGE
   G. name is also interesting.
   H. name also is interested.
   J. name, also interesting

9. A. NO CHANGE
   B. they consider
   C. they are considering
   D. it is considered

10. F. NO CHANGE
    G. from subspecies and subspecies
    H. between subspecies to subspecies
    J. subspecies and subspecies

11. A. NO CHANGE
    B. which
    C. to
    D. OMIT the underlined portion.

12. F. NO CHANGE
    G. good
    H. best
    J. and does well

13. Which of the following would be the best placement of the last sentence of the passage?
    A. At the beginning of the first paragraph
    B. At the beginning of the second paragraph
    C. At the end of the second paragraph
    D. At the beginning of the third paragraph

14. F. NO CHANGE
    G. have
    H. have been
    J. are starting to

15. Which of the following additions would be the best conclusion to this paragraph?
    A. Giraffes may be just as unique as human beings.
    B. Giraffes are evolving and changing their color patterns to meet their environments.
    C. Giraffes are the most colorful creatures in the animal kingdom.
    D. Giraffes are my favorite animal.

Go on to next page

Passage 2

Alex Haley, *Roots* Author

[1]

[1]*Roots* author Alex Haley turned his African
                                              ―――――――――
                                                  16
ancestors into a book who's emotional impact on
                       ―――――
                         17
Black Americans cannot be overestimated. [2]Born
in 1921 in Ithaca, New York, his early years were
                             ――――――――――――――――――
                                     18
spent with his grandmother in Henning, Tennessee.
―――――   ―――――――――
                                           19
[3]The oldest of three sons in his family. [20]

[2]

As a child, Alex wasn't desirous of becoming a
―――
                        21
writer. As an adult, Alex took a variety of jobs,
――――――
eventually joining the Coast Guard and becoming a
cook. Unchallenged by his daily routine in the U.S.
Coast Guard, Haley wrote articles which he sent to
             ―――――――――――――――――
                     22
many different magazines, hoping to catch an
editor's attention. Eventually his submissions were
                    ――――――――――
                        23
accepted, and occasionally he received payment
for his work. Haley's literary abilities afforded him
                                         ――――――――――
                                              24
an opportunity to change his career. It is not every
―――――――――――――
cook who can become a military journalist. By 1959
when Haley retired from military service, he held
the title of Chief Journalist.

---

16. F. NO CHANGE
    G. stories about his African ancestors
    H. his (African) ancestors
    J. African, his ancestors' stories

17. A. NO CHANGE
    B. whos'
    C. who is
    D. whose

18. F. NO CHANGE
    G. Alex's early years were spent
    H. Alex spent his early years
    J. the years that Alex was early, he was spending

19. A. NO CHANGE
    B. Tennessee — the oldest of
    C. Tennessee because he was the oldest of
    D. Tennessee. Alex was the oldest of

20. Which of the following is true about sentence 3 of paragraph 1?
    F. It should be the first sentence of the passage.
    G. It should be deleted because it adds little to the narrative and doesn't forward the passage.
    H. It disagrees with information presented earlier in the passage.
    J. It repeats information given elsewhere in the passage.

21. A. NO CHANGE
    B. Alex's desires to become a writer were unstated when he was a child.
    C. Alex didn't write much as a child.
    D. OMIT the underlined portion.

22. F. NO CHANGE
    G. articles written by Haley
    H. Haley, writing articles
    J. and writing articles

23. A. NO CHANGE
    B. Although
    C. Because
    D. Nonetheless

24. F. NO CHANGE
    G. allow him an opportunity
    H. enabled him an opportunity
    J. give him an opportunity

Go on to next page

[3]

Alex Haley wrote many articles on a variety of topics, both domestic and international. Eventually, he did family history research in the National Archives in Washington, D.C. Haley took more than a dozen years to do the research and he traveled
                                                25
more than a half a million miles to work in huge archives and small libraries ranging over three continents. Researching his ancestors took them to
                                                              26
Juffure, a small village in The Gambia. The Gambia's historian spoke about Kunta Kinte, who was sent to the United States on a British slave ship. After Haley completed his research, then he knew he had to tell
                27
everyone the story of Kunta Kinte. The author emphasized that this was the saga of not only the
                                    28
Haley family but also the story of Black Americans. That Black Americans agreed was amply demonstrated by the fascination surrounding the miniseries developed from the book. The miniseries *Roots* has been repeated and continues to earn high ratings every time it shows on television. 29

25. A. NO CHANGE
    B. research; but he traveled
    C. research which traveled
    D. the research, during which he traveled

26. F. NO CHANGE
    G. takes him
    H. took him
    J. takes us

27. A. NO CHANGE
    B. After Haley completed his research, he knew
    C. When Haley, after completing his research, knew
    D. Then, after having completed his research, Haley knew

28. F. NO CHANGE
    G. was not only the saga of
    H. was of not only his saga but
    J. saga was not only of

Question 29 refers to the passage as a whole.

29. This passage was written as a homework assignment to "Discuss the literary abilities of Alex Haley." Did the passage fulfill the assignment?
    A. Yes, because the derivation of *Roots* is discussed.
    B. Yes, because the reader learns the sources of Haley's ideas.
    C. No, because the emphasis is on Haley's life, not his skill as a writer.
    D. No, because the focus is more on Haley's family than on Haley.

Go on to next page

Passage 3

One Man's Opinion About Time Travel

by Carl Mack

Want to go back in time and <u>discussing</u> philosophy with Aristotle, rule with Nero, dine with Lincoln? If you want to travel in time, <u>a space ship</u>. But given that you are on earth now, why would you need a space ship to return to a place you already are? The answer can be explained with a little science (or at least what I, a non-scientist, think is logical). The earth is rotating <u>on its axis, it is</u> also orbiting the Sun. The Sun is traveling along the outer arm of the Milky Way galaxy which is traveling through space <u>on it's endless</u> journey to the infinite. <u>Because</u> in the minute you were thinking the earth has moved from where it was to where it is now, <u>moving you with it so you do not notice any change</u>. <u>This is why you think you are not moving when you are.</u> To simplify things, think of the earth as a car traveling down a road and you are a passenger in the car. If the car is moving at one mile an hour and you jump back in time one hour (discounting all the movement of the earth itself)<u>; you</u> would find yourself sitting on the road with the car one mile away heading toward you. When you left the time you were in and went back in time, you did not take the car with <u>you; therefore,</u> it moved back in time and space to when and where it was one

30. F. NO CHANGE
    G. be discussing
    H. discuss
    J. have discussed

31. A. NO CHANGE
    B. a space ship is needed
    C. you need a space ship
    D. using a space ship

32. F. NO CHANGE
    G. on it's axis, it is
    H. on its axis and also it is
    J. on its axis; it is

33. A. NO CHANGE
    B. on its endless
    C. on it's never-ending
    D. not ending its

34. F. NO CHANGE
    G. Due to the fact that
    H. Despite
    J. OMIT the underlined portion

35. A. NO CHANGE
    B. and, moving you with it, so you do not notice any change
    C. moves you with it so you do not notice any change
    D. moving, and you move with it, so you are not noticing any change

36. F. NO CHANGE
    G. Because of this, you think you're not moving, but you are moving.
    H. You're moving when you think you're not moving, and this is why.
    J. OMIT the underlined portion.

37. A. NO CHANGE
    B. ,
    C. :
    D. .

38. F. NO CHANGE
    G. you, therefore;
    H. you; therefore;
    J. you, therefore,

hour earlier. The same if you moved in time
accounting for the earth's movement. You would
end up somewhere in space waiting for the earth to
catch up to you!

And this is the reason because you need a
space ship, so you could travel to where the earth
was at that time to which you return. Not only do
you have to jump back in time, you have to go back
to a time earlier than you wanted so you can travel
to the earth and arrive "on time."

They say that the proof that time travel is
impossible is that there are no time travelers here
right now, it could be that time travel is possible
but space travel has not advanced enough to get
them here yet. 43

39. A. NO CHANGE
    B. Being the same if you moved
    C. The same being true if you moved
    D. The same would be true if you moved

40. F. NO CHANGE
    G. And this being the reason why you
    H. Because of this is the reason you
    J. You

41. A. NO CHANGE
    B. Scientists say
    C. They are saying (scientists)
    D. OMIT the underlined portion

42. F. NO CHANGE
    G. now. It
    H. now, and therefore it
    J. and

43. Which of the following best summarizes the idea of this passage?
    A. Time travel is impossible.
    B. Time travel would require going backwards to return to the same time.
    C. Time travel would require more technology than we currently have.
    D. Time travel would allow people from different eras to converse.

Passage 4

The Findings of the Paleontologists

[1]

Paleontologists have called the preserved burrows "devil's corkscrews" (or *Daemonelix*) when the time they were first found. At that time there were then, scientists thought the corkscrews might be holes left by the giant tap roots of some unknown plant. But when, however, *Palaeocastor* skeletons were found in the bottoms of the spirals, almost everyone had to concede that they were truly beaver burrows. Admittedly, the skeleton of a *Nothocyon* been found in one burrow; but this predator probably followed a beaver home for supper and just stayed. Three other kinds of beavers lived around Agate in the early Miocene epoch, but their bones have never been found in the burrows, in fact, no one knows what they did for homes. Perhaps there burrows were much shallower or were in the river banks where running water soon destroyed them.

44. F. NO CHANGE
    G. calling
    H. have been called by
    J. used to be called

45. A. NO CHANGE
    B. then
    C. since
    D. while

46. F. NO CHANGE
    G. There were at that time
    H. Then at that time
    J. At that time

47. A. NO CHANGE
    B. the bottoms of
    C. the roots
    D. it

48. F. NO CHANGE
    G. knowing
    H. there were
    J. OMIT the underlined portion.

49. A. NO CHANGE
    B. was
    C. his
    D. is being

50. F. NO CHANGE
    G. burrow — however, this
    H. burrow. But this
    J. burrow, but this

51. A. NO CHANGE
    B. burrows. In fact, no one
    C. burrows, no one, in fact,
    D. burrows, because in fact no one

52. F. NO CHANGE
    G. there, burrows
    H. their burrow's
    J. their burrows

[2]

[1] The paleontologists' findings seem incompatible with the divisions of epochs, periods, and eras until one considers that the divisions were based on breaks in the European sedimentary record reflecting local events that did not necessarily show up in North America's sediments. [2] Paleontologists can tell that no dramatic change <u>layed</u> in store for the fauna at the beginning of the Miocene epoch and that many Oligocene genera carried over into the new epoch. [3] Most of the primitive animals that had survived in the <u>extensive forests become extant</u> when the forests began to <u>retreat: but for the most part, the</u> record continued undisturbed. [4] This is to be expected where the accumulation of sediments continued <u>nonstop</u> without interruption. 57 58 59

53. A. NO CHANGE
    B. lay
    C. lies
    D. was laying

54. F. NO CHANGE
    G. extensive forests, became extant
    H. extensive forests became extinct
    J. OMIT the underlined portion.

55. A. NO CHANGE
    B. retreat. However, for the most part, the
    C. retreat. Moreover, for the most part, the
    D. retreat. But most of the part of the

56. F. NO CHANGE
    G. nonstopping
    H. nonstop but
    J. OMIT the underlined portion.

57. Is the word reflecting in sentence 1 of paragraph 2 used appropriately in this passage?
    A. Yes, because it means "indicating" or "corresponding."
    B. Yes, because it refers to the smooth, mirrorlike lake in which the fossils were found.
    C. No, because reflecting means "thinking back on, examining."
    D. No, because it means the same as record, making the sentence redundant.

Question 58 refers to the passage as a whole.

58. The passage as a whole is best expressed by which of the following titles?
    F. Tracking Ancient Rodents
    G. What Fossils Reveal
    H. A Paleontologist's Duties
    J. The Extinction of Species

59. Which of the following represents the best order of the sentences in the second paragraph?
    A. 2 — 3 — 4 — 1
    B. 3 — 2 — 1 — 4
    C. 3 — 4 — 1 — 2
    D. 2 — 4 — 3 — 1

Go on to next page

Passage 5

Vietnam

In 111 B.C., ancestors of the present-day Vietnamese, inhabiting part of what is now southern China and northern Vietnam, were conquered, there being the warlike forces of China's Han dynasty. Chinese rule lasted more than 1,000 years, since A.D. 939, when the Vietnamese ousted their conquerors and began a southward expansion, that, by the mid-eighteenth century, reached the Gulf of Siam.

The Vietnamese were rent by internal political divisions, however, and for nearly two centuries contending families in the north and south struggled to control the powerless kings of the Le dynasty. During this period, Vietnam affectively was divided near the 17th parallel. Just a few kilometers above the demarcation line established at the 1954 Geneva Conference.

Vietnam having been reunited following a devastating civil war in the eighteenth century but soon fell prey to the expansion of European colonialism. While the French conquest of Vietnam began in 1858 with an attack on what is now the city of Da Nang. France imposed control gradually, to meet heavy resistance, and only in 1884 was Vietnam officially incorporated into the French empire.

60. F. NO CHANGE
    G. due to the warlike
    H. by the warlike
    J. OMIT the underlined portion.

61. A. NO CHANGE
    B. when
    C. from
    D. until

62. F. NO CHANGE
    G. expansion that is reaching, by the mid-eighteenth century,
    H. expansion, by the mid-eighteenth century, reaching,
    J. expansion, by mid-eighteenth century having been reached

63. A. NO CHANGE
    B. divisions; however, and
    C. divisions. And however,
    D. divisions, although

64. F. NO CHANGE
    G. in affect
    H. in effect
    J. ineffective

65. A. NO CHANGE
    B. parallel, just a
    C. parallel, that is just a
    D. parallel; just a

66. F. NO CHANGE
    G. being
    H. was
    J. OMIT the underlined portion.

67. A. NO CHANGE
    B. When the
    C. Whenever the
    D. The

68. F. NO CHANGE
    G. meeting
    H. and meeting
    J. about to have met

Vietnam's resistance was the precursor of nationalist activity directed against foreign rule. By 1930, the Vietnam Nationalist Party had staged the first significant armed uprising against the French, but its virtual destruction in the ensuing French repression left the leadership of the anticolonial movement to those more adapt at underground organization and survival — the Communists. In that same year, the recently formed Indochinese Communist Party (ICP) took the lead in setting up short-lived "soviets" in Nghe An and Ha Tinh provinces, an action that identified the ICP with peasant unrest.

The Vietnamese communist movement began in Paris in 1920 when Ho Chi Minh became a charter member of the French Communist Party. Two years later, Ho went to Moscow to study Marxist doctrine, then he went to China. While in China, he formed the Vietnamese Revolutionary Youth League, setting the stage for the formation of the ICP in 1930. French repression of nationalists and Communists forced some of the insurgents underground. Other dissidents were imprisoned, some emerging later to play an important role in the anticolonial movement. 74 75

69.
A. NO CHANGE
B. but it's
C. but, it's
D. so its

70.
F. NO CHANGE
G. adept at
H. adopted from
J. adept with

71.
A. NO CHANGE
B. took the lead in setting up
C. taking the led in setting up
D. taking the lead in setting up

72.
F. NO CHANGE
G. doctrine; then went
H. doctrine, and then going
J. doctrine, then went

73.
A. NO CHANGE
B. Other dissidents was imprisoned,
C. Other dissidents imprisoned
D. Other dissidents, imprisoned,

Questions 74 and 75 refer to the passage as a whole.

74. This passage may have been written for which of the following purposes?
F. to ridicule the futility of fighting Communism
G. to provide an historical overview of the government of Vietnam
H. to criticize foreign powers that attempt to control Vietnam
J. to show Ho Chi Minh's role in the development of modern communism

75. Which of the following topics would be most appropriate for the next paragraph in this passage?
A. the Vietnamese war for independence
B. the Vietnamese development of nuclear weapons
C. the change of Vietnam from an agrarian to an industrialized society
D. the role of the United States in developing a stronger human-rights program in Vietnam

Mathematics Test

60 Minutes — 60 Questions

DIRECTIONS: Each question has five answer choices. Choose the best answer for each question and shade the corresponding oval on your answer grid.

1. A sales department wants to make a 12% profit on its product. If the cost of the product is $87, what will the selling price of the product have to be to achieve the desired profit?
    A. $98.44
    B. $97.44
    C. $95.04
    D. $92.14
    E. $90.00

2. A board exactly 1⅛ yards long is cut into three pieces. The first piece is 25 inches. The second piece is 10 inches. How long is the third piece?
    F. 15 inches
    G. 14 inches
    H. 13½ inches
    J. 13 inches
    K. 10½ inches

3. Three friends, Mike, Ken, and Debi, earned an average of $50,000 each on a project. Their total earnings were exactly 40% of the total earnings of everyone in their company. How much were the total earnings of the entire company?
    A. $600,000
    B. $450,000
    C. $375,000
    D. $340,000
    E. $40,000

4. Given that $(a + 5)(a - 6) = 0$, which of the following is a true statement?
    F. a could be 5 or 6
    G. a could be −5 or −6
    H. a could be −5 or _6
    J. a could be +5 or −6
    K. a could be 0

5. An office receives 80 calls a day for 6 days. In order to average 100 calls per day for 12 days, how many calls must the company get in the next 6 days?
    A. 1,200
    B. 1,100
    C. 1,020
    D. 720
    E. 120

6. If x is an integer between 6 and 10, which of the following could be a true statement?
    F. $x^2 = 144$
    G. $\sqrt{x} = 2+$
    H. $2x = 14.5$
    J. $3x = 24$
    K. ½$x = 1.5$

7. If one of the angles in a triangle is obtuse, which of the following is a true statement regarding the other two angles in the triangle?
    A. They are in a ratio of 2:1.
    B. They total 90 degrees.
    C. One must be a right angle.
    D. Both angles must be acute.
    E. Both angles must be obtuse.

8. 5% of $(a + b) = $ 10% of b. Which of the following must be a true statement?
    F. $a > b$
    G. $a < b$
    H. $a = b$
    J. $a + b = 0$
    K. $a < 0, b < 0$

Go on to next page

9. A square (Figure I) and an isosceles triangle (Figure II) have equal areas. $x =$

   Figure 1: square with side 8
   Figure 2: right isosceles triangle with legs x

   A. $4\sqrt{2}$
   B. $8\sqrt{2}$
   C. $4\sqrt{3}$
   D. $8\sqrt{3}$
   E. $12\sqrt{3}$

10. The sides of a triangle are 6, 8, and 10. What is the degree measure of the angle between the sides measuring 6 and 8?
    F. 15
    G. 30
    H. 45
    J. 60
    K. 90

11. The cost of a textbook increased by 25% from 1998 to 1999. In 2000, the cost of the textbook was ¼ below its 1998 cost. By what percentage did the cost of the textbook decrease from 1999 to 2000?
    A. 0
    B. 20
    C. 25
    D. 40
    E. 75

12. Which of the following is a factor of $a^2 - 8a + 15$?
    F. $a + 5$
    G. $a + 3$
    H. $a - 1$
    J. $a - 3$
    K. $a - 15$

13. Jim was y years old m years ago. How many years old will he be in terms of y in 12 years?
    A. $y + m + 12$
    B. $y\,m + 12$
    C. $y - m + 12$
    D. $y\,m - 12$
    E. $y - m - 12$

14. $\left(5x^2 y^5\right)^2 \left(3x^3 y^4\right)^3 = ?$
    F. $675x^{13}y^{22}$
    G. $675x^{36}y^{120}$
    H. $15x^{36}y^{120}$
    J. $15x^{13}y^{22}$
    K. $15x^7 y^{14}$

15. A circle with a radius of 4 inches has ¼ the area of a circle with a radius of how many inches?
    A. 1
    B. 2
    C. 8
    D. 16
    E. 64

16. A hiker walks nonstop for 2 hours and 20 minutes and travels 7 miles. At what rate did he walk?
    F. 2 mph
    G. 2⅒ mph
    H. 2½ mph
    J. 3 mph
    K. 3½ mph

17. A dollhouse is to be an exact replica of a collector's own home on a reduced scale. If the main bedroom of the dollhouse is 18 inches long by 24 inches wide, the real bedroom of 12 feet long will be how many feet wide?
    A. 24
    B. 18
    C. 16
    D. 10
    E. 8

18. Triangles I and II (not shown) are similar figures. The angles of triangle I are in the ratio 1:2:3. If the perimeter of triangle I is $15 + 5\sqrt{3}$, and the shortest side of triangle II is 15, then what is the perimeter of triangle II?
    F. $150 + 20\sqrt{3}$
    G. $60 + 15\sqrt{3}$
    H. $60 + 5\sqrt{3}$
    J. $45 + 15\sqrt{3}$
    K. 45

Go on to next page

19. When asked her age, Lael responded, "Take the square root of 625, add it to the square of 5, and take 40 percent of the resulting sum." Which of the following expresses Lael's age?

   A. $L = \sqrt{(625+5)\,40}$
   B. $L = .40 \cdot \sqrt{625} + 5^2$
   C. $L = .40 \cdot \sqrt{625} \cdot 5^2$
   D. $L = .40 + \sqrt{625} + 5^2$
   E. $L = .40(\sqrt{625} + 5^2)$

20. In a classroom of children, every child has either blond, brown, or red hair. The probability of randomly selecting a child with red hair is ⅙. The probability of randomly selecting a child with brown hair is ⅓. If 30 children have blond hair, how many children are in the classroom?

   F. 30
   G. 45
   H. 60
   J. 90
   K. 120

21. If a is six greater than b, and the sum of a and b is −18, then $b^2 =$

   A. 144
   B. 36
   C. 16
   D. 4
   E. 0

22. What is the interior degree measure of figure ABCDE?

   F. 900
   G. 720
   H. 540
   J. 360
   K. 300

23. A city is visited one month by 200 German, 320 American, 140 Moroccan, 180 French, and 240 Japanese tourists. If a circle graph were made representing the various categories, the angle made by the segment representing the French would be how many degrees?

   A. 360
   B. 270
   C. 60
   D. 1
   E. ⅙

24. Nine friends intend to buy class rings at $85.00 each. The rings cost $864 per dozen if bought in a full dozen batch. If the friends can bring in three more students to purchase rings, how much would each friend save on the price of the ring?

   F. $15.00
   G. $14.33
   H. $13.00
   J. $12.75
   K. $11.90

25. For all x and y, $(3x^2y + xy^2) - (2x^2y - 2xy^2) = ?$
   A. $x^2 - x$
   B. $x^2y - xy^2$
   C. $x^2y + 3xy^2$
   D. $5x^2 - xy^2$
   E. $xy^2 + 3x^2y^2$

26. If line segment XY (not shown) goes from (−2, 6) to (4, 6), what are the coordinates of the midpoint of XY?

   F. (−1,6)
   G. (0,0)
   H. (1,6)
   J. (3,0)
   K. (3,6)

27. The ratio of olives to dates is 3:5 and the difference between the number of dates and the number of olives is 18. What is the total number of olives and dates?

   A. 144
   B. 72
   C. 40
   D. 27
   E. 24

Go on to next page

28. Given that *x* is an integer, for what value of *x* is $x + \frac{2}{3}x > 15$ and $x + 4 < 15$?
    F. 8
    G. 9
    H. 10
    J. 11
    K. 12

29. A third of the product of 6 and 4 is the same as 3 less than 2*x*. What is *x*?
    A. 8
    B. 7
    C. 6
    D. 1½
    E. ⅚

30. A gambler's lucky number is 12. On any roll of two dice, what is the probability that he will roll his lucky number?
    F. ½
    G. ⅓
    H. ⅙
    J. 1/12
    K. 1/36

31. Isosceles right triangle ABC has a perimeter of $20 + 10\sqrt{2}$. What is the area of the triangle?
    A. $200\sqrt{2}$
    B. 200
    C. $100\sqrt{2}$
    D. 100
    E. 50

32. Paul wants to buy a new aquarium with the same volume as the old. His old aquarium measures 6 × 4 units on the base and is 10 units tall. If his new aquarium has a base in which each side is 50 percent longer than the corresponding side in the old aquarium, approximately how many units tall will the new aquarium be?
    F. 4.4
    G. 4.5
    H. 4.9
    J. 5.0
    K. 5.1

33. Triangles ABC and DEF are similar figures. What is the perimeter of triangle DEF?

    Area of ABC = 32

    A. $56 + 28\sqrt{2}$
    B. 84
    C. $84\sqrt{2}$
    D. $84 + 28\sqrt{2}$
    E. $90\sqrt{2}$

34. Given that $-|3 - 3a| = -12$, which of the following could be *a*?
    F. 5
    G. 4
    H. 3
    J. 2
    K. 1

35. Triangle ABC is an equilateral triangle with an area of 32. Triangle DEF is an isosceles right triangle of area 64. Which of the following represents the ratio of the sum of the interior angles in triangle ABC to the sum of the interior angles in DEF?
    A. 4:1
    B. 3:1
    C. 2:1
    D. 1:1
    E. 1:2

36. Marcy bought eight items costing *x* cents each. She gave the clerk *y* dimes. In terms of *x* and *y*, how much change should Marcy get back?
    F. $y - 8x$
    G. $10y + 8x$
    H. $10y - 8x$
    J. $8x - y$
    K. $8x - 10y$

37. Arc AB = 3 units. What is the circumference of Circle O in units?

Angle $AOB = 10°$
Circle O

A. $108/\pi$
B. 36
C. 36π
D. 108
E. 108π

38. Kim starts at point X and walks 50 yards straight north. Scott starts at the same point X and walks due east. The shortest distance between Kim and Scott is 120 yards. How many yards did Scott walk?

F. 13,000
G. 11,900
H. $\sqrt{13,000}$
J. $\sqrt{11,900}$
K. 50

39. What point on the graph of $x^2 - y = 4$ has an x coordinate of 3?

A. (3, −5)
B. (3, $\sqrt{5}$)
C. (3, 4)
D. (3, 5)
E. (3, 13)

40. An equilateral triangle has an altitude of $10\sqrt{3}$ units. What is the perimeter of the triangle?

F. 80
G. 60
H. 30
J. $20\sqrt{3}$
K. 20

41. An automatic water system fills an empty pool half full in one hour. Each hour thereafter the system fills one-half of the capacity that is still empty. After how many hours is the pool $1/64$ empty?

A. 12
B. 10
C. 7
D. 6
E. 5

42. If m pencils cost n cents, which of the following expresses the cost of p pencils?

F. mnp cents
G. $m + \frac{mp}{n}$ cents
H. $m + \frac{p}{n}$ cents
J. $n + \frac{p}{m}$ cents
K. $\frac{np}{m}$ cents

43. Hal can assemble 600 widgets in 2½ hours. Faye can pack 200 widgets in 45 minutes. If Faye wants to work for exactly 4½ hours and finish the same number of widgets as Hal, how many hours will Hal have to work?

A. 5
B. 4½
C. 4¼
D. 4
E. 3⅗

44. The cost of a swimsuit goes up 50 percent in June, down 20 percent in July, and down another 30 percent in August. The cost of the swimsuit in August is what percent of the cost of the swimsuit before June?

F. 110
G. 100
H. 90
J. 84
K. 61

45. A wheel covers a distance of 300π meters in 15 revolutions. What is the radius of the wheel?
A. 30π
B. 25
C. 20
D. 10π
E. 10

46. A prime number times a composite number must be
F. prime
G. composite
H. zero
J. a fraction
K. even

47. Sector AOC has an area of 120π square units. What is the circumference of the circle?

Angle ABC = 6°
O is the midpoint of the circle

A. 34,600π
B. 1,200π
C. 120π
D. 120/π
E. $\sqrt{120/x}$

48. On a circle with the equation $x^2 + y^2 = 25$, if the x-coordinate is –3, the y-coordinate could be
F. –3
G. 0
H. 4
J. 9
K. 16

49. $(a+3)^2 + (a-4)^2 =$
A. $2a^2 - 2a + 25$
B. $2a^2 + 14a + 25$
C. $a^2 + 2a + 25$
D. $a^2 - 2a - 25$
E. $2a^2 - 2a - 4$

50. A jar that is now empty is going to be filled with red marbles and blue marbles. The person filling the jar wants the probability of drawing a red marble at random from the jar to be twice as great as the probability of drawing a blue marble at random. If the jar is going to contain 36 marbles, how many more must be red marbles than blue marbles?
F. 30
G. 24
H. 20
J. 18
K. 12

51. In the right triangle XYZ below, what is the value of tan Z?

A. 7/25
B. 7/24
C. 24/25
D. 25/24
E. 24/7

52. Which of the following is best expressed by the figure below?

F. $x > -4$
G. $x < -4$
H. $-4 \leq x < 0$
J. $-4 < x \leq 0$
K. $-5 < x \leq 1$

53. If $4cx - \frac{3d}{e} = 4cy$, then $x - y = ?$
A. $-\frac{3d}{4ce}$
B. $-\frac{3d}{e} + \frac{1}{4c}$
C. $\frac{3d}{4e} - c$
D. $\frac{3d}{4ce}$
E. $\frac{3e}{e} + 4c$

Go on to next page

Chapter 19: How to Ruin a Perfectly Good Day, Part I: Practice Exam 1   **201**

54. For all $a \neq 0$, and $b \neq 0$, what is the slope of the line passing through (a,b) and $(-a,-b)$?

    F. 0
    G. 1
    H. a/b
    J. b/a
    K. $-b/a$

55. From a lookout point on a cliff, the angle of depression to a boat on the water is 14 degrees, and the distance from the boat to the shore just below the cliff is 2 km. How far is the lookout from the water surface?

    A. $\dfrac{2}{\sin 14°}$
    B. $\dfrac{2}{\tan 14°}$
    C. $\dfrac{2}{\cos 14°}$
    D. $2 \sin 14°$
    E. $2 \tan 14°$

56. A computer is printing a novel. It prints 60 pages in the first hour, after which it breaks. Two hours later, the computer is fixed and resumes printing at the rate of 60 pages per hour. To finish the job on time, another computer that prints at the same rate is brought in and begins printing when the first computer is repaired. The two computers finish printing one hour later. The graphs of the number of pages printed (p) as a function of time (t) would most resemble which of the following?

    F.
    G.
    H.
    J.
    K.

57. Which of the following is equivalent to $\dfrac{\sin^2 \theta + \cos^2 \theta}{\sec^2 \theta}$?

    A. $\cos^2 \theta$
    B. $\sin^2 \theta$
    C. $\tan^2 \theta$
    D. $\dfrac{1}{\cos^2 \theta}$
    E. $\sin^2 \theta + 1$

58. On average, a cow and a half can give a pint and a half of milk in 36 hours. How many pints can three cows give on average in 72 hours? (All cows give milk at the same rate.)

    F. 3
    G. 4
    H. 5
    J. 6
    K. 7

Go on to next page

Part VII: I'd Rather Wait for the Movie: Full-Length Practice ACTs

59. From an observer on the ground, the angle of elevation to a hot-air balloon is 21 degrees and the distance from the observer to a point on the ground directly underneath the balloon is 1,500 meters. How many meters high is the balloon?

Balloon not to scale

x

21°

1,500 meters

- A. 1,500/cos 21°
- B. 1,500/tan 21°
- C. 1,500 sin 21°
- D. 1,500 cos 21°
- E. 1,500 tan 21°

60. If A measures between 0° and 180° and tan A = 4/3, what are the possible values of cos A?
- F. −3/5 only
- G. −3/5 and 3/5
- H. −4/5 and 4/5
- J. 3/5 only
- K. 4/5 only

STOP DO NOT TURN THE PAGE UNTIL TOLD TO DO SO.
DO NOT RETURN TO A PREVIOUS TEST.

Reading Test

35 Minutes — 40 Questions

DIRECTIONS: Each of the four passages in this section is followed by ten questions. Answer each question based on what is stated or implied in the passage and shade the corresponding oval on your answer grid.

Passage 1

Natural Science

Thrombosis refers to abnormal clotting that causes the blood flow in a blood vessel to become obstructed. Venous thrombosis refers to such an obstruction in a vein, often at some site of inflam- (05) mation, disease, or injury to the blood vessel wall. The clot (thrombus) may remain fixed at the site of origin, adhering to the wall of the vein. Or the clot (or a fragment of it) may break loose to be carried elsewhere in the circulatory system by the blood. (10) The migratory clot or fragment is then called an embolus.

In pulmonary embolism, the clot or fragment breaks free from its site of origin, usually a deep vein of the leg or pelvis, and is carried by the blood (15) through progressively larger veins into the inferior vena cava, a very large abdominal vein that empties into the right side of the heart. The embolus is pumped through the right side of the heart and into the pulmonary artery, whose branches supply (20) blood to the lungs. Depending on its size, the embolus may pass through the larger pulmonary branches, but may eventually enter a branch too narrow to allow it to pass. Here it lodges, obstructing blood flow to the lung tissues supplied by that (25) vessel and its finer divisions "downstream" from the embolus.

The clinical consequences of pulmonary embolism vary with the size of the embolus and the extent to which it reduces total blood flow to the (30) lungs. Very small emboli cause so little circulatory impairment that they may produce no clinical signs or symptoms at all. In fact, among the estimated 300,000 patients who experience pulmonary embolism each year, the great majority suffer no (35) serious symptoms or complications, and the disorder clears up without significant aftereffects.

However, in a significant percentage of patients, the pulmonary embolism is massive, sometimes reducing total pulmonary blood flow by 50 percent (40) or more; and the consequences may be grave: seriously strained circulation, shock, or acute respiratory failure. Massive pulmonary embolism causes some 50,000 deaths each year in the U.S.

Certain classes of patients are more likely than others to develop venous thrombosis with its atten- (45) dant risk of pulmonary embolism. Disorders that increase susceptibility include venous inflammation (phlebitis), congestive heart failure, and certain forms of cancer. Women are more susceptible during pregnancy and during recovery from child- (50) birth than at other times, and those taking birth control pills appear to be at slightly higher risk than are women who do not. Postoperative patients constitute a high-risk group, particularly following pelvic surgery and orthopedic procedures involving (55) the hip. Any operations requiring that the patient be immobilized for prolonged periods afterward exacerbate the risk of this problem. Among patients recovering from hip fractures, for example, the incidence of venous thrombosis may run as high as (60) 50 percent.

Venous thrombosis can sometimes be diagnosed by the presence of a swollen extremity with some evidence of inflammation or a clot that can be felt when the affected vein is examined. But some- (65) times venous thrombosis produces no clear-cut clinical signs so that other tests may be needed to confirm the diagnosis.

One such test entails injecting fibrinogen tagged with a radioactive isotope of iodine into the (70) blood. Fibrinogen has a strong affinity for blood clots and is incorporated into them, carrying its radioactive label with it. The clot can then be located with a radiation-sensing device.

Another diagnostic technique, called venogra- (75) phy, involves injecting a dye (one that shows clearly on X-rays) into the vein where obstruction is suspected. The X-ray venogram provides very detailed information on the extent and location of the obstruction. (80)

A third technique uses sensitive instruments that measure blood flow in vessels of the extremities to detect any circulatory impairment that may result from thrombosis.

Signs of nonfatal pulmonary embolism may (85) include sudden shortness of breath, chest pain, increased heart rate, restlessness and anxiety, a fall in blood pressure, and loss of consciousness. But clinical symptoms may vary by their presence or

(90) absence and in their intensity, and their similarity to symptoms that may result from other disorders can make the diagnosis of pulmonary embolism difficult on this basis alone.

Pulmonary angiography (X-ray visualization of
(95) the pulmonary artery and its branches after injection of a radiopaque dye) is the most reliable diagnostic technique, but it is a complex test that cannot be done routinely in all patients. A somewhat simpler test involves injecting extremely fine
(100) particles of a radioactively labeled material such as albumin into a vein and then scanning the lungs with a radiation detector while the particles traverse the pulmonary blood vessels.

1. The purpose of the first paragraph is
   A. to analyze the causes of blood clots.
   B. to describe types of blood clots.
   C. to predict who is most likely to get a blood clot.
   D. to inform the readers of steps to take for the prevention of blood clots.

2. Which of the following best describes the difference between a thrombosis and an embolus?
   F. A thrombosis is in the lung; an embolism may be anywhere.
   G. A thrombosis is usually fatal; an embolism is rarely fatal.
   H. A thrombosis remains stationary; an embolism moves within the circulatory system.
   J. A thrombosis is larger than an embolism.

3. Which of the following may you infer about pulmonary embolism?
   A. It may cure itself.
   B. It is invariably fatal.
   C. It is more severe in children than in adults.
   D. It is directly related to diet.

4. According to the passage, a common origin for a pulmonary thrombosis is in the
   F. heart.
   G. brain.
   H. leg.
   J. arm.

5. In lines 45–46, the phrase "attendant risk" means
   A. risks faced by those who aid others.
   B. risks that accompany something else.
   C. minimal, almost nonexistent risks.
   D. risks for women only, not for men.

6. In lines 57 and 58, "exacerbate" means
   F. reduce.
   G. cure.
   H. heal.
   J. make worse.

7. Which of the following may you substitute for "clinical signs" (line 67)?
   A. Hospitals
   B. Deaths
   C. Diseases
   D. Symptoms

8. Which of the following may be the best title for the passage?
   F. How to Cure Embolisms
   G. How Blood Clots Develop
   H. Means of Preventing Blood Clots and Embolisms
   J. Description and Diagnosis of Blood Clots

9. The three tests discussed in lines 69–84 are introduced for which of the following purposes?
   A. to lament the high cost of diagnosis
   B. to prove that any blood clot can eventually be diagnosed
   C. to describe the means of confirming a suspected diagnosis
   D. to reject the premise that all blood clots are fatal

10. According to the author, using clinical symptoms to diagnose pulmonary embolisms
    F. is cheaper and more time-effective than using high-tech machinery.
    G. should be done cautiously and in conjunction with other tests.
    H. may be done only in the least-acute cases.
    J. cannot be done routinely on all patients.

Go on to next page

Passage 2

Prose Fiction

(From *Nicholas Nickleby* by Charles Dickens)

This was a young lady who could be scarcely eighteen, of very slight and delicate figure, but exquisitely shaped, who, walking timidly up to the desk, made an inquiry, in a very low tone of voice, relative to some situation as governess, or companion to a lady. She raised her veil, for an instant, while she preferred the inquiry, and disclosed a countenance of most uncommon beauty, though shaded by a cloud of sadness, which, in one so young, was doubly remarkable. Having received a card of reference to some person on the books, she made the usual acknowledgment, and glided away.

She was neatly, but very quietly attired; so much so, indeed, that it seemed as though her dress, if it had been worn by one who imparted fewer graces of her own to it, might have looked poor and shabby. Her attendant — for she had one — was a red-faced, round-eyed slovenly girl, who, from a certain roughness about the bare arms that peeped from under her draggled shawl, and the half-washed-out-traces of smut and blacklead which tattooed her countenance, was clearly of a kin with the servant-of-all-work on the farm: between whom and herself there had passed various grins and glances, indicative of the freemasonry of the craft.

The girl followed her mistress; and before Nicholas had recovered from the first effect of his surprise and admiration, the young lady was gone. It is not a matter of such utter improbability as some sober people may think, that he would have followed them out, had he not been restrained by what passed between the fat lady and her bookkeeper.

"When is she coming again, Tom?" asked the fat lady.

"Tomorrow morning," replied Tom, mending his pen.

"Where have you sent her to?" asked the fat lady.

"Mrs. Clark's," replied Tom.

"She'll have a nice life of it, if she goes there," observed the fat lady, taking a pinch of snuff from a tin box.

Tom made no other reply than thrusting his tongue into his cheek, and pointing the feather of his pen towards Nicholas — reminders which elicited from the fat lady an inquiry of, "Now, sir, what can we do for you?"

Nicholas briefly replied, that he wanted to know whether there was any such post to be had, as secretary or amanuensis to a gentleman.

"Any such!" rejoined the mistress; "a dozen such. An't there, Tom?"

"I should think so," answered that young gentleman; and as he said it, he winked towards Nicholas with a degree of familiarity which he, no doubt, intended for a rather flattering compliment, but with which Nicholas was most ungratefully disgusted.

Upon reference to the book, it appeared that the dozen secretaryships had dwindled down to one. Mr. Gregsbury, of Manchester Buildings, Westminster, wanted a young man, to keep his papers and correspondence in order; and Nicholas was exactly the sort of young man that Mr. Gregsbury wanted.

"I don't know what the terms are, as he said he'd settle them himself with the party," observed the fat lady; "but they must be pretty good ones, because he's a member of Parliament."

Inexperienced as he was, Nicholas did not feel quite assured in the face of this reasoning, or the justice of this conclusion; but without troubling himself to question it, he took down the address, and resolved to wait upon Mr. Gregsbury without delay.

"I don't know what the number is, "said Tom, "but Manchester Buildings isn't a large place; and if the worst comes to worst, it won't take you very long to knock at all the doors on both sides of the way till you find him out. I say, what a good-looking girl that was, wasn't she?"

"What girl?" demanded Nicholas sternly.

"Oh yes. I know — what gal, eh?" whispered Tom, shutting one eye, and cocking his chin in the air. "You didn't see her, you didn't — I say, don't you wish you was me, when she comes tomorrow morning?"

Nicholas looked at the ugly clerk, as if he had a
(90) mind to reward his admiration of the young lady by
beating the ledger about his ears, but he refrained
and strode haughtily out of the office; setting at
defiance, in his indignation, those ancient laws of
chivalry, which not only made it proper and lawful
(95) for all good knights to hear the praise of the ladies
to whom they were devoted, but rendered it incumbent upon them to roam about the world, and
knock on the head all such matter-of-fact and unpoetical characters, as declined to exalt, above all the
(100) earth, damsels whom they had never chanced to
look upon or hear of — as if that were any excuse!

11. Which of the following is the best way of rewriting the expression "preferred the inquiry" (line 7) without changing the author's original meaning?
   A. liked one question better than another
   B. asked the question
   C. recommended one specific question
   D. answered a question

12. The author probably chose the word "glided" in line 12 to
   F. create a feeling of subterfuge and cunning on the part of the young woman.
   G. show how unusual the young woman's conduct was in a person so young.
   H. make the reader feel the young woman's shyness and quietness, or grace.
   J. indicate the speed with which the entire transaction took place.

13. The first sentence in the second paragraph
   A. demonstrates a bias towards brighter clothing.
   B. expresses contempt and scorn at the girl's unfashionable attire.
   C. contrasts the quality of the clothing with the shabbiness of the surroundings.
   D. indicates that the author believes that "the woman makes the clothes," rather than "the clothes make the woman."

14. Which of the following is another way to express the author's statement, ". . . was clearly of a kin with the servant-of-all-work on the farm . . ." (lines 22 and 23)?
   F. held the same status as the farm servant
   G. was obviously a relative of the farm servant
   H. had previously worked as a laborer on a farm
   J. was trying to better her position in life

15. The statement that "It is not a matter of such utter improbability as some sober people may think . . . " (lines 29–31) means that
   A. the narrator was intoxicated at the time this event occurred.
   B. the event was obviously inevitable.
   C. it would not be as surprising or as unexpected as some people might think
   D. it is completely impossible.

16. The conversation between Tom and the fat lady about the young woman's coming again tomorrow (lines 34–43) indicates that
   F. the girl comes to the office every day as part of her routine.
   G. the girl will probably not enjoy the post to which she was sent.
   H. the girl will begin working for Tom and the fat lady the next day.
   J. the girl wants to see the narrator again.

17. "'I should think so,' answered that young gentleman, and as he said it, he winked towards Nicholas with a degree of familiarity which he, no doubt, intended for a rather flattering compliment . . ." (lines 54–57). The author implies by this statement
   A. that Tom and Nicholas are friends.
   B. that Tom recognized and approved of Nicholas's interest in the young woman who had just left.
   C. that Tom meant to imply that Nicholas was such a man that his services would be greatly valued.
   D. that the young gentleman knew that the fat lady was going to cheat Nicholas.

18. The fat lady's comments about Mr. Gregsbury's being a member of Parliament (lines 67–70)
   F. are meant to reassure Nicholas as to the superiority of the position offered.
   G. are untrue.
   H. are intended to demonstrate the high-class clientele of which the fat lady boasts.
   J. are given as an excuse for her having but the one listing.

Go on to next page →

19. In the context of the passage, "to wait upon" (line 75) means

A. to be delayed by.
B. to visit.
C. to serve.
D. to doubt.

20. Which of the following most closely captures the meaning of the last paragraph of the passage?

F. Nicholas and the clerk both chivalrously agreed that the young woman was beautiful and were determined to fight each other for her affections.
G. Nicholas was insulted that the clerk would think that he, Nicholas, would be interested in a woman as obviously low class as the young lady.
H. Nicholas had a duty to defend the young woman against what he perceived as slurs upon her character made by the clerk.
J. The clerk had motivated Nicholas to forget the job and go seek the young woman in order to tell her of his feelings toward her.

Passage 3

Natural Science

Tales abound of the large snake of Trinidad, Surinam, and Bolivia known as the bushmaster. The bushmaster, found primarily in South and Central America, is the largest venomous (poisonous) (05) snake in the New World. The names of this snake tell much about it. The Latin name of the bushmaster is Lachesis muta. The Lachesis comes from Greek mythology, and refers to one of the three Fates. The Greeks believed that the Fates were (10) women who determined how long the "string" of a person's life would be. When the Fates cut the string, the person's life would cease. The bite of the Lachesis muta, the bushmaster snake, can indeed kill. It has been known to kill even humans (15) (although the actual death or injury may come from the bacteria on the snake's fangs, rather than from the venom itself). The muta part of the name is similar to our common word mute, and derives from the fact that although the snake shakes its tail — as (20) does the rattlesnake, to which it is related — when it senses danger, because there are no rattles on the bushmaster's tail, no noise is made.

A second name for the bushmaster is concha pita, meaning pineapple tail. This name reflects the (25) fact that the snake is covered in raised scales. The bushmaster can vary in color (most frequently in shades of brown), but is often tan with dark brown markings in the shape of diamonds. The snake's coloring serves as an excellent camouflage in the forests where it lies. Bushmasters are usually soli- (30) tary animals, coming together only during breeding. After breeding, the bushmaster female lays up to 12 eggs in a group called a clutch. While the eggs are in the clutch, the bushmaster exhibits a strong maternal instinct, coiling around and protecting the (35) eggs. This maternal instinct is quite rare among reptiles. When the eggs hatch — usually in two to three months — the young are immediately capable of survival on their own.

The bushmaster is a type of pit viper. The "pit" (40) in the snake's name comes from the fact that it has a hollow pit close to the eye. The pit is covered by skin to protect it. The purpose of the pit is to sense heat. The heat is given off by the bushmaster's prey, which consists of warm-blooded animals. The (45) most common prey of the pit viper is a rodent. Usually, a viper will bite its prey, then retreat, letting the venom do the actual killing of the smaller animal. Should the animal wander away during its death throes, the bushmaster can follow the (50) animal's scent to find it later. Some bushmasters, however, bite their prey, then hold their fangs in the animal, often lifting it off the ground. Bushmasters

can patiently stalk their prey, hiding under the
(55) leaves or trees of the forest and waiting for the prey to pass. For this reason, some scientists refer to bushmasters as ambush predators.

The bushmaster itself has few enemies. Some larger species of snakes that are not susceptible to
(60) the pit viper's venom, such as certain constrictors, can feed on the bushmaster. And like all snakes, the bushmaster may be attacked by the large birds of prey. However, in the final analysis, the greatest foe of the snake is encroaching civilization. More and
(65) more of the animal's habitat — forests that until recently were considered remote and uninhabitable by humans — is being cleared. The bushmaster, while not an endangered species, is undergoing an alarming decline in numbers.

(70) Some think that the bushmaster's reputation for ferocity is misplaced. True, the animal is daunting by its sheer size. Some can reach lengths of 12 feet. However, except when hunting or attempting to breed, bushmasters are relatively placid, unag-
(75) gressive creatures. Most of the injuries reported from bushmasters occurred when hikers accidentally stepped on drowsing snakes (whose coloration and silent warning system rarely alert humans to the snake's presence). They are noctur-
(80) nal, and thus more aggressive at night than in the daytime.

21. The primary purpose of the passage is to
   A. explain why bushmaster snakes are the most poisonous snakes in the world
   B. distinguish between the truths and myths regarding the bushmaster snake
   C. suggest ways to use the bushmaster snakes to benefit mankind
   D. explain the origins of the bushmaster's name

22. Which of the following best describes the question that remains unanswered in the passage?
   F. Why is the snake colored the way it is?
   G. What is the purpose of the pits in the viper's head?
   H. What does the bushmaster eat?
   J. How does a bushmaster attract its mate?

23. According to the passage, which of the following characteristics of a bushmaster is rare among reptiles?
   A. the pits around its head
   B. the number of eggs it lays in one clutch
   C. its maternal instincts
   D. the lack of rattles on its tail

24. It can be inferred from the passage that
   F. the bushmaster is not the world's largest venomous snake
   G. the bushmasters have more brightly colored skins in the tropics
   H. a bushmaster attacks only when threatened
   J. because the central American rainforests are being threatened, the bushmaster is an endangered species

25. Which of the following is the reason the bushmaster is called an ambush predator?
   A. It lives primarily in bushes in the Amazon.
   B. It hides from its prey and then attacks it secretly.
   C. It attacks only smaller animals.
   D. It feeds off only live flesh, not carrion.

26. Which of the following does the author mean in lines 70–71 by stating that "the bushmaster's reputation for ferocity is misplaced"?
   F. The bushmaster is fierce only when outside of its normal habitat.
   G. The bushmaster is becoming more and more fierce because it is endangered.
   H. People are wrong in considering the bushmaster fierce.
   J. People fear the bushmaster.

27. Which of the following is most reasonable to infer from the second to last paragraph?
   A. Bushmasters may become endangered soon.
   B. Bushmasters' venom is not deadly to any birds.
   C. Bushmasters' venom is not deadly to humans.
   D. Bushmasters cannot survive.

28. The passage suggests that the reason hikers are more frequently attacked by bushmasters is
   F. hikers disturb the snakes at sleep
   G. hikers enter the territories most fiercely defended by the snakes
   H. hikers disturb the snake's breeding grounds
   J. snakes are out more in the night than in the daytime

Go on to next page

29. The main point of the last paragraph is that
- A. bushmasters sleep during the day
- B. bushmasters will attack to protect their young and their food
- C. bushmasters are quiet and hard to detect
- D. bushmasters are not as aggressive as some people believe

30. Which of the following questions is NOT answered in the passage?
- F. Who are the primary enemies of the bushmaster?
- G. How does a bushmaster locate its prey?
- H. Why is the bushmaster considered aggressive?
- J. Why is a bushmaster's maternal instinct stronger than that of other snakes?

Passage 4

Social Science

Line Symbolism in architecture is often overlooked by those who simply enjoy the beauty of the buildings. The United States Capitol is one such example of a building that is rarely examined more than
(05) superficially, yet has a wealth of symbols of interest to the American people. Starting off with one small wing in 1800, the Capitol has been the site of the inauguration of most of the presidents since Thomas Jefferson in 1801. Abraham Lincoln's
(10) inaugural took place under scaffolding of increased construction in 1861. During Lincoln's term, he responded to critics who complained about the cost of the construction by saying that the Capitol is a symbol of the unity of the nation, and that
(15) "if people see the Capitol going on, it is a sign we intend the Union shall go on." Lincoln may be said to have begun and ended his presidency in the Capitol: His body lay in state in the Rotunda after his 1865 assassination.

(20) Farmers are symbolically represented by the products depicted on columns in the original Senate wing, including corn and tobacco. (One ponders the fact that the sculptors hired to create such American symbols came from abroad.) Of course,
(25) some architectural items are more overt than symbolic, such as the Statue of Freedom that is atop the Capitol dome. On the base of the statue is incised "E Pluribus Unum," which is Latin for "Out of many, one," and is also found on the Great Seal of the
(30) United States.

In 1814, the British, fighting the war of 1812, captured Washington and set fire to most of its buildings, including the Capitol. While there was much damage inflicted upon the building, including
(35) the gutting of the interiors and the scarring of exteriors, there was not complete destruction during the conflagration because of a fortuitous rainstorm that hit Washington that evening. It was followed the next day by a windstorm that killed British
(40) officers and set off gunpowder explosions and destroyed houses. The British officers decided to retreat and the Capitol was spared.

One of the most striking features of the Capitol is its collection of artworks. Most tell a story about American history; some also present interesting
(45) facts about their artists. Samuel Morse, before he invented the telegraph for which he is best known, was a painter. He painted a night session of the House that featured each individual member, having painstakingly convinced each member to sit
(50) for him in order that he could get the likeness correct. A painting of the Marquis de Lafayette (who, incidentally, was the first foreign visitor to speak before a Joint Meeting of Congress) hangs in the House. Paintings trace the expansion of the country
(55) as well. An Emanuel Leutze 1862 painting called "Westward the Course of Empire takes Its Way" showed pioneers crossing a divide. And it's not just paintings that portray American history. A Thomas Crawford bronze door shows Washington saying
(60) goodbye in New York to his officers. The frieze on the Rotunda depicts William Penn's treaty with the Indians. Statues abound, including, perhaps surprisingly, one of a Confederate general, Floridian Edmund Kirby Smith. Women are remembered as
(65) well. Amusingly nicknamed "Women in a Bathtub," an eight-ton block of marble honors a trio of suffragettes: Elizabeth Cady Stanton, Susan B. Anthony, and Lucretia Mott. Also found are statues of Ethan Allen, the Revolutionary War hero from Vermont,
(70) Robert Fulton, the creator of the steamboat, and John Gorrie, M.D., a physician who patented the first ice-cream making machine in 1851, in an attempt to find something to cool down his fevered patients.
(75)

31. The primary point of the first paragraph is
- A. Presidents are usually sworn into office on the steps of the Capitol.
- B. The Capitol is over 200 years old.
- C. The Capitol holds much symbolism for Americans.
- D. A beautiful building cannot truly be appreciated unless one understands its symbolism.

32. What did the author mean by saying that Lincoln ended his presidency in the Capitol?
    F. Lincoln said goodbye to his party members on the steps of the Capitol.
    G. Lincoln was involved in a scandal in the Capitol that brought down his presidency.
    H. Lincoln's body was returned to the Capitol after he'd been shot.
    J. Lincoln used the Capitol, not the White House, as his office of the Presidency.

33. Which of the following would the author most probably use to describe the fact that American symbols found in the Capitol were sculpted by foreign artists?
    A. irony
    B. ingenuity
    C. perspicacity
    D. pride

34. As it is used in line 25, the word "overt" most nearly means
    F. large
    G. obvious
    H. mysterious
    J. artistic

35. In line 37, "conflagration" most nearly means
    A. rainstorm
    B. evening
    C. bombing
    D. fire

36. Which of the following may best be implied by paragraph three?
    F. American forces were superior to British forces of the time.
    G. The British were too superstitious to fight after the occurrences that seemed to favor the American cause.
    H. The Capitol was completely destroyed by the British and had to be rebuilt.
    J. The Capitol was saved from destruction by natural forces.

37. According to the passage, one function of the art in the Capitol is
    A. to support and finance American art classes
    B. to provide physical proof to Americans of the use of their tax dollars
    C. to portray American history
    D. to put on public display various artworks presented to the President and Congress over the years

38. The passage answers all of the following questions EXCEPT
    F. How did the sculpture "Women in a Bathtub" get its nickname?
    G. What does *E Pluribus Unum* mean?
    H. Who was the first foreign citizen to speak before a joint session of Congress?
    J. Other than paintings, what type of artwork is found in the Capitol?

39. It is reasonable to infer that the author uses the phrase "perhaps surprisingly" in lines 63–64 to imply
    A. one wouldn't expect a tribute to a former enemy in the Capitol
    B. one wouldn't expect a Southerner to be honored in the North
    C. most statues are of civilians, not military people
    D. most statues are of more famous people, not a relatively unknown general

40. Which of the following was most probably the author's reason for listing all the people portrayed in statues in the Capitol?
    F. to prove that there is an equal representation of men and women
    G. to signify the different types of artworks found in the building
    H. to demonstrate the variety of people who have contributed to America
    J. to provide a touch of comic relief

Science Reasoning Test

35 Minutes — 40 Questions

DIRECTIONS: Following are seven passages and then questions that refer to each passage. Choose the best answer and blacken in the corresponding oval on your answer grid.

Passage 1

The amount of moisture in the air is designated as humidity. Weather reports typically present relative humidity, the percentage of the maximum amount of moisture the air can contain that is currently in the air. Air can contain more moisture at higher temperatures than at lower temperatures.

Relative humidity can be measured by comparing the temperature reading on a wet-bulb thermometer with the reading on a dry-bulb thermometer. Less humid air causes more moisture to evaporate from the wet bulb, thus lowering the temperature reading. Table 1 shows the relative humidity that is calculated at various air temperatures (dry-bulb) as a function of the difference between the wet-bulb and dry-bulb readings.

Table 1	\multicolumn{10}{c}{Difference Between Wet-Bulb and Dry-Bulb Reading (°C)}
Dry-Bulb Reading (°C)	1	2	3	4	5	6	7	8	9	10
0	81	64	46	29	13					
2	84	68	52	37	22	7				
4	85	71	57	43	29	16				
6	86	73	60	48	35	24	11			
8	87	75	63	51	49	29	19	8		
10	88	77	66	55	44	34	24	15	6	
12	89	78	68	58	48	39	29	21	12	
14	90	79	70	60	51	42	34	26	18	10
16	90	81	71	63	54	46	38	30	23	15
18	91	82	73	65	57	49	41	34	27	20
20	91	83	74	66	59	51	44	37	31	24
22	92	83	76	68	61	54	47	40	34	28
24	92	84	77	69	62	56	49	43	37	31
26	92	85	78	71	64	58	51	46	40	34
28	93	85	78	72	65	59	53	48	42	37
30	93	86	79	73	67	61	55	50	44	39

Humid air feels warmer to a human than does dry air at the same temperature because the moisture in the air makes it harder for the human body to cool itself by evaporating water from its body. Table 2 shows what various temperatures feel like to a typical human at different relative humidities.

Go on to next page

Table 2	Relationship Between Relative Humidity and Apparent Temperature (°C)										
	Air Temperature (°C)										
	21.1	23.9	26.7	29.4	32.2	35.0	37.8	40.6	43.3	46.1	48.9
Relative Humidity	Apparent Temperature (°C)										
0%	17.8	20.6	22.8	25.6	28.3	30.6	32.8	35.0	37.2	39.4	41.7
10%	18.3	21.1	23.9	26.1	29.4	32.2	35.0	37.8	40.6	43.9	46.7
20%	18.9	22.2	25.0	27.8	30.6	33.9	37.2	40.6	44.4	48.9	54.4
30%	19.4	22.8	25.6	28.9	32.2	35.6	40.0	45.0	50.6	57.2	64.4
40%	20.0	23.3	26.1	30.0	33.9	38.3	43.3	50.6	58.3	66.1	
50%	20.6	23.9	27.2	31.1	35.6	41.7	48.9	57.2	65.6		
60%	21.1	24.4	27.8	32.2	37.8	45.6	55.6	65.0			
70%	21.1	25.0	29.4	33.9	41.1	51.1	62.2				
80%	21.7	25.6	30.0	36.1	45.0	57.8					
90%	21.7	26.1	31.1	38.9	50.0						
100%	22.2	26.7	32.8	42.2							

1. Which of the following is the best estimate of the apparent temperature when the air temperature is 35.0°C and the relative humidity is 75%?
   A. 51.6
   B. 54.0
   C. 56.9
   D. 57.3

2. Which of the following statements about the relationship between air temperature and apparent temperature is true?
   F. As air temperature increases, the relative humidity that produces an equivalent apparent temperature increases.
   G. As air temperature increases, the relative humidity that produces an equivalent apparent temperature remains constant.
   H. As air temperature increases, the relative humidity that produces an equivalent apparent temperature decreases.
   J. There is no relationship between air temperature and equivalent apparent temperature.

3. When the dry-bulb reading is 12°C, what is the wet-bulb reading, in °C, when the relative humidity is 78%?
   A. 2
   B. 10
   C. 12
   D. 14

4. The dry-bulb reading is the same as the air temperature. For a dry-bulb reading of 24°C and wet-bulb reading that is 4 degrees different, which of the following is the approximate apparent temperature in °C?
   F. 20
   G. 25
   H. 28
   J. 69

5. According to Table 1, under which of the following conditions is the amount of moisture in the area the least?
   A. Dry-bulb reading of 0°C; wet-bulb reading 4°C different
   B. Dry-bulb reading of 8°C; wet-bulb reading 6°C different
   C. Dry-bulb reading of 16°C; wet-bulb reading 8°C different
   D. Dry-bulb reading of 24°C; wet-bulb reading 10°C different

Go on to next page

Passage 2

A pharmaceutical company has developed a new drug for treating hay fever. It claims that the new drug causes less drowsiness than the current best-selling brand. To test this claim, the company ran the following three studies.

Study 1

Subjects were asked to perform a motor coordination task that requires a high degree of alertness. Subjects who made fewer errors were judged to be less drowsy. Eight subjects were given a standard dosage of the new drug, and eight other subjects were given a standard dosage of the old drug. Four persons of each group of eight were tested one hour after ingesting the drug while the other four persons were tested eight hours after ingesting the drug. Realizing that drug effects often depend on a subject's weight, the researchers weighed each subject who participated in the study. The number of errors and weights for each subject are presented in Table 1.

Table 1 Number of Errors on Coordination Task After Ingesting Drug

Old Drug

One hour after ingestion			Eight hours after ingestion		
Subject	Errors	Weight (kg)	Subject	Errors	Weight (kg)
1	38	75	5	37	71
2	52	55	6	33	73
3	44	70	7	52	53
4	57	54	8	45	55
Average	47.75		Average	41.75	

New Drug

One hour after ingestion			Eight hours after ingestion		
Subject	Errors	Weight (kg)	Subject	Errors	Weight (kg)
9	30	73	13	32	70
10	49	53	14	52	50
11	42	55	15	46	51
12	34	70	16	35	71
Average	38.75		Average	41.25	

Study 2

After observing a wide range in the number of errors made by the subjects, the researchers repeated Study 1 but restricted the study to males who weighed 72 kilograms (kg). The results of this study appear in Table 2.

Table 2 Coordination Task Errors for 72-kg Males

Old Drug

One hour after ingestion		Eight hours after ingestion	
Subject	Errors	Subject	Errors
1	39	5	33
2	44	6	36
3	42	7	34
4	40	8	36
Average	41.25	Average	34.75

New Drug

One hour after ingestion		Eight hours after ingestion	
Subject	Errors	Subject	Errors
9	30	13	31
10	31	14	31
11	34	15	29
12	34	16	32
Average	32.25	Average	30.75

Go on to next page

Study 3

This study was identical to Study 2 except that 54-kg females were used. The results of this study are shown in Table 3.

Table 3 — Coordination Task Errors for 54-kg Females

Old Drug

One hour after ingestion		Eight hours after ingestion	
Subject	Errors	Subject	Errors
1	54	5	49
2	56	6	49
3	53	7	51
4	54	8	50
Average 54.25		Average 49.75	

New Drug

One hour after ingestion		Eight hours after ingestion	
Subject	Errors	Subject	Errors
9	44	13	47
10	48	14	48
11	44	15	46
12	46	16	48
Average 45.5		Average 47.25	

6. Which of the following is the most reasonable conclusion that can be made on the basis of Study 1?
   F. The new drug is more effective than the old drug one hour after ingestion but not eight hours after ingestion.
   G. Performance on the motor coordination task deteriorates as time after ingestion of the old drug increases.
   H. As compared to the old drug, the new drug improved the ability of experimental subjects to perform the motor coordination task.
   J. The new drug causes less drowsiness than the old drug one hour after ingestion but not eight hours after ingestion.

7. Which of the following best summarizes why the researchers conducted Studies 2 and 3?
   A. They wished to examine the effects of weight on drowsiness produced by the drug.
   B. They were interested in whether the drug would affect men and women differently.
   C. They wanted to eliminate a factor that caused variability in the results.
   D. Most people who suffer from hay fever weigh approximately what the subjects in those studies weighed.

8. In comparison to Study 1, what is a primary limitation of Study 2?
   F. Study 2 does not measure the effects of the drugs on females.
   G. Study 1 suggests that the new drug may be more effective for a variety of subjects.
   H. Study 1 shows that the new drug caused less drowsiness in a wider range of subjects.
   J. Study 2 produced results that were more difficult to interpret.

9. If Study 3 included a group that was tested two hours after ingesting the old drug, which of the following predictions for the average number of errors made by this group would be reasonable?
   I. 44
   II. 51
   III. 52
   IV. 56
   A. II only
   B. I and II only
   C. II, III, and IV only
   D. I, II, III, and IV

10. Suppose that further study revealed that the group of subjects given the old drug and tested at eight hours in Study 1 was, under normal conditions, particularly proficient at performing the motor coordination task. How would this finding affect the overall results of the study?

F. It would add evidence that the new drug causes less drowsiness than the old drug at eight hours after ingestion.
G. It would suggest that side effects associated with the old drug are more common eight hours after ingesting the drug than at only one hour after ingestion.
H. It would suggest that the new drug is more effective than the old drug at any time after ingestion.
J. It would require that the entire experiment be repeated with the same subjects being tested at both one hour and eight hours.

11. If later studies show that the new drug is at least as effective as the old drug in relieving hay fever and that the new drug produces no side effects other than drowsiness, would it be reasonable to recommend the new drug over the old drug to lightweight individuals suffering from hay fever?

A. Yes, but only if such individuals are given a lower dose than what was used in the current three studies.
B. Yes, because the evidence supports the claim that the new drug is at least as effective and produces less drowsiness.
C. No, because the individuals may operate dangerous machinery within eight hours after ingesting the drug.
D. No, because the new drug differs from the old system with regard to how it affects the immune system, which is responsible for hay fever.

Passage 3

A wide beach protects bluffs by spreading out the energy of waves and keeping them from eroding the soil and rocks that comprise the bluff (see Figure 1).

Figure 1: Simplified illustration of waves hitting a wide beach.

When water levels rise, bluffs are vulnerable to erosion because much of the beach is now underwater, and the bluffs now bear the brunt of the waves' force (see Figure 2).

Figure 2: Simplified illustration of waves hitting a bluff when water level rises above beach.

To gain a better understanding of how natural forces can affect future water levels and bluff erosion, scientists studied the relationship between some key meteorological factors and water depth (deeper water means a higher water level) near the shore of an inland lake.

Study 1

Scientists measured precipitation and lake depth over a 30-year period and plotted the average depth against annual precipitation, as shown in Figure 3.

Figure 3: The average depth against annual precipitation.

Go on to next page

Study 2

Because temperature affects water evaporation rate and a higher evaporation rate lowers water levels, scientists plotted the average depth against the mean annual temperature. This relationship is shown in Figure 4.

Figure 4: The average depth versus the mean annual temperature.

Study 3

Wind is another factor that affects water evaporation rate, so scientists plotted the average depth against wind speed, as shown in Figure 5.

Figure 5: The average depth versus wind speed.

12. Suppose that only 10 cm of precipitation occurs in one year. Which of the following is the most reasonable lake depth estimate for that year?
    F. 5.5 m
    G. between 5.0 m and 5.5 m
    H. less than 5.0 m
    J. 2.5 m

13. What is the most likely relationship between temperature and evaporation rate?
    A. When temperature increases, evaporation rate increases.
    B. When temperature increases, evaporation rate decreases.
    C. When temperature increases, evaporation rate is unaffected.
    D. When temperature decreases, evaporation rate increases.

14. After a year of low precipitation, high temperatures, and strong winds, the lake depth would probably be
    F. low.
    G. average.
    H. high.
    J. extremely high.

15. Are strong winds definitely good for the bluff?
    A. Yes, because strong winds tend to lower water levels and help stimulate plant growth.
    B. Yes, because strong winds deposit soil on the bluff and reduce soil fertility.
    C. No, because strong winds raise temperatures.
    D. No, because strong winds produce more powerful waves, which can crash into the bluff.

16. Which of the following is the dependent variable of the investigation?
    F. precipitation
    G. lake depth
    H. mean annual temperature
    J. wind speed

17. Without any additional information, which of the following would further knowledge of how weather affects the bluff?
    I. counting the number of homes built on the bluff
    II. investigating the feasibility of constructing a protective seawall
    III. measuring erosion as a result of precipitation, temperature, and wind speed
    IV. measuring the tides over the course of several years
    A. III only
    B. I and III only
    C. II and IV only
    D. II, III, and IV only

Passage 4

The use of gasoline is directly related to the number of pollutants, such as hydrocarbons, nitrous oxide, and carbon monoxide, present in the air. As a result, drivers should take steps to minimize their gasoline consumption. One way to reduce this consumption is to drive at slower speeds. Figure 1 shows how gasoline mileage is affected by freeway driving speeds.

Go on to next page

Chapter 19: How to Ruin a Perfectly Good Day, Part I: Practice Exam 1   217

Figure 1: Gas mileage as a function of speed.

18. Which of the following will produce the most pollutants on a 100-mile trip?
  F. a compact car driven at 50 mph
  G. a midsize car driven at 60 mph
  H. a full-size car driven at 50 mph
  J. a full-size car driven at 60 mph

19. You are in the desert with no gas in sight, and your gas gauge shows that you have very little gas left. Should you speed up to get to your destination?
  A. No, because you use more gas at a higher speed.
  B. No, because you need more time to find a gas station.
  C. Yes, because the desert has very little pollution.
  D. Yes, because your car operates for less time and, as a consequence, burns less gas.

20. A full-size car driven at 55 mph will get approximately how many miles per gallon?
  F. 23
  G. 25
  H. 32
  J. 37

21. On the basis of the graph, which of the following statements is the most reasonable regarding compact gas mileage at 25 mph?
  A. Gas mileage is about 40 miles per gallon.
  B. Gas mileage is about 50 miles per gallon because gas mileage increases eight miles per gallon for every 10 mph increase in speed.
  C. Gas mileage is about 80 miles per gallon because gas mileage doubles when speed is cut in half.
  D. Gas mileage can't be determined with any reasonable certainty because 25 mph is outside the range of numbers presented in the graph.

22. Which of the following graphs best represents the relationship between freeway speed and pollutants emitted?

F.

G.

H.

J.

Go on to next page

Passage 5

From stimulating the brains of patients undergoing neurosurgery, scientists have determined that a strip of the brain just in front of the central sulcus controls the motor neurons throughout the body. That is, this part of the brain controls the neurons that control the voluntary muscles. This motor area is illustrated in Figure 1.

Figure 1: Side view of the brain.

Further work has mapped out the specific parts of this motor area that control certain parts of the body. The regions of the left half of the brain, which controls the right side of the body, are illustrated in Figure 2. The right side of the brain, which controls the left side of the body and is not illustrated, shows a mirror image of the left side of the brain.

Figure 2: Simplified front view of left brain through motor area. Bands indicate region of brain that control stated part of body.

23. Which of the following is/are true regarding the organization of the motor area, shown in Figure 2?
    I. No systematic relationship exists between how the motor area is organized and how the body is organized.
    II. The sequence of controlling regions in the motor area is similar to the sequence of body parts.
    III. Some parts of the body are controlled by larger regions of the motor area than others.
    A. II only
    B. III only
    C. I and II only
    D. II and III only

24. From an inspection of Figure 2, which of the following areas involves the most complex coordination of muscles?
    F. Hip
    G. Shoulder
    H. Hand
    J. Brow

Right half   Left half

Figure 3: Sides are in reference to patient's right and left, not yours.

25. Damage to the part of the motor area marked in the above figure would most likely affect movement in which of the following areas of the body?
    A. Right lips
    B. Right knee
    C. Left knee
    D. Left jaw

26. The brain is organized so that related functions are under control of areas that are close to one another in the brain. Which of the following is the most likely location for the part of the brain that controls speech production?

    F. location F
    G. location G
    H. location H
    J. location J

27. Damage to the part of the motor area marked in Figure 4 will most likely affect
    A. vision.
    B. hearing.
    C. the ability to feel touching on the face.
    D. the ability to move facial muscles.

Left half

Figure 4: Left half of the brain.

Passage 6

Homing pigeons received their name because of their ability to find their way home even when they are hundreds of kilometers away. Scientists know that pigeons do not use visible landmarks to navigate, because the birds can find their way home even after they have been transported in a covered box and released in an unfamiliar area. Scientists have offered several explanations for this acute navigational ability. Following are two of these hypotheses.

Sun Compass

Pigeons use the sun as a compass to orient themselves. Evidence for this theory comes from an experiment in which pigeons were placed in a circular cage with identical food cups evenly spaced just outside the cage. After being trained to go to the cup due east of the cage's center, pigeons were observed to go to the same cup even after the cage was rotated and the background scenery was changed. Pigeons failed to go to the east cup when the skies were overcast or when the experimenters used mirrors to alter the apparent position of the sun.

The pigeons use their internal clocks in conjunction with the sun to find their way home. For example, if the internal clock of a pigeon indicates noon while the bird observes the sun about to set, the pigeon knows that it is far east of its home and

Go on to next page

flies west to get there. A northern hemisphere bird that is due south of home at noon sees that the sun is in the correct position as far as east and west are concerned but observes that the sun is higher in the sky than normal and therefore flies north to get home. Support for this mechanism comes from observing birds whose internal clocks have been experimentally shifted. Their orientation, with respect to the sun, is consistent with their internal clock, but because the clock is off, the pigeons fly in the wrong direction.

Magnetic Field

Pigeons do not rely on a sun-internal clock calculation to orient themselves. Clock-shifted birds are just as accurate and fast as normal birds at finding their way home on overcast days.

Disruptions in the magnetic field surrounding the birds, on the other hand, affect the birds' orientation under such conditions. When bar magnets are placed on pigeons, they fly in random directions on overcast days. Similar results were obtained when scientists used electrical wires to induce an electrical field in a particular direction. When the wires induced a magnetic field that pointed up through the birds' heads, the pigeons flew away from home. When the field pointed in the opposite direction, the birds flew toward home. These findings, along with the discovery that pigeons are capable of responding to a magnetic field much weaker than that of earth, indicate that pigeons use the earth's magnetic field for orientation.

28. According to the sun-compass hypothesis, how would the pigeons with the disrupted magnetic fields orient on a sunny day?
    F. They would fly in random directions.
    G. They would fly toward home.
    H. They would fly in a direction that is a compromise between the information provided by the magnetic field and the information provided by the sun.
    J. They would fly straight but in a direction away from home.

29. Scientists have found that large disturbances in the earth's magnetic field affect the pigeons' flight direction on sunny days. Which of the following is the most reasonable statement that can be made on the basis of this finding?
    A. The sun-compass hypothesis is false.
    B. Pigeons don't use the sun for orientation.
    C. The Earth's magnetic field is the only factor that affects pigeon navigation.
    D. The finding supports the magnetic-field hypothesis.

30. Which finding presented in the passage is consistent with the sun-compass hypothesis but inconsistent with the magnetic-field hypothesis?
    F. The caged pigeons don't fly to the right cup on overcast days.
    G. The clock-shifted pigeons fly the wrong way on a sunny day.
    H. The clock-shifted pigeons fly home on an overcast day.
    J. Magnetic-field disturbances affect pigeon navigation.

31. The author of the magnetic-field hypothesis assumes that
    A. pigeons with magnets are not affected by the mere presence of metal.
    B. magnets have absolutely no effect on pigeons on sunny days.
    C. no birds use internal clocks to navigate.
    D. pigeons do not use the sun to navigate.

32. According to the entire passage, which of the following statements are most reasonable to make regarding clock-shifted pigeons that are placed at their home?
    I. They will fly away from their home on a sunny day because the clock-sun calculation will indicate that they are away from home.
    II. They will stay home on a sunny day because they will recognize familiar landmarks.
    III. They will stay home on an overcast day because the magnetic field will indicate that they are home.
    F. I and II only
    G. I and III only
    H. II and III only
    J. I, II, and III

33. Some evidence indicates that homing pigeons can use barometric pressure to navigate. How does this evidence relate to the sun-compass and magnetic-field hypotheses?
    A. This evidence disproves both hypotheses.
    B. This evidence is inconsistent with both hypotheses.
    C. This evidence is consistent with the sun-compass hypothesis but inconsistent with the magnetic-field hypothesis.
    D. This evidence may be consistent with both hypotheses.

Go on to next page

34. Research shows that pigeons can orient to light that mimics conditions present on a partially overcast day in which blue sky is present but the sun's disk is blocked. If clock-shifted pigeons navigate home on such a day, which hypothesis is supported?

F. Sun-compass, because the pigeons responded correctly to the light.
G. Sun-compass, because the sun was blocked.
H. Magnetic-field, because the pigeons responded correctly to the light.
J. Magnetic-field, because the internal clock shift did not throw the birds off.

Passage 7

A typical chemical reaction can be represented A + B → AB. A and B are reactants that react to form product AB.

Chemists have measured the rate at which various products of reactions are formed and have found that the rate varies with the concentration of the reactants. For example, when the concentration of reactant A is doubled, the rate of formation of product AB may change, depending on the nature of the chemical reaction. The rate can remain the same, double, quadruple, or change in other ways. The concentration of reactant B affects the rate of product formation, but reactant B's effect can be different from that of reactant A. For example, you can have a reaction in which doubling the concentration of A doubles the rate of product formation, while doubling B's concentration quadruples the rate.

To learn more about the chemical reaction $H_3AsO_4 + 3I^- + 2H^+ \rightarrow H_3AsO_3 + I^{3-} + H_2O$, scientists ran a series of experiments to determine how the concentration of each reactant affects the rate of formation of the product H_3AsO_3.

Experiment 1

Scientists combined 0.01 moles of H_3AsO_4, 0.20 moles of I^-, and 0.10 moles of H^+ in a liter of solution. H_3AsO_3 was formed at the rate of 2.8 units. Scientists repeated the reaction three times, using different amounts of H_3AsO_4 each time. The results are summarized in Table 1.

Table 1 Results of Combining Chemicals

Concentration (moles/liter)

H_3AsO_4	I^-	H^+	Formation rate (rate units)
0.01	0.20	0.10	2.8
0.02	0.20	0.10	5.6
0.03	0.20	0.10	8.4
0.04	0.20	0.10	11.2

Experiment 2

This experiment was identical to Experiment 1 except that the scientists varied the concentration of I^- while holding the concentration of the other reactants constant. The results of these experimental trials are presented in Table 2.

Table 2 Results of Holding the Concentration of Other Reactants Constant

Concentration (moles/liter)

H_3AsO4	I^-	H^+	Formation rate (rate units)
0.01	0.20	0.10	2.8
0.01	0.40	0.10	5.6
0.01	0.60	0.10	8.4
0.01	0.80	0.10	11.2

Experiment 3

This experiment was identical to the other two, except that the concentration of H^+ was the one that varied. The results are presented in Table 3.

Table 3 Results of Varying H^+ Concentration

Concentration (moles/liter)

H_3AsO_4	I^-	H^+	Formation rate (rate units)
0.01	0.20	0.10	2.8
0.01	0.20	0.20	11.2
0.01	0.20	0.30	25.2
0.01	0.20	0.40	44.8

Go on to next page

35. A chemist must make as much H₃AsO₄ as possible in a minute. If she can change the concentration of only one reactant, which reactant should she choose?
    A. H₃AsO₄
    B. I⁻
    C. H⁺
    D. Any reactant

36. Why did the chemists vary the concentration of only one reactant at a time?
    F. Varying the concentration of more than one reactant causes a violent explosion.
    G. When the concentration of more than one reactant varies and the formation rate changes; how each reactant affects the formation rate is unclear.
    H. Measuring the concentration of more than one reactant at the same time is difficult.
    J. When the concentration of more than one reactant is varied, the amount of product formed is too great to make an accurate determination of the formation rate.

37. If the concentrations of H₃AsO₄, I⁻, and H⁺ are 0.02 moles/liter, 0.40 moles/liter, and 0.10 moles/liter, respectively, what is the formation rate?
    A. 2.8 rate units
    B. 5.6 rate units
    C. 8.4 rate units
    D. 11.2 rate units

38. If scientists combine 0.01 moles H₃AsO₄, 0.20 moles of I⁻, and 0.10 moles of H⁺ in two liters of solution instead of the one liter that was used in the first trial of each experiment, what happens to the formation rate?
    F. The formation rate decreases.
    G. The formation rate remains the same.
    H. The formation rate increases for a few seconds and then decreases.
    J. The formation rate increases.

39. If a fifth trial is performed in Experiment 3 at which 0.80 moles/liter of H⁺ are used and all other concentrations remain unchanged, what is the likely formation rate?
    A. 22.4 rate units
    B. 44.8 rate units
    C. 89.6 rate units
    D. 179.2 rate units

40. What happens to the formation rate of H₂O when the concentration of one or more reactant is increased?
    F. The formation rate decreases.
    G. The formation rate is zero.
    H. The formation rate remains the same.
    J. The formation rate increases.

STOP DO NOT TURN THE PAGE UNTIL TOLD TO DO SO.
DO NOT RETURN TO A PREVIOUS TEST.

Getting Down to the Nitty-Gritty: Subscores

Three of the tests of the ACT feature subscores as an added bonus (think of these as a "gift with purchase"). In 20-plus years of tutoring for the ACT (I started when I was a mere child, you see), few students have cared about the subscores. By the time you get through with this book, you should pretty much know which sections are your best and which are your weakest. However, you'll see subscores on your score report, so a few words about them are necessary.

English Test

The English Test has 40 questions in the Usage/Mechanics subscore area, and 35 questions in the Rhetorical Skills subscore area — a total of 75 questions. (See Chapter 5 for more info on the types of questions on the English Test.) Because I wrote these practice exams to give you more practice with the types of questions my experience shows students have the best chance of getting correct with practice, this breakdown isn't really applicable to the practice exams in this book. Besides, students get headaches trying to understand the fine distinctions between what is rhetorical and what is not. Don't worry about it.

Mathematics Test

The actual ACT Mathematics Test usually has 24 prealgebra/elementary algebra problems, 18 intermediate algebra/coordinate geometry problems, and 18 plane geometry/trig problems — a total of 60 questions. Good news! The ACT has only four trig questions, so if you haven't had the subject yet, don't panic!

However, because this book is a teaching book and not the actual ACT, I'm not going to put you through the trauma of subscores. Besides, there are many gray areas in which one person is convinced that a problem is elementary algebra but another argues it's intermediate algebra, or worse. Here's the simple solution: Be able to do all the problems (easy for me to say!), and don't worry about typecasting and labeling them.

Reading Test

The Reading Test subscores couldn't possibly be any easier. You get a subscore for questions in social studies/sciences (20 questions, based on two passages) and arts/literature (20 questions, based on two passages).

Science Reasoning Test

The Science Reasoning test has no subscores.

Score One for Our Side: The Scoring Key

The ACT scoring may be weird (Why a 36? Why not a 21 or a 49 or a 73?), but it is very straightforward. Follow the simple directions below to score your practice exam.

1. **Count the number of correct responses in each of the practice tests: English, Mathematics, Reading, and Science Reasoning (see the Answer Key at the end of this chapter).**

   Do NOT subtract any points for questions you missed or questions you didn't answer. Your score is based only on the number of questions you answered correctly. That number is called your *raw score*.

2. **Locate your raw score on the following table. Move to the left or right and find the *scaled score* that corresponds to your raw score.**

   For example, a raw score of 50 on the English Test gives you a scaled score of 21.

3. **Add your four scaled scores. Divide that sum by 4. The resulting number is your *composite score*.**

   For example, say that your scaled scores were 23, 31, 12, and 19; your composite score would be 85 ÷ 4 = 21.25 or 21.

		Raw Scores			
Scale Score	English	Mathematics	Reading	Science Reasoning	Scale Score
1	0–1	0	0	0	1
2	2	–	1	–	2
3	3	1	2	1	3
4	4–5	–	3	–	4
5	6–7	–	4	–	5
6	8–9	2	5	2	6
7	10–11	3	6	3	7
8	12–13	–	7	4	8
9	14–16	4	8	5	9
10	17–19	5	9	6	10
11	20–22	6–7	10	7	11
12	23–25	8	11–12	8–9	12
13	26–28	9–10	13	10	13
14	29–31	11–12	14	11–12	14
15	32–35	13–14	15	13–14	15
16	36–37	15–17	16	15	16
17	38–40	18–19	17	16–17	17
18	41–43	20–22	18–19	18–19	18
19	44–45	23–24	20	20–21	19
20	46–48	25–26	21	22	20
21	49–50	27–29	22	23–24	21
22	51–53	30–32	23	25	22
23	54–55	33–34	24	26–27	23
24	56–57	35–37	25	28	24
25	58–59	38–40	26–27	29	25
26	60–62	41–42	28	30	26
27	63–64	43–45	29	31	27
28	65–66	46–48	30	32	28
29	67	49–50	31	33	29
30	68–69	51–53	–	34	30
31	70	54–55	32	35	31
32	71–72	56	33	36	32
33	73	57	34	37	33
34	–	58	35	38	34
35	74	59	36	39	35
36	75	60	37–40	40	36

Answer Key

English Test

1. B		39. D	
2. J		40. J	
3. B		41. B	
4. H		42. G	
5. A		43. B	
6. J		44. F	
7. A		45. C	
8. G		46. J	
9. B		47. A	
10. F		48. J	
11. B		49. B	
12. F		50. J	
13. D		51. B	
14. F		52. J	
15. A		53. B	
16. G		54. H	
17. D		55. B	
18. H		56. J	
19. D		57. A	
20. G		58. G	
21. D		59. A	
22. F		60. H	
23. A		61. D	
24. F		62. F	
25. D		63. A	
26. H		64. H	
27. B		65. B	
28. G		66. H	
29. C		67. D	
30. H		68. G	
31. C		69. A	
32. J		70. G	
33. B		71. B	
34. J		72. J	
35. A		73. A	
36. J		74. G	
37. B		75. A	
38. F			

Mathematics Test

1. B	31. E
2. J	32. F
3. C	33. A
4. H	34. F
5. D	35. D
6. J	36. H
7. D	37. D
8. H	38. J
9. B	39. D
10. K	40. G
11. D	41. D
12. J	42. K
13. A	43. A
14. F	44. J
15. C	45. E
16. J	46. G
17. C	47. C
18. H	48. H
19. E	49. A
20. H	50. K
21. A	51. B
22. H	52. J
23. C	53. D
24. H	54. J
25. C	55. E
26. H	56. G
27. B	57. A
28. C	58. J
29. D	59. E
30. K	60. J

Reading Test

1. B	21. D
2. H	22. J
3. A	23. C
4. H	24. F
5. B	25. B
6. J	26. H
7. D	27. A
8. J	28. F
9. C	29. D
10. G	30. J
11. B	31. C
12. H	32. H
13. D	33. A
14. F	34. G
15. C	35. D
16. G	36. J
17. C	37. C
18. F	38. F
19. B	39. A
20. H	40. H

Science Reasoning Test

1. B	21. D
2. H	22. J
3. B	23. D
4. G	24. H
5. A	25. B
6. J	26. F
7. C	27. D
8. H	28. G
9. C	29. D
10. F	30. F
11. B	31. A
12. H	32. G
13. A	33. D
14. F	34. J
15. D	35. C
16. G	36. G
17. A	37. D
18. J	38. F
19. A	39. D
20. G	40. J

Chapter 20

Practice Exam 1: Answers and Explanations

*N*ow you've done it. You've completed the practice exam, checked your answers against the key, and found your score on the Raw Score chart.

Hang on! Invest another hour or so to go through this chapter, reading why one answer was correct and the others weren't. Along the way, you find zillions of tips and traps, valuable information that you can use when you face the Big One.

Keep in mind that any words marked *like this* are vocabulary words to add to your vocabulary list.

English Test

If you want highly technical explanations discussing the future pluperfect and subordinate subjunctive, you're in the wrong place. We've written these explanations for real people, not for grammarians. The explanations put things in terms of everyday speech, not textbook rules and regulations.

Passage 1

1. **B.** The easy way to choose between "me" and "I" is to ignore the other person. That is, read the sentence as, "My mother took I to the zoo." You would never say that; you would say, "My mother took me to the zoo." Choice D is incorrect because the other person needs to come before the "me."

2. **J.** The original has two subjects, the zoo and the it. Use only one. The pronoun *which* changes the second part of the sentence to a *subordinate clause* (one that can't stand on its own) and eliminates the run-on problem of choice G.

3. **B.** The original sentence is a *fragment,* an incomplete sentence. Use choice B to express a complete thought.

   Did you notice the dreaded word "being" in choice C? *Being* often indicates sloppy English; you need to be especially careful when you see this word, because it usually (not always) indicates a wrong answer.

4. **H.** *Among* compares more than two items; *between* compares exactly two. (As a way to remember this, note the *tw* in between and the *tw* in two.) Here, the sentence compares the giraffe and the zebra, two animals, requiring the word "between."

   If you chose J, you got careless and didn't reread the sentence with your answer inserted. This final step can catch awkward sentences and save you a lot of points.

5. **A.** This was a pretty hard question; pat yourself on the back if you got it right. *Latter* is an *-er* form, and compares two items. Here, the sentence compares just two animals, the giraffe and the zebra. The word *last* is an *-st* form and compares three or more items. (If you missed this question, flip to Chapter 4.)

6. **J.** The original sentence is a fragment, an incomplete sentence. It just hangs in the air, not expressing a completed thought. (You find yourself asking, "Well, what about the keeper?")

   Did you double-check the *-ing* verbs, "coming" and "noticing," in choices F, G, and H? Although not all *-ing* words are wrong, they are wrong often enough on this exam to make you very, very nervous. Always look suspiciously at *-ing* verbs.

7. **A.** A double negative is a positive in English, just as it is in math. "Not inappropriate" means "appropriate." From the rest of the passage, you learn that a name meaning "tallest of all" is appropriate, given that the giraffe is the tallest animal.

   In some other languages, such as Spanish, a double negative does not make a positive and may not change the meaning of the sentence (as the double negative in this example does). Those of you who speak languages other than English need to be especially careful not to make a mistake with double negatives.

8. **G.** If you chose F, you probably have what we call Smart Students Disease: You automatically, instinctively corrected the error in the sentence. Go back and look at the original, and you'll notice that it's missing the verb.

   If you find that you have a lot of NO CHANGE answers, you're probably suffering from this insidious disease (too many brain cells can be as big of a problem as too few!). If you have a few minutes left at the end of the section, go back and check all your NO CHANGE answers to be sure that you didn't correct the errors in your head but not on paper.

9. **B.** Always, always, always check what *it* refers to. In this case, *it* (singular) refers to the scientists (plural). You need to use a plural pronoun to refer to a plural noun: *they*. Choice C doesn't fit when reinserted into the sentence.

10. **F.** The correct formation is "from . . . to," not "from . . . and" or "between . . . to." Choice J changes the meaning of the sentence.

11. **B.** The word "being" is often wrong on this exam. The expression "being that" is very sloppy grammar. Use "which" to express the same thought. Choice D is the trap answer. Don't fall into the habit of choosing OMIT every time you see it. (Subconsciously, you may want to omit the whole darn exam, but that doesn't count!) Take a minute to reread how the sentence would work without the underlined portion.

12. **F.** *Well* is an adverb and answers the question "how?" How does the giraffe blend in? It blends in well. If you chose G, see Chapter 4 for information on *good* versus *well*. If you chose H or J, you changed the meaning of the sentence. A good general rule is to correct the error, and then get outta there. In other words, don't do any more work, or make any more changes, than absolutely necessary.

13. **D.** The sentence talks about how different the markings of giraffes are, which is the topic of the third paragraph.

    This type of question is considered by many students to be more like the Reading Test than English Usage. It requires you to go back and reread most of the passage. If you are rushed for time (and most of us are in this section), our suggestion is that you "guess and go," making a quick guess and hoping you can come back to think more about the problem later. (Be sure not to leave the answer entirely blank. **Remember:** The ACT has no penalty for wrong answers. Even a wild guess may be correct.)

14. **F.** The subject of the verb is "the theory," which is singular, requiring the singular verb *has*. If you thought that "markings" or "fingerprints" was the subject of the sentence, you missed the point.

15. **A.** The last paragraph talks about how unique the giraffes are, how their markings distinguish them from each other. Choices B and C are tricky. Yes, the last paragraph talks about how giraffes have different colors and blend in well with their surroundings, but it doesn't say anything about their evolving. Don't read too much into the paragraph. And choice D may be true, but just because a statement is true does not mean that it is the answer to that specific question.

Passage 2

16. G. The original sounds as if Mr. Haley were a magician who changed a person into a book! The sentence means to say that stories about people were put into a book. Choice H has the same problem as the original, converting people into books. Choice J makes absolutely no sense when inserted into the sentence.

17. D. This question should have been a very simple one. *Who's* means *who is,* as in, "Who's going to miss a question this easy?" The correct word is *whose,* which is the possessive of *who.* I want to know *whose* grammar skills are so weak he missed this question.

There is no such word as "whos'." The only place we can imagine that word is in the Dr. Seuss book, *Horton Hears a Who.* The plural of one Who, we suppose, would be two Whos, and they could own something. But if you find yourself thinking of Dr. Seuss stories in the middle of this exam, you're someone whose score is going to be a lot lower than that of someone who's concentrating on what he's doing.

18. H. The original sounds as though the early years were born in New York, when obviously it was Alex who was born there. When a sentence begins with a subordinate clause (a clause that can't stand by itself), the first noun or pronoun after the comma usually has to do the action of that clause. In this case, start the underlined portion with Alex, eliminating choices F and J. Choice G is tricky. It starts with Alex . . . , or does it? It actually starts with Alex's years, again sounding as if the years were born in New York. Also, choice G is passive voice — rarely preferable to the active voice.

19. D. The original is a sentence fragment, an incomplete sentence: The oldest of three sons. . . . Who was the oldest of three sons? The sentence is missing a subject. Predict that you need the second sentence to start with Alex, and you have the right answer quickly.

Choices B and (especially) C look good on their own, but when you plug them back into the sentence, they don't correct the error.

20. G. To many students, this question seems to be more like a Reading Test question than strictly a grammar question. The fact that Alex was the oldest of three sons doesn't mean much in the context of the passage. His brothers are never again mentioned, nor is it mentioned whether his family situation influenced him or his writing. In short, the line just dies. It goes nowhere. It can safely be eliminated because it doesn't do anything to spur on the writing in the passage.

21. D. The underlined portion does not fit with the rest of the paragraph, which discusses Alex's military career. Although the route Alex took to become a writer is discussed, his motivation is not.

22. F. The sentence is correct as written. Did you double-check that the first noun after the subordinate clause did the action of the clause? "Unchallenged by his daily routine in the U.S. Coast Guard, Haley. . . ." Haley is the one who was unchallenged. Often the first noun after the subordinate clause is wrong, making a nonsense sentence, such as, "When she was two, the fortune-teller predicted Ms. Ferraro would be president." Chances are, it was Ms. Ferraro who was two at the time of the prediction, not the fortune-teller. Rearrange the sentence to read, "When she was two, Ms. Ferraro was told. . . ."

23. A. "Eventually his articles were published" makes sense. The other answers change the meaning of the sentence. Did you note the correct spelling of "nonetheless" in choice D? Nonetheless is all one word. (Do you care? My best friend is so rabidly antispelling that she has a sign on her desk that says, "Misspellers of the world, untie!")

24. F. "Afforded him an opportunity" is a correct expression. Note that choice G would have been correct had it said "allowed" rather than "allow." Choices H and J would have been correct had the passage said "enabled him to gain an opportunity" or "gave him an opportunity." Be careful not to rewrite the answer choices, unconsciously supplying words that are not actually printed on the paper.

25. D. The traveling and the research were done at the same time, eliminating choice B. Choice C sounds as if the research did the traveling, whereas it was Mr. Haley who actually traveled. The original version is a *run-on sentence,* two sentences incorrectly joined. If you're confused by run-ons, go to Chapter 4 to discover the four ways to correct them.

26. H. The original sounds as though the ancestors went to a small village, whereas Mr. Haley went to the village. Choice G and choice J are incorrect because they are present tense. The research occurred in the past, requiring the past tense: took.

> Verb mistakes are among the most common errors in the English portion of the ACT. Verbs may be in the wrong number (singular versus plural) or the wrong tense. Always double-check the verb.

27. B. If you chose A, you read this too quickly. "After Haley . . . then he knew. . . ." You do not need both the word "after" and the word "then." Choice B eliminates the unnecessary "then."

> If two answer choices appear to be identical, one probably adds or deletes the critical word and is the correct answer choice. If you are confused, choose one of those two. (Always keep in mind: The ACT has no penalty for wrong answers. Feel free to guess anytime you're not sure of the correct answer.)

28. G. Do you remember the point tested with the formation "not only . . . but also"? The rule (covered in Chapter 4, in case you've forgotten) is that "not only" and "but also" must be in parallel positions in the sentence. In other words, if "not only" is in front of a noun, "but also" must be in front of a noun. This question is even a little trickier than that. "Not only" is in front of "the Haley family" which is the object, but "but also" is in front of "the story" which is the subject. Change this sentence to read as follows: was not only the saga . . . but also the story.

> You should have buzzers and alarms going off in your brain whenever you encounter one of the terrible twosomes. Diction questions, although not automatically wrong, need to be checked carefully. As I often say, "Sure, I'm paranoid . . . but am I paranoid enough?"

29. C. The passage gives an overview of Haley's history and how he came to write *Roots.* However, it doesn't analyze, or even mention, any other work. The reader gains no insight into Haley's ability, just into his background.

Passage 3

30. H. Verbs in a series must be in parallel, or similar form. You need to say, discuss . . . rule . . . dine.

> Verbs ending in *-ing* are often used incorrectly. Be very, very suspicious when you see one.

31. C. The original version is a sentence fragment, an incomplete sentence. Choice C makes the sentence logical and coherent. Choice B is grammatically correct, but is in the passive voice. In standard written English, the active voice is preferable (confused on these two? Flip to Chapter 4 and enlarge your brilliance). Choice B is put there to trap lazy students, who read until they find a "good enough" answer instead of reading all the choices and selecting the best one. Choice D would leave the sentence as a fragment.

Bonus trivia: Speaking of outer space, did you hear about the new restaurant on the moon? Great food, no atmosphere!

32. J. The original version is a run-on, two sentences incorrectly joined. A *comma splice* (two independent clauses or sentences joined by a comma) is too weak; use a semicolon instead. A semicolon is a kinder, gentler period, serving the same function. Choice G changes the correct its (possessive) to the incorrect it's (the contraction of "it is"). Choice H may have trapped you if you didn't invest the necessary few seconds to plug the answer choice back into the sentence. Choice H makes the sentence read, ". . . on its axis and also it is also . . ." saying "also" twice.

Chapter 20: Practice Exam 1: Answers and Explanations

33. **B.** The possessive form "its" is correct here; "it's" is the contraction of it is. (These and other commonly confused word duos are covered in excruciating detail in Chapter 4.) Choice C has the wrong form, "it's." Choice D, although using the correct form "its," changes the meaning of this sentence. Be careful not to change more than is necessary.

34. **J.** The word because is unnecessary and serves only to make the sentence longer and more confusing (and it's already pretty labyrinthine!).

   TIP: Rewrite the entire sentence in your mind to clarify what the author is trying to say. Then go to the answer choices and see which one best fits your own revision. Choice G says the same thing as the original, but in a more wordy way. Choice H makes no sense in the sentence.

35. **A.** The original is the best way of making the point. Choice C wouldn't work when reinserted into the sentence (don't forget to take that step). Choice B makes the sentence a fragment, an incomplete thought. Choice D is unnecessarily wordy.

36. **J.** The underlined portion states the same thought that was expressed in the previous sentence, and thus is unnecessary.

37. **B.** A comma indicates a pause, not a complete stop. Read the sentence aloud, and you'll notice that you pause for a second after "... of the earth itself," and then keep on the same thought. A semicolon is too strong, because it connects completely independent sentences (that is, each part before and after the semicolon must be able to stand alone as a complete sentence). A colon is incorrect, because it introduces a list of things to come. A period here would make what comes before it a fragment, an incomplete sentence.

38. **F.** The original is correct. When separating two sentences, the proper form is semicolon, coordinating conjunction (such as therefore and however), comma.

   TIP: If you're confused on this, go to Chapter 4. (Don't you wish you were like the ruler Sigismund who said the famous line that's quoted in all English classrooms: "I am the King of Rome and I am above grammar." When I was in high school, I named my dog Sigismund in the man's honor.)

39. **D.** The original version is a fragment, an incomplete sentence, as are choices B and C.

   TIP: The word "being" is often used incorrectly and needs to be looked at with extreme suspicion.

40. **J.** A good writer is concise and succinct. Always look at the shortest answer to see whether it can possibly fit. In this case, choices F, G, and H are redundant and unnecessarily wordy.

   TIP: The word "because" is often used incorrectly. The expression "the reason is because" is a typical redundancy.

41. **B.** "They" is a pronoun and must have an *antecedent,* a word it replaces. Who are they? We're not told, so we must have a noun. Choice C is too wordy. Choice D would make the sentence a fragment.

   TRAPS & TRICKS: Did you choose D automatically? Although I understand that, if you had your way, you'd omit the entire passage and all the answers, you, alas, are not in charge here. Omit is not correct every single time it appears; if you choose that answer, be sure to go back and see how the new sentence would read without the underlined portion.

42. **G.** The easiest way to clarify this portion is to make two separate sentences. Choice H is verbose. Choice J makes the sentence nonsense when inserted alone.

43. **B.** The passage discusses how time travel would require one to go backward in a spaceship to arrive at the same time. It doesn't state that time travel is impossible; if you chose answer A, you were expressing your own opinion. Choice C is probably a true statement, but is not the main idea of the passage.

Passage 4

Just because a statement is correct or is a fact, doesn't mean it's the answer to the question. "Lincoln is the capital of Nebraska" is a fact, but it doesn't answer this question. Choice D was mentioned briefly in the first paragraph, but is not the main idea of the entire passage.

44. **F.** The past tense, "have called," is correct in this sentence because the burrows were found previously. Choice G has an *-ing* word. As you probably remember, *-ing* words are often misused and abused in this portion of the exam. Choices J and H change the meaning of the sentence; they sound as if the scientists themselves were called "dirt corkscrews."

45. **C.** The correct expression is "since the time they were found," meaning from that time on. The other answers make no sense when reinserted into the sentence.

If you're running out of time (a definite possibility by this point in the exam), search for a one-word question like this. You can answer such a question very quickly. All questions count the same; it's logical to head for the short ones first.

46. **J.** Choices F and H are redundant: They both have "at that time" and "then." Choice G creates a clause without a noun: "There were at that time scientists thought. . . ." A *who* is missing.

Have you noticed how often the shortest answer is the correct answer? Although you can't automatically assume that the shortest answer is always correct, check it out carefully.

47. **A.** This question tests a little reading comprehension rather than pure grammar. The previous and the subsequent sentences make it clear that the passage is talking about corkscrew spirals or holes in the ground. Choices B and C make no sense when reinserted in the sentence. Choice D has no **antecedent** (the noun which the pronoun is replacing). What is "it"? Remember, *it* is one of the *Beware!* words that you were cautioned to examine carefully.

48. **J.** "But" and "however" serve the same function in this sentence. Both words are not needed; eliminate the underlined one. Choices G and H do not fit when reinserted into the sentence.

Are you remembering to reinsert your answer choices and reread the entire sentence? If not, you are probably falling for some traps.

49. **B.** The "been" is a form of "being," one of the *beware!* words, words that should immediately capture your attention. On this exam, "being" is frequently used incorrectly, as it is here. Usually, you can't substitute "been" for "is," "are," "was," or "were."

50. **J.** A simple comma suffices. A semicolon connects two independent clauses, clauses that can stand on their own. You would not say as a complete sentence, "But this predator probably followed a beaver home for supper and just stayed." The "but" usually indicates a subordinate clause that is preceded by a comma.

Are you about ready to enter a Clinic for the Terminally Confused? Don't worry about the terminology. Just know that a semicolon is much stronger than a comma. If you come to a dead stop when reading, use a semicolon. If you merely pause, use a comma.

51. **B.** The comma in this case is not strong enough to connect two independent sentences. Insert a period and a capital letter to make these separate sentences. Choice D is tempting, but it is unnecessarily verbose ("because in fact").

52. **J.** *Their* is the possessive. *There* is a place. (*Their* books are over *there*.) Because "their" is already possessive, you don't also need the possessive "burrow's." Choice G looks good alone, and it fits when inserted into the sentence; but it does not make sense with the rest of the passage.

Always be sure that your answer fits into the entire passage by checking everything, not just the new sentence; always check a few sentences before and after it.

Chapter 20: Practice Exam 1: Answers and Explanations 233

53. **B.** The correct conjugation of "lie" is: lie, lay, have lain. (Doesn't this make it easy? The past tense of lie is lay.) The verbs to lie and to lay are often tested. Be absolutely certain that you know the distinction between them (*lie* has no object; *lay* requires an object) and their conjugation. I discuss these verbs in more detail in Chapter 4.

54. **H.** *Extinct* means no longer in existence (you may feel about now that your brain is extinct). *Extant* means in existence, able to be seen. (No matter how many times you wish that the ACT would be extinct, it remains extant.) The sentence implies that the animals no longer exist. Eliminate choices F and G. Omitting the underlined portion (choice J) makes nonsense of the sentence.

Don't fall into the bad habit of choosing the OMIT answer every time that you see it. Be sure to reread the sentence that results when you omit the underlined words. Often, the resulting sentence makes no sense at all.

55. **B.** A colon usually introduces a list of items. (Rochelle told her boyfriend, "If you want us to stay together, you're going to have to get a few things straight: (1) I am not to be referred to as your 'hot momma'; (2) any jewelry you give me cannot come from the gumball machine; and (3) your mother is never again to call me by your former girlfriend's name.") Colons rarely connect separate sentences. Choices C and D change the meaning of the sentence.

Did you fall for the trap in Choice D? The meaning of "but most of the part" is very different from "however, for the most part." The expression *for the most part* simply means primarily or mostly. You might say, "I'm avoiding the traps for the most part, only missing one or two." "For the most part" is an idiomatic expression.

56. **J.** Did this question trap you? If so, you probably read only the underlined portion, not the context of the entire sentence. The original is redundant; it says the same thing twice — "nonstop, without interruption." *Nonstop* means *without interruption*. Use one or the other, not both.

57. **A.** The local events correspond to, or are indicated by, what is shown in the sedimentary record. *Reflect* has several meanings. Although the other answers discuss those alternate meanings, the original is one of the correct uses.

58. **G.** The passage was primarily about identifying animals based on their fossils. Choice F summarizes the first paragraph only, not the second. Choice H is much too broad; the passage was primarily about the fossils, not what the paleontologists did with them. Choice J is too specific. Extinction was only briefly mentioned in the second paragraph.

If you are running out of time and know that you won't get to the grammar, try a "reading comp" question at the end. To answer this question, for example, you merely had to skim what is actually a pretty short passage. (Careful! This advice does not mean that all "box" questions are short and easy to do. Distinguish this "content" question, which is easy to answer, from a "structure" question, such as number 59, which is both difficult and time-consuming.)

59. **A.** An ordering-the-sentences question is an excellent type of question to make a wild guess on. (Don't just skip it entirely. The ACT has no penalty for wrong answers, so guessing when you don't know the answer is always worthwhile.) Ordering-the-sentences questions take much more time than most other question types and are somewhat subjective. I have had students pound their fists on my table and scream at me, arguing that their construction of the paragraph was preferable to mine. You can argue 'til you're blue in the face, but the test-makers' interpretation is final.

If you decide to invest some time answering this type of question, start by identifying the topic or main sentence. It usually has an introductory tone, setting up the rest of the paragraph. Here, sentence 2, talking about changes in store, is a typical *beginning* or *topic* sentence. Knowing that sentence 2 is first enables you to eliminate choices B and C. You may be even more willing to guess, now that your odds are down to 50-50.

When you do an "ordering" question, try to identify the topic sentence and, if necessary, the last sentence. Doing so is usually much easier than arranging the more generic "filler" sentences in middle of the passage.

Passage 5

60. H. The Han Dynasty conquered the Vietnamese. Find the most succinct, concise way to say this.

Did you notice the *beware!* word *being?* Whenever you see that word, get very nervous. It is often used incorrectly throughout this exam.

If you chose J, you didn't read the sentence as a whole without the underlined portion. If you eliminate it, you see that the sentence makes no sense as written " . . . were conquered, forces of China's Han Dynasty." The Vietnamese themselves were not Chinese forces, but they were conquered by Chinese forces. Any time you choose to omit an underlined portion, go back and reread the new sentence to be sure that you haven't changed the meaning.

61. D. The Dynasty, or rule, lasted from 111 B.C. until A.D. 939. This is almost a reading comprehension question. Had you read the phrase "since A.D. 939" by itself, it would seem logical. You have to read the entire sentence (and often a few sentences above or below it) to choose the correct grammar.

62. F. If you look at the underlined portion by itself, it looks bizarre because it has two commas, before and after "that." However, the purpose of a comma is to express a pause or hesitation. Read this aloud, and you will see that the commas are correctly placed. Choices G and H have an *-ing* word, "reaching." Double-check all *-ing* words because they often introduce errors or unnecessarily clumsy sentences. Choice J has the wrong tense.

63. A. If you got this question correct, kudos to you! Normally, the word "however" is part of the construction that separates independent sentences. For example, "I was careful; however, I still missed the question." In this case, however, the commas do not separate independent sentences (if they did, they would be wrong), but simply pause, or make a parenthetical aside. Choice D changes the meaning of the sentence. Choice C is tempting, but it would turn the second sentence into a fragment: "And however for nearly two centuries contending families in the north and south struggled to control the powerless kings of the Le Dynasty." You may remember, from junior-high grammar, that you should not begin a sentence with the conjunction "and." Although that is a good idea in general, it is not a hard-and-fast rule. There may be a few times in which *and* can correctly begin a sentence. ("You told me you loved me!" she sobbed. "And I meant it when I said it!" he assured her.)

64. H. *Affect* with an *a* means touch or concern. "How does having your boyfriend flirt with another girl affect your relationship?" The idiomatic expression *in effect* means primarily or generally. The *effect* is the result of something. *In effect* means a situation, basically, has that result. "When I saw him flirting with his former girlfriend, I gave Leon his ring back, in effect ending our relationship." Choice J changes the meaning of the entire sentence. *Ineffective* means not skillful, not efficient. "Leon's efforts to win his girlfriend back were ineffective, even pathetic."

65. B. The original has a fragment, "Just a few kilometers above the demarcation line established at the 1954 Geneva Conference." This clause cannot stand on its own. Change the second "sentence" into a subordinate clause, tagging on the end of the previous sentence.

Choice D may have trapped you. A semicolon functions the same way that a period functions (by connecting two independent sentences). Choice C turns the sentence into a run-on — two sentences incorrectly joined.

66. H. If the word "but" weren't there, the original form would work: "Vietnam, having been reunited, soon fell prey. . . ." However, the word "but" (which is not underlined and therefore cannot be changed) requires the simple past tense, "was."

If you missed this question, you probably fell for the common trap of reading only the underlined portion and a small portion around it. Reading the entire sentence is critical.

Chapter 20: Practice Exam 1: Answers and Explanations

67. **D.** The word "while" turns the entire sentence into a subordinate clause, an incomplete sentence, a fragment. Eliminating "while" allows the sentence to stand alone. *While* is a good word to double-check each time that you encounter it. Subordinate terms such as "while," "although," and "despite" often (on this exam) begin sentence fragments.

68. **G.** Notice that this is an exception to the tip that *-ing* words are usually wrong. The original sounds as if France's purpose in imposing control gradually was in order to meet heavy resistance. The sense of the sentence indicates something entirely different. Choice H has an unnecessary "and." (I live by the motto, "When in doubt, leave it out." It's a good thing I'm a grammar teacher, not a surgeon!) Choice J has the wrong verb tense.

69. **A.** This question tests *its* (possessive) versus *it's* (it is). Here, "its" refers to the uprising, making the possessive correct. That narrows the answers down to A and D. "So" indicates a corresponding thought; "but" correctly indicates here a contrary thought.

70. **G.** *Adept* means skillful and is usually followed by at. (You're skillful or adept at taking the ACT.) *Adopt* means to take as one's own; *adopted from* means taken from. *Adapt* means to fit or adjust. You have to adapt to a new schedule in order to find time to study for the ACT.

71. **B.** Led is the past tense of lead. I led you right into a trap. The required word here is the noun, **lead,** meaning the front position. (Rudolph takes the lead when pulling Santa's sleigh.) Choice D has the wrong verb tense, turning the sentence into a fragment.

72. **J.** The original is a run-on. A mere comma is not strong enough to join independent clauses.

    If you chose G, you fell for the trap. A semicolon does join independent clauses, but "then went to China" (note that "he" is missing) is not an independent clause. Choice H is awkward (a common failing of *-ing* words) and isn't parallel. Choice J, by eliminating the "he," makes the second clause subordinate, correcting the run-on.

73. **A.** Choice B has the singular verb "was" with the plural subject "dissidents." Choice C sounds as if the dissidents were doing the imprisoning, rather than being imprisoned. Choice D turns the sentence into a fragment.

74. **G.** ACT passages are rarely negative; they don't ridicule or criticize. Eliminate choices F and H. Choice J is too specific. Ho Chi Minh was mentioned only in the last paragraph.

    The purpose of a passage is usually very broad and general: to introduce a topic, to give an overview, or to discuss or explain an idea. When in doubt (remember that the ACT has no penalty for guessing), choose the most generic answer.

75. **A.** The passage is about the various governments that Vietnam has had and the wars that put those governments in power. The next paragraph would continue the thought of the last paragraph, the paragraph that discussed the burgeoning anticolonial movement.

    Nothing in the passage even hints at nuclear weapons (choice B) or human rights (choice D). And even if Vietnam were industrialized (it's still primarily agrarian, although you don't have to know that to get this question correct), the passage does not discuss that topic.

Mathematics Test

1. **B.** Multiply 87 by .12 (which is the same as 12%) to get $10.44. Add that to the original 87, for a total of 97.44.

   There's a small shortcut you can take. Multiply 87 by 1.12, because that's the same as 112%, to get 97.44 immediately. You cut out one additional step.

2. J. This problem requires just simple subtraction and knowing that there are 3 feet in a yard. That means that 1½ yards is 3 feet + 1 foot or 4 feet, for a total of 48 inches. Subtract: 48 – 25 = 23; 23 – 10 = 13.

You could have eliminated choices H and K immediately. You are cutting off whole inches, not fractions. If you chose either H or K, you got confused on ⅓ of a yard (which is a foot) versus ⅓ of an inch.

3. C. The three friends averaged $50,000 each. That means their total was $150,000 (3 × 50,000 = 150,000). Make the equation: 150,000 = 40% Total, or 150,000 = .4T. Divide both sides through by what's next to the variable. 150,000/.4 = T. T = 375,000.

Were you looking for an answer like, "It cannot be determined" among the choices? If so, you were probably confused because you don't know exactly how much money each individual made. Maybe Debi made $100,000 and both Mike and Ken together made $50,000. It's irrelevant. The only important point is that three people together made $150,000.

4. H. One of the two parenthetical expressions must equal zero, because the product of zero and anything else is zero. That means that either $a = 5$ (because –5 + 5 = 0) or $a = 6$ (because 6 – 6 = 0).

Although this is an easy problem, it's also an easy problem to miss with a careless mistake. As soon as you see that the answer choices are "variations on a theme," with the positive and negative signs making all the difference, go back and double check that you didn't make a silly mistake.

5. D. If the office wants 100 calls a day for 12 days, it wants 1,200 calls (100 × 12 = 1,200). It has 480 calls (80 × 6 = 480). Subtract: 1,200 – 480 = 720.

If you chose E, you fell for the trap! The question does not ask how many calls per day the office receives, but how many calls altogether. Sure, if the office needs to have 720 calls in 6 days, that's 120 calls per day (720/6 = 120), but that's not what the question wants to know. *Remember:* The mere fact that the answer you got is staring you in the face does not mean that's the correct answer to the problem.

6. J. The key here is knowing that an integer is a whole number (for example, 1.5 is not an integer). If number sets are fuzzy in your memory, go back to the thrilling pages of Chapter 12. For F to be true, x would have to be 12, which is too large. For G to be true, x would have to be 4, which is too small. For H to be true, x would have to be 7.25, which is not an integer. For K to be true, x would have to be 4.5, which is both too small and not an integer. Only choice J works, because if $3x = 24$, $x = 8$.

7. D. The key here is math vocabulary (which is covered in Chapter 10). An *obtuse* angle is more than 90 degrees. (I always think of obtuse angles as obese angles, "fatter" than a 90-degree angle.) The interior angles of a triangle total 180 degrees. If one angle is greater than 90 degrees, the sum of the other two angles must be less than 90 degrees. An *acute* angle is greater than 0, but less than 90 degrees (think of it as "a cute" little angle). Each of the remaining two angles, therefore, must be acute.

8. H. An easy way to deal with percentages is to use the number 100. In this case, say that $(a + b) = 100$. Then 5% of 100 = 5. That means that 10% of b = 5. Solve for b: $.10b = 5$. Divide both sides through by what's next to the variable: $b = 5/.10 = 50$. If $a + b = 100$, then $a = 50$ and $a = b$.

Are you saying, "Yeah, but what if I plug in something besides 100? How do I know it works with other numbers? Okay, we'll prove it to you. Try plugging in another number. (If you want to make life harder, go ahead!) Choose something truly bizarre, like –37. Let $(a + b) = -37$. Then 5% of –37 = –1.85. If –1.85 = 10% of b, solve for b. $-1.85 = .1b$. Divide both sides through by what's next to the variable: $-1.85/.1 = -18.5$. $b = -18.5$. If $(a + b) = -37$, and $b = -18.5$, then $a = -18.5$ as well. Son of a gun, it works! (But the moral of the story is: Plug in 100 when dealing with percentages. Life is so much easier.)

9. B. The area of a square is side squared. In this case, that's 8^2, or 64. That means the area of the triangle is also 64. The area of a triangle is ½ base times height. In this case, that's ½x times x, or ½x^2. Make the equation: ½x^2 = 64. Multiply through by 2 to get rid of

Chapter 20: Practice Exam 1: Answers and Explanations 237

the fraction: $x^2 = 128$. Take the square root by simplifying: $\sqrt{128} = \sqrt{64} \times \sqrt{2}$. The square root of 64 = 8, giving you a final answer of $8\sqrt{2}$.

10. **K.** This problem can be solved very quickly if you recognize that 6, 8, and 10 is double the ratio of 3:4:5. A 3:4:5 ratio (a very common ratio), is for the sides of a 30:60:90 triangle. (This ratio is covered in Chapter 7.)

    Note that 30, 60, and 90 are all answer choices. If you chose G, you fell for the trap, thinking that the angle between the two shortest sides must be the smallest angle. Wrong. Draw a 30:60:90 triangle. The 3 (or in this case, the 6) side is opposite the 30-degree angle, but next to the 90. The 4 (or in this case, the 8) is opposite the 60 degree angle, but next to the 90. That means that the angle between the two smaller sides is 90 degrees.

11. **D.** If you chose answer A or answer E, you fell for a trap. Answer A caught careless students who thought, "The price rises 25% then falls ¼, or 25%, for a 0% change." Wrong. An easy way to solve a problem like this is to plug in 100 for the original price of the book. In 1998, the book cost $100. If the price rose by 25%, it went up $25 to a total of $125. In 2000, the price was ¼, or 25%, below its 1998 cost. That means that it was $25 below the original $100, or $75.

    Here's where the trap comes in. Reading the question carefully tells you that you want to know the percent decrease from 1999 to 2000, which here is from 125 to 75. The formula (given in the math review) for percent increase or decrease is:

    Number increase or decrease ÷ starting (original) number.

    In other words, the denominator is the number you begin with, which in this case is 125 (because the question asks for the change from 1999, not from 1998). The number decrease is 50 (125 – 75 = 50). Finally, $^{50}\!/_{125} = ^{4}\!/_{10} = 40\%$.

    Choice E traps readers who forget that you are trying to find a percentage decrease and find just the year 2000 price.

12. **J.** The easiest way to do this problem is to look at the last term in the expression, the 15. What two numbers multiply to 15? You could choose 3 and 5, or –3 and –5. If you chose 3 and 5, you'd have $(a + 3)(a + 5)$, giving you a squared $+8a + 15$. You need $(a - 3)(a - 5)$ which multiplies (using the FOIL: First, Outer, Inner, Last method described in Chapter 8) to $a^2 - 8a + 15$.

13. **A.** A simple way to do this problem is to plug in numbers. Say that Jim is 20 years old now. Let $m = 5$. That means that 5 years ago, he was 15, such that $y = 15$. In 12 years, he will be 20 (his current age) + 12 = 32. Look for an answer that works out to 32. Choice A: $y(15) + m(5) + 12 = 32$.

14. **F.** First, square or cube each expression: $(5x^2y^5)(5x^2y^5) = 25x^4y^{10}$ Then $(3x^3y^4)(3x^3y^4)(3x^3y^4) = 27x^9y^{12}$. Next, multiply the products.

    Before you go through all the pencil-pushing to find 25×27, look at the exponents: $x^4 \cdot x^9 = x^{4+9} = x^{13}$. You've immediately narrowed the answers down to F and J. Because $25 \times 27 > 15$, eliminate J. What looked like a "pain in the posterior" problem is over with in a flash.

    This question is relatively easy if you remember how to work with bases and exponents. To multiple like bases, add the exponents. To work with a "power to a power," that is, with one exponent inside a parenthesis and one outside, multiply the exponents. (If I've totally left you in the dust, go to Chapter 8. This jazz is easier than it looks.)

15. **C.** The area of a circle is π times radius squared, or 16π for the first circle. Because 16π is ¼ of 64π, you want a circle with an area of 64π, which means its radius must be 8: $8^2 \times \pi = 64\pi$.

    If you chose A, you went backward and didn't think the problem through. If the second circle has a bigger area, it must have a bigger — not smaller — radius. The fact that 1 is ¼ of 4 is irrelevant. If you chose D, you simply took 4 times the first circle's radius. Remember that you get the ratio of the areas of similar figures by squaring the ratio of their sides (or radii). In other words, if the radii are in a ratio of 1:2, their areas are in a ratio of 1:4.

16. **J.** The formula for rate, time, and distance is RT = D: *rate × time = distance*. Plug what you know into the formula: *rate* × 2 hours 20 minutes = 7 miles. Then convert 2 hours 20 minutes to 7/3 hours (because an hour has 60 minutes, 20 minutes is 1/3 hour). Change the 7 miles (distance) to thirds as well: 21/3. Now, you have R × 7/3 = 21/3 and R = 3.

17. **C.** Find the ratio of the sides, noting that the dollhouse is in inches while the regular house is in feet. 18 inches = 1.5 feet and 1.5 to 12 = 15/120 or 1/8. That means the width must be in a 1/8 or 1:8 ratio as well. First, 24 inches = 2 feet. Then 2/16 = 1/8.

Did you notice that you can eliminate answers A, D, and E by using common sense? You can eliminate A because the length of the real bedroom is not 18 feet, and the dollhouse is built to scale; the width cannot be 24 feet. Because the floor is wider than it is long (24 inches to 18 inches in the dollhouse), the answer must be more than 12 feet.

18. **J.** Two figures are similar if their sides (and angles) are in proportion. (See Chapter 7 for a quick refresher on similar figures.) In this case, if the triangles are similar, then the angles of triangle II are also in the ratio 1:2:3, which just happens to be a 30:60:90 triangle. (See Chapter 7 for a refresher on the interior angles of a triangle and on properties of special triangles, like the 30:60:90 triangle.)

The ratio of sides in a 30:60:90 triangle is $\sqrt{2}$:3. This means that the "side $\sqrt{3}$" side of triangle I is the $5\sqrt{3}$ side. Therefore, the "side" is 5, and the "2side" is 10. (Check by adding these once more: $5 + 5\sqrt{3} + 10 = 15 + 5\sqrt{3}$.) If the shortest side of triangle I is 5 and the shortest side of triangle II is 15, the triangles are in a 1:3 ratio. That means that every side of triangle II is three times as long as every side of triangle I. The sides of triangle II, therefore, are 15, $15\sqrt{3}$, 30. Add these together to get the perimeter $45 + 15\sqrt{3}$.

19. **E.** On this type of problem, be sure that you note what the question is asking for. It doesn't want the solution to the equation, but rather the equation itself. Often, you will find going backward easier. "Forty percent of everything" means .40 times everything else, eliminating choices A and D. The square of 5 is simply 5^2, but be careful not to take the square root of that answer (eliminating choice B). Because you add $\sqrt{625}$ and 5^2, eliminate choice C. Only E is left.

Read every choice. If you're rushed (and who isn't?), you may do too much work by anticipating what the question is asking for and actually solving out the question. No one here really wants to know Lael's age, just the equation for finding it.

20. **H.** Add together the number of redheaded children (1/6) and brown-haired children (1/3, which can be written as 2/6) to get 3/6 or 1/2. If half the children don't have blond hair, the other half of the children do have blond hair. That means that the blondes, 30, are half of the number of children, making the total 60.

21. **A.** Set up the equations: $a - b = 6$ (because a is six greater than *b*, the difference between them is 6) and $a + b = -18$. Line them up vertically, and add:

$a - b = 6$

$a + b = -18$

$2a = -12$

$a = -6$

$-6 + b = -18$

$6 = -12$

$(-12)^2 = 144$

The key to this problem is lining up the equations vertically, then adding them so that one variable (in this case, the *b*) drops out. Solve for the other variable, then substitute that back into one of the equations.

Chapter 20: Practice Exam 1: Answers and Explanations

22. H. The interior angles of any polygon are found by using this formula, discussed in detail in Chapter 10: $(n - 2) \times 180°$, where n stands for the number of sides. Here $n = 5$ and $(5 - 2)180 = 3(180) = 540$.

Notice that it makes no difference whether the figure is regular (all sides and angles are the same) or irregular. The exam may give you some truly bizarre-looking figures; don't let them intimidate you. The interior angle formula is the same no matter how grotesque the figure is.

23. C. The total number of tourists is the sum of $200 + 320 + 140 + 180 + 240 = 1,080$. The French are $180/1080$ or $1/6$ of the total.

Tourists Visiting City M

Japanese 240
Germans 200
Americans 320
Moroccans 140
French 180

If you chose E, you fell for the trap and didn't finish working the problem out to answer what the question was asking. A circle has 360°, and $1/6$ of 360 is 60°.

24. H. This problem was easier than it looked. If the rings cost \$864 for 12, divide 864 by 12 to get 72. The price per ring drops from 85 to 72, a difference of 13.

25. C. Remove the parentheses: $3x^2y + xy^2 - 2x^2y + 2xy^2$.

The last item is added because of the negative sign in front of the second set of parentheses: $-1(-2xy^2) = 2xy^2$. Confusing signs is one of the most common careless errors in algebra problems.

Combine like terms: $3x^2y - 2x^2y + xy^2 + 2xy^2 = x^2y + 3xy^2$.

26. H. Line segment XY must be a horizontal line parallel to the x-axis, because the y coordinate does not change. If the line segment goes from –2 to +4, it is 6 units long. The midway point would be 3 units along. Start at –2 and count: From –2 to –1 is one unit. From –1 to 0 is two units. From 0 to 1 is 3 units.

If you said K, you fell for the trap. Yes, you're moving three units to the right, but you're moving *from* –2. You go only from –2 to 1, not to 3.

27. B. Add the numbers in the ratio: $3 + 5 = 8$. The total must be a multiple of 8, eliminating answers A and D. Try each of the remaining answers. If the total is 72, there are 9 groups (because 8 into 72 is 9). Multiply: $9 \times 3 = 27$ and $9 \times 5 = 45$. Subtract: $45 - 27 = 18$. (***Bonus trivia:*** Did you know that olive trees can live to be more than 2,000 years old? Just think, this question may be plaguing students two millennia from now!)

28. H. There are two ways to do this problem: The official, gives-you-brain-cramp way, and the easy, Dummies way. Which do you prefer? Us, too. Here's the easy way: Plug in the answer choices. We suggest you start with the middle term. That way, you can see whether the answer is too high or low, and choose your next plug-in accordingly.

If x is 10, then $10 + 2/3(10) = 10 + 6.66 =$ about 17, certainly more than 15. The first equation is valid. Try the second. Is $10 + 4 < 15$? Yes. The answer is C.

Just to prove to those Doubting Thomases in the crowd, try another answer. Choose G: $9 + 2/3(9) = 9 + 6 = 15$. The first equation doesn't work; don't even bother with the second. If you take the time to check, you'll see that none of the other answers work.

When you make up your own numbers to plug in, you have to check every single answer, in case more than one can work (if more than one works, plug in something else and try again). But when you plug in the answer choices, you can stop as soon as one works. On the ACT, only one answer can be correct.

29. D. This question tests your ability to convert from English to algebra. Talk it through in your mind: Three less than $2x$ means $2x - 3$. The product of 6 and 4 means 6×4. A third of it is ⅓ (24) or 8. Combine $8 = 2x - 3$. Finally, $11 = 2x$ and $x = 11½$.

Did you choose E? Tsk, tsk. You forgot to change your sign and got $8 - 3 = 5$ rather than $8 + 3 = 11$.

30. K. The only way to roll a 12 is to roll double sixes. The probability of rolling any number on a fair six-sided die (one of a pair of dice) is 1 out of 6, or ⅙. (*Fair dice* are not loaded. The ACT would never corrupt the youth of America by even thinking about cheating!) Multiply consecutive probabilities:

⅙ (for the first die) × ⅙ (for the second die) = 1/36.

Probability is discussed in detail in Chapter 11. ACT-type problems have basically only two probability rules, both easy. I suggest that you learn them and get yourself some quick points. (The probability of your getting a probability question on the ACT is probably 100 percent.)

31. E. The area of a triangle is ½ base times height. The sides of an isosceles right triangle are in the ratio: side:side:side$\sqrt{2}$ (this ratio is discussed in Chapter 10). Therefore, $25 + 5\sqrt{2} = 20 + 10\sqrt{2}$. Solve for $s = 10$. The sides of an isosceles right triangle are the base and height, such that ½ (10) (10) = 50.

32. F. The formula for the volume of a rectangular solid (like a box or a fish tank, for instance) is *length × width × height* ($l \times w \times h$). The volume of the first tank is $6 \times 4 \times 10 = 240$. The sides of the base of the second tank are half again as long as those of the first tank: If one side of the first tank is 6, the second tank has a side of 6 + ½(6), or $6 + 3 = 9$. If the other side of the first tank is 4, the second tank has a side of length 4 + ½(4), or $4 + 2 = 6$. Multiply these: $9 \times 6 = 54$. Because the volumes are to be the same, $54 \times h = 240$. Divide by 54 to get $4.\overline{44}$ or approximately 4.4.

33. A. The area of a triangle is ½ *base × height*, written as ½bh. If Area = 32, then ½$bh = 32$, and $bh = 64$.

Be very careful not to go the opposite way, and say that $bh = 16$. The base is 8, so $8h = 64$, making $h = 8$. Therefore, the figure is an isosceles right triangle. Because similar figures have sides in proportion, DEF is also an isosceles right triangle, making its base 28.

You could use the Pythagorean theorem to say that $a^2 + b^2 = c^2$, or you could remember from Chapter 7 that isosceles right triangles have their sides in the ratio of side: side: side$\sqrt{2}$. (This theorem is one of the PTs, or Pythagorean triples, that are so useful on this test. They're definitely worth memorizing; see Chapter 10.) That means the hypotenuse DE is $28\sqrt{2}$. To find the perimeter, add all the sides: $28 + 28 + 28\sqrt{2} = 56 + 28\sqrt{2}$.

If you chose B, you just added all the numbers and said to heck with that pesky square root sign. No can do. You cannot add roots and nonroots. If you chose C, you kept the square root sign but added everything together anyway. If adding roots and nonroots confuses you, go to Chapter 11 for a quick refresher.

34. F. The straight lines indicate absolute value, which is always positive. Therefore, $3 - 3a$ must equal 12 or -12. If $3 - 3a = 12$, $|3 - 3a| = 12$ and $-|3 - 3a| = -12$. If $3 - 3a = -12$, $|3 - 3a| = 12$ and once again $-|3 - 3a| = -12$. For $3 - 3a = 12$: $-3a = 9$ and $a = -3$, which is not one of the answer choices. For $3 - 3a = -12$: $-3a = -15$ and $a = 5$.

Chapter 20: Practice Exam 1: Answers and Explanations

Why not take a simple shortcut? Plug in the answer choices. The ACT is nice enough to give you the answer; all you have to do is plug and chug through the answer choices until you find it. Here, only choice F works.

Note how carefully the question asks which *could* be true. The answer choices never try to trap you by putting in two correct answers. If more than one value works in a problem, the ACT will offer only one as an answer choice.

If you chose H, you forgot to change the sign when you moved the 3 to the other side of the equal sign.

35. **D.** This problem is much easier than it looks. The sum of the interior angles of any triangle is 180 — whether the triangle is equilateral, isosceles, or scalene (no sides are equal), no matter what the size of the triangle is. The interior angles of a triangle always total 180°, so 180:180 = 1:1.

If you chose A, C, or E, you let yourself be tricked by the areas of the triangle.

36. **H.** The easy way to do this problem is to plug in numbers. Say the items cost 1 cent each for a total cost of 8 cents. Marcy forked over 2 dimes, for a total of 20 cents. Her change is the difference: 20 – 8 = 12. Go through each answer choice, plugging in 1 for x and 2 for y. Whichever answer comes out to be 12 is the winner. Choice F becomes 2 – 8 = –6. Nope. Choice H is 20 – 8 = 12. That's it.

When you plug in numbers that you choose randomly, you must, absolutely must, go through all the answer choices. Once in a while, more than one answer choice is correct, based on the numbers you've chosen. What do you do then? You choose different numbers and do the problem again with the answer choices that have yet to be eliminated. The chance of the same thing occurring (that is, of having two answers fit with those given numbers) is astronomical.

37. **D.** Because a circle has 360°, arc AB is $^{10}\!/_{360}$, or $^{1}\!/_{36}$, of the circumference. Make the equation: $3 = ^{1}\!/_{36}$ C. *Cross-multiply* (multiply each side by 36): 36 × 3 = C. Finally, C = 108.

Did you fall for the trap answer E? Yes, the circumference of a circle is $2\pi r$ or πd, but in this case, the π is already built into the length of the arc. Don't feel too bad if you missed this question. Most of the time, a circumference (or an area, for that matter) does have a π in it. This was just the exception I put in to drive you nuts.

38. **J.** If you chose F, I gotcha! Did you think that this was a 5:12:13 triangle, one of the famous PT (Pythagorean theorem) triples? Sorry, not this time (but I like the fact that you thought of the triples, which do show up often on this test). Draw the figure like this:

Notice that the 120 is the hypotenuse, which in a 5:12:13 triangle is 13, not 12. No shortcuts here: Do the calculations: $a^2 + b^2 = c^2$. Then $50^2 + b^2 = 120^2$. Then $2{,}500 + b^2 = 14{,}400$. Finally, $b^2 = 14{,}400 - 2{,}500 = 11{,}900$.

If you chose G, you avoided one trap but fell for a second. The 11,900 represents a side *squared*. To find the side, take the square root of 11,900.

39. **D.** Plug 3 in for x in the equation: $y = 5$ when $x = 3$. The coordinates are (3, 5).

40. G. An altitude divides the triangle into two 30:60:90 triangles, as shown.

You know this because an altitude is always perpendicular (90 degrees) to the base. An equilateral triangle has three 60-degree angles. That means the angle at the left bottom is 60, the angle in the middle is 90, and the angle at the top has been split into two, making it 30 degrees, as shown in the figure.

The ratio of the sides of a 30:60:90 triangle is side: side: side$\sqrt{3}$:2side. (This concept is discussed in greater depth in Chapter 10.) The side opposite the 60 is the "side$\sqrt{3}$" side, or the $10\sqrt{3}$. That means "side" is 10 — but if you chose C, you fell for the trap. *Half* of the bottom is the side of the small triangle, meaning the full bottom of the overall triangle is 20. Three equal sides sum up to 60.

Like many people, you may be taking both the ACT and the SAT. Although the SAT gives you some formulas in the directions (including "side: side$\sqrt{3}$:2side"), the ACT does not. You have to memorize more math formulas and rules for the ACT than for the SAT. It's back to Chapter 10 once again!

41. D. The easy way to do this problem is to take it one step at a time. After one hour, the pool is at ½ empty. Then after the next hour, it is at ¼ (because ½ of ½ = ¼) empty. Keep a little chart, as follows:

Hour	Capacity Left
1	½
2	¼
3	⅛
4	⅟₁₆
5	⅟₃₂
6	⅟₆₄

Scan the answer choices before you begin solving the problem. Doing so tells you how precise you need to be. Because three of the answers are so close (C, D, E), you had to solve the problem exactly. Had the answers been far apart, like 12, 6, 0, you could have estimated.

42. K. The easy way to do this problem is to plug in numbers. Let $m = 5$ and $n = 10$. If five pencils cost ten cents, each pencil costs ¹⁰⁄₅ or two cents. So you know the cost of one pencil is n/m. Because m is in the denominator, your answers are already narrowed down to H and K. Multiply the cost per pencil (n/m) by the number of pencils (p) to get $n/m \times p = np/m$.

43. A. First, find out how many 45-minute increments are in 4½ hours, or 270 minutes: ²⁷⁰⁄₄₅ = 6. Faye, therefore, assembles 6 batches of 200 widgets, or 1,200 widgets. Hal assembles 600 in 2½ hours, or 1,200 in 5 hours.

Don't bother figuring out how many Hal does in 1 minute, or in 45 minutes, or in any other increment. You're doing too much work. Because 1,200 is 2 × 600, he works twice 2½ hours, or 5 hours. You can talk the problem through instead of heading for Power Math.

44. J. Say that the suit was originally $100. A 50 percent increase raises the price to $150. A 20 percent, or ⅕ drop in the price, puts the cost at $120. First, ⅕ × 150 = 30. Then 150 − 30 = 120. A 30 percent decrease from 120 is 84. First, .3 × 120 = 36. Then 120 − 36 = 84. Now you can easily see what percent of the original (100) the new price (84) is. That's the beauty of starting with 100. Yes, the answer is true no matter what number you choose, but why make life any harder than it already is?

Choice G is the trap answer. Did you simply write down +50 − 20 − 30 = 0, meaning there was no change? If so, the new cost would be 100 percent of the old cost, *but,* as explained above, the decreases are not all percentages of the same number.

45. E. A revolution of a wheel is the same as the circumference of a wheel. If the wheel goes 15 revolutions and 300π meters, you divide 300 by 15, and each revolution is 20π. Remember that Circumference = π × diameter. First, $d = 20$. Then $d = 2r$. Finally, $r = 10$.

46. G. A little vocabulary lesson here: *Prime numbers* are numbers that have no positive integer factors other than 1 and themselves. Examples are 2, 3, 5, and 7. *Composite numbers* do have positive integer factors other than 1 and themselves. Examples are 4, 6, and 9. Because a composite number already has more factors than just 1 and itself, multiplying it by yet another number keeps it composite.

To do a problem of this sort, plug in numbers. Try to plug in numbers that eliminate answer choices, as in this example: 3 (prime) × 9 (composite) = 27. The answer is not a prime number, nor zero, nor a fraction, nor even, so eliminate answers F, H, J, and K.

47. C. An *inscribed angle* (one that has a vertex on the circle) has half the measure of its central angle so that AOC = 12°. (If you forgot this, go back to the circles portion in Chapter 10.) Because a circle has 360°, AOC is 12⁄360 or 1⁄30 of the circle. Follow these steps: 120π = 1⁄30 area and 120π × 30 = area and 3,600π = area.

The *area* of a circle is πr^2. Here, $\pi r^2 = 3{,}600\pi$. (When you see a perfect square such as 3,600, you know that you're on the right track.) First, $60^2 = 3{,}600$ and $r = 60$ (not 6 or 600, both easy, careless mistakes to make). Finally, the *circumference* of a circle is $2\pi r$, or 120π.

Did I getcha? Did you immediately eliminate choice C because it's the same as the area of the sector? When it comes to the ACT, expect the unexpected. Bizarre is the norm.

48. H. Don't be intimidated if you don't remember anything about circles or their equations. Simply plug the −3 into the equation, and solve for y. First, $-3^2 + y^2 = 25$. Then $9 + y^2 = 25$ and $y^2 = 16$. Then $y = -4, 4$. Either −4 or +4 works.

Now, if you insist on getting excessively paranoid, don't freak out and think that two answer choices would be −44 and +4. You'll get one or the other, not both. The question very carefully asks you which *could* be y, not which *must* be y.

Just as a quick review, the equation of a circle is $(x - h)^2 + (y + k)^2 = r$ where the center is at (h, k) and r is the radius. In this problem, $x^2 + y^2 = 25$ could be written as $(x - 0)^2 + (y - 0)^2 = 5^2$. Therefore, the center is at (0, 0), and the radius is 5. This could be drawn as shown:

A look at the graph shows that when $x = -3$, $y = 4$ or -4.

To check this, you can show that the distance from $(0, 0)$ to $(-3, 4)$ is equal to 5, the length of the radius. You can make a 3:4:5 triangle,

Or you can use the distance formula:
$$\sqrt{(-3-0)^2 + (4-0)^2} = \sqrt{-3^2 + 4^2} = \sqrt{9+16} = \sqrt{25} = 5$$

49. A. You can, of course, FOIL (First, Outer, Inner, Last, as discussed in Chapter 11). Multiply each expression out, and then add the products. Personally, I refuse to do this much work. If you've been clever enough to pay attention to my suggestions about memorization, you know that $(a + 3)^2$ would follow the same rule as $(a + b)^2$, and automatically know that it is $(a^2 + 2ab + b^2)$, substituting a 3 for the b. That gives you $a^2 + 6a + 9$. Next, $(a - 4)$ is the same as $(a - b)$, which you have (of course) memorized as $(a - b) = a^2 - 2ab + b^2$. Substitute the 4 for the b to get $a^2 - 8a + 16$. Now add vertically:

$$\begin{aligned} a^2 + 6a + 9 \\ \underline{a^2 - 8a + 16} \\ 2a^2 - 2a + 25 \end{aligned}$$

When the answers have "variations on a theme," such as positive and negative versions of the same numerals, be sure to watch your signs carefully. You should double-check this type of problem as soon as you've finished it.

Did you at least eliminate choices C and D? You know that $a^2 + a^2 = 2a^2$. Don't forget to narrow down the answers as you go, to avoid making a careless mistake.

Chapter 20: Practice Exam 1: Answers and Explanations 245

50. **K.** If there are going to be two colors of marbles, red marbles must be ⅔ of the total and blue marbles must be ⅓. That way, the probability of drawing a red marble is twice as great as the probability of drawing a blue marble. Multiply: ⅔ × 36 = 24 and ⅓ × 36 = 12. The difference between 24 and 12 is 12.

51. **B.** Do you remember that great saying you learned in trig: SOH CAH TOA ("soak a toe, uh")? It means:

    Sine = **O**pposite/**H**ypotenuse (SOH)

    Cosine = **A**djacent/**H**ypotenuse (CAH)

    Tangent = **O**pposite/**A**djacent (TOA)

    Here is an illustration:

    To find tan Z in this problem, identify the side opposite angle Z and the side adjacent to angle Z.

    tan Z = Opposite/Adjacent = 7/24

52. **J.** The unshaded circle means that point is not included on the graph. Therefore, the –4 is not part of the graph. Eliminate choice C. The shaded circle means that point is included on the graph. Look for an answer that says the graph can be equal to 0. Choice D works well.

    Choice A is far too broad. Numbers greater than –4 are infinite! Choice B is also too broad, for the same reason: Numbers less than –4 are infinite. Choice E is the trap answer. The graph does not go all the way to –5 or all the way to –1. A careless test-taker who didn't take the time to examine this graph closely deserves to miss this question.

53. **D.** Get x and y on one side and all the terms that have nothing to do with x and y on the other side:

    $4cx - \frac{3d}{e} = 4cy$ and $4cx - 4cy - \frac{3d}{e} = 0$ and $4cx - 4cy = \frac{3d}{e}$

    Factor out $4c$ to leave $x - y$: $4c(x - y) = \frac{3d}{e}$

    Divide by $4c$: $x - y = \frac{3d}{4ce}$

54. **J.** Remember to use the equation

    slope $\frac{y_2-y_1}{x_2-x_1}$. Then $\frac{y_2-y_1}{x_2-x_1} = \frac{b-(-b)}{a-(-a)} = \frac{2b}{2a} = \frac{b}{a}$.

    Note: Which point you choose for y_2 doesn't matter, but once you choose y_2 (or b), you must choose the x coordinate in the ordered pair for x_2 (or a).

55. **E.** To find the angle of depression, first draw a horizontal line from the lookout point. The 14° angle is formed with this line. The horizontal line is parallel to the water's surface. When parallel lines are cut by a transversal, the alternate interior angles are *congruent* (the same):

    This means that you can draw a right triangle with a 14° angle:

    You know the side adjacent to (next to) the 14° angle. You are trying to find the opposite side. The trigonometric function needed is the tangent $\left(\frac{opposite}{adjacent}\right)$ so tan 14° = $x/2$. Solve for x by multiplying both sides by 2 to get rid of the fraction: 2 tan 14° = x.

56. **G.** Stop, stop — you don't need to drag out your graphing calculator. This problem requires more common sense than anything else. First, look for a graph showing that nothing was printed for two hours. This narrows the field quickly to choices G and H because the horizontal portion shows that the number of pages (p) remained steady. Choice G is better than choice H because the horizontal portion is longer (representing a longer time) than either of the increasing portions. The computer was broken for two hours, but each printing segment lasted only one hour. Choice G also makes sense in that the second printing phase is steeper than the first. With two computers during the second phase, the segment should have twice the slope of the first.

57. **A.** The key to answering the question is to remember the equation $\cos^2\Theta + \sin^2\Theta = 1$. If you have trouble remembering this, think of a right triangle with a hypotenuse of 1, as in $x^2 + y^2 = 1$ (remember the Pythagorean theorem?).

Because $\cos\Theta = \frac{adjacent}{hypotenuse} = \frac{x}{1} = x$ and $\sin\Theta = \frac{opposite}{hypotenuse} = \frac{y}{1} = y$, then $x^2 + y^2 = 1$.

You can just rewrite this as $\cos 2\Theta + \sin 2\Theta = 1$.

To get back to our problem, use this equation:

$$\frac{\sin^2\theta + \cos^2\theta}{\sec^2\theta} = \frac{1}{\sec^2\theta}$$

$\sec\Theta = \sec\theta = \frac{1}{\cos\theta}$, so $\sec 2\Theta = \sec^2\theta = \frac{1}{\cos^2\theta}$

Finally, substitute the following:

$$\sec^2\theta = \frac{1}{\cos^2\theta} = \frac{1}{\sec^2\theta} = \frac{1}{\frac{1}{\cos^2\theta}} = 1 \times \frac{\cos^2\theta}{1} = \cos^2\theta$$

TIP: If this problem is really, really tough for you, you're not alone. Many students find this jazz difficult. Keep in mind as you're going through these questions that you don't have to get all the problems right to get a very good score; you can afford to miss several of them.

58. J. This problem is one of the oldest in the books and is included to try to get students to waste time doing a lot of Power Math, setting up algebraic equations full of *p*'s and *c*'s. Forget it. Talk this problem through.

The first thing you want to do is realize that you can't have a cow and a half, so double that to get three cows. Twice as many cows (three instead of 1½) can give twice as much milk (three pints instead of 1½) in the same number of hours.

HEADS UP: Be very careful not to double all the variables, including the 36 hours, at once. Double two variables at a time.

You now have the right number of cows. You want to double the number of hours ($36 \times 2 = 72$). The same number of cows in double the time can give double the milk: $3 \times 2 = 6$ pints. This problem is much easier than it looks . . . unless *you* made it hard.

59. E. The unknown height is opposite the 21° angle. Because 1,500*m* is the side adjacent to 21°, you can use the tangent=opposite/adjacent. First, $\tan 21° = x/1{,}500$. Solve for *x*: 1,500 $\tan 21° = x$.

60. J. If, like most people, you don't remember anything about the unit circle, draw a right triangle and remember this:

```
        /|
       / | 4 (opp. A)
      /  |
     /A__|
     3 (adj. A)
```

If one leg is 3 and the other is 4, use $a^2 + b^2 = c^2$ to find the length of the hypotenuse: $9 + 16 = 25$ and $\sqrt{25} = 5$.

If you're really on the ball, you remembered the PT (Pythagorean theorem) triple (discussed in detail in Chapter 10) of 3:4:5 triangle to come up with a hypotenuse of 5, without doing any of that busywork.

$\cos A = \frac{adjacent\ A}{hypotenuse}$, so $\cos A = \frac{3}{5}$

To verify that the answer is choice J rather than F or G, draw a unit circle:

Because tan A = $\frac{\text{opposite } A}{\text{adjacent } A}$, tan A = $\frac{\sin A}{\cos A}$ in the unit circle.

Because tan A is positive, sin A and cos A must both be positive or both negative. Between 0° and 90°, sin A and cos A are both positive. But between 90° and 180°, sin A is positive and cos A is negative, ruling out any possibility that A is between 90° and 180° and that cos A is negative.

Depending on what math level you're taking in school, you may not have even learned this in class yet. Don't worry; the ACT has only a few questions like this. And look on the bright side: Quickly guessing on this question frees up more time for you to return to the other questions you can get right — if only you had the time.

Reading Test

Passage 1

1. **B.** The first paragraph simply introduces blood clots, mentioning fixed and migratory clots. Did you remember that *describe* is one of the Big Three? Three words are often (not always, but frequently enough to merit your attention) the correct answers to a "what is the purpose" question: discuss, describe, explain.

2. **H.** The first paragraph tells you that **thrombosis** is clotting; an **embolism** is simply a migratory clot. The other answers may or may not be true. The passage doesn't give you that information.

3. **A.** Lines 32–36 state that, among pulmonary embolism patients, "the great majority suffer no serious symptoms or complications, and the disorder clears up without significant aftereffects."

   Dramatic words, such as "invariably," are usually (not invariably) wrong. If you're making a guess (always worth doing, because the ACT has no penalty for wrong answers), eliminate answers with strong, emphatic words (always, must) and look for wimpy words (may, possibly).

   As for choices C and D, the passage did not discuss either children or diet.

4. **H.** Lines 13–14 state that the site of a pulmonary embolism is often a deep vein of the leg or pelvis.

   A question that begins "According to the passage" is usually very straightforward. This type of question is worth an investment of your time. Go back to the passage and find the precise answer.

   If you knew that "pulmonary" referred to the lungs, you may have looked for the answer "lung" immediately. Fortunately, I didn't put in that trap answer, but you can't count on the ACT to be as nice as I am. Take the time to find the *exact* answer in the passage.

Chapter 20: Practice Exam 1: Answers and Explanations   249

5. **B.** Although you may have been able to answer this based on common sense, the theme of the first half of the passage is that thrombosis may turn into an embolism. Choice A is outta left field — nothing was said about aiding others. Obviously, this was the cheap trick answer, playing on the word "attendant."

You have no information about the degree of risk (choice C), although the list of disorders is pretty daunting. And although women are classified according to childbirth status, the passage never contrasted women and men (choice D).

6. **J.** By citing a high percentage of patients who have venous thrombosis after recuperating from hip fractures, the passage implies that the risk of thrombosis is worsened.

In this example, the passage used "exacerbate" in its normal, everyday sense. (The ACT exacerbates, or makes worse, your tension headache.) This will not always be so. A word may have a dozen meanings. Don't be surprised if the ACT uses the least common of those meanings in a passage.

7. **D.** The clinical signs refer to the swollen extremity or inflammation mentioned in the preceding sentence.

Every question in a section counts the same. A basic "definition question" like this one is easy to answer quickly. If you're short on time (and who isn't on the reading passages?), this is a good type of question to focus on.

8. **J.** A "best title" is often the most broad and general statement that is offered. Choice G is mentioned, but only in one brief part of the passage. Choices F and H were never discussed.

You can often predict the answer to a main-idea or best-title question. Pretend that your buddy comes up behind you just as you finish reading the passage and asks you what it was about. Your first reaction is the best title: "Oh, I just read this dull passage about what blood clots are and how to recognize them."

9. **C.** This question should have been very easy — if you remembered to "expand your search." Often, when a passage sends you to certain lines, the answer isn't there. It's a little above or a little below those lines. Lines 67–68 at the end of the preceding paragraph stated that ". . . other tests may be needed to confirm the diagnosis." The next few paragraphs describe such tests.

This is the third correct answer in this passage that uses the word "describe" (see questions 1 and 8). Many ACT passages, especially science passages, describe a problem or situation. Don't immediately choose describe every time you see it, but definitely give describe serious consideration. (I like to think of describe's use as being "guilty until proven innocent." I assume that describe is correct unless I can find something clearly better.)

To *lament* (choice A) is to grieve over. Although you may lament having to take the ACT, few ACT passages themselves lament anything. Choice B has the dramatic word *prove*. Few things are definitively proven in ACT passages. Also, you can probably eliminate choice B by common sense — can *all* of *anything* be diagnosed?

10. **G.** The second-to-last paragraph (the ***penultimate*** paragraph, if you like to use pretentious language) mentions that pulmonary embolisms are difficult to diagnose on the basis of clinical symptoms alone.

You probably could have chosen G based on its wimpy language alone. Dramatic or emphatic answers rarely are correct; hedging or wishy-washy answers are often correct. How can you go wrong saying something like, "should be done cautiously and in conjunction with other tests?" Any physician makes a diagnosis cautiously and usually uses more than one test.

Did you fall for the trap answer, choice J? Lines 94–98 mention a complex test that cannot be done routinely on all patients — but these lines are talking about pulmonary angiography, not clinical symptoms. If you simply skimmed until you found familiar words, you were conned by this cheap trick. ***Remember:*** Just because the answer choice is mentioned in the passage does not mean that it is the correct answer to this specific question.

Passage 2

11. B. The previous sentence tells you that the young lady made an inquiry. She raised her veil while making this inquiry, or, in other words, asking the question. Choices A and C are there to catch careless readers who use their common sense to answer the question ("Well, obviously, to prefer is to like better, as in 'I'd prefer to be hanging out with my friends than studying for this test'") rather than go back to see how the word is used in context.

12. H. This question is slightly harder than number 11. In that question, you are simply asked to define how the term is used. Here, you need to know *why* the author chose that particular word. This question is more subjective, requiring you to understand the author's feelings about the person in question. Here, Dickens describes the young lady as being slight and delicate and timid (lines 2–3) and neatly and quietly attired (line 13). Therefore, he uses the word "glided" to indicate that quietness.

This type of question is especially difficult for someone whose first language is not English. If you don't understand the passage well enough to "get into the author's head" and know how the author is feeling, guess quickly and go on to the next question. (Don't forget to guess — the ACT has no penalty for wrong answers.)

13. D. The author struggles to say tactfully that, while on any other woman, the dress would have looked like what it was ("poor and shabby"), this woman was so attractive and genteel that on her, even low-quality clothing looked good. (Hmmm . . . I wonder whether I can ever teach my boyfriend to be quite so tactful?)

14. F. If you chose G, you probably didn't go back to see how the word was used in context, but only used your knowledge that the word *kin* means a relative (your parents and siblings are your kin, for example). Even though doing so chews up your time, go back to the passage and read a little bit above and below the indicated portion. The slovenly girl is the attendant of, or assistant to, the attractive young girl, and serves in the same class as the assistant or "servant-of-all-work" on a farm.

15. C. First, recognize that *sober* in this sense has nothing to do with being drunk. *Sober* can also mean serious, not frivolous ("consider soberly which college you want to spend four years of your life attending"). Dump the cheap trick answer, choice A.

Dramatic answers, answers with strong, powerful, exclusive words *(all, every, must)* are often wrong. An answer like B, with *obviously,* is rarely right. An answer like D, with *completely,* is almost never right. On the other hand, a wishy-washy answer, with a word like *some* (choice C), is often correct.

In this instance, the author means that Nicholas would have followed the young woman out (to the surprise of others who may have thought more seriously about their conduct and may have acted less impetuously).

16. G. The girl was given a card to get a job, and left — yet Tom indicated that she would be back the next day. From this, you may infer that Tom believes the girl will not take, or will not stay long at, the position. The statement of the fat lady that "She'll have a nice life of it, if she goes there" may be construed as sarcasm, showing that the fat lady agrees that the girl would not like the post.

Nothing in the passage indicates that the girl comes in daily (choice F). It's clear that the girl does not work for Tom and the fat lady, because she was asking about a post of governess. Choice J is tempting (to Nicholas at least), but you get no indication that the girl even noticed that Nicholas was present.

17. C. If you didn't go back to the passage and read this portion in context, you may have chosen A or B. Choice A is exactly wrong; the passage goes on to say that Nicholas was disgusted by Tom's conduct.

Chapter 20: Practice Exam 1: Answers and Explanations

Don't choose an answer simply because it is a true statement. Be sure that it answers the specific question asked. Choice B may be a true statement (Tom saw and agreed with Nicholas's admiration of the young woman), but that statement is not the reason for the quote given here. Tom commented and winked at Nicholas in order to flatter him by indicating that Nicholas's skills would be valued by many employers.

18. **F.** The fat woman makes the comment that Mr. Gregsbury is a Member of Parliament only after saying that she didn't know what the terms of the position were. From this you may infer that the purpose of the comment was to reassure Nicholas that the job would be a good one.

Choice G may or may not be true; you have no way of knowing whether the fat lady's comment is true or false. Choice H seems logical, until you go back to the passage and find that the fat lady (in this excerpt at least) did no boasting whatsoever of any of her clientele. Choice J may have trapped you. True, there was only one listing, but that fact didn't seem to upset the fat lady any.

19. **B.** Given that the next paragraph discusses Nicholas's going to the building and knocking upon every door until he finds Mr. Gregsbury, you may infer that Nicholas is going to visit the man.

If you chose C, you got careless. Any vocabulary word must be interpreted in context. You have to go back to the passage and see how that word is used there. While "to wait upon" could mean serve, as a waitress waits upon diners, it has no such connotation in this passage.

20. **H.** If you chose F, you simply focused on the word "chivalrously" and ignored the greater meaning of the sentence. The last paragraph lightly mocks the ideas of chivalry, saying that a "knight" has a duty to knock about anyone who does not praise his lady-love, even if he's never met that lady-love. Therefore, Nicholas had a duty (which he ignored) to defend the young woman's honor.

Passage 3

21. **D.** A primary purpose is general and broad, not specific. Choice B gives information that is stated in the passage, but only briefly, not as the purpose of writing the passage. Choice C is not mentioned at all. Choice A is the trap answer. The passage does state that bushmasters are poisonous, but not why.

22. **J.** If you are rushed for time, this is a good question to guess at quickly and come back to later. (The ACT has no penalties for wrong answers, which means that you need never leave an answer blank.) The best way to answer this question is by the process of elimination: Find three questions that were answered, and whatever is left is the correct answer. Paragraph 2 states that the bushmaster's coloring aids in its camouflage. Paragraph 3 tells why the bushmaster has the pits in its head. Paragraph 3 also tells what the bushmaster eats (rodents). Although the passage does talk about the maternal instincts of the bushmaster, it does not discuss mating habits or attracting a mate.

23. **C.** Paragraph 2 states, "This maternal instinct is quite rare among reptiles."

When a question begins with the words, "According to the passage," it is usually a freebie for you, a complete gift. If you know that you are not going to be able to answer all the questions in time, or if your brain is mush and you are losing focus (I speak from experience!), look for an "According to the passage" question. This is one question that you are almost guaranteed to get correct.

If you chose D, you fell for the trap. Yes, paragraph 1 states that unlike the rattlesnake, the bushmaster has no rattles on its tail, but nothing is said about this lack of rattles being rare among reptiles. The author is differentiating just two snakes, not making a generalization.

24. **F.** The first paragraph states that the bushmaster is the largest venomous snake in the *New World*. From this careful distinction (not "the largest snake in the world," but the largest snake "in the New World"), you can infer that larger snakes are found elsewhere in the world.

251

Choice H is tempting, but is a trap. The bushmaster perhaps attacks humans only when threatened, but the passage implies that the bushmaster does attack its prey for food, even though the prey (like rodents) cannot be considered threatening.

25. **B.** The third to last paragraph discusses how bushmasters hide from and then ambush their prey.

    You didn't really fall for that piece of lame humor in choice A, did you? "Ambush" has nothing to do with bushes in the Amazon!

26. **H.** Words have more than one meaning. Much of the ACT reading test asks you to interpret how the author uses the words, not just their straightforward dictionary meanings. To *misplace* does mean to lose, but that's not how the author means the term in this instance. He is saying that people have the wrong idea, that bushmasters are not really fierce.

    The key to answering this question is to continue reading. The real answer is in the rest of the paragraph. Careless and lazy readers who go only where they are directed and don't continue will miss this type of question every time.

27. **A.** The paragraph discusses how the bushmasters' numbers are declining, although the bushmaster is not yet an endangered species. The author implies, without coming right out and stating so, that the bushmaster may become endangered as more and more of its habitat is removed. Choice H is far too dramatic. A common trap on the ACT is offering a very strongly worded answer that is rarely correct.

28. **F.** The last paragraph states that the hikers step on sleeping snakes, unable to see the snakes because of their coloration or hear them because of the snake's lack of rattles. Choice J is the trap answer. It's true that the bushmaster is nocturnal, out more in the evening than the daytime, but that's not given as the reason the hikers are attacked by the snakes.

    Just because something is true doesn't mean that it's the right answer to the question.

29. **D.** This question is tricky. Choice A states a fact; bushmasters do sleep during the day, but that isn't the main point of the paragraph. Choice B states a fact that seems logical, based on what we all know about wildlife in general (most animals — including humans — will attack to protect their young and their food), but that's not the main point of the paragraph. Choice C is discussed in the last paragraph, which states that the bushmaster's coloration and silent warning system rarely alert humans to the snake's presence . . . but that's not the main point of the paragraph. The main point (as introduced by the topic sentence of the paragraph) is that the bushmaster is not as ferocious and aggressive as its reputation would make you believe.

    When a question asks you for the main idea, whether of the entire passage or of just a paragraph, try to predict an answer before you look at the choices. Pretend that someone just asked you what you're reading. Your response, which in this case may be something like, "People think that this snake is more dangerous than it really is," is the main idea.

30. **J.** If you are rushed for time, a negatively phrased question ("Which was NOT . . .") is a good one to guess at quickly. Answering this question is really like answering three separate questions, because you have to find three questions the passage *does* answer, and then by process of elimination, identify which question it does *not* answer. Paragraph 4 talks about enemies of the bushmaster. Paragraph 3 discusses how a bushmaster locates its prey. The last paragraph explains why some people consider the bushmaster aggressive.

    Choice J can be a little tricky. The author mentions that the bushmaster has a strong maternal instinct that is rare in snakes, but he never tells *why* the bushmaster had that instinct. (If you missed this question, don't feel too bad. Many people miss negatively phrased questions, which is why I suggest that you not invest too much time in them.)

Passage 4

31. C. Choices A and B are true statements but are much too specific to be a main idea. A main idea, whether of a paragraph or of the passage, is broad and general. Choice D is tricky, but goes too far. The passage neither states nor implies that a building cannot be appreciated without understanding symbolism; it simply informs the reader of the symbolism within the Capitol.

32. H. In lines 18–19, you are told that Lincoln's body lay in state under the Rotunda after Lincoln was assassinated. The other answers are neither given nor implied in the passage.

When you're asked what the author means, be sure to go back to the passage and find the answer in the context of the passage. Don't try to use your common sense or dredge up what little you remember from American history.

Bonus trivia: Speaking of Lincoln, did you know that one of his nicknames was the Perpendicular Pronoun? The 6'4" president was criticized for using the word "I" in his speeches, something considered improper at the time.

33. A. Irony is the opposite of what might be expected. One example always given is "the irony of the firehouse burning down." Here, it is *ironic,* or opposite of what you'd expect, that the symbol of America, the Capitol, is filled with works by foreign artists. In choice B, *ingenuity* means cleverness, resourcefulness. Choice C, *perspicacity* means shrewdness, perceptiveness.

Did you choose C on the theory, "Ooooh, big word, I don't know what it means, it must be the right answer!"? If so, you're not alone. Many students automatically choose the longest, hardest word. Usually, the totally bizarre word you've never seen before is put there to trick you. Don't choose a word you don't know unless by process of elimination you're absolutely positive that the words you do know are wrong.

34. G. This type of question is merely plug 'n' chug; plug each answer choice into the context and see which one works best. The sentence says, ". . . more overt than symbolic," meaning there isn't hidden symbolism, but an open, obvious meaning.

35. D. Paragraph three talks about the buildings being on fire, then says the conflagration was prevented from destroying everything by the rainstorm. From this you may deduce that a conflagration is a fire, and the fire was doused by the rainstorm.

If you chose A, you fell for the trap. The conflagration itself was not the rainstorm; just the opposite.

36. J. The paragraph talks about how the fire was put out by a rainstorm, and the windstorm killed British forces. From this, you may infer that Nature helped save the Capitol. Choice F is a value judgment: Who's to say who is superior and who is inferior? Value judgments are rarely correct answers. Choice G is a trap. It may be true that the British superstitiously thought that the world was conspiring against them and in favor of the Americans, but that implication is quite a stretch for you to make. Choice H is just plain wrong. The paragraph tells you that the Capitol was damaged, but not destroyed.

37. C. Sometimes the obvious answer is in fact the correct answer. Paragraph four specifically says that most artworks tell a story about American history. The other answers may in fact be true, but are not given in the passage. When a question begins with the words, "According to the passage," the answer is usually given very directly. This type of question, in my opinion, is a gift to you. The only way to get it wrong is to outsmart yourself, making the question seem harder than it really is.

38. F. An EXCEPT question (or any negatively phrased question, such as, "The author would most likely DISAGREE with which of the following statements?" or "Which of the following is NOT true?" is often a time-wasting question, a good one to guess at quickly and go on. The only way to get this question correct is to find the answers to the three other questions. You were told the definition of *E Pluribus Unum* ("Out of many, one,") in paragraph two. Paragraph four tells you that Lafayette was the first foreigner to address a joint session of Congress. The last paragraph gives several examples of the

254 Part VII: I'd Rather Wait for the Movie: Full-Length Practice ACTs

subject matter of the paintings. The nickname "Women in a Bathtub" was mentioned in the last paragraph, but no explanation of the nickname was given.

39. **A.** The passage talks about such patriots as Washington and Jefferson and Lafayette and Penn. The author probably finds it surprising that a statue of a former enemy is found among the others.

TIP

A little common sense goes a long way. Use the process of elimination to get this question right. Nothing in the passage implies that only Northerners were honored. You know there are statues of women as well as of men. And some of the people honored, like Washington and Lafayette, are in fact military heroes, not civilians.

40. **H.** The author mentions men and women, Confederates and foreigners, doctors and Indians. It is reasonable to assume that his purpose is to show the diversity of people who have helped make America the nation it is. If you chose J, you were indulging in a little wishful thinking! Yes, mentioning the man who invented ice cream may have been slightly funny, but it's unlikely the author was trying to provide any comedy in this passage.

Science Reasoning

Passage 1

Before going to the questions, make sure you have some idea about how the tables work. To figure the relative humidity in Table 1, find a dry-bulb reading in the left-hand column and move rightward to the appropriate difference between wet-bulb and dry-bulb readings. For example, for a dry-bulb reading of 20°C, the relative humidity is 59% when the wet-bulb reading is 5 degrees different from the dry-bulb reading. The major trend to note in Table 1 is that humidity increases with higher temperatures (as you move down the table) and decreases with increased differences between the two bulb readings (as you move to the right).

For Table 2, note that the apparent temperature, as explained in the sentence immediately preceding the table, is what a given combination of humidity and air temperature would feel like to a typical human. The table shows, for example, that the apparent temperature at 70% relative humidity and an air temperature of 23.9°C is 25.0°C. The trends here are that apparent temperature increases with increasing humidity, consistent with the common knowledge that high humidity is uncomfortable, and that apparent temperature increases with increasing air temperature, consistent with the commonsense notion that the hotter it gets, the hotter it feels.

1. **B.** All four of the choices are between the 51.1 for 70% and the 57.8 for 80% (see Table 2). Because 75% is halfway between 70% and 80%, the number you're looking for should be close to half way between 51.1 and 57.8.

   Choice B is a little less than half way, but the number should actually be closer to 51.1, the number for 70%. 51.1 is closer to 45.6, the number for 60%, than it is to 57.8, the number for 80%. In other words, as the relative humidity levels progress evenly, the apparent temperature intervals in this range are getting larger. The gap between the apparent temperatures for 75% and 80% should be larger than the gap between such temperatures for 70% and 75%. Choice B is 2.9 away from 51.1 and 3.8 away from 57.8.

2. **H.** The choices all have to do with the point at which air temperature and apparent temperature are equivalent. According to Table 2, at an air temperature of 21.1°C, the apparent temperature is the same at 60% and 70% relative humidity. When the air temperature is 23.9°C, this equivalence occurs at 50% humidity. At 26.7°C, the humidity is between 40% and 50%. This trend of having lower humidity to make the two temperatures equal continues as air temperatures increase (as one moves to the right on the table). Choice H is the only choice that expresses this relationship.

Remember that one of the main skills to have when approaching Data Representation and Research Summaries passages is to pick up on trends.

3. B. Did you look at Table 1, find the dry-bulb reading of 12°C, look across until you got to 78% relative humidity, look up the table until you saw the number 2, and then put down choice A? The problem is that the 2 represents the *difference* between the dry-bulb reading and the wet-bulb reading. Read the introductory material to see that the wet-bulb reading is lower than the dry-bulb reading because the evaporation of water from the wet bulb lowers the reading. So the wet-bulb reading in this case is 2°C lower than 12°C, or 10°C (choice B). If you were not able to pick up on the idea that the wet-bulb reading is lower than the dry-bulb reading, you can at least figure that there is a difference of 2 from 12, making the answer choice B or D. While even a wild guess is appropriate on the ACT (because there is no penalty for wrong answers), a 50-50 guess is certainly worth making.

4. G. To answer this question correctly, you must combine information from the two tables.

Notice that trap answer F comes from simply subtracting 4 from 24 and that trap answer H is obtained by adding 24 and 4. If you got either of these choices, you probably picked up on the word "different" in this question and didn't engage the brain cells sufficiently to think through how to get the apparent temperature.

Wrong answer J corresponds to the relative humidity that occurs in the situation described in this question. To answer the question, you must take this 69% relative humidity and go to Table 2. The 69% figure is close to 70%, so use the 70% row and move under the column marked 23.9, which is close to 24, the dry-bulb reading, and hence air temperature, in this question. The row and column match up at 25.0, making the answer choice G.

5. A. While low moisture causes a greater difference between the two bulbs, as explained in the introduction, don't go for choice D so quickly. A look at Table 1 reveals that the relative humidities for choices A, B, C, and D are 29%, 29%, 30%, and 31%, respectively. To find the actual, as opposed to relative, amount of moisture in the air, one must, according to the introduction, multiply these percentages by the maximum amount of moisture that the air can hold at the various temperatures. Because this maximum amount increases with increasing temperature, choice A must be the answer over choice B because the 29% is multiplied by a lower number in choice A. Choices C and D can be dismissed because both the percentages and the numbers these percentages are multiplied by (the maximum moistures) are higher.

Passage 2

The important point to understand from the introductory paragraph is that the purpose of the study is to test which drug makes subjects less drowsy.

Although the pharmaceutical company is probably concerned with how effectively its drug alleviates hay fever, this factor is not measured in this study.

The description of Study 1 tells you that drowsiness was tested by counting the number of errors that subjects made on a task that requires alertness. Picture yourself as an experimental subject. If you are drowsy from a pill as you perform a motor task that requires alertness, how do you think you'll do? You'll probably make many mistakes. The statement that subjects who made fewer errors were judged to be less drowsy concurs with your imagined scenario. The rest of the description of Study 1 tells you that the two drugs were compared at two different times, creating four groups of subjects. Each group had four subjects, making the study symmetrical and straightforward to follow.

As with Data Representation passages, be sure to examine the data and look for major trends. Table 1 reveals that the subjects taking the new drug made fewer errors on the average than those taking the old drug. This difference was far more pronounced for the groups that were tested one hour after ingestion. The errors associated with the old drug were much lower at eight hours than at one hour. This finding makes sense once you realize that the effects of drugs tend to wear off with time. The new drug did not show this decrease in the number of errors, perhaps because it wasn't making its subjects too drowsy to begin with.

How does weight figure in? A scan of Table 1 shows that the heavier subjects made fewer errors than the lighter subjects. The drowsiness caused by the drug seems to be greater in those who are lighter. Some reflection on outside knowledge should help you understand this finding: Who gets a higher dosage of a pain reliever, an adult or a baby? An adult who received a baby's dose would not feel much lessening of the pain.

Now that you've gotten a handle on Study 1 and Table 1, you can readily see what happened in the next two studies. Study 2 was basically a repeat of Study 1 except that the experimenters took out a factor that caused some variability. Table 2 shows much of what Table 1 shows but also indicates that the new drug caused fewer errors than the old drug even at eight hours. The difference in averages of the two eight-hour groups may not seem great (34.75 vs. 30.75), but such a difference is probably significant when the table shows how little variability there is within each group of four.

Study 3 was identical to Study 2 except that the subjects were lighter and female. The number of errors was higher (remember how the lighter subjects made more errors in Study 1), but the trend of the results was virtually identical to that of Study 2.

6. **J.** Note the purpose of the study mentioned in the introduction and the description of Study 1. This study was designed to test the extent to which the drugs make test subjects drowsy. It did not examine how effective the drugs were in relieving hay fever; eliminate choice F. Choice J follows nicely from the analysis of Study 1 presented above. Don't choose answer G just because the numbers decrease. You must remember that lower numbers mean *fewer* errors, or a *better* performance. Choice H is wrong because there are no data showing how well the subjects did on the task before taking the drug. Such information is needed before one can conclude anything about the drug's improving performance.

7. **C.** Once again, the analysis of the results completed before looking at the questions makes answering a question much easier. As stated in that analysis, the researchers eliminated a source of variability by using subjects who were all of the same weight. Choice C expresses this idea. With less variability, researchers can be more confident that any differences observed between drugs or between times is a consequence of the drug taken or the time since ingestion. Small differences between groups don't mean much if the results for both groups range widely. Such small differences may be significant if one group is consistently a little higher than the other group.

    Choice D is the easiest choice to eliminate. Where in this study can anybody learn the weight of typical hay fever sufferers? A comparison of Studies 2 and 3 could provide some information regarding choice A, but such information is already provided in Study 1. Remember that the question is basically asking why the researchers went on to conduct Studies 2 and 3. Choice B is tempting because the subjects in Study 2 were male and the subjects in Study 3 were female, but the description of the studies does not mention the sex of the subjects as something that was of major concern to the researchers. Besides, the way Studies 2 and 3 are designed, it's impossible to look at them and determine whether the greater number of errors in Study 3 came about because the subjects were lighter or because the subjects were female.

8. **H.** Here's your chance to use some common sense. Study 2, as discussed above, may have produced results with less variability, in contrast to what is stated in incorrect choice J, but all Study 2, taken by itself, shows is that the new drug is probably better with regard to producing drowsy side effects only for males of a certain weight. Choice H is correct because it points out that Study 1 used a wider range of subjects. Choice F may look enticing, but you do not know the sex of the subjects in Study 1. Perhaps the subjects in Study 1 were also all male. Eliminate choice G because the studies were concerned with drowsiness, not the effectiveness of the drug.

Chapter 20: Practice Exam 1: Answers and Explanations 257

9. **C.** Here's a way to save yourself some time. Scan the choices and notice that option II has to be included because it appears in each of the four choices. Don't waste time trying to justify option II.

Table 3 indicates that the average for the one-hour group was 54.25 while the average for the eight-hour group was 49.75. It is quite reasonable to expect that the average for the two-hour group could be in between these two averages, so option III should be included, and choices A and B are out. You may consider that both options I and IV are within range, but think about the logic of option I. Why would the drug cause fewer errors at two hours than at either one or eight hours? The results suggest that the drug's side effects wear off with time, so it does not seem reasonable that there would be fewer errors at two hours than at eight hours. You may now eliminate choice D because option I is out.

The only answer left is correct choice C. Move on before you drive yourself crazy trying to understand why the number of errors could be higher at two hours (option IV) than at either one or eight hours. The test-maker has given you a break by the way the options are arranged in the answer choices.

Okay, okay! You insist upon knowing why option IV is reasonable? The drowsiness produced by the drug may not have peaked at one hour. Perhaps it peaks after one hour before subsiding at eight hours or so. In addition, option IV is closer to the old-drug averages in Table 3 than is option I.

10. **F.** The question tells you that the average you see for the old drug group eight hours after ingestion is probably a bit lower than what would have been obtained had subjects who were not particularly proficient at the motor task been used. With regular, everyday, less-coordinated people, the average would probably be higher than the 41.75 shown. With this higher average, the gap between the new and old drugs would be higher than the current 0.5 and would strengthen the claim, which can be made with Studies 2 and 3, that the new drug produces less drowsiness at eight hours.

The next two choices have key flaws. To make a case for choice G, you would have to know that the old drug at eight hours normally produces more errors than the old drug at one hour. You may not assume that less-coordinated subjects would make that many additional errors. Another problem with choice G is that it mentions side effects in general while the study simply investigated drowsiness. The best way to get rid of choice H is to realize that the choice mentions the drugs' effectiveness, which was not investigated in these studies.

Choice J makes some sense. Many studies do use the same subjects for different parts of a study. One advantage of such an experimental design is that different groups are equated for overall ability because the different groups have the same people. One problem with choice J, though, is that the subjects may do better at eight hours not because the drowsiness has worn off but because the subjects already had a chance to practice at one hour.

A more serious problem with choice J is that it uses the extreme word "require." Remember that absolute choices are rarely correct on the ACT.

11. **B.** Even if you wanted to be ultraconservative and not recommend the new drug, the reasons given in choices C and D aren't logical. You have no way of knowing what the patients will do, and even if you did, such information doesn't have much to do with the new drug versus the old drug. In fact, the evidence points to the superiority of the new drug at both one and eight hours. If the individual is going to operate dangerous machinery, it's better that he or she do so with the new drug, which doesn't produce as much drowsiness. Choice D doesn't follow from the information in the question or in the studies, so get rid of it because the ACT does not expect you to start using some specialized knowledge of the immune system. In addition, choice D provides no indication as to which drug is superior regarding its effect on the immune system.

Choice B is consistent with the studies and the information in the question and does not make any outlandish statement such as, "The new drug is vastly superior to the old drug with respect to all short-term and long-term effects." Choice A is out primarily because the ACT does not want you to practice medicine without a license. You would have to know a lot more about the new drug's pharmacological actions before making such a statement. Another point is that the new drug seemed better than the old drug when the dosages of the drugs were equated. Why would you say that the new drug is okay only if the dosage is reduced?

Passage 3

The first two paragraphs and figures provide background information, as is often done on the ACT. Don't worry about understanding all the details. The main point is that when water levels rise, the waves are more likely to hit the bluff. When this happens, the bluff erodes.

Don't waste time thoroughly analyzing each study or Figures 3–5. Often, you can use common sense on these science passages. Study 1 shouldn't shock you; you should expect that precipitation leads to greater lake depth.

Study 2 is somewhat more complex than Study 1. The key is to observe in Figure 4 that higher temperatures are associated with lower water levels (less depth). This relationship makes sense if you reason that high temperatures increase evaporation rate (don't you dry off fast when you get out of a pool on a hot day?), which, as stated, lowers water levels.

The results of Study 3 are similar to those of Study 2. Like high temperatures, strong winds lead to high evaporation, which, as you have seen, lowers water levels. This relationship is illustrated in Figure 5. Link Studies 2 and 3 together in your mind to help you nail down this high temperature, strong wind, high evaporation, less water association.

12. **H.** A quick look at Figure 3 reveals that lake depth goes down as precipitation goes down. Because lake depth is 5.0 m when precipitation is 15 cm/year, choices F and G are unreasonable. Choice J is too precise and is also improbable. A doubling of precipitation from 15 cm/year to 30 cm/year results in only a 0.5 m change in lake depth. The change from 10 cm/year to 15 cm/year is not as great as the 15-to-30 change, so the lake depth changing from 2.5 m to 5.0 m would not make sense. Choice H, although not certain, is a safe thing to say and is the answer. Such safe answers are good bets on the ACT.

13. **A.** Experimenters conducted Study 2 under the premise that temperature affects evaporation rate. The researchers already know that high evaporation rates lower water levels. Figure 4 shows an association between high temperature and low water levels. If high temperatures result in low water levels, and high evaporation rates result in low water levels, high temperatures probably lead to high evaporation.

    Remember, common sense counts when answering a question in this section. Choice A is logical and fits in with basic science. You have probably observed that liquids disappear faster when the temperature is hot. Also, when evaporating, water changes from a liquid to a gas. Which state is associated with a higher temperature? The gas, so high temperatures and high evaporation go together.

14. **F.** Although what happens to lake depth cannot be determined with certainty (because several unmentioned factors are involved), the question asks what probably will happen. Therefore, the most obvious choice is safe. Low precipitation is associated with low water levels. High temperatures and strong winds increase evaporation rates, which lower water levels. When all three factors are connected to low water levels, you can safely say that the water level will be low.

15. **D.** Study 3 provides some evidence that strong winds can be good for the bluff because such winds lower water levels. With low water levels, more waves will hit the beach rather than the bluff. However, the word "definitely" in the question makes choice A incorrect. Other factors, one of which is mentioned in choice D, also exist. Does the fact that powerful waves can lead to erosion on the bluff make sense? Yes, it does, reinforcing choice D as the answer.

As with choice A, choice B is wrong because you can't definitely say things are good. In addition, wind is more likely to erode the soil on the bluff rather than deposit soil on it. Choice C is out because you can't say that wind raises temperatures (which may be good for the bluff).

16. **G.** The lake depth depends on the temperature and the amount of precipitation and wind. In a cause-and-effect relationship, the cause is the independent variable, and the effect or result is the dependent variable.

    Another reason to pick choice G is that the other three choices all work the same way in this investigation. The other choices are all factors that the scientist examines for their effects on lake depth. If you want to select choice F, you would also have to select choices H and J. Because three answers can't all be correct, these choices must all be wrong.

17. **A.** Because statements I and II mention nothing about the weather, strike them out. Doing so quickly eliminates choices B, C, and D, leaving choice A as the answer. Statement III helps because it is similar to the passage's investigation but more direct; it measures something on the bluff instead of water level, which can affect the bluff. Statement IV is out because tides are the result of gravitational pull from the moon and the sun, which is not a weather factor. Even if you are unsure of this fact, no choice presents III and IV only.

Passage 4

At last, a graph you can actually relate to. You probably know that a compact car gets more miles per gallon than a full-size car does, as shown by the graph. The graph also shows that for each car size, gas mileage is better at slower speeds — which is why, logically enough, speed limits were lowered during the energy crisis of the 1970s.

The information presented before the graph is no big shock. When cars burn gas, they pollute the air. The more gas burned, the more pollution. To put this idea together with the graph, figure that the cars that get better gas mileage use less gas to travel a given distance; therefore, they do not pollute as much as large cars do.

18. **J.** Reasoning backward from the preceding summary, the car that produces the most pollutants is the one that uses the most gas. Which car uses the most gas? The one that gets the worst gas mileage, choice J.

19. **A.** When you drive a car faster, you get fewer miles per gallon than when you drive that car slower. This means that you have to use more gas to go a given distance.

    Eliminate choice B because time isn't the critical factor in your finding a gas station. The probability of your finding a gas station increases with the distance driven, not the time driven.

    You probably eliminated choices C and D as soon as you saw that they began with "Yes." (Good for you!) Choice C looks tricky but is wholly irrelevant. If you are facing being stranded in the middle of the desert, you probably don't care too terribly much whether your car is going to pollute. The key factor is whether you run out of gas. (Besides, just because an environment is relatively unpolluted does not give you license to pollute it.) Choice D is only half true. You will operate your car for less time; however, gas consumption is a function of distance, not time.

20. **G.** The logical solution is to figure that the answer is in between the miles per gallon for a full-size car driven at 50 mph and 60 mph. These figures are 26 and 24, respectively, making 25 the answer.

    Choice F is illogical. That gas mileage is worse than what a full-size car driven at 60 mph gets. Remember, gas mileage should be higher when speed is reduced.

    If you chose H or J, you made the test-maker's day. These answers are designed to trap careless readers who didn't notice that the figures are the mileage that midsize and compact (not full-size) cars would get at 55 mph.

21. D. If you got this question right, congratulations — you're thinking like a scientist. Making projections beyond the range of numbers presented in a graph is risky. In the graph, statistics are given for speeds between 50 and 70 mph. The 25-mph figure cited is far outside of this range.

Try hard not to outsmart yourself. You can't simply figure that if slowing down between 70 and 50 mph increases gas mileage, further decreases in speed will improve gas mileage even more. Too many factors that you don't know about are involved (for example, the engine may have to work harder when lower gears are used at lower speeds).

You need to recognize when you may make a reasonable extrapolation and when you may be going too far, right into a trap. In the previous question, you can logically estimate a number (because 55 is between 50 and 60, both of which were on the chart). In this question, you can't logically make an estimate because the chart does not cover the number in question.

22. J. More gas is used when speed increases, which means that more pollutants are emitted when speed increases. Only choice J shows that pollutants increase as speed increases for the entire range of speeds.

Passage 5

Did you take one look at this problem and tell a friend, "Pull the plug; I'm obviously brain dead!"? You don't need to be intimidated by the terms. No one expects you to be a neurosurgeon. All the ACT wants you to understand is that certain parts of the brain control certain muscles in the body. The figures simply indicate the locations of these controlling regions.

23. D. Scan the Roman numeral options. A quick glance at Figure 2 reveals that III is true. Much more of the motor area is dedicated to the hand, for example, than to the trunk, narrowing the field to Choices B and D. If you're in a rush or just want to get this horror over with, make a guess. A 50-50 chance is pretty good odds on this exam.

Now here's where you can use your test-taking skills, rather than using, well, your brain. Did you notice that options I and II are contradictory? As a result, one option, but not both, can be correct. A choice that presents I and III is not available (and remember, you already deduced that statement III is right), so the only thing left is the correct answer, II and III. Statement II, in fact, is correct. You can see how, starting from the inside of the brain, the regions progress from toes, at the bottom of the body, to the head.

Roman numeral questions can be very time-consuming. I often tell my students to skip these questions and to leave them for last. However, if you can immediately say that one statement is either definitely true or definitely wrong, you have narrowed the choices down immensely. Before skipping this sort of question, at least take a look at it. You may be in for one of the few pleasant surprises offered by the ACT.

24. H. One simple way to reason through this question is to see that the hand is much larger than the areas for hip, shoulder, and brow. (If Choice F is the answer, then why not G or J? They're all about the same size.) And don't forget to use your common sense. You can logically think that the more complex areas of the body require more brain control.

25. B. Figure 2 shows that the dot is in the knee area, narrowing the choices to B and C. Because the left half of the brain controls the right side of the body (see the text before Figure 2), the correct answer is Choice B.

In this figure, you see a classic example of how thinking about the diagram and the accompanying notes for a few moments before jumping right into the problems can help. The paragraph below the first figure states that one side of the brain controls the opposite side of the body (left brain, right body, and vice versa). Knowing that fact sends you quickly to the right answer.

Chapter 20: Practice Exam 1: Answers and Explanations 261

26. **F.** To know what areas H and J do, you would have to have specific science knowledge. Unless you're a brain surgeon, you probably don't have all this info right at your fingertips. Remember that the ACT does not expect you to have specific knowledge but only to deduce information from a chart, table, graph, or picture. The passage tells you nothing about areas H and J.

    Area G is near the top of the brain, which, according to Figure 2, is involved with the lower part of the body. Area F is near the face, lips, and jaw area. These parts of the body have more to do with speech (although you've heard of body language, your knees don't really chatter up a storm), making F the more logical choice.

27. **D.** This question (the entire question set, actually) deals with the motor area of the brain, so focus on choices that mention muscles. Hey! Doing so is a quick process of elimination: Choice D is the only possible answer.

    Once again, don't sweat about Choices A, B, and C. Knowing how the brain controls these functions requires too much specialized knowledge for the ACT. The ACT wants to make sure that your brain functions, not that you know how it functions.

Passage 6

The introduction is certainly simple enough. Try to rephrase it in your own words: Pigeons are able to find their way home, but exactly how they do so is not known.

Try to identify one key point in each paragraph. In Paragraph 1 of the sun-compass hypothesis, all you need to understand is that the birds seem to use the sun's position to locate the cup. Don't get hung up trying to figure out more than that.

The main idea of the second paragraph is about internal clocks; when the internal clock provides incorrect information, errors result. This information suggests that the birds use the clock and compare the clock's info with the position of the sun.

This type of question isn't called Conflicting Viewpoints for nothing. Just as you have the main idea of the first hypothesis, just as you think you've grasped the logic, along comes a second hypothesis. The magnetic-field hypothesis states that pigeons don't always use their internal clocks with the sun. But be careful not to go too overboard with this conclusion. All the findings say is that when the sun is not available, the birds do not compare their internal clocks with the sun to orient themselves. This is not to say that pigeons never use the sun, even though the author of the magnetic-field hypothesis chooses to ignore it. The findings simply suggest that the sun is not essential for orientation. Because the pigeons found their way home, they seem capable of using other information.

Finally, rephrase the gist of the second paragraph. The paragraph presents some evidence that shows that magnetic fields influence pigeon orientation. This evidence suggests that pigeons may use the earth's magnetic field to find their home but does not mean that they must use the field.

28. **G.** The sun-compass hypothesis says that homing pigeons use the sun. Because the pigeons can see the sun, they will use the sun and fly home. Choices F and H are more consistent with the other hypothesis, which suggests that the magnetic field is a major player in the birds' orientation. Choice J has real problems: It's inconsistent with both hypotheses. If the sun is key, the birds will fly in the correct direction unless their internal clock is altered. If the magnetic field is the most important element, the birds will continue to fly in random directions because the fields are distorted.

29. **D.** The magnetic-field hypothesis states that pigeons use the earth's magnetic field to orient themselves. A finding that shows that changes in this field change the way pigeons fly is certainly consistent with this hypothesis. The experiments with the magnets and electrical wires produced similar results, which were used to support the magnetic-field hypothesis.

Were you shrewd enough to notice that choices A and B basically say the same thing? Because you can't have two correct answers, both answers must be wrong. Besides, choices A and B are much too extreme. The sun may be overruled by a large disturbance in the magnetic field, but to say that the sun has no effect is going too far. Choice C has the same problem with extremism. The word "only" is too limiting (choices containing "only" are rarely correct). The pigeons still seem to use the sun under normal conditions.

30. **F.** If you chose J, you were 180 degrees wrong: Choice J is the major piece of support for the magnetic-field hypothesis. Choice H is almost as bad as choice J; this info was also used by the magnetic-field author. Choice G is consistent with the sun-compass hypothesis, but the magnetic-field author can respond by saying that the magnetic field is a factor that is sometimes overruled on sunny days. By process of elimination, F is correct. With no sun, the sun-compass hypothesis would predict that the pigeons would have trouble. On the other hand, the magnetic-field hypothesis would predict that the magnetic field should guide the pigeon, especially on a day when the sun was blocked.

31. **A.** Because a question like this one is hard to predict an answer for, go through the answer choices. Choice A appears good. The author has to make this assumption because if pigeons were affected by the mere presence of metal, the author could not conclude that the magnets were responsible for throwing the pigeons off. Metal may be disorienting the pigeons. The material may not have to be magnetic.

Choice B is too extreme (remember, a hedging answer is almost always better than a definite answer, so go for the wimpy words) and seems to contradict the author's idea that magnets are important. No information regarding what happens when magnets are worn on sunny days is available.

The downfall of choice C is also extremism. The author may accept that internal clocks may be used on sunny days. What makes this choice particularly bad is that it generalizes to all birds. You have no information regarding other bird species, so you have no way of knowing what the author assumes about this point.

And finally, choice D is wrong because the author may accept that the sun can be used under certain conditions. The author's main point is that magnetic fields are used.

32. **G.** Here's a case where opposites don't attract. If two statements are contradictory, they can't both be right. Eliminate choices F and J immediately because they include both I and II together. Doing so means that statement III has to be correct (because the remaining answer choices, G and H, both contain statement III). Don't strain any brain cells trying to think about it. (Okay, if you insist: Statement III is consistent with the magnetic-field discussion. When the sun is wiped out as a factor, the magnetic field plays an important role.)

Option I looks good because of its similarity to the sun-compass evidence cited in the passage. Option II is out because the beginning of the passage rules out landmarks. With I in and II out, only choice G can be the answer.

33. **D.** A major idea to get from this passage is that the two hypotheses present factors that homing pigeons may use. The evidence does not suggest that the sun or the earth's magnetic field is essential. (Both hedging and looking for exceptions when dealing with science passages are a good idea. Very rarely will you see an absolute, something that must be true. Note the very safe, wimpy language in the correct answer, choice D.) Evidence that brings up another possible factor does not contradict either hypothesis. This reasoning eliminates choices A and B. Choice C is easily dumped. If barometric pressure is consistent with one hypothesis, it has to be consistent with the other.

34. **J.** According to the sun-compass hypothesis, clock-shifted pigeons should make mistakes when light is present. The pigeons did not make mistakes, so choices F and G are out. The magnetic-field hypothesis, on the other hand, uses evidence of clock-shifted pigeons' not making errors to build up support for its claim. Choice G is wrong because pigeons did not respond correctly to the light, when you consider that a clock-light calculation should have pointed them in another direction. The pigeons did respond

correctly, but they did not use the light to do so. If they had, they would have gone another way. Choice J, the correct answer, is similar to what is presented in the first paragraph of the magnetic-field hypothesis.

Passage 7

Start off by summarizing to yourself the passage's main idea, which tells you why the passage was written. Although the introduction may seem long and complicated, all it is saying is that the concentration of what you start with affects how fast you get a product as the chemical reaction takes place.

When looking at the experiments, don't get hung up on the chemical formulas. You can skim over them for the moment. (And remember: You are not required to have any background science to answer these questions. You do not need to memorize the Periodic Table or know anything about chemistry.) Just try to identify the information the tables give and the conclusions you can draw from the tables.

The key factor to note is that an increase of any reactant increases the formation rate. Increases in H^+ lead to larger increases in formation rate than do increases in the other two reactants.

35. C. H_3AsO_3 is the product, so the change that increases the formation rate the most is the change that produces more H_3AsO_3 in a given amount of time. As you deduced from your analysis of the introduction, increases in H^+ lead to the largest increases in formation rate.

36. G. The chemists varied only one concentration at a time, so you can easily observe how each reactant affects the formation rate. For example, Table 1 shows that doubling the concentration of H_3AsO_4 doubles the formation rate, while Table 3 shows that doubling the concentration of H^+ quadruples the formation rate. If both these reactants are doubled, the formation rate is eight times the original rate, but without knowing anything beforehand, scientists are not able to tell which reactant, if any, has a greater effect on the rate.

In general, you can interpret experiments more easily when the experimenters change only one factor at a time. This type of experimental methodology question is a frequent one on the ACT.

The other choices do not make sense. Why would an explosion occur (choice F)? No explosion occurs even when the concentration of a given reactant is four times the original amount. You can reasonably think that changing the concentration of a couple of reactants by small amounts would not lead to any calamities. This type of reasoning also rules out choice J. In Experiment 3, scientists measure a rate that is almost 20 times the original rate. Even if measuring greater rates is difficult, the scientists can take care not to change the concentrations of two or three reactants by too great an amount.

Choice H is not at all PC (politically correct). The ACT will not have you believe that scientists are not up to a task. Even if measuring two or more concentrations is difficult, you can rest assured that the scientists will find a way. Besides, who said that the concentrations had to be measured at the same time? Why not measure each concentration separately and then dump all the reactants in at once?

37. D. How do the concentrations compare with the original concentrations, the concentrations that appear in the top line of each table? The concentrations of the first reactants are doubled, while the concentration of H^+ is the same. Table 1 shows that when the concentration of H_3AsO_3 is doubled, the formation rate doubles from 2.8 to 5.6 rate units. Table 2 reveals that doubling the concentration of I^- also doubles the formation rate. When each concentration is doubled, as in Table 2, the formation rate will be 2×2 or four times the rate obtained when the original concentrations are used ($4 \times 2.8 = 11.2$).

38. F. With two liters of solution instead of one and the same amounts of reactants, the concentration of each reactant decreases. In each experiment, increasing concentration increases formation rate, so decreasing concentration decreases formation rate.

39. D. Get rid of choices A and B immediately. Why would the rate go down when the concentration of H⁺ goes up? Throughout Table 3, the rate increases. A sudden reversal makes no sense.

Don't fight the ACT. Rarely, very rarely, does the Science Reasoning Test contain traps (as opposed to some other tests, such as the mathematics). The logical conclusion is usually correct; the reasonable interpretation of a table or chart or graph is usually the right one.

Did you choose Choice C? Don't feel bad. It is tempting to think that doubling the concentration of H⁺ from 0.40 moles/liter to 0.80 moles/liter would double the formation rate, but look at Table 3. Did doubling the concentration from 0.10 to 0.20 merely double the rate? No, doubling the concentration quadrupled the rate, making choice C too low. The answer is Choice D, which is quadruple the rate when the concentration of H⁺ is only 0.40 moles/liter.

40. J. Uh-oh: Where did H_2O come from? Don't panic. The equation written in the introduction indicates that H_2O is formed when H_3AsO_3 is formed. Well, what happens to the formation rate of H_3AsO_3 when reactant concentration increases? All the experiments show that this formation rate increases. Because H_2O is also formed when H_3AsO_3 is formed, the increase in the formation rate of H_2O makes sense.

Don't think that questions in this test necessarily follow the same order of the passage. That is, question one doesn't have to come from the introduction and question six from the last paragraph. As you just saw, the last question can be from the first part of the passage. That's one reason I suggest that you jot down your thoughts — your summary of the passage — in the margin of the test booklet. You may need to go back and refer to your notes a few times.

Chapter 21

How to Ruin a Perfectly Good Day, Part II: Practice Exam 2

You now are ready to take a sample ACT. The following exam consists of four tests: a 45-minute English Test, a 60-minute Mathematics Test, a 35-minute Reading Test, and a 35-minute Science Reasoning Test. You probably are familiar with the format of each test by now.

Please take this test under normal exam conditions. (This is serious stuff!)

1. Sit where you won't be interrupted (even though you'd probably welcome any distractions).
2. Use the answer grid provided.
3. Set your alarm clock for the intervals indicated at the beginning of each test.
4. Do not go on to the next test until the time allotted for the test you are taking is up.
5. Check your work for that test only.
6. Do not take a break during any test.
7. Give yourself one ten-minute break between tests two and three.

After you've completed the entire test, check your answers with the answer key at the end of this chapter. A section explaining your score precedes the answer key.

Chapter 22 gives detailed explanations of the answers. Go through the answer explanations to all the questions, not just the ones that you missed. You will find a plethora of worthwhile information, material that provides a good review of everything that you've learned in the other chapters of the book. I've even tossed in a few good (?) jokes to keep you somewhat sane.

Answer Sheet

Begin with Number 1 for each new section.

English Test

1. Ⓐ Ⓑ Ⓒ Ⓓ
2. Ⓕ Ⓖ Ⓗ Ⓙ
3. Ⓐ Ⓑ Ⓒ Ⓓ
4. Ⓕ Ⓖ Ⓗ Ⓙ
5. Ⓐ Ⓑ Ⓒ Ⓓ
6. Ⓕ Ⓖ Ⓗ Ⓙ
7. Ⓐ Ⓑ Ⓒ Ⓓ
8. Ⓕ Ⓖ Ⓗ Ⓙ
9. Ⓐ Ⓑ Ⓒ Ⓓ
10. Ⓕ Ⓖ Ⓗ Ⓙ
11. Ⓐ Ⓑ Ⓒ Ⓓ
12. Ⓕ Ⓖ Ⓗ Ⓙ
13. Ⓐ Ⓑ Ⓒ Ⓓ
14. Ⓕ Ⓖ Ⓗ Ⓙ
15. Ⓐ Ⓑ Ⓒ Ⓓ
16. Ⓕ Ⓖ Ⓗ Ⓙ
17. Ⓐ Ⓑ Ⓒ Ⓓ
18. Ⓕ Ⓖ Ⓗ Ⓙ
19. Ⓐ Ⓑ Ⓒ Ⓓ
20. Ⓕ Ⓖ Ⓗ Ⓙ
21. Ⓐ Ⓑ Ⓒ Ⓓ
22. Ⓕ Ⓖ Ⓗ Ⓙ
23. Ⓐ Ⓑ Ⓒ Ⓓ
24. Ⓕ Ⓖ Ⓗ Ⓙ
25. Ⓐ Ⓑ Ⓒ Ⓓ
26. Ⓕ Ⓖ Ⓗ Ⓙ
27. Ⓐ Ⓑ Ⓒ Ⓓ
28. Ⓕ Ⓖ Ⓗ Ⓙ
29. Ⓐ Ⓑ Ⓒ Ⓓ
30. Ⓕ Ⓖ Ⓗ Ⓙ
31. Ⓐ Ⓑ Ⓒ Ⓓ
32. Ⓕ Ⓖ Ⓗ Ⓙ
33. Ⓐ Ⓑ Ⓒ Ⓓ
34. Ⓕ Ⓖ Ⓗ Ⓙ
35. Ⓐ Ⓑ Ⓒ Ⓓ
36. Ⓕ Ⓖ Ⓗ Ⓙ
37. Ⓐ Ⓑ Ⓒ Ⓓ
38. Ⓕ Ⓖ Ⓗ Ⓙ
39. Ⓐ Ⓑ Ⓒ Ⓓ
40. Ⓕ Ⓖ Ⓗ Ⓙ
41. Ⓐ Ⓑ Ⓒ Ⓓ
42. Ⓕ Ⓖ Ⓗ Ⓙ
43. Ⓐ Ⓑ Ⓒ Ⓓ
44. Ⓕ Ⓖ Ⓗ Ⓙ
45. Ⓐ Ⓑ Ⓒ Ⓓ
46. Ⓕ Ⓖ Ⓗ Ⓙ
47. Ⓐ Ⓑ Ⓒ Ⓓ
48. Ⓕ Ⓖ Ⓗ Ⓙ
49. Ⓐ Ⓑ Ⓒ Ⓓ
50. Ⓕ Ⓖ Ⓗ Ⓙ
51. Ⓐ Ⓑ Ⓒ Ⓓ
52. Ⓕ Ⓖ Ⓗ Ⓙ
53. Ⓐ Ⓑ Ⓒ Ⓓ
54. Ⓕ Ⓖ Ⓗ Ⓙ
55. Ⓐ Ⓑ Ⓒ Ⓓ
56. Ⓕ Ⓖ Ⓗ Ⓙ
57. Ⓐ Ⓑ Ⓒ Ⓓ
58. Ⓕ Ⓖ Ⓗ Ⓙ
59. Ⓐ Ⓑ Ⓒ Ⓓ
60. Ⓕ Ⓖ Ⓗ Ⓙ
61. Ⓐ Ⓑ Ⓒ Ⓓ
62. Ⓕ Ⓖ Ⓗ Ⓙ
63. Ⓐ Ⓑ Ⓒ Ⓓ
64. Ⓕ Ⓖ Ⓗ Ⓙ
65. Ⓐ Ⓑ Ⓒ Ⓓ
66. Ⓕ Ⓖ Ⓗ Ⓙ
67. Ⓐ Ⓑ Ⓒ Ⓓ
68. Ⓕ Ⓖ Ⓗ Ⓙ
69. Ⓐ Ⓑ Ⓒ Ⓓ
70. Ⓕ Ⓖ Ⓗ Ⓙ
71. Ⓐ Ⓑ Ⓒ Ⓓ
72. Ⓕ Ⓖ Ⓗ Ⓙ
73. Ⓐ Ⓑ Ⓒ Ⓓ
74. Ⓕ Ⓖ Ⓗ Ⓙ
75. Ⓐ Ⓑ Ⓒ Ⓓ

Mathematics Test

1. Ⓐ Ⓑ Ⓒ Ⓓ Ⓔ
2. Ⓕ Ⓖ Ⓗ Ⓙ Ⓚ
3. Ⓐ Ⓑ Ⓒ Ⓓ Ⓔ
4. Ⓕ Ⓖ Ⓗ Ⓙ Ⓚ
5. Ⓐ Ⓑ Ⓒ Ⓓ Ⓔ
6. Ⓕ Ⓖ Ⓗ Ⓙ Ⓚ
7. Ⓐ Ⓑ Ⓒ Ⓓ Ⓔ
8. Ⓕ Ⓖ Ⓗ Ⓙ Ⓚ
9. Ⓐ Ⓑ Ⓒ Ⓓ Ⓔ
10. Ⓕ Ⓖ Ⓗ Ⓙ Ⓚ
11. Ⓐ Ⓑ Ⓒ Ⓓ Ⓔ
12. Ⓕ Ⓖ Ⓗ Ⓙ Ⓚ
13. Ⓐ Ⓑ Ⓒ Ⓓ Ⓔ
14. Ⓕ Ⓖ Ⓗ Ⓙ Ⓚ
15. Ⓐ Ⓑ Ⓒ Ⓓ Ⓔ
16. Ⓕ Ⓖ Ⓗ Ⓙ Ⓚ
17. Ⓐ Ⓑ Ⓒ Ⓓ Ⓔ
18. Ⓕ Ⓖ Ⓗ Ⓙ Ⓚ
19. Ⓐ Ⓑ Ⓒ Ⓓ Ⓔ
20. Ⓕ Ⓖ Ⓗ Ⓙ Ⓚ
21. Ⓐ Ⓑ Ⓒ Ⓓ Ⓔ
22. Ⓕ Ⓖ Ⓗ Ⓙ Ⓚ
23. Ⓐ Ⓑ Ⓒ Ⓓ Ⓔ
24. Ⓕ Ⓖ Ⓗ Ⓙ Ⓚ
25. Ⓐ Ⓑ Ⓒ Ⓓ Ⓔ
26. Ⓕ Ⓖ Ⓗ Ⓙ Ⓚ
27. Ⓐ Ⓑ Ⓒ Ⓓ Ⓔ
28. Ⓕ Ⓖ Ⓗ Ⓙ Ⓚ
29. Ⓐ Ⓑ Ⓒ Ⓓ Ⓔ
30. Ⓕ Ⓖ Ⓗ Ⓙ Ⓚ
31. Ⓐ Ⓑ Ⓒ Ⓓ Ⓔ
32. Ⓕ Ⓖ Ⓗ Ⓙ Ⓚ
33. Ⓐ Ⓑ Ⓒ Ⓓ Ⓔ
34. Ⓕ Ⓖ Ⓗ Ⓙ Ⓚ
35. Ⓐ Ⓑ Ⓒ Ⓓ Ⓔ
36. Ⓕ Ⓖ Ⓗ Ⓙ Ⓚ
37. Ⓐ Ⓑ Ⓒ Ⓓ Ⓔ
38. Ⓕ Ⓖ Ⓗ Ⓙ Ⓚ
39. Ⓐ Ⓑ Ⓒ Ⓓ Ⓔ
40. Ⓕ Ⓖ Ⓗ Ⓙ Ⓚ
41. Ⓐ Ⓑ Ⓒ Ⓓ Ⓔ
42. Ⓕ Ⓖ Ⓗ Ⓙ Ⓚ
43. Ⓐ Ⓑ Ⓒ Ⓓ Ⓔ
44. Ⓕ Ⓖ Ⓗ Ⓙ Ⓚ
45. Ⓐ Ⓑ Ⓒ Ⓓ Ⓔ
46. Ⓕ Ⓖ Ⓗ Ⓙ Ⓚ
47. Ⓐ Ⓑ Ⓒ Ⓓ Ⓔ
48. Ⓕ Ⓖ Ⓗ Ⓙ Ⓚ
49. Ⓐ Ⓑ Ⓒ Ⓓ Ⓔ
50. Ⓕ Ⓖ Ⓗ Ⓙ Ⓚ
51. Ⓐ Ⓑ Ⓒ Ⓓ Ⓔ
52. Ⓕ Ⓖ Ⓗ Ⓙ Ⓚ
53. Ⓐ Ⓑ Ⓒ Ⓓ Ⓔ
54. Ⓕ Ⓖ Ⓗ Ⓙ Ⓚ
55. Ⓐ Ⓑ Ⓒ Ⓓ Ⓔ
56. Ⓕ Ⓖ Ⓗ Ⓙ Ⓚ
57. Ⓐ Ⓑ Ⓒ Ⓓ Ⓔ
58. Ⓕ Ⓖ Ⓗ Ⓙ Ⓚ
59. Ⓐ Ⓑ Ⓒ Ⓓ Ⓔ
60. Ⓕ Ⓖ Ⓗ Ⓙ Ⓚ

Chapter 21: How to Ruin a Perfectly Good Day, Part II: Practice Exam 2

Reading Test	Science Test
1. Ⓐ Ⓑ Ⓒ Ⓓ	1. Ⓐ Ⓑ Ⓒ Ⓓ
2. Ⓕ Ⓖ Ⓗ Ⓙ	2. Ⓕ Ⓖ Ⓗ Ⓙ
3. Ⓐ Ⓑ Ⓒ Ⓓ	3. Ⓐ Ⓑ Ⓒ Ⓓ
4. Ⓕ Ⓖ Ⓗ Ⓙ	4. Ⓕ Ⓖ Ⓗ Ⓙ
5. Ⓐ Ⓑ Ⓒ Ⓓ	5. Ⓐ Ⓑ Ⓒ Ⓓ
6. Ⓕ Ⓖ Ⓗ Ⓙ	6. Ⓕ Ⓖ Ⓗ Ⓙ
7. Ⓐ Ⓑ Ⓒ Ⓓ	7. Ⓐ Ⓑ Ⓒ Ⓓ
8. Ⓕ Ⓖ Ⓗ Ⓙ	8. Ⓕ Ⓖ Ⓗ Ⓙ
9. Ⓐ Ⓑ Ⓒ Ⓓ	9. Ⓐ Ⓑ Ⓒ Ⓓ
10. Ⓕ Ⓖ Ⓗ Ⓙ	10. Ⓕ Ⓖ Ⓗ Ⓙ
11. Ⓐ Ⓑ Ⓒ Ⓓ	11. Ⓐ Ⓑ Ⓒ Ⓓ
12. Ⓕ Ⓖ Ⓗ Ⓙ	12. Ⓕ Ⓖ Ⓗ Ⓙ
13. Ⓐ Ⓑ Ⓒ Ⓓ	13. Ⓐ Ⓑ Ⓒ Ⓓ
14. Ⓕ Ⓖ Ⓗ Ⓙ	14. Ⓕ Ⓖ Ⓗ Ⓙ
15. Ⓐ Ⓑ Ⓒ Ⓓ	15. Ⓐ Ⓑ Ⓒ Ⓓ
16. Ⓕ Ⓖ Ⓗ Ⓙ	16. Ⓕ Ⓖ Ⓗ Ⓙ
17. Ⓐ Ⓑ Ⓒ Ⓓ	17. Ⓐ Ⓑ Ⓒ Ⓓ
18. Ⓕ Ⓖ Ⓗ Ⓙ	18. Ⓕ Ⓖ Ⓗ Ⓙ
19. Ⓐ Ⓑ Ⓒ Ⓓ	19. Ⓐ Ⓑ Ⓒ Ⓓ
20. Ⓕ Ⓖ Ⓗ Ⓙ	20. Ⓕ Ⓖ Ⓗ Ⓙ
21. Ⓐ Ⓑ Ⓒ Ⓓ	21. Ⓐ Ⓑ Ⓒ Ⓓ
22. Ⓕ Ⓖ Ⓗ Ⓙ	22. Ⓕ Ⓖ Ⓗ Ⓙ
23. Ⓐ Ⓑ Ⓒ Ⓓ	23. Ⓐ Ⓑ Ⓒ Ⓓ
24. Ⓕ Ⓖ Ⓗ Ⓙ	24. Ⓕ Ⓖ Ⓗ Ⓙ
25. Ⓐ Ⓑ Ⓒ Ⓓ	25. Ⓐ Ⓑ Ⓒ Ⓓ
26. Ⓕ Ⓖ Ⓗ Ⓙ	26. Ⓕ Ⓖ Ⓗ Ⓙ
27. Ⓐ Ⓑ Ⓒ Ⓓ	27. Ⓐ Ⓑ Ⓒ Ⓓ
28. Ⓕ Ⓖ Ⓗ Ⓙ	28. Ⓕ Ⓖ Ⓗ Ⓙ
29. Ⓐ Ⓑ Ⓒ Ⓓ	29. Ⓐ Ⓑ Ⓒ Ⓓ
30. Ⓕ Ⓖ Ⓗ Ⓙ	30. Ⓕ Ⓖ Ⓗ Ⓙ
31. Ⓐ Ⓑ Ⓒ Ⓓ	31. Ⓐ Ⓑ Ⓒ Ⓓ
32. Ⓕ Ⓖ Ⓗ Ⓙ	32. Ⓕ Ⓖ Ⓗ Ⓙ
33. Ⓐ Ⓑ Ⓒ Ⓓ	33. Ⓐ Ⓑ Ⓒ Ⓓ
34. Ⓕ Ⓖ Ⓗ Ⓙ	34. Ⓕ Ⓖ Ⓗ Ⓙ
35. Ⓐ Ⓑ Ⓒ Ⓓ	35. Ⓐ Ⓑ Ⓒ Ⓓ
36. Ⓕ Ⓖ Ⓗ Ⓙ	36. Ⓕ Ⓖ Ⓗ Ⓙ
37. Ⓐ Ⓑ Ⓒ Ⓓ	37. Ⓐ Ⓑ Ⓒ Ⓓ
38. Ⓕ Ⓖ Ⓗ Ⓙ	38. Ⓕ Ⓖ Ⓗ Ⓙ
39. Ⓐ Ⓑ Ⓒ Ⓓ	39. Ⓐ Ⓑ Ⓒ Ⓓ
40. Ⓕ Ⓖ Ⓗ Ⓙ	40. Ⓕ Ⓖ Ⓗ Ⓙ

English Test

45 Minutes — 75 Questions

DIRECTIONS: Following are five passages with underlined portions. Alternate ways of stating the underlined portions are to the right of the passages. Choose the best alternative; if the original is the best way of stating the underlined portion, choose NO CHANGE.

You also have questions that refer to the passage or ask you to reorder the sentences within the passage. These questions are identified by a number in a box. Choose the best answer and blacken in the corresponding oval on your answer grid.

Passage 1

Food Trends

by Joel Shapiro

<u>It has</u> been a recent trend in the food service industry toward lower fat content, and less sodium. This trend, which was spearheaded by the medical community as a method of fighting heart disease, has had some unintended side <u>effects obesity</u> and heart disease — the very thing the medical community was trying to fight.

Fat and salt are very important parts of a diet. <u>It is</u> required to process the food that we eat, to recover from injury, to stay hydrated, and for several other bodily functions. <u>Fat and salt are required parts of diet.</u> When fat and salt are removed from food, the food tastes as if it is missing something. As a result, people will eat more food to try to make up for that something missing. Even worse, the amount of junk food that people eat goes up. <u>Such as potato chips, soda, candy, and doughnuts, my favorite.</u> Junk food is full of fat and salt; by eating more junk food people will get more salt and fat than they need in their diet.

1.
   A. NO CHANGE
   B. There have
   C. There has
   D. Having

2.
   F. NO CHANGE
   G. effects, including obesity
   H. affects, such as obesity
   J. affects: obesity

3.
   A. NO CHANGE
   B. It's
   C. They are
   D. OMIT the underlined portion

4.
   F. NO CHANGE
   G. Fat, and also salt, are required parts of diet.
   H. When on a diet, fat and salt are required.
   J. OMIT the underlined portion

5.
   A. NO CHANGE
   B. Junk food includes potato chips, soda, candy and my favorite, doughnuts.
   C. Junk food, including potato chips, soda, candy and my favorite doughnuts.
   D. Potato chips, soda, candy and doughnuts are my favorite junk foods.

Go on to next page

There is another interesting side effect of removing salt and fat from food — less flavor. It took me several years to figure out why the food that I get at restaurants has had <u>lesser</u> flavor as time went by, while the food that I prepare at home has strong flavors. I <u>discover</u> the answer in a bowl of chili. I had been making chili (my family's favorite dish and one that I serve at least once a week) with low-fat meats, following the current trend toward low-fat food. One day at the grocery, the store had run out of the low-fat meat, so I bought some meat with much higher fat content than I normally get. The chili made from this meat had a much better flavor than <u>the previous chili.</u>

From that point <u>on, I experimented,</u> with ingredients that were not low in fat. The resulting dishes were much more satisfying than before. In addition, I found that people didn't eat as much. <u>After talking to several,</u> I discovered that they found the meals much more satisfying than they had in the past. Therefore, they ate less. <u>As a result of eating less, ending up eating</u> fewer calories than they had with the low fat meals. 12

6. F. NO CHANGE
   G. less and less
   H. lesser and lesser
   J. the least

7. A. NO CHANGE
   B. discovering
   C. discovered
   D. had discovered

8. F. NO CHANGE
   G. the previous chili's
   H. that of the previous chili
   J. the previous chili's did

9. A. NO CHANGE
   B. on; I experimented,
   C. on, I experimented;
   D. on, I experimented

10. F. NO CHANGE
    G. After talking with several,
    H. After talking to several people,
    J. Talking afterwards to several,

11. A. NO CHANGE
    B. As a result, they are eating less, ending up eating
    C. As a result, consuming less,
    D. As a result of eating less, they consume

12. The writer wants to add the following sentence:
    While salt has no calories, it also affects how much food is consumed.
    This sentence would most logically be placed:
    F. before Sentence 1
    G. after Sentence 1
    H. before sentence 4
    J. at the end of the first paragraph

13. A. NO CHANGE
    B. the meal doesn't taste well
    C. the meal doesn't taste good
    D. the meal isn't tasting good

[1] Salt is a more difficult ingredient to judge. [2] If there is too much, the meal isn't tasting well, and diners will push the food aside uneaten. [3] If there isn't enough, then the dish tastes like something is missing and diners will eat more food to obtain enough salt. [4] Salt also helps bring out the flavors of the dish. [5] The trick is to find just the right amount. [6] I generally do this by tasting. [7] As I cook, I taste the sauce or food that I am preparing. [8] If it tastes like "something is missing," then I add a little salt. [9] Stir it in and give it a few minutes, and then try it again. [10] Eventually, it's just right.

Fat and salt are important parts of any diet and also important to the food that you cook. Having enough in your meals will reduce the urge to snack between meals (often on unhealthy, empty-calorie treats) and will improve the taste and flavor of your food. However, be careful not to go overboard. Like anything, it is possible to have too much of both, not good for the health. [15]

14. F. NO CHANGE
     G. which is not good for the health.
     H. not being good for the health.
     J. and that is for the health not good.

15. The author wants to conclude the passage by emphasizing the importance of having the right amounts of fat and salt, rather than eliminating them altogether. Which version does that best?
     A. NO CHANGE
     B. But don't eliminate these vital ingredients totally, or you won't like the way your food tastes.
     C. However, if you have no salt or fat, you are likely to overeat and become obese.
     D. Having no salt or fat is just as bad as having too much, maybe even more so.

Go on to next page

Passage 2

Native American Government

The question has been asked how Native American tribes, whom govern themselves do so. Most tribal governments are organized democratic, that is, with an elected leadership. The governing body is referred to as a council, it is composed of persons elected by vote of the eligible adult tribal members. The presiding official is the chairman, although some tribes use other titles, such as principal chief, president, or governor. An elected tribal council, recognized as such by the Secretary of the Interior and the people working for him, have authority to speak and act for the tribe and to represent it in negotiations with federal, state, and local governments.

Just what do tribal governments do? They generally define conditions of tribal membership, regulate domestic relations of members, prescribe rules of inheritance for reservation property not in trust status, levy taxes, regulate property under tribal jurisdiction, control conduct of members by tribal ordinances, and they administer justice.

16. F. NO CHANGE
    G. who govern themselves,
    H. governing them
    J. whom, governing themselves,

17. A. NO CHANGE
    B. organized democratically
    C. organized in a democracy
    D. OMIT the underlined portion

18. F. NO CHANGE
    G. council; however, it is
    H. council, but is
    J. council, and is

19. A. NO CHANGE
    B. such as a principle
    C. like a principle
    D. like principle

20. F. NO CHANGE
    G. had
    H. has
    J. having

21. A. NO CHANGE
    B. be representing it
    C. to represent them
    D. representing them

22. F. NO CHANGE
    G. regular
    H. regulating
    J. having regulated

23. A. NO CHANGE
    B. and administering
    C. and administer
    D. and to be administering

What role do Native Americans have in the American political system? They have the same obligations for military service as do other U.S. citizens. They have fought in all American wars since the Revolution, they served on both sides in the Civil War. Eli S. Parker, a Seneca from New York, was at Appomattox as an aide to General Ulysses S. Grant when Lee surrendered, and the unit of Confederate Brigadier General Stand Watie, a Cherokee, was the last to surrender. It was not until World War I that Native American's demonstrating patriotism (6,000 of the more than 8,000 who served were volunteers) moved Congress to pass the Indian Citizenship Act of 1924. One reads in your history books about using the Navajo Marines of their language as a battlefield code, the only such code that the enemy could not break. Today, one out of every four Native American men is a military veteran, and 45 to 47 percent of tribal leaders is a military veteran. [29]

24. F. NO CHANGE
    G. They did fight
    H. It has fought (the tribal)
    J. Fighting

25. A. NO CHANGE
    B. when the Native Americans, who demonstrated
    C. that the Native Americans' demonstrated
    D. when the Native Americans'

26. F. NO CHANGE
    G. in history books
    H. in their history books
    J. in one of their history books

27. A. NO CHANGE
    B. about the use by Navajo Marines of their language
    C. about Navajos using their Marine language
    D. , the Navajo Marines' language use

28. F. NO CHANGE
    G. is military veterans
    H. are military veterans
    J. are a military veteran

Question 29 refers to the entire passage.

29. Which of the following best describes the author's purpose in writing this passage?
    A. to argue the need for governmental withdrawal from Native American affairs
    B. to explain tribal structure and Native American military participation
    C. to hypothesize causes of racial tension between Native Americans of warring tribes
    D. to predict the roles of Native Americans in future wars

Go on to next page

Passage 3

Mountains and Volcanoes

[1] The theory of plate tectonics <u>hold that as</u>
                                    30
the expanding oceanic crust is thrust beneath
the continental plate <u>margins: it penetrates</u> deep
                        31
enough into the Earth to be partly remelted.
[2] Pockets of molten rock (magma) <u>result</u>.
                                     32
[3] Before Lassen Peak was emplaced, Mount
Tehama had collapsed, but its caldera was
breached, and no large lake ever developed
as did Crater Lake in Oregon. [4] About 500,000
years ago, Mount Tehama <u>gradually building up</u>
                          33
<u>here throughout countless</u> eruptions. [5] These
become the feeding chambers for volcanoes, <u>like</u>
                                                34
the great Pacific Ring of Fire stratovolcano, Mount
Tehama; remnants of its caldera flanks are Brokeoff
Mountain, Mount Diller, Pilot Pinnacle, and Mount
Conard.

[6] If you connect these peaks in a circle on
the map, you can envision Mount Tehama's base,
which was more than 18 kilometers (11 miles)
wide. [7] The park's plant life mixes species of
the Sierra Nevada to the south <u>from</u> those of the
                                  35
Cascade Range. [8] The result is <u>more species than</u>
                                    36
<u>you can break a stick over</u>. The park <u>boast some</u>
                                         37
715 plant species, but nearby Mount Shasta has only

30. F. NO CHANGE
    G. hold when
    H. holds that whichever
    J. holds that as

31. A. NO CHANGE
    B. margins, it penetrates
    C. margins; however, it penetrates
    D. margins and penetrating

32. F. NO CHANGE
    G. resulting
    H. results
    J. resulted

33. A. NO CHANGE
    B. was bilt up here, going through countless
    C. had built up here throughout uncounted
    D. built up here through countless

34. F. NO CHANGE
    G. as
    H. as if
    J. likely

35. A. NO CHANGE
    B. with
    C. form
    D. to

36. F. NO CHANGE
    G. more species than you can shake a stick at
    H. as many species as you can find in two shakes of a stick
    J. so many species that they break the sticking point

37. A. NO CHANGE
    B. boasts and has
    C. boasts some
    D. boast some more of the

485 species. Of 38 transitional species, about 24 Sierran species are at the northern limit of their range here; therefore, about 14 Cascadian species are at their southern limits. 39 40
                                          38

What was life like on these peaks? Sometimes historians have difficulty determining that. The Lassen area, for example, was a meeting point for four groups of Native Americans: Atsugewi, Yana, Yahi, and Maidu. Because of its weather and snow
                                    41
conditions, generally high elevation, and seasonally mobile deer populations, the Lassen area was not conducive to year-round living. These Native American groups encamped here in warmer months for hunting and gathering. The Native Americans left few artifacts. History generally describes the
        42
period from 1840 on, even though mountain man Jedediah Smith passed through in 1828 on his overland trek to the West Coast. Two pioneer trails, developed by William Nobles and Peter Lassen, are associated with the park. 43

38. F. NO CHANGE
    G. , therefore;
    H. ,
    J. : and

Question 39 refers to the entire passage.

39. Using a cliché in sentence 8 does which of the following?
    A. It changes the meaning of the passage.
    B. It introduces a new concept.
    C. It forestalls an opposing argument.
    D. It inserts inappropriate humor into a serious discussion.

40. Which of the following would be the correct order of sentences in the first paragraph?
    F. 3 — 5 — 4 — 2 — 1
    G. 2 — 3 — 4 — 5 — 1
    H. 2 — 5 — 3 — 1 — 4
    J. 1 — 2 — 5 — 4 — 3

41. A. NO CHANGE
    B. Since
    C. Therefore,
    D. OMIT the underlined portion

42. F. NO CHANGE
    G. have few artifacts.
    H. with few artifacts left.
    J. leaving few artifacts.

43. Which of these best describes the effect of the last paragraph?
    A. It summarizes the information given in the previous paragraphs.
    B. It presents a personal opinion that contradicts the beginning of the passage.
    C. It introduces a new concept.
    D. It supports the author's hypothesis.

Go on to next page

Passage 4

One Boy's Role Model

As a young boy, I having dreamed of following in the footsteps of explorer Richard Halliburton, who it is fair to say has been my hero since childhood. Let other boys dream of being Viking warriors or knights in shining armor. I have always wanted to be a world-famous explorer, going places no one has ever been, or returning to places where civilization flourished long ago. Richard Halliburton lived the life I always wanted to live and wrote about it in ways that motivated me as a youngster and still have the power to thrill me as a man. I am especially fascinated by his stories of his trip to Pompeii, which he calls the city that rose from the dead. A few miles past Naples, Italy, along the slopes of Vesuvius. This city is found, which is much the same as it was in A.D. 79, with wine jars still lying in place and the ruts in the streets from the passing chariots still visible.

[1] He calls these chilling effects the volcano's "tantrums" and mentions that while the locals treat them causally, he himself cannot help but think of what future explorers would think if they found his body, complete with tourist guide, wristwatch, and toothbrush. [2] My favorite is, "Good health to anybody who invites me to dinner." [3] Neither too wordy or too concise, the explorer's writing appeals to the secret fears of all of us by mentioning that as he sat in his hotel room that evening and looked out over the landscape, he could see flashes of red light shooting up from the summit of Vesuvius.

44. F. NO CHANGE
    G. As a young boy, I dreamed of
    H. As a young boy, I am dreaming of
    J. Dreaming, as a young boy, of

45. A. NO CHANGE
    B. who fairly says
    C. who, its' fair to say
    D. of whom it is fairly said

46. F. NO CHANGE
    G. enslaved with
    H. captivated to
    J. enriched of

47. A. NO CHANGE
    B. Vesuvius, is found this city,
    C. Vesuvius: This city is found,
    D. Vesuvius, finding this city

48. F. NO CHANGE
    G. laying
    H. being to lay
    J. lain

49. A. NO CHANGE
    B. whereas the locals treat them causally
    C. although the locals treat them causally
    D. while the locals treat them casually

50. F. NO CHANGE
    G. invite me to dinner
    H. invite him to dinner
    J. OMIT the underlined portion

51. A. NO CHANGE
    B. or concise, too
    C. nor too concise
    D. nor concisely

52. F. NO CHANGE
    G. and looks out over
    H. and is looking out over
    J. , having looked

Go on to next page

Chapter 21: How to Ruin a Perfectly Good Day, Part II: Practice Exam 2   **277**

[4] Halliburton <u>makes his writing breathing</u> by showing the homey points that we all can <u>relate to. The graffiti on the walls.</u> [5] He also mentions the signboards and posters <u>in very perfect condition</u> that show the announcements of new plays and the contests of the <u>gladiators. Sure to</u> inspire every young boy's imagination to feats of daring and bravery. 57 58 59

53.
A. NO CHANGE
B. makes his writing vivid
C. , making lively writing,
D. made his writing breath

54.
F. NO CHANGE
G. relate with — the graffiti on the walls.
H. relate to, one example is the graffiti on the walls.
J. relate to, such as the graffiti on the walls.

55.
A. NO CHANGE
B. in perfect condition
C. , which are in completely perfect condition,
D. — perfect —

56.
F. NO CHANGE
G. gladiators, they're sure to
H. gladiators and sure to
J. gladiators, which are sure to

57. Which of the following represents the best order of the first four sentences for the second paragraph to make the most sense?
A. 1 — 2 — 3 — 4
B. 4 — 3 — 1 — 2
C. 4 — 2 — 3 — 1
D. 2 — 3 — 1 — 4

Questions 58 and 59 refer to the entire passage.

58. In which of the following places would you be most likely to find this passage?
F. an encyclopedia
G. a newspaper editorial
H. a memoir
J. a geography textbook

59. Why did Halliburton mention a toothbrush (paragraph 2, sentence 1)?
A. to show how far hygienic practices have come
B. to add a touch of humor to the prospect of having his body found in a lava flow
C. to ridicule the idea of treating a volcano casually
D. to emphasize the completely destructive effects of volcanoes

Go on to next page

Passage 5

Bird Mating Habits

The courting ritual of many birds <u>that</u> includes
elaborate dances and posturing. Some birds have
intricate <u>set routines that never vary,</u> patterns that
are repeated over and over again in a dance as old
as the species itself. Other birds appear to be
improvising, making up steps as they go along,
adapting their movements to fit the situation. Some
of the dancers <u>appears</u> more warlike than roman-
tic, with puffed-out chests and aggressive strutting.
Some of the dancers even charge the object of
their affections. A type of pheasant called the
tragopan pops out from behind a rock to show
himself to the female. [63] While one would <u>except</u>
the female to be surprised or at least startled,
more often than not she is what one zoo curator
called "amazingly unimpressed."

Another part of the mating ritual is <u>to be
providing</u> an appropriately enticing home,
<u>often called a bower,</u> for the female. The nesting
areas are decorated with everything and anything
the bird can find, including twigs, feathers, small
rocks, <u>also bits of trash bags</u> and broken glass.
Some experts have noted that the birds with the
less attractive plumage, dull light brown birds with
no exceptionally attractive coloring, create the
<u>more colorful and elaborate</u> bowers, perhaps as
compensation.

---

60. F. NO CHANGE
    G. which
    H. those
    J. OMIT the underlined portion

61. A. NO CHANGE
    B. sets of routines, and they never vary these,
    C. routines and sets, never varying
    D. routines

62. F. NO CHANGE
    G. appear
    H. who appear
    J. they appear

63. The author used the phrase "pops out" most likely
    A. to express the awkwardness of the bird
    B. to show his unfamiliarity with this type of bird
    C. to paint a picture of the bird's appearance
    D. to further the idea of the aggressiveness of some birds

64. F. NO CHANGE
    G. accept
    H. expect
    J. be expecting

65. A. NO CHANGE
    B. to have provision for
    C. to have provided
    D. to provide

66. F. NO CHANGE
    G. often called a bower —
    H. often called, a bower
    J. often, called a bower

67. A. NO CHANGE
    B. and also bits of trash bags,
    C. bits of trash bags,
    D. trash, and bag bits

68. F. NO CHANGE
    G. most colorful and elaborate
    H. mostly colorful and elaborate
    J. more than colorful and elaborate

Chapter 21: How to Ruin a Perfectly Good Day, Part II: Practice Exam 2

Not all birds are plain-colored. The male tragopan (found in southern Tibet) has a bright yellow face and a red head. The wattled pheasant has a dark body but a fan of snowy, almost painfully white tail feathers. He also has a blue wattle around the head, and <u>red irises in the eye region</u>. The bird of paradise can range from black to bright orange and blue. You may know that a peacock has "eyes" on its tail feathers, but did you know that a pheasant <u>is with them</u>, too? The Argus pheasant can raise his wing feathers which are decorated with a pattern that seems to resemble eyes. <u>This is why the Argus pheasant got its name,</u> after Argus, the watchman in Greek mythology who had a hundred eyes. Some birds are so stunning that people who observed them in captivity, brought back by explorers, theorized that the birds must have come from the Garden of Eden, the only place that could possibly support such beauty.

The courtship dances of birds <u>have been emulated by humans. In New Guinea, for example.</u> Warriors wear large headdresses made with bird of paradise feathers, and dye their bodies to resemble those of their favorite birds. The dances the men perform are thought by some to resemble the mating dances of those same birds. 74 75

69. A. NO CHANGE
    B. red irises
    C. red in the irises region
    D. red irises in the regions of the eye

70. F. NO CHANGE
    G. with them
    H. has them
    J. also has them

71. A. NO CHANGE
    B. The Argus pheasant was named
    C. This is the reason why they named the Argus pheasant
    D. Therefore, the name is the Argus pheasant

72. F. NO CHANGE
    G. has been initiated
    H. has been emulated by humans
    J. by humans have been emulated

73. A. NO CHANGE
    B. For example, in New Guinea.
    C. In, for example, New Guinea.
    D. Take New Guinea, for example.

Questions 74 and 75 refer to the passage as a whole.

74. If the passage were to continue, it would most likely discuss which of the following?
    F. The costumes the male dancers wear to attract the females.
    G. The dances the males perform.
    H. The origins of the names of the birds the human males imitate.
    J. Homes the human males build to provide for their mates.

75. Suppose the writer had been assigned to write an essay detailing the courtship ritual of birds. Did the author complete his task successfully with this essay?
    A. No, because only a few birds were mentioned.
    B. No, because the author digressed by talking about human mating rituals.
    C. Yes, because the author discusses how the males attract the females.
    D. Yes, because the author gives a common theory and provides examples and counterexamples.

STOP DO NOT TURN THE PAGE UNTIL TOLD TO DO SO.
DO NOT RETURN TO A PREVIOUS TEST.

Mathematics Test

60 Minutes — 60 Questions

DIRECTIONS: Each question has five answer choices. Choose the best answer for each question and shade the corresponding oval on your answer grid.

1. Five cheerleaders and ten football players contributed to a coach's retirement party. Each cheerleader gave the same amount of money, exactly twice as much as each football player gave. If together the 15 friends donated $480, how much money did each football player give?
   A. $5
   B. $15
   C. $22
   D. $24
   E. $26

2. What is the fourth term in the arithmetic sequence 2, 5, 8 . . . ?
   F. 9
   G. 10
   H. 11
   J. 12
   K. 13

3. Let $x = -3$. Which of the following is equal to $2x - (3y - 3x) + 4y$?
   A. $y + 15$
   B. $y + 12$
   C. $y - 12$
   D. $y - 15$
   E. $7y - 15$

4. What is the measure of angle LMX?

   $LN = MN$
   $\angle LNM = 120°$

   F. 150°
   G. 120°
   H. 100°
   J. 60°
   K. 30°

5. Jarnelle can assemble 300 widgets in an hour. To be eligible for a raise, she must be able to raise her rate of assembly by 25 percent. At the new rate, how many widgets could Jarnelle assemble in 8 hours? (Assume a steady rate with no breaks.)
   A. 6,125
   B. 3,000
   C. 375
   D. 300
   E. 75

6. To solve the following proportion, a must be which of the following?
   $$\frac{3}{5} = \frac{a}{25}$$
   F. 20
   G. 18
   H. 15
   J. 12
   K. 5

7. What is the number of square units in the area of an isosceles right triangle with a hypotenuse $5\sqrt{2}$?
   A. $2\sqrt{2}$
   B. 25
   C. $12.5\sqrt{2}$
   D. 12.5
   E. $10 + 5\sqrt{2}$

8. Which of the following is another way of expressing $6a - [(a - 3) - a]$?
   F. $4a + 3$
   G. $5a - 3$
   H. $6a - 3$
   J. $5a + 3$
   K. $6a + 3$

Go on to next page

9. Veronica buys a car on sale for 25 percent off the original price but has to pay a 5 percent luxury tax on the sale price. If the before-sale price of the car is $18,000, how much does Veronica pay for the car?
   A. $18,900
   B. $14,400
   C. $14,175
   D. $13,500
   E. $4,500

10. A floor with a length three times its width has a perimeter of 640 feet. What is its area in square feet?
    F. 100,000
    G. 19,200
    H. 14,400
    J. 8,800
    K. 6,000

11. If $a = 3$; $b = 10$, which of the following is the closest approximation to
    $$\frac{a + b(a-b)^2(a^2-b)}{b(a^2+b)}?$$
    A. 10
    B. 2.5
    C. −1
    D. −2.5
    E. −8

12. Three angles, x, y, and z, lie along a straight line. If $x = \frac{1}{2}y$, and $y = \frac{2}{3}z$, how much is $z - x$?
    F. 90°
    G. 85°
    H. 80°
    J. 70°
    K. 60°

13. What is the answer when $5a^3b^4 + 3a^2b^3$ is subtracted from $a^3b^4 - 2a^2b^3$?
    A. $-4a^3b^4 - 5a^2b^3$
    B. $-4a^3b^4 + a^2b^3$
    C. $6a^3b^4 + a^2b^3$
    D. $4a^3b^4 + a^2b^3$
    E. $4a^3b^4 + 5a^2b^3$

14. If a 30:60:90 triangle has a perimeter of $30 + 10\sqrt{3}$, what is its area in square units?
    F. $2000\sqrt{3}$
    G. 2000
    H. $100\sqrt{3}$
    J. $50\sqrt{3}$
    K. $10\sqrt{3}$

15. The average scores of students on a final exam are as shown on the chart below.

Dustin	Kristiana	Leoni	Tim	Deidre
75	82	79	91	93

    What is the positive difference between the mean and the median of their scores?
    A. 84
    B. 82
    C. 12
    D. 5
    E. 2

16. Rectangle ABCD (not shown) has a diagonal of 6 units and one side measures 3 units. What is the perimeter, in units, of the rectangle?
    F. 24
    G. $12 + 12\sqrt{3}$
    H. $12 + 6\sqrt{3}$
    J. $6 + 6\sqrt{3}$
    K. 6

17. Which of the following is true of the pair of numbers 4 and 6?
    A. Their least common multiple is 24.
    B. Their least common denominator is 4.
    C. Neither number has any prime factors.
    D. The least prime factor of both numbers is 3.
    E. The least common multiple of both numbers is 12.

18. For all x and y, $(3x^2y + xy^2) - (2x^2y - 2xy^2) = ?$
    F. $x^2 - x$
    G. $x^2y - xy^2$
    H. $x^2y + 3xy^2$
    J. $5x^2y - xy^2$
    K. $x^4y^2 + 3x^2y^4$

Go on to next page

19. What is the number of square units in the total surface area of this cylinder, including both ends?

A. 16π
B. 40π
C. 100π
D. 104π
E. 112π

20. What is the slope of a line parallel to the line $2x + 3y = 6$?
F. ⅔
G. 1
H. ¾
J. ⅔
K. 0

21. What is $(2a^2 + ab - 8) - (3a^2 - 2ab + 8)$?
A. $ab + a^2$
B. $3ab + a^2 - 16$
C. $3ab + a^2$
D. $3ab - a^2 - 16$
E. $ab - a^2 - 16$

22. Jessica and Josh want an average score of 95 for five exams. Jessica's scores are 93, 92, 90, 100. Josh's scores are 95, 97, 89, and 94. For each student to average a 95 for the five exams, how many more points does Josh need to get than Jessica on the last test?
F. 5
G. 4
H. 2
J. 1
K. 0

23. Simplify $2y - (4 - 3y) + 3$.
A. $-y - 12$
B. $-y + 7$
C. $5y - 7$
D. $5y - 1$
E. $5y + 1$

24. If the shaded area in the square below is $144 - 36π$, what is the diagonal of the square?

F. $11\sqrt{2}$
G. $12\sqrt{3}$
H. $12\sqrt{2}$
J. $6\sqrt{2}$
K. 6

25. Solve for the number of degrees in x.

A. 10°
B. 20°
C. 30°
D. 40°
E. 50°

26. A machine sorts ball bearings. Due to a mechanical problem, the machine drops half the ball bearings per cycle. If the machine finishes its fifth cycle with 11 balls still remaining in the machine, how many balls were in the machine at the end of the first cycle?
F. 704
G. 352
H. 176
J. 88
K. 44

27. Five friends are going to share computer time. Each of the five will pay $22.20 for his share. If the friends want to drop their individual price paid down to under $12.00 each, how many additional friends must join in sharing the price of the computer time? (Assume all friends pay equal shares.)
A. 8
B. 5
C. 4
D. 3
E. 2

Go on to next page

28. If $\frac{1}{a} = 4$ and $\frac{1}{b} = 5$, how much is $\frac{1}{ab}$?

   F. $\frac{1}{20}$
   G. $\frac{1}{9}$
   H. 9
   J. 20
   K. 200

29. The circumference of Circle O is 10π units. What is the area of triangle *ABC* in square units?

   A. 10
   B. $10 + 10\sqrt{2}$
   C. 20
   D. 25
   E. 50

30. $4^{-x} = 64$. What is the value of *x*?

   F. –4
   G. –3
   H. 0
   J. 3
   K. 4

31. In the right triangle *XYZ* below, what is the value of tan *Z*?

   A. $\frac{7}{25}$
   B. $\frac{7}{24}$
   C. $\frac{24}{25}$
   D. $\frac{25}{24}$
   E. $\frac{24}{7}$

32. After a slow reader increased her speed by 25 percent, she was still 50 percent slower than a fast reader. *Before* the slow reader increased her speed, the fast reader's speed was what percent of the slow reader's speed?

   F. 300
   G. 250
   H. 225
   J. 200
   K. 125

33. The current pushes a swimmer back 2 feet for every 2 yards she swims. If she needs to cover 500 yards and each stroke takes her 5 yards, how many strokes must she take?

   A. 1,000
   B. 700
   C. 500
   D. 150
   E. 100

34. A farmer can plow *x* rows in *y* minutes. Which of the following represents the number of rows the farmer can plow in *w* hours?

   F. $60xyw$
   G. $\frac{x+7}{60} \cdot w$
   H. $\frac{w}{60} \cdot x$
   J. $\frac{w+x+y}{60}$
   K. $60\frac{x}{y} \cdot w$

35. If $f(x) = 1 + x^3$, what is $f(-5)$?

   A. 126
   B. 124
   C. –124
   D. –125
   E. –126

36. Two interior angles of an octagon sum up to 480. What is the average measure of each of the remaining interior angles in the figure?

   F. 180
   G. 175
   H. 150
   J. 125
   K. 100

37. Square RSTU has a perimeter of 48. If A, B, C, and D are the midpoints of their respective sides, what is the perimeter of square ABCD?
    A. 32
    B. $24\sqrt{2}$
    C. 24
    D. $12\sqrt{3}$
    E. $12\sqrt{2}$

38. What is the perimeter of the figure shown below?

    F. 75
    G. 60
    H. 59
    J. 56
    K. 50

39. Given that a + b = 26, and $a \neq b$, what is the largest possible value for *ab*?
    A. 169
    B. 168
    C. 165
    D. 26
    E. 13

40. If $x \neq 4$, solve for $\dfrac{\sqrt{x}+2}{\sqrt{x}-2}$.
    F. -1
    G. $\dfrac{x+4}{x-4}$
    H. $-\sqrt{x}-1$
    J. $\dfrac{x+4\sqrt{x}+4}{x-4}$
    K. $-\sqrt{x}+4$

41. $64^{2/3} = ?$
    A. 0
    B. 4
    C. 8
    D. 16
    E. 32

42. Set A = (2, 3, 4, 5, 6, 7, 8, 9)
    Set B = (3, 6, 9, 12, 15)
    Let *a* be a number from Set A and *b* be a number from set B. Define *a* @ *b* as the sum of all prime numbers from Set A and all nonprime numbers from Set B. What is the value of *a* @ *b*?
    F. 61
    G. 60
    H. 59
    J. 51
    K. 50

43. A cookie jar has nine chocolate chip cookies, six oatmeal cookies, and four sugar cookies in it (there are no other cookies in the jar). Paul pulls out and eats a chocolate chip cookie, an oatmeal cookie, a chocolate chip cookie, a sugar cookie, and an oatmeal cookie. What percent probability is there that the next time he reaches into the jar, he'll pull out a chocolate chip cookie?
    A. 66⅔
    B. 50
    C. 40
    D. 33⅓
    E. ½

44. A street has a number of billboards. Starting at the beginning of the street, the billboard advertising milk is the 13th; from the other end of the street, the billboard is the 14th. How many billboards are there along the street?
    F. 24
    G. 25
    H. 26
    J. 27
    K. 28

Go on to next page

45. The trinomial $x^2 + 7x - 8$ can be factored as the product of two linear factors, in the form $(x + a)(x + b)$. What is the polynomial sum of these two factors?

A. $2x - 7$
B. $2x + 7$
C. $2x - 6$
D. $2x + 6$
E. $2x - 8$

46. $3a + 5b = 10$. Solve for b in terms of a.

F. $5 - \frac{5}{2}a$
G. $2 - \frac{3}{2}a$
H. $2 - \frac{3}{5}a$
J. $2a - \frac{3}{2}$
K. $2a - \frac{3}{5}$

47. If $-4mx - \frac{3b}{c} = 4my$, then $x + y = ?$

A. $\frac{-3b}{4mc}$
B. $\frac{-3b}{8mc}$
C. $\frac{-3b}{16m^2c}$
D. $\frac{-6b}{4m^2c}$
E. $\frac{-3b}{c} - 4m$

48. What is the solution set of $a(a + 4) = 12$?

F. $\{6, -2\}$
G. $\{-6, 6\}$
H. $\{-6, 2\}$
J. $\{12, 0\}$
K. $\{4\}$

49. What is the simplified form of $x[(3 + x)(4x) + 2]$?

A. $4x^3 + 12x^2 + 2x$
B. $2x^3 + 12x^2 + 2x$
C. $12x^3 + 4x^2 + 2x$
D. $4x^3 + 2x^2 + 4x$
E. $4x^3 + 4x^2 + 12$

50. A car passed a designated point on the freeway and traveled for 2 hours at 80 m/hr. Then, in an effort to save gas, the driver slowed to 70 m/hr for 1 hour. The driver stopped for gas and lunch for 1 hour and then traveled 80 m/hr for 1 hour. The graph of the driver's distance (d) from the designated point as a function of time (t) would most resemble which of the following?

F.
G.
H.
J.
K.

Go on to next page

51. What is the sum of the two solutions to the equation $x^2 - 5x + 6 = 0$?
    A. −5
    B. −1
    C. 1
    D. 5
    E. 6

52. Which of the following represents the graph of the solution set of $x + 1 \leq 8$?

    F. [number line with ray extending left from filled point at 7]

    G. [number line with ray extending left from open point at 7]

    H. [number line with ray extending right from filled point at 7]

    J. [number line segment with open endpoints from −5 to 5]

    K. [number line segment with filled endpoints from −5 to 5]

53. A line's equation is $x + 2y = 4 - (x + y)$. Its equation may also be expressed as $y = ?$
    A. $\frac{3}{4} + \frac{2x}{3}$
    B. $\frac{4}{3} + \frac{2x}{3}$
    C. $\frac{4}{3} - \frac{2x}{3}$
    D. $\frac{1}{4} - \frac{2x}{3}$
    E. $\frac{2x}{3}$

54. Which of the following is equivalent to $\frac{\sin^2\theta + \cos^2\theta}{\sec^2\theta}$?
    F. $\cos^2\theta$
    G. $\sin^2\theta$
    H. $\tan^2\theta$
    J. $\frac{1}{\cos^2\theta}$
    K. $\sin^2\theta + 1$

55. What is the simplified form of $\frac{7}{2 + \sqrt{3}}$?
    A. 21
    B. $7 + \sqrt{3}$
    C. $7 - 7\sqrt{3}$
    D. $14 + 7\sqrt{3}$
    E. $14 - 7\sqrt{3}$

56. For all $a \neq 0$, what is the slope of the line passing through $(2a, -b)$ and $(-a, -b)$ in the usual (x, y) coordinate plane?
    F. 0
    G. $\frac{2b}{3a}$
    H. $\frac{3a}{2b}$
    J. $3a$
    K. Undefined

57. Three painters take ten hours to paint four rooms. How many hours will 9 painters take to paint 12 rooms?
    A. 1⅓
    B. 3⅓
    C. 6
    D. 10
    E. 30

58. Which of the following is equal to $\frac{10.8(10^{-3})}{400(10^{-5})}$?
    F. $.027(10^2)$
    G. $.0027(10^{-2})$
    H. $.27(10^{-2})$
    J. $.0027(10^2)$
    K. $27(10^{-2})$

59. Georgia buys q quarts of milk at d dollars per quart and b boxes of cereal at $d + 1$ dollars per box. Which of the following expressions represents the total amount spent?
    A. $qd + bd + 1$
    B. $(q + b)(d + 1)$
    C. $(q + b)(2d + 1)$
    D. $d(q + b) + b$
    E. $bd(q + b)$

60. Find the area of rectangle ACEG.

GX = 4

F. $8\sqrt{2}$
G. $8\sqrt{3}$
H. 16
J. $16\sqrt{2}$
K. $16\sqrt{3}$

Reading Test

35 Minutes — 40 Questions

DIRECTIONS: Each of the four passages in this section is followed by ten questions. Answer each question based on what is stated or implied in the passage, and shade the corresponding oval on your answer grid.

Passage 1

Natural Science

When people hear the word "prehistoric," they think of animals, especially dinosaurs. But there were prehistoric plants as well, and they were just as unusual to modern sensibilities as the animals of (05) those ancient times. Among the most interesting of prehistoric plants are the cycads, which flourished 65 million to 240 million years ago. The plants are extant today, in areas as widely scattered as South America, Africa, Australia and Malaysia. Although (10) they primarily live in the wet tropical or semi-tropical habitats, some species can not only survive but thrive in arid regions as well. Scientists long considered the widespread distribution of the cycad a mystery, as the seeds were too large to be (15) carried by wind or ocean currents or birds. One popular theory connects the migration of cycads to the theory of Continental Drift. Briefly, Continental Drift hypothesizes that at one point millions of years ago, there existed just one continent, a super-(20) continent named Pangaea. Over the years, the continents separated, drifting apart and taking their flora and fauna with them. Thus, the plants that otherwise would be not as widely dispersed are found in far-flung areas.

(25) If these plants provided sustenance to the gargantuan animals of that time (several times as large as any animals alive today), the plants must have been huge as well. Today's cycads have trunks that can grow up to 50 feet tall. But it is the cones that (30) are perhaps the most impressive. There are two different types of cones, pollen cones (which grow on the male plants) and seed cones (which grow on the female plants), and these can be as long as 36 inches and weigh up to nearly 100 pounds.

(35) One variety of seed pods produces bright red seeds. These seeds are ground into flour and used as foodstuffs by people in Africa. Some Japanese cooks mix brown rice with the powdered seeds of some cycads and ferment the mixture into a miso. In America, the Seminole Indians of Florida used the (40) pith of cycads to make bread. Unfortunately, some ground cycad seeds have been found to be carcinogenic (cancer-causing) if not properly prepared.

There are also leaves on the cycad plant, which grow into a sort of crown and thus make (45) many people who merely glance at a cycad think it is a palm tree. The trunks may occasionally grow underground, leaving an impression that the leaves are growing directly out of the ground. In fact, many parts of the cycads are underground. Inside (50) the roots of the cycad are blue-green algae. The conversion of atmospheric nitrogen into ammonia is one way the cyanobacteria supply the cycad with inorganic nitrogen. It is fascinating to note that even though the cyanobacteria are in the (55) dark underground, they have the same membrane structure and pigments of other bacteria that thrive in the sunlight. Why does this strange structure remain? One theory is that evolution has not yet had sufficient time to change the portions that at (60) one point had been essential to the plant's survival.

1. The main purpose of the passage is
   A. to discuss similarities between prehistoric animals and prehistoric plants
   B. to refute the theory that cycads were spread via birds
   C. to contrast and compare prehistoric and current plant life
   D. to provide an overview of cycads

2. In line 8, the word "extant" most nearly means
   F. extinct
   G. prehistoric
   H. narrowly distributed
   J. still existing

3. According to the author, which of the following is a mystery to scientists?
   I. why the cycad is found in such different locales
   II. what caused the continents to drift apart
   III. why prehistoric plants were so much larger than current plants
   A. I only
   B. II only
   C. II and III only
   D. I, II, and III

4. In line 12, "arid" most nearly means
   F. scented
   G. dry
   H. unpopulated
   J. large

5. The author's purpose in mentioning Pangaea is to
   A. explain why the cycad is extinct today
   B. prove the cycad was once the largest plant on earth
   C. suggest one cause for the cycad's widespread distribution
   D. refute the theory that the continents were once connected

6. In line 25, "sustenance" most nearly means
   F. nourishment
   G. danger
   H. medicine
   J. continuation

7. The author mentions all of the following EXCEPT
   I. the differences between seed cones and pollen cones
   II. Medicinal properties of the seeds of the cycad
   III. dangers in using the seeds of the cycad
   A. I only
   B. II only
   C. III only
   D. II and III only

8. The author claims that people confuse a cycad with a palm tree because
   F. they both produce coconuts
   G. the cycad grows in the same tropical regions as does the palm tree
   H. the cycad's leaves may resemble the fronds of a palm tree
   J. both plants are approximately the same size

9. According to the passage, one function of cyanobacteria is
   A. to allow the cycad to live underground
   B. to supply the cycad with inorganic nitrogen
   C. to help the cycad reproduce
   D. to enable the cycad to live long periods without water

10. The author of the passage would most likely agree with which of the following statements?
    F. Bacteria above and below ground do not usually have the same pigments.
    G. Cycads will be much more widely distributed in the future than they are currently.
    H. Cycads seeds offer a possible cure for cancer.
    J. The cycads and the palm trees probably descended from a common ancestor.

Go on to next page

Passage 2

Prose Fiction. This passage is adapted from George Eliot's *Middlemarch*.

Line
　　The human soul moves in many channels, and Mr. Casaubon, we know, had a sense of rectitude and honorable pride in satisfying the requirements of honor, which compelled him to find other reasons for his conduct than those of jealousy and vindic-
(05) tiveness. The way in which Mr. Casaubon put the case was this:

　　"In marrying Dorothea Brooke I had to care for her well-being in case of my death. But well-being is not to be secured by ample, independent posses-
(10) sion of property; on the contrary, occasions might arise in which such possession might expose her to the more danger. She is ready prey to any man who knows how to play adroitly either on her affection-
(15) ate ardor or her quixotic enthusiasm; and a man is standing by with that very intention in his mind — a man with no other principle than transient caprice, and who has a personal animosity towards me — I am sure of it — an animosity which he has
(20) constantly vented in ridicule, of which I am as well assured as if I had heard it. Even if I live I shall not be without uneasiness as to what he may attempt through indirect influence. This man has gained Dorothea's ear; he has fascinated her attention; he
(25) has evidently tried to impress her mind with the notion that he has claims beyond anything I have done for him. If I die — and he is waiting here on the watch for that — he will persuade her to marry him. That would be calamity for her and success for him.
(30) She would not think it calamity; he would make her believe anything; she has a tendency to immoderate attachment which she inwardly reproaches me for not responding to, and already her mind is occupied with his fortunes. He thinks of an easy conquest and
(35) of entering into my nest. That I will hinder! Such a marriage would be fatal to Dorothea. Has he ever persisted in anything except from contradiction? In knowledge he has always tried to be showy at small cost. In religion he could be, as long as it suited him,
(40) the facile echo of Dorothea's vagaries. When was sciolism ever disassociated from laxity? I utterly distrust his morals, and it is my duty to hinder to the utmost the fulfillment of his designs."

　　The arrangements made by Mr. Casaubon on
(45) his marriage left strong measures open to him, but in ruminating on them his mind inevitably dwelt so much on the probabilities of his own life that the longing to get the nearest possible calculation had at last overcome his proud reticence and had deter-
(50) mined him to ask Lydgate's opinion as to the nature of his illness.

　　He had mentioned to Dorothea that Lydgate was coming by appointment at half past three, and in answer to her anxious question, whether he had felt ill, replied, "No, I merely wish to have his opin-
(55) ion concerning some habitual symptoms. You need not see him, my dear. I shall give orders that he may be sent to me in the yew-tree walk, where I shall be taking my usual exercise."

　　When Lydgate entered the yew-tree walk he saw
(60) Mr. Casaubon slowly receding with his hands behind him according to his habit, and his head bent forward. It was a lovely afternoon; the leaves from the lofty limes were falling silently across the somber evergreens, while the lights and shadows slept side
(65) by side; there was no sound but the cawing of the rooks, which to the accustomed ear is a lullaby, or that last solemn lullaby, a dirge. Lydgate, conscious of an energetic frame in its prime, felt some compassion when the figure which he was likely soon to
(70) overtake turned around and in advancing towards him showed more markedly than ever the signs of premature age — the student's bent shoulders, the emaciated limbs, and the melancholy lines of the mouth.
(75)
　　"Poor fellow," he thought, "some men with his years are like lions; one can tell nothing of their age except that they are full grown."

　　"Mr. Lydgate," said Mr. Casaubon with his invariably polite air, "I am exceedingly obliged to
(80) you for your punctuality. We will, if you please, carry on our conversation in walking to and fro."

　　"I hope your wish to see me is not due to the return of unpleasant symptoms," said Lydgate, filling up a pause.
(85)

11. Which of the following best expresses the same idea as that given in the first sentence of the passage?
   A. Mr. Casaubon is justifiably proud of not being jealous or vindictive.
   B. Mr. Casaubon justified his actions to himself in a way that didn't make him seem jealous or vindictive.
   C. Mr. Casaubon was ashamed of his jealousy and vindictive toward those who pointed it out to him.
   D. Mr. Casaubon is afraid of his wife's jealousy and vindictiveness.

12. Mr. Casaubon feels that leaving his money to Dorothea in case of his death
    F. would be unfair to his children from a previous marriage.
    G. would leave her vulnerable to fortune-hunters.
    H. would be the right and proper thing to do.
    J. would be fair because getting his money was the only reason that Dorothea married him in the first place.

13. Which of the following may you infer about the animosity of the man whom Mr. Casaubon fears is "standing by" to take Dorothea after Mr. Casaubon's death (line 16)?
    A. He has never directly expressed any animosity toward Mr. Casaubon.
    B. He has valid reasons for his animosity, which Mr. Casaubon is uneasily aware of.
    C. His intentions toward Dorothea are not honorable.
    D. He was a rival of Mr. Casaubon's for Dorothea long ago.

14. In lines 8–45, you learn that Mr. Casaubon
    F. is afraid of the other man's corrupting Dorothea.
    G. has convinced himself that frustrating the other man is his responsibility.
    H. hopes to avoid a confrontation with the other man.
    J. is uneasily aware that Dorothea prefers the other man to him.

15. The sentence, "The arrangements made by Mr. Casaubon on his marriage left strong measures open to him . . ." emphasizes that
    A. Mr. Casaubon believed that Dorothea was marrying him only for his money.
    B. Dorothea was unaware of Mr. Casaubon's fears and neuroses.
    C. Mr. Casaubon was a cautious man and may have had his concerns over Dorothea's remarriage from the start.
    D. Dorothea demanded that Mr. Casaubon divulge his arrangements to her before she agreed to marry him.

16. ". . . his mind inevitably dwelt so much on the probabilities of his own life that the longing to get the nearest possible calculation . . ." (lines 46–48). Which of the following expresses most nearly the same thought as in this quotation?
    F. He worried about his success at gambling and wanted advice from an outside expert.
    G. He regretted his past actions and sought to find out what repercussions they may have.
    H. He wondered how long he had left to live and wanted an estimate of his time remaining.
    J. He was obsessed with himself and cared for no one else.

17. Which of the following attitudes best describes Lydgate's feelings upon seeing Mr. Casaubon?
    A. confusion
    B. embarrassment
    C. self-pity
    D. ebullience

18. You may infer which of the following was the author's reason for describing the loveliness of the day (lines 63–68)?
    F. to show Lydgate's tranquil frame of mind
    G. to contrast the beauty of his surroundings with the unattractiveness and frailty of Mr. Casaubon
    H. to foreshadow impending doom to Mr. Casaubon and his wife
    J. to emphasize Mr. Casaubon's wealth in comparison to his ill health

19. The author indicates that Lydgate's comment (lines 83–85)
    A. was a professional pleasantry with which he always began a visit.
    B. was intended to encourage Mr. Casaubon to discuss his illness.
    C. was designed to make Mr. Casaubon conscious of his infirmity.
    D. was made to end an awkward silence.

20. Which of the following most likely happens to the reader's attitude toward Mr. Casaubon as he goes through this excerpt?
    F. It changes from contempt toward the man to pity for him.
    G. It becomes progressively less tolerant of the man and more disgusted with his behavior.
    H. It becomes indifferent, as the reader no longer cares what happens to Mr. Casaubon but focuses on Lydgate.
    J. It becomes more understanding, finally seeing the reasons Dorothea married her husband.

Go on to next page

Passage 3

Social Science. This passage is adapted from *How to Develop Self-Esteem in Your Child* by Dr. Bettie Youngs (copyright 1991 Bettie Youngs).

What is the work of childhood? Each stage of a child's development presents its own set of tasks and demands, all focused on gaining self-knowledge: selfhood. The work of each stage is (05) pretty well-defined.

Until the age of two, a child primarily views himself as part of his mother (or father, if he is the primary caretaker). Upon reaching two, he develops the ability to be aware that he is in reality sepa- (10) rate from her. This situation presents him with the task of establishing autonomy — separateness. The two words that best describe his new-found selfhood, that he is in fact a separate person, are no and mine. Possession is the tool he uses to enforce (15) that sense of separate self.

Having realized his separateness, the three-year-old goes on to master his environment. Mastery plays an important role in his perception of self. It influences his feelings of being capable or not capa- (20) ble. His need for success in his endeavors at this stage is crucial. He labors over each of his accomplishments. He is slow and methodical and takes forever to do each task. Needing feedback to know if he has been successful, he strives for recognition (25) of these achievements. ("Watch me, Mommy! Watch me, Mommy!") That he has something to offer nurtures his sense of competence and proves his value.

Parents are the name of the game for the five-year-old. At this age, the mother is the center of the (30) child's world. He not only wants to please her, but he also wants to be near her, wants to talk with her, wants to play with her, and wants to help her around the house. The five-year-old's adoration of his parents is unquestionably heartwarming. The (35) result is almost totally parent-pleasing behavior. In his determination to do everything just right, he'll ask permission for the simplest thing, even when he needn't; and he will then beam with pleasure when the parent smiles and gives permission.

(40) Age six can be described as the stage of "me-ness." Self-centeredness comes before other-centeredness. While children were in the preschool stage, they discovered that they were separate from their parents, although they still kept their parents as the center of their existence. At six, they must (45) shift the focus from their parents to themselves. They now place themselves at the center of their world instead of parents or others. Although they may appear to be excessively self-centered and unconcerned with the needs and feelings of others, (50) this is an important milestone in their development. They are now ready to undertake the task of being receptive to their own interests and attempting to understand them.

At age 16, it is not uncommon for a child to (55) experience feelings of being confused, embarrassed, guilty, awkward, inferior, ugly, and scared, all in the same day. In fact, a teenager can swing from being childish and petulant to being sedate, or from acting rational to irrational, all in the same (60) hour. It's a time of confusion and uncertainty. The goal is to experience intimacy; he needs to belong. This is a time of duality. The 16-year-old wants to be with others, yet he wants to be alone; he needs his friends, but he will sabotage them if they appear to (65) outdo him; he'll root for a friend out loud, but he'll secretly wish for his friend's failure. Age 16 is a time when he wants total independence, but he is not capable of it. He doesn't really want to live without his parents, although he believes that they are (70) roadblocks hindering his life.

The final stage of development in childhood is establishing total independence. In changing from being dependent on others to being self-dependent, children confront some pretty big (and frightening) (75) issues. They have three tasks. Their first task is to determine vocation. A child needs to ask what he is going to do with his life. Underlying this task is the self-esteem need to be somebody, to experience positive feelings of strength, power, and compe- (80) tence. Second, he needs to establish values. The goal is to sort out his own values and to decide which ones to keep and which ones to discard. Following this step is the only way that he can develop integrity. Perhaps most striking is his need (85) to establish a workable and meaningful philosophy of life. Reevaluating his moral concepts will mean searching for his own personal beliefs, complete with facing religious, ethical, and value-laden ideologies. Developing personal convictions will be (90) influenced by his level of self-esteem, especially if a conflict exists among what he believes, what his family believes, and what his friends find acceptable. Third, he needs to establish self-reliance.

21. The author's primary purpose in writing this passage is
    A. to show the importance of early childhood learning, which provides the foundation for life.
    B. to analyze the causes behind low self-esteem in children.
    C. to denounce child psychologists.
    D. to discuss the various behaviors associated with the ages of children.

22. According to the author, the ultimate goal of children is
    F. recognition.
    G. selfhood.
    H. praise.
    J. competence.

23. The author uses the comment "Watch me, Mommy! Watch me, Mommy!" to make the point that three-year-olds
    A. recognize they are individuals, separate from their parents.
    B. do tasks in order to please their parents.
    C. need outside acknowledgment of their accomplishments at a specific age of development.
    D. are prone to repeating themselves.

24. Which of the following is another way of stating "Parents are the name of the game" (line 28)?
    F. Parents design games and activities to entertain and stimulate their children.
    G. The names parents give their children determine their sense of self-worth.
    H. Parental gamesmanship influences children's development.
    J. Parents are of prime importance to their children.

25. You may infer from paragraph five that the author considers a lack of sensitivity in six-year-olds
    A. abnormal and rare.
    B. unacceptable in adults, but cute in small children.
    C. precocious; such egotism doesn't usually begin until the teenage years.
    D. vital in order for children to recognize their separateness from their parents.

26. Which of the following phrases from paragraph six best expresses the idea of the paragraph?
    F. "The goal is to experience intimacy."
    G. "This is a time of duality."
    H. "Age 16 is a time when he wants total independence."
    J. "He believes that [his parents] are roadblocks hindering his life."

27. As used in line 77, "vocation" means
    A. rest and relaxation.
    B. geographical area.
    C. romance.
    D. career.

28. Which of the following does the author not mention as a factor in the development of convictions?
    I. educational level
    II. age group
    III. self-esteem
    F. I only
    G. II only
    H. II and III only
    J. I, II, and III

29. Which of the following best describes the organization of the passage?
    A. from most-important to least-important concepts
    B. from theories to proven facts
    C. chronological
    D. from beliefs to predictions

30. You may infer that all stages of childhood have as their ultimate goal
    F. fiscal security.
    G. recognition.
    H. independence.
    J. parental respect.

Go on to next page

Passage 4

Humanities

The months are familiar to everyone. Nearly any small child can rattle off the twelve months of the year. When students learn foreign languages, one of the first exercises they practice is saying the (05) names of the months. Despite all that familiarity, however, one important piece of knowledge is still missing: an explanation of how and why the names of the months came into existence. Who decided on the names? Were the months named after people? (10) Did the months always have the same names throughout history? The story of the months is a fascinating one and deserves more attention.

Every month's name tells a story. January is named after Janus, a Roman god who was depicted (15) as having two faces, one looking forward and one looking back. Janus is the Latin term for an arch or gate (janua is door). The god Janus needed both of his faces. As the guardian of doors or gateways, he had to be vigilant for friends and foes coming from (20) either direction. Of course, January is the first month of the year, but it wasn't always so. Until around 150 B.C., January was the eleventh month of the year.

February is one of the few months not named (25) after a person. February is a form of februare, which was the Latin word for "to purify." This month's name came from the February 15 feast of purification. On that feast day, people attempted to atone for their sins and, by so doing, hoped to appease (30) the gods sufficiently to ensure healthy children and abundant crops in the next year.

March is named for Mars, whom many people have read about as the god of war. Few people realize that originally Mars was the god of springtime (35) and new blossoms. Warriors would "take the winter off" from fighting, resting while the weather was too bad for battle. In the spring — around what we now think of as March — battles would resume. From this time line, Mars soon became more well-known (40) as the god of war than of springtime.

Not every month's name has a definitive provenance. Scholars debate the origins of the name of April. Some writers and researchers claim that the word is from the Latin term aperire, meaning to (45) open. The buds of new plants opened at this time of year. Other scholars believe the name April is perhaps the namesake of the Greek goddess Aphrodite (abbreviated to Aphro). Aphrodite and Ares — whose Latin name was Mars — were a couple. (50) Romantics prefer to think that as April follows March, Venus/Aphrodite followed Mars.

May is also named after a goddess, Maika. She was the goddess of plants. Because plants often blossom in May, naming the month after the goddess has an indisputable logic. Not much else is (55) known about Maika.

Not every month retained its original name over the years. For example, July and August weren't always known by those names. The original name for July was Quintilis, "fifth month." (Previously, (60) the Latin calendar began with what is now March. Therefore, the month of July was originally the fifth month: March, April, May, June, July.) August was previously called Sextilis, "sixth month." Likewise, September, October, November, and December were (65) the seventh, eighth, ninth, and tenth months. (The roots sept, oct, nov, and dec are common in many other words we use today. A septuagenarian is a person in his seventies; an octogenarian is a person in his eighties, and so on.) How did July and August (70) get their new names? When Julius Caesar was assassinated, Mark Anthony ordered the Roman senate to rename the fifth month, when Caesar was born, after him. Quintilis became Julius, or July. Almost forty years later, Julius Caesar's relative, Augustus Caesar, (75) had August named after him. Augustus was born in September but chose to give August his name because that was the month in which he had made several of his most important conquests.

The number of days in the months has changed (80) throughout the years as well. It was a Roman superstition that even numbers were unlucky. Therefore, all months in the Roman calendar had an odd number of days, usually 31 or 29. Even the number of days in the year has changed. In order to bring (85) the Roman calendar back into sync with the solar year, one memorable year, 46 B.C., actually contained 445 days! The calendar of 365 days officially began on January 1, 45 B.C. Even that, however, was not sufficient to make the year balanced and equiv- (90) alent with nature. To remedy the discrepancy, in 1582, Pope Gregory XIII stated that the day after October 4 should be October 15!

Of course, not every year has exactly 365 days. Some, known as leap years, have 366 days. A trivia (95) question that many people believe they can answer is, "When do leap years occur?" Most people answer, "Every four years." They gloss over one very important fact, however. Not every fourth year is a leap year. The century years — 1600, 1700, (100) 1800, 1900, and 2000 — are not leap years unless they are evenly divisible by 400. For example, 1600 and 2000 are leap years, but 1700, 1800, and 1900 are not.

Go on to next page

31. As it is used in line 2, "rattle off" most nearly means
    A. shake until it drops off.
    B. recite quickly.
    C. eliminate.
    D. upset.

32. The main purpose of the passage is
    F. to explain how the months got their names.
    G. to show why there are twelve, not just ten, months.
    H. to explain the role of superstition in the naming of the months.
    J. to suggest new, alternate names for the months.

33. The passage states that Janus needed both of his faces for which of the following reasons?
    A. He was the caretaker of warriors in battle.
    B. He was the god of the beginning of the year.
    C. He had to look in both directions as the god of doors and gateways.
    D. He had more days in his month than in the other months.

34. According to the passage, which of the following months was named for a feast?
    F. February
    G. March
    H. April
    J. May

35. With which of the following statements would the author most likely agree?
    A. Many people have misconceptions about the origin of the name of March.
    B. Many people believe that all the months are named after gods and goddesses.
    C. Scholars agree on the origins of the names of the months.
    D. The number of days in any month is determined by its lunar cycle.

36. As it is used in line 86, the expression "into sync" most nearly means
    F. within the receptacle
    G. in line
    H. politically correct
    J. into the future

37. The passage discusses all of the following EXCEPT
    A. how July and August got their names
    B. why July changed its name
    C. how the calendar is balanced with the natural cycle
    D. why Romans considered even numbers unlucky

38. Which of the following is the main idea of the seventh paragraph?
    F. Roman emperors had the power to change the calendar.
    G. The Roman calendar was different from the calendar we have today.
    H. Extra months were necessary to make the Roman calendar consistent with the calendars of the rest of the world.
    J. The names of the months of the Roman calendar have changed over time.

39. The author of the passage states which of the following about leap years?
    I. They are every fourth year.
    II. No century year is a leap year.
    III. Century years are leap years if they are also millennium years.
    A. None
    B. I only
    C. II and III only
    D. I, II, and III

40. In line 98, the author uses the phrase "gloss over" to mean
    F. polish
    G. finish
    H. ignore
    J. shine

STOP DO NOT TURN THE PAGE UNTIL TOLD TO DO SO.
      DO NOT RETURN TO A PREVIOUS TEST.

Science Reasoning Test

35 Minutes — 40 Questions

DIRECTIONS: Following are seven passages and then questions that refer to each passage. Choose the best answer to each question and blacken in the corresponding oval on your answer grid.

Passage 1

In the pole vault, the pole acts to convert the energy generated by an athlete running down a runway into a force that lifts the athlete over a crossbar. The most advanced vaulters use stiff poles that quickly convert the horizontal energy into the lifting force. Beginning vaulters are not strong, fast, or skillful enough to bend a stiff pole as needed to generate substantial vertical lift. Beginning vaulters must use more flexible poles.

To test the suitability of two materials for use in poles, scientists subjected three miniature poles to two laboratory tests. Pole No. 1, made of fiberglass, is 50 cm long, with a diameter of 1 cm and a mass of 1 kg. Pole No. 2, also made of fiberglass, is also 50 cm long but has a diameter of 1.5 cm and a mass of 2.25 kg. Pole No. 3, made of carbon fiber, is 50 cm long, 1.5 cm in diameter, and has a mass of 1 kg.

Study 1

Scientists tested the three poles to determine how much force is required to bend the poles to an 85-degree angle. Table 1 shows the results.

Table 1	Results of Bent-Pole Test
Pole	**Force in Newtons (N)**
1	4.9
2	5.8
3	6.3

Study 2

Scientists bent each pole to an 85-degree angle and then allowed the pole to snap back to a straight position. Table 2 shows the time required for each pole to snap back.

Table 2	Results of Snap-Back Test
Pole	**Time in Milliseconds (msec)**
1	733
2	626
3	591

1. According to the results, what is the relationship between the force required to bend a pole and the time needed for the pole to snap back to its regular position?
   A. The greater the force required to bend the pole, the more time required for the pole to snap back.
   B. The greater the force required to bend the pole, the less time required for the pole to snap back.
   C. For only the fiberglass poles, the greater the force required to bend the pole, the more time required for the pole to snap back.
   D. For only the fiberglass poles, the greater the force required to bend the pole, the less time required for the pole to snap back.

2. On the basis of Study 1, what is the relationship between pole mass and stiffness?
   F. The greater the mass, the stiffer the pole.
   G. For a fiberglass pole, the greater the mass, the stiffer the pole.
   H. The less the mass, the stiffer the pole.
   J. Mass and stiffness have no relationship.

3. Which of the following is a controlled variable in this study?
   A. pole diameter
   B. force required to bend poles
   C. time for poles to return to vertical
   D. force generated when poles return to vertical

Go on to next page

Chapter 21: How to Ruin a Perfectly Good Day, Part II: Practice Exam 2   **297**

4. Kinetic energy results from the actual motion of an object, while potential energy is a measure of the energy that results if an object moves from a certain location. During a pole vault, at which times is virtually all the energy in the form of potential energy?
   F. when the vaulter is running down the runway
   G. when the pole is bent
   H. as the pole unbends and sends the vaulter upward
   J. as the vaulter falls into the pit

5. Ideally, vaulters like to use long poles because the poles reach closer to the crossbar. If a pole is too long, though, a vaulter has difficulty carrying it down the runway because of its mass. Given these considerations, which material is best suited for a very long pole?
   A. Fiberglass, because it snaps back relatively slowly.
   B. Fiberglass, because it has a relatively high mass-to-volume ratio.
   C. Carbon fiber, because it's hard to bend.
   D. Carbon fiber, because it has a relatively low mass-to-volume ratio.

6. On the basis of the entire study, which poles, if they were proportionately enlarged for use by a vaulter, are most appropriate for a beginning and experienced vaulter, respectively?
   F. Pole No. 1, Pole No. 2
   G. Pole No. 1, Pole No. 3
   H. Pole No. 1, either Pole No. 2 or Pole No. 3
   J. Pole No. 2, Pole No. 3

Passage 2

Very few humans live to the age of 100. Another way of saying this is that almost all members of the human population who were born in a given year will die within 100 years. Scientists, health professionals, and life insurance agents are interested in examining how many people in a population will live to be a certain age. One way to measure this information is to look at how much of the population has died after a certain number of years. This information is presented in Figure 1.

7. According to Figure 1, approximately what percentage of the human population lives to at least 80 years of age?
   A. 10 percent
   B. 40 percent
   C. 60 percent
   D. 80 percent

8. The increase in percentage of deaths is highest for which of the following intervals?
   F. 0 to 20 years
   G. 20 to 40 years
   H. 40 to 60 years
   J. 60 to 80 years

9. Suppose infant mortality (children dying at birth or very shortly thereafter) is eliminated. How will the graph change?
   A. The quick rise that is seen just after 0 years will disappear.
   B. The graph will be higher at 20 years.
   C. The graph will be less steep between 60 and 80 years.
   D. The graph will rise until past 120 years.

10. According to the graph, by what age do the largest number of people die?
    F. 25 years
    G. 45 years
    H. 75 years
    J. 95 years

11. For a person born the same year this population started, what is the maximum number of years he could live and still observe an 80 percent chance of still being alive?
    A. 15 years
    B. 35 years
    C. 55 years
    D. 80 years

Go on to next page

Figure 1: Human deaths as a function of time.

Passage 3

A radioactive substance is one that contains atoms whose nuclei change into other types of atomic nuclei. For example, a uranium nucleus can lose two protons and two neutrons and become a thorium nucleus. Atoms of some radioactive substances change more frequently than others. Over time, the rate of change for any substance slows as a greater percentage of atomic nuclei change to a final, more stable state.

Devices can measure the number of atomic changes that take place at a given time. Each of these changes is commonly called a disintegration. Table 1 and Table 2 show the disintegration rates for two unknown substances.

Table 1   Substance A Disintegrations

Time (hours)	Disintegration Rate (millicuries)
0	200
5	100
10	50
15	25
20	12.5

Table 2   Substance B Disintegrations

Time (hours)	Disintegration Rate (millicuries)
0	2000
4	1000
8	500
12	250
16	125

12. About how many millicuries will be measured from Substance B after 20 hours?
    F. 0
    G. 12.5
    H. 62.5
    J. 200

13. If Substance A originally had 10,000,000 radioactive atoms, how many atoms are present at 15 hours?
    A. 666,667
    B. 1,250,000
    C. 3,333,333
    D. 5,000,000

14. When is the disintegration rate of Substance B 1,500 millicuries?
    F. at about 2 hours
    G. at exactly 2 hours
    H. at about 3 hours
    J. at exactly 3 hours

15. The half-life of a radioactive substance is the time it takes for half of the radioactive atoms to disintegrate. Which substance has a shorter half-life?
    A. Substance A, because only 50 millicuries are present after 10 hours
    B. Substance A, because it will all be gone after 25 hours
    C. Substance B, because the disintegration rate fell to half its original value in only 4 hours, instead of 5 hours
    D. Substance B, because it was measured for only 16 hours instead of 20

16. Radioactive substances are potential health hazards. The particles emitted from radioactive substances can damage parts of the human body. Humans should take great care to limit the amount of radioactivity to which they are exposed. Which of the following is safest for a human to handle?
    F. Substance A after 5 hours
    G. Substance A after 20 hours
    H. Substance B after 8 hours
    J. Substance B after 16 hours

Passage 4

When sunlight heats the earth's surface, much of that energy is radiated back to the atmosphere. Although some of this re-radiated energy escapes to space, a significant amount of it is reflected back to the earth's surface by molecules in the atmosphere. These molecules — water, nitrous oxide, methane, and carbon dioxide — trap re-radiated energy as glass in a greenhouse does and warm the earth. Hence, the term "greenhouse effect" has been used to refer to the warming of the earth caused by the gases' keeping heat within the earth's atmosphere.

Scientists agree that the greenhouse effect results in higher temperatures on earth but disagree as to whether recent increases in atmospheric carbon dioxide will lead to undesirable global warming. Two scientists discuss this possibility.

Scientist 1

Ancient ice cores from Antarctica indicate that the concentration of carbon dioxide in the atmosphere and global mean temperatures have followed the same pattern of fluctuations in levels over the past 160,000 years. Therefore, the increase in atmospheric carbon dioxide concentration from 280 parts per million to 360 parts per million that has occurred over the past 150 years points to significant and detrimental climatic changes in the near future. The climate has already changed: the average surface temperature of the earth has increased 0.6°C in the past hundred years, with the ten hottest years of that time period all occurring since 1980. Although 0.6°C may not seem large, changes in the mean surface temperature as low as 0.5°C have dramatically affected crop growth in years past. Moreover, computer models project that surface temperatures will increase about 2.0°C by the year 2100 and will continue to increase in the years after even if concentration of greenhouse gases is stabilized by that time. If the present trend in carbon dioxide increase continues, though, carbon dioxide concentration will exceed 1,100 parts per million soon after 2100 and will be associated with a temperature increase of approximately 10.0°C over the present mean annual global surface temperature.

Scientist 2

The observed increases in minor greenhouse gases such as carbon dioxide and methane will not lead to sizeable global warming. Water vapor and clouds are responsible for more than 98% of the earth's greenhouse effect. Current models that project large temperature increases with a doubling of the present carbon dioxide concentration incorporate changes in water vapor, clouds, and other factors that would accompany a rise in carbon dioxide levels. The way these models handle such feedback factors is not supported by current scientific knowledge. In fact, there is convincing evidence that increases in carbon dioxide concentration would lead to changes in feedback factors that would diminish any temperature increase associated with more carbon dioxide in the atmosphere. The climatic data for the past hundred years show an irregular pattern in which many of the greatest jumps in global mean temperature were too large to be associated with the observed increase in carbon dioxide. The overall increase of 0.45°C in the past century is well under what the models would have predicted given the changes in carbon dioxide concentration. As with the temperature models, recent increases in atmospheric carbon dioxide have not risen to the extent predicted by models dealing solely with carbon dioxide levels. The rate of carbon dioxide concentration increase has slowed since 1973. Improved energy technologies will further dampen the increase so that the carbon dioxide concentration will be under 700 parts per million in the year 2100.

17. Which of the following is an assumption made by Scientist 1?
    A. Feedback factors have little effect on the magnitude to which increased carbon dioxide will increase temperature.
    B. Humans will not be able to limit their activities that contribute to rising carbon dioxide levels.
    C. A rise in the global mean temperature of 1.0°C is not significant.
    D. Temperature fluctuations will match carbon dioxide changes when carbon dioxide changes are abrupt.

18. A scientific article stated that "Scientists will soon develop computer models that accurately account for feedback factors." Which of the scientists' viewpoints, if any, is(are) consistent with this statement?
    F. Scientist 1 only
    G. Scientist 2 only
    H. Both Scientists 1 and 2
    J. Neither Scientist 1 nor 2

19. Which of the following is the most likely reason that the two scientists present different figures for the temperature rise that has occurred over the past hundred years?
    A. It has been difficult to determine the mean global temperature with complete accuracy.
    B. Scientist 2 uses figures that do not take account of the rise in atmospheric carbon dioxide.
    C. Scientist 1 notes that all ten of the hottest years in the last hundred years have come since 1980.
    D. It has not been established that global warming is a threat to the earth.

Go on to next page

20. Indicative of rising temperatures, a large block of the Larson B Ice Sheet in Antarctica recently broke off, raising water levels around the world and increasing the vulnerability of coastal areas to flooding. In light of this information, which of the following predictions would be most consistent with Scientist 1's viewpoint?
   F. Feedback factors will retard the future rate of ice sheet disintegration.
   G. The amount of ice that will break off will double with a doubling of atmospheric carbon dioxide.
   H. The breakup of the ice sheet will minimize global warming.
   J. Coastal areas will be more prone to flooding in the next hundred years.

21. Scientists 1 and 2 would most likely agree with which of the following statements about atmospheric carbon dioxide levels?
   A. Increasing carbon dioxide levels affect other factors.
   B. Humans will never be able to stabilize atmospheric carbon dioxide levels.
   C. The rate of increase in carbon dioxide levels will rise throughout the next hundred years.
   D. Carbon dioxide levels are directly linked to temperature.

22. The manner in which Scientist 1 presents her claim about the significance of increased global temperatures over the past hundred years is most vulnerable to which of the following criticisms?
   F. The carbon dioxide increases that she presents have taken place over the past 150 years.
   G. She does not specify which years since 1980 have been hottest.
   H. She does not specify whether the change in crop growth she cites was caused by an increase or decrease in temperature.
   J. The figures she presents for temperature increases over the next hundred years are greater than the figure for the past hundred years.

23. Scientist 2 implies the truth of which of the following statements?
   A. Humans will be able to adapt to any problem produced by global warming.
   B. A change in atmospheric water vapor could significantly affect global temperatures.
   C. Atmospheric carbon dioxide levels will never reach 1,100 parts per million.
   D. Atmospheric carbon dioxide levels will eventually stop increasing.

Passage 5

Angiosperms, or flowering plants, typically produce flowers seasonally. The various angiosperm species produce their flowers at different times of the year. For example, some flowers bloom in early spring, while others bloom in the summer. Research has shown that these flowering plants respond to changes in day length. A cocklebur, for example, does not produce flowers during the time of year that has days longer than 15.5 hours. When the length of day drops below this figure, flowering occurs. This type of flower is known as a short-day (SD) plant. Long-day (LD) plants do the opposite. These plants do not flower until the length of day exceeds a certain critical value. Plants that do not respond to changes in day length are called day-neutral (DN) plants. The following experiments investigate what aspect of changing day length is responsible for the plants' responses.

Experiment 1

Botanists raise both SD and LD plants in a greenhouse under long-day conditions. As expected, SD plants do not flower, and the LD plants do flower. When a brief period of darkness interrupts a long day, the plants continue to flower.

Experiment 2

Scientists raise both SD and LD plants in a greenhouse under short-day conditions. The SD plants do flower, and the LD plants do not flower. When a brief flash of light interrupts the long night, the SD plants stop flowering, and the LD plants began to flower.

Experiment 3

Experimenters perform a yearlong study in which they raise both SD and LD plants in several greenhouses. The light/dark cycle corresponds to the day length changes that occur over the course of a year. Daytime temperatures differ in each greenhouse. All SD plants flower at the same time of year. As expected, all LD plants flower at a different time than the SD plants do, but the LD plants all flower at the same time when compared to one another.

Experiment 4

Conditions are identical to those of Experiment 3, except that daytime temperatures are the same across greenhouses, while nighttime temperatures vary. SD and LD plants still flower at different times of the year, but the plants vary considerably as far as when each plant begins to flower. For example, SD plants in greenhouses with warmer nighttime temperatures flower at a different time than do SD plants in cooler greenhouses.

24. On the basis of Experiments 1 and 2, which of the following is the most critical factor in determining whether SD and LD plants will flower?
   F. the total number of daytime hours
   G. the total number of nighttime hours
   H. the number of uninterrupted daytime hours
   J. the number of uninterrupted nighttime hours

25. Cocklebur, an SD plant, and spinach, an LD plant, are both raised on an 8-hour day, 16-hour night cycle. If a brief flash of light is presented in the middle of the 16-hour night, what is the most likely result?
   A. Neither plant will flower.
   B. Cocklebur will flower; spinach will not.
   C. Spinach will flower; cocklebur will not.
   D. Both plants will flower.

26. Which of the following variables is not directly controlled by the experimenters?
   F. type of plant
   G. flowering
   H. amount of light
   J. temperature

27. Are the results of Experiments 3 and 4 consistent with the results of Experiments 1 and 2?
   A. No, because Experiments 3 and 4 use a wider variety of plants.
   B. No, because the temperature is not changed in Experiments 1 and 2.
   C. Yes, because both sets of experiments suggest that the plants respond to a night factor rather than a day factor.
   D. Yes, because both SD and LD plants are used in all the experiments.

Go on to next page

28. Which of the following best represents the shape of a graph plotting flowering activity as a function of day length for an LD plant that starts to flower when day length exceeds 15 hours?

F.

Flowering Activity vs. Day Length (hours), 0 to 20: linear line increasing from origin.

G.

Flowering Activity vs. Day Length (hours), 0 to 20: flat low line, then sharp rise after about 15 hours.

H.

Flowering Activity vs. Day Length (hours), 0 to 20: horizontal flat line.

J.

Flowering Activity vs. Day Length (hours), 0 to 20: linear line decreasing.

29. Near the equator, day length varies little throughout the year. That is, days and nights are close to 12 hours each during every season. Which of the following plants would most likely flower (assuming proper soil, water, and other essential conditions) if grown near the equator?

I. an LD plant that flowers only when the day length exceeds 12 hours
II. an SD plant that flowers only when the day length falls below 12 hours
III. an SD plant that flowers only when day length falls below 8 hours
IV. a DN plant

A. IV only
B. I, II, and III
C. I, II, and IV only
D. I, II, III, and IV

Passage 6

Matter exists in three phases: solid, liquid, and gas. In general, these phases are defined by how far apart the particles in the substance are. Particles are typically closest together in a solid and farthest away from one another in a gas.

Temperature is clearly related to phases. When temperature rises, particles move faster and away from one another. As temperature increases, matter changes from a solid to a liquid to a gas.

Pressure also affects phases of matter. A substance that is a gas at a certain temperature and low pressure may become a liquid at the same temperature if pressure is increased.

The figures that follow summarize the relationship among temperature, pressure, and phase for both bromine and water:

Go on to next page

Figure 1: Bromine phases.

Figure 2: Water phases.

30. At 60°C and 1.00 atm, water is
    F. a solid.
    G. a liquid.
    H. a gas.
    J. melting (changing from a solid to a liquid).

31. Sublimation occurs when a solid changes to a gas without going through a liquid phase. Under which of the following conditions can sublimation occur?
    A. bromine at –20°C and 0.05 atm
    B. bromine at 0°C and 0.80 atm
    C. water at 0°C and 0.80 atm
    D. water at 80°C and 0.50 atm

32. At 30°C, as pressure is decreased from 0.6 atm to 0.3 atm, which of the following is true?
    F. Bromine changes from a gas to a liquid.
    G. Bromine changes from a liquid to a gas.
    H. Water changes from a solid to a liquid.
    J. Water changes from a gas to a liquid.

33. For which of the following are the particles farthest apart?
    A. bromine at –10°C and 1.00 atm
    B. bromine at 50°C and 0.80 atm
    C. water at 0°C and 0.40 atm
    D. water at 100°C and 0.60 atm

34. At high altitudes, pressure is lower, and softening spaghetti in boiling water (temperature at which liquid changes to a gas) takes longer. Which of the following is the most reasonable explanation for this effect?
    F. Ice crystals form on the spaghetti.
    G. Air temperature is lower at high altitudes.
    H. The boiling point is lower at lower pressure. Lower temperatures are not as effective in softening spaghetti.
    J. At lower pressure, water boils at a higher temperature. Reaching this temperature takes longer.

Passage 7

Radon is a gas that is emitted from the earth's crust in small quantities. Radon can readily be detected in wells. An accidental discovery of excessive radon emission in an earthquake-prone area led seismologists to study the association between radon emission and earthquakes. Such an association could prove valuable in perfecting ways to predict earthquakes.

Study 1

Scientists selected four sites that had experienced recent earthquakes and measured radon emissions in wells located near the epicenter (the point on the earth's surface above the focus of an earthquake). At each well, the scientists recorded the percent that the radon emission exceeded the average radon emission found in wells throughout the world. This percentage was called the differential. These measurements are depicted in Figures 1 through 4.

Figure 1

```
        3.8
         W
4.4
 W
       0.2
        W          2.7
                    W
3.6
 W      0.1
         W
```
China
Magnitude - 7.9
Average Differential - 2.5

Figure 2

```
    1.8          2.0
     W            W

  1.9       2.1
   W         W
                     1.5
                      W
```
Iran
Magnitude - 6.9
Average Differential - 1.9

Figure 3

```
             2.1
   3.0        W
2.7  W
 W

                3.0
                 W
       2.8
        W
```
California, USA
Magnitude - 7.2
Average Differential - 2.7

Figure 4

```
     3.8
      W        3.2
                W
  4.2
   W  •  4.1
          W
        2.1
         W
                1.7
                 W
```
Chile
Magnitude - 7.5
Average Differential - 3.2

Legend for all figures

● - epicenter

Number - percent that radon emission is greater than normal (differential)

W - well

Scale: 1 cm = 100 km

Study 2

To study whether the differential varied with the magnitude of an earthquake, seismologists made a scatter plot of the average differential against earthquake magnitude for each site. Figure 5 shows this scatter plot.

35. Which of the following is the most reasonable conclusion that can be drawn from Study 1?
- **A.** No association is present between earthquakes and increased radon emissions.
- **B.** Some evidence suggests an association between earthquakes and increased radon emissions.
- **C.** Radon emissions of wells more than 1,000 km from the epicenter did not increase.
- **D.** The radon emission right at the epicenter is more than 5 percent greater than normal levels for the entire earth.

36. Which of the following would strengthen the claim that increased radon emissions are associated with earthquakes?
- I. more well sites in the vicinity of each epicenter showing higher than normal radon emissions
- II. a location that had a 7.9 magnitude quake and an average emission differential of 3.6
- III. more earthquakes at the epicenters depicted in Figures 1 through 4
- **F.** II only
- **G.** III only
- **H.** I and II only
- **J.** I and III only

37. Can it be determined from the results that radon emissions cause earthquakes?
- **A.** No, because the results merely suggest that earthquakes and increased radon emissions occur at about the same time.
- **B.** No, because the differentials would have to exceed 4 percent at all well sites to make such a condition.
- **C.** Yes, because every well site had higher-than-normal radon emissions.
- **D.** Yes, because the radon comes from beneath the earth's surface.

Figure 5: Scatter plot of average differential and earthquake magnitude.

38. Which of the following is an important control condition that is lacking in the studies?
    F. radon emissions from a well very distant from the epicenter
    G. radon emissions from sites that experienced earthquakes of magnitude greater than 8.0
    H. radon emissions from sites that haven't had an earthquake in over 400 years
    J. radon emissions from the Study 1 sites when no earthquake took place

39. What type of study needs to be done to help determine whether radon emissions can be used to predict earthquakes?
    A. measuring radon emissions before an earthquake takes place
    B. measuring radon emissions as an earthquake takes place
    C. measuring radon emissions around epicenters for quakes weaker than 6.9
    D. measuring radon emissions around epicenters for quakes stronger than 7.9

40. What is most puzzling about the China results?
    F. The China earthquake was the strongest earthquake studied.
    G. One well showed a differential of 4.4, higher than that of any other well in the studies.
    H. The wells closest to the epicenter had lower differentials than those farther away.
    J. Readings were taken from six wells.

STOP DO NOT TURN THE PAGE UNTIL TOLD TO DO SO.
DO NOT RETURN TO A PREVIOUS TEST.

Getting Down to the Nitty-Gritty: Subscores

Three of the tests of the ACT feature subscores as an added bonus (think of these as a "gift with purchase"). In 20-plus years of tutoring for the ACT (I started when I was a mere child, you see), few students have cared about the subscores. By the time you get through this book, you should pretty much know which sections are your best and which are your weakest. However, you'll see subscores on your score report, so a few words about them are necessary.

English Test

The English test has 40 questions in the Usage/Mechanics subscore area and 35 questions in the Rhetorical Skills subscore area — a total of 75 questions. (See Chapter 5 for more info on the types of questions on the English Test.) Because I wrote these practice exams to give you more practice with the types of questions that my experience shows students have the best chance of getting correct with practice, this breakdown isn't really applicable to the practice exams in this book. Besides, students get headaches trying to understand the fine distinctions between what is rhetorical and what is not. Don't worry about it.

Mathematics Test

The actual ACT Mathematics Test usually has 24 prealgebra/elementary algebra problems, 18 intermediate algebra/coordinate geometry problems, and 18 plane geometry/trig problems — a total of 60 questions. Good news! The ACT has only four trig questions, so if you haven't had the subject yet, don't panic.

However, because this book is a teaching book and not the actual ACT, I'm not going to put you through the trauma of subscores. Besides, there are many gray areas in which one person is convinced that a problem is elementary algebra but another argues it's intermediate algebra or worse. Here's the simple solution: Be able to do all the problems (easy for me to say!), and don't worry about typecasting and labeling them.

Reading Test

The Reading Test subscores couldn't possibly be any easier. You get a subscore for questions in social studies/sciences (20 questions, based on 2 passages) and arts/literature (20 questions, based on 2 passages).

Science Reasoning Test

The Science Reasoning test has no subscores.

Score One for Our Side: The Scoring Key

The ACT scoring may be weird (Why a 36? Why not a 21 or a 49 or a 73?), but it is very straightforward. Follow these simple directions to score your practice exam.

1. **Count the number of correct responses in each of the practice tests: English, Mathematics, Reading, and Science Reasoning.**

    Do NOT subtract any points for questions you missed or questions you didn't answer. Your score is based only on the number of questions you answered correctly. That number is called your *raw score*.

2. **Locate your raw score on the following table. Move to the left or right and find the scaled score that corresponds to your raw score.**

    For example, a raw score of 50 on the English Test gives you a scaled score of 21.

3. **Add your four scaled scores. Divide that sum by 4. The resulting number is your composite score.**

    For example, if your scaled scores were 23, 31, 12, and 19, your composite score would be 85 ÷ 4 = 21.25, or 21.

Raw Scores

Scale Score	English	Mathematics	Reading	Science Reasoning	Scale Score
1	0–1	0	0	0	1
2	2	–	1	–	2
3	3	1	2	1	3
4	4–5	–	3	–	4
5	6–7	–	4	–	5
6	8–9	2	5	2	6
7	10–11	3	6	3	7
8	12–13	–	7	4	8
9	14–16	4	8	5	9
10	17–19	5	9	6	10
11	20–22	6–7	10	7	11
12	23–25	8	11–12	8–9	12
13	26–28	9–10	13	10	13
14	29–31	11–12	14	11–12	14
15	32–35	13–14	15	13–14	15
16	36–37	15–17	16	15	16
17	38–40	18–19	17	16–17	17
18	41–43	20–22	18–19	18–19	18
19	44–45	23–24	20	20–21	19
20	46–48	25–26	21	22	20
21	49–50	27–29	22	23–24	21
22	51–53	30–32	23	25	22
23	54–55	33–34	24	26–27	23
24	56–57	35–37	25	28	24
25	58–59	38–40	26–27	29	25
26	60–62	41–42	28	30	26
27	63–64	43–45	29	31	27
28	65–66	46–48	30	32	28
29	67	49–50	31	33	29
30	68–69	51–53	–	34	30
31	70	54–55	32	35	31
32	71–72	56	33	36	32
33	73	57	34	37	33
34	–	58	35	38	34
35	74	59	36	39	35
36	75	60	37–40	40	36

Answer Key

English Test

1. C		39. D	
2. G		40. J	
3. C		41. A	
4. J		42. F	
5. B		43. C	
6. G		44. G	
7. C		45. A	
8. F		46. F	
9. D		47. B	
10. H		48. F	
11. D		49. D	
12. G		50. F	
13. C		51. C	
14. G		52. F	
15. A		53. B	
16. G		54. J	
17. B		55. B	
18. J		56. J	
19. A		57. C	
20. H		58. H	
21. A		59. B	
22. F		60. J	
23. C		61. D	
24. J		62. G	
25. C		63. D	
26. G		64. H	
27. B		65. D	
28. H		66. F	
29. B		67. C	
30. J		68. G	
31. B		69. B	
32. F		70. H	
33. D		71. B	
34. F		72. F	
35. B		73. D	
36. G		74. G	
37. C		75. C	
38. F			

Mathematics Test

1. D		31. B	
2. H		32. G	
3. D		33. D	
4. F		34. K	
5. B		35. C	
6. H		36. K	
7. D		37. B	
8. K		38. K	
9. C		39. B	
10. G		40. J	
11. D		41. D	
12. K		42. H	
13. A		43. B	
14. J		44. H	
15. E		45. B	
16. J		46. H	
17. E		47. A	
18. H		48. H	
19. E		49. A	
20. F		50. J	
21. D		51. D	
22. J		52. F	
23. D		53. C	
24. H		54. F	
25. B		55. E	
26. H		56. F	
27. B		57. D	
28. J		58. F	
29. D		59. D	
30. G		60. K	

Reading Test

1. D		21. D	
2. J		22. G	
3. A		23. C	
4. G		24. J	
5. C		25. D	
6. F		26. G	
7. B		27. D	
8. H		28. F	
9. B		29. C	
10. F		30. H	
11. B		31. B	
12. G		32. F	
13. A		33. C	
14. G		34. F	
15. C		35. A	
16. H		36. G	
17. B		37. D	
18. G		38. J	
19. D		39. A	
20. F		40. H	

Science Reasoning Test

1. B		21. A	
2. G		22. H	
3. A		23. B	
4. G		24. J	
5. D		25. C	
6. G		26. G	
7. B		27. C	
8. J		28. G	
9. A		29. C	
10. H		30. G	
11. C		31. A	
12. H		32. G	
13. B		33. D	
14. F		34. H	
15. C		35. B	
16. G		36. H	
17. D		37. A	
18. H		38. J	
19. A		39. A	
20. J		40. H	

Chapter 22

Practice Exam 2: Answers and Explanations

Now you've done it! You've completed the practice exam, checked your answers against the key, and found your score on the Raw Score chart.

Hang on! Invest another hour or so to go through this chapter, reading why one answer was correct and the others weren't. Along the way, you'll find tons of tips and traps — valuable information that you'll be able to use when you face the Big One.

Keep in mind that any words marked *like this* are vocabulary words to add to your vocabulary list.

English Test

Passage 1

1. **C.** The word "it" should send off warning bells and buzzers. "It" is often misused and abused. The word "it" should have an *antecedent*, a word it refers to and replaces. Here, there's no antecedent. Choice B is wrong because the "recent trend" is singular, requiring the singular verb (has) not the plural verb (have). Choice D turns the sentence into a *fragment*, which is an incomplete thought.

2. **G.** Chapter 4 discusses the difference between effect and affect. An *effect* is a result and is correct here (to *affect* is to concern or influence: Your not knowing the distinction between these two words can adversely affect your ACT score). Knowing effect is correct enables you to narrow the answer choices down to F and G. Choice F is wrong because there needs to be a break between "effects" and "obesity," either punctuation or a conjunction.

3. **C.** The pronoun refers to two things, fat and salt, such that you need the plural pronoun "they," not the singular pronoun "it." Choice D would make the sentence a fragment.

   Some students get into the bad habit of choosing OMIT every time they see it. Although I can understand your urge to toss out everything you can get your hands on (including those annoying proctors who call time before you're finished), doing so isn't always the best policy.

4. **J.** The sentence repeats what was said in the second sentence of the paragraph and doesn't add anything. Good writing is short and to the point. Be careful not to change something just for the sake of change; make a change only if it corrects a grammatical mistake or improves the passage.

5. **B.** Although you may desperately be seeking for an answer that says, "None of the above; they all stink," alas, no such choice exists. Choice B is the best of the sorry lot.

The original is a fragment, an incomplete sentence. Choice C is also a fragment. Choice D changes the meaning of the sentence (making it sound as if all four selections are the favorites).

6. **G.** The author means to imply that the restaurant food is getting progressively blander. "Lesser" is rarely right on its own. It's most commonly used in a phrase such as "a lesser man would have thrown his book out the window, but I held on to mine." Usually, "less" is correct. Choice J is wrong because least implies a comparison of at least three items, not the two (home cooking and restaurant food) discussed here.

7. **C.** From the context of the passage, you know that the verb needs to be in the past tense; thus, "discovered" is correct.

Often, to determine the tense of a verb, you need to read a little bit ahead in the passage. The next sentence says that "I had been making. . . ." If you read the underlined portion only or otherwise read it out of context, you're likely to fall for the trap that the test-makers have set for you.

8. **F.** The original version is fine, as it implies that the current chili has a better flavor than the previous chili did. Note that if you put G or H or J, you're saying this chili has a better *flavor* than did the flavor of the previous chili.

This is a particularly difficult question. You find out in Chapter 4 that you have to compare similar items. For example, you wouldn't say, "The flavor of the ice cream is better than the cake," because there you're comparing flavor to cake, whereas you mean to compare the flavor of the ice cream to the flavor of the cake. That type of mistake is common on the ACT, but in the case of question 8, the original was fine.

9. **D.** A comma is a short pause; a semicolon is a complete stop. There must be a complete sentence (an independent clause) before and after a semicolon, which eliminates choices B and C. Choice A is wrong because there is no need for a pause after "experimented."

Commas can be confusing. My general rule is, "When in doubt, leave it out." Although commas are often necessary, my experience has been that people overuse them.

10. **H.** Talking with several what? The original sentence leaves you hanging. Clarify it by adding the word "people."

11. **D.** Beware of *-ing* words. Although they're not always incorrect, they're misused often enough to make you paranoid and neurotic whenever you see them. The original version is a fragment, as is choice C. Choice B is wordy and redundant when inserted into the question. Choice D not only adds the subject "they" but makes the sentence better by changing the second verb to "consume."

12. **G.** This type of question is a real time-waster. If finishing this section on time is difficult for you, skip this type of question. Remember that no penalty in assessed on the ACT for wrong answers; always fill in some sort of guess. Simply don't waste time here because to answer the question correctly, you have to go back and reread the paragraph, probably several times.

In this instance, put the addition after sentence 1, such that you expand on the idea in sentence 2 that when there isn't enough salt, people will eat more food.

13. **C.** This question should have been relatively simple. As discussed in Chapter 4, "good" describes a characteristic, as in good food, good meal, or good cook. "Well" tells how something is done: You cook well. The only way the food couldn't taste well is if the food has taste buds and they are not functioning as they should! Choice D has two errors. It sounds as though the meal itself is doing the tasting, and — if that were so — it would taste well, not good.

14. **G.** Adding the word "which" makes the sentence correct. Choice H has the dreaded word "being," which is often found in trap answers. Choice J sounds like Yoda from *Star Wars,* with the order of the words stilted and awkward.

15. **A.** What a horrible selection of answer choices! Each one is wordy and unnecessary. The author already does a good job in the final passage of concluding with his opinion that too much salt and fat are bad, but those ingredients can't be totally eliminated. The answer choices don't present a better way of stating that idea.

Passage 2

16. **G.** This question primarily tests "who" versus "whom." "Who" is a subject and does the action of the sentence. In this case, "who" is doing the governing. "Whom" is an object and receives the action. For example, you may say, "Whom do they govern?" In that case, the "whom" would be the ones being governed or receiving the action of the governing.

    Again, if you confuse who and whom, substitute "him," with an *m* for "whom" with an *m*. If "him" works, "whom" is necessary. If "him" does not work, use "who." Knowing that "who" is required eliminates choices F and J. Choice H does not fit when reinserted into the sentence.

17. **B.** An adverb, which usually ends in *-ly,* answers the question *how.* How are most tribal governments organized? Democratically. Choice C is tempting. Choice C *is* grammatically correct, but choice C is also unnecessarily awkward and prolix. (No, prolix isn't an expensive brand of watch. *Prolix* just means wordy.) It isn't necessary to say a government is organized in a democracy, but rather, democratically. Choice D makes no sense. Omitting the underlined portion makes the sentence read, "Most tribal governments are, that is, with an elected leadership."

    Many students fall into a bad habit on this exam. They choose the *OMIT* answer every time that they see it. OMIT has no better or worse chance of being correct than does any other answer choice.

18. **J.** The original is a run-on sentence, two sentences (independent clauses) incorrectly joined. The ability to use a period instead of a comma is a good hint that the sentence is a run-on. Eliminating the subject of the second sentence, "it," makes the second portion subordinate and thus part of one complete sentence. Choice G sounds tempting, but it changes the meaning of the sentence. The conjunction "however" indicates that the second sentence is changing (or in some way contradicting) the first sentence. This situation is not the case here. The same error eliminates choice H. The sentence does not need a *but.*

19. **A.** This question tests the distinction between "principal" and "principle." *Principal* (with a *-pal*) means main or primary. (You may have learned in about sixth grade that "The principal is your pal, your buddy.") *Principle* (with an *-le*) is a rule. Eliminating the *-le* option immediately narrows the choices down to only one.

    This type of question is one that you should always be able to get right. It tests a diction error, two commonly confused words. Diction errors are discussed at length in Chapter 4. Be sure that you have these diction twosomes memorized before the exam. Correcting a diction error is, in general, much easier than correcting, for example, a verb-tense error or answering a question on the meaning of the passage.

20. **H.** If you missed this easy question, pack your bags — you're going on a guilt trip. This situation is a typical subject-verb agreement problem. The subject of the sentence is "an elected tribal council." Council is singular and requires the singular verb "has."

    Did you let yourself get bamboozled by the prepositional phrase? "Of the Interior and the people working for him" is a prepositional phrase (*of* is a preposition). Prepositional phrases do not affect subject-verb agreement (this concept is covered in Chapter 4).

21. **A.** *Tribe* is singular. You say "the tribe *is*" not "the tribe *are.*" (Tribe is a collective noun. Collective nouns look plural, but they are always singular. Collective nouns are discussed in Chapter 4.) Because *tribe* is singular, it requires a singular pronoun, "it," rather than "them." Eliminate choices C and D because of the plural pronoun *them.*

Have you noticed how often you may use a diction rule or a "twosomes" concept to narrow the answers quickly down to two? Be sure that you have *memorized* all the twosomes discussed in Chapter 4.

Choice B has an *-ing* verb, always a suspicious character. If you insert it back into the sentence, you'll see that "be representing" changes the flow of the sentence: ". . . authority to speak and act for the tribe and be representing it. . . ." Verbs in a series must be in parallel forms: to speak, to act, to represent.

22. **F.** The sentence is satisfactory as is. Verbs in a series must have parallel forms. "Tribal governments define . . . regulate . . . prescribe . . . levy," and so on.

Did you notice the error in Choice G? *Regular* is not the same word as *regulate*. Be careful not to anticipate, to read the word you expect to see rather than the word that's actually on the page.

23. **C.** No need to break into a cerebral sweat for this pretty simple question. Verbs in a series must be in parallel form. This very long sentence has a number of verbs, and all are in the simple present: "define," "regulate," "prescribe," "levy," "regulate," and "control." The last verb must be in the same form as well: "administer," eliminating choices B and D immediately. The original unnecessarily adds a subject, *they*.

24. **J.** Ahh, did you immediately eliminate J because of the *-ing* verb? If so, I gotcha! You know that *-ing* verbs almost always are wrong — but not always. In this case, the original looks correct until you read the entire sentence. "They have fought . . . they served." Because the "they served" portion is not underlined, it cannot be changed. The beginning of the sentence must become a subordinate clause (one that cannot stand alone). Subordinate clauses often begin with *-ing* verbs: "Fighting in all wars . . . they have served. . . ." Besides that, F, G, and H are run-ons.

Beware of taking my tips as gospel and using them automatically. The tips and tricks you are learning in this book are not chiseled in stone. They are *tips,* not rules. Personally, I think of *-ing* words as guilty until proven innocent. They're probably wrong, but at least give them a chance and check them out.

25. **C.** *Demonstrated patriotism* caused Congress to pass the Indian Citizenship Act. "Demonstrating patriotism" has an *-ing* verb and should be looked at with suspicion. Choice D leaves out the verb entirely.

This situation presents a persnickety grammatical point, one that is difficult even for native English speakers. If all of the answers sound correct to you, just make a quick guess and go on. (Remember that the ACT does not subtract penalty points for wrong answers. Guessing is always to your advantage.)

26. **G.** The original, using both "one" and "you," is all mixed up. Use either one selection or the other, but do not use both. Choice J is tempting because it has the word "one," but this choice is actually using the plural pronoun "their," which is incorrect. *One* does not read in *their* books. Eliminate H for the same reason.

27. **B.** Choice C is tempting, but it changes the meaning of the sentence. The Navajos did not use the Marine language; they used the Navajo language. Getting so involved in the grammar that you forget the reading comprehension concepts is very easy. Be sure, when you correct a grammatical mistake, that you have not introduced a new mistake in the meaning of the sentence. Choice A is totally awkward (if it's hard to read aloud, it's probably the wrong answer). Choice D doesn't fit when reinserted into the sentence.

28. **H.** You need to use a plural verb: "Forty-five to forty-seven percent of tribal leaders *are*. . . ." Although the word *percent* looks singular, you have to determine what the percent is. This example presents one of the rare instances in which a prepositional phrase *does* affect subject-verb agreement. (Sometimes you have to look at the object of the preposition. For example, 50 percent of the *house* is infested with termites, but 50 percent of the *houses* in the neighborhood *are* infested with termites.) Because "of tribal leaders" is plural, use a plural verb, *are,* and a plural noun, *veterans*.

And speaking of termites, a quick joke: What did the termite say when he walked into the saloon?

"Is the bar tender here?"

29. **B.** This question is like the main idea question that you would find after a regular reading comprehension passage. To answer this question, you probably have to reread the entire passage, ignoring the grammar concepts and focusing on the meaning of the passage.

Before you make a wild guess, look at the answer choices; look especially at the verbs. You can eliminate choice A based on the verb "to argue." Very few passages are passionate enough to *argue* a point of view. In choice C, "to hypothesize" is wrong. Nothing about this passage is theoretical; it simply gives the facts. In choice D, "to predict" is wrong. The passage tells you what has been and what is, not what will be.

The main idea of a passage is often described by one of three words: discuss, describe, or explain. The primary purpose of a passage is to discuss something, to describe something, or to explain something. If you're making a wild guess, choose one of those verbs.

Passage 3

30. **J.** The subject of the sentence is "the theory." "Theory" is singular, requiring a singular verb, "holds." This narrows the answers down to H and J. In H, "whichever" makes no sense when reinserted into the sentence.

An underlined portion that features a verb often tests subject-verb agreement. Go back and identify the specific subject, ignoring (in most cases) the prepositional phrase.

31. **B.** A simple comma indicating a pause is sufficient. A semicolon separates independent sentences. In other words, the part before the semicolon and the part after the semicolon must each be a complete sentence. The part before the semicolon here would be a fragment, an incomplete sentence. Choice D introduces an unnecessary *-ing* verb (always be suspicious of *-ing* verbs) that would ruin the parallelism of the sentence ("is thrust . . . penetrating").

32. **F.** The subject of the sentence is "pockets," which is plural, requiring a plural verb, *result*. If you thought the subject was "rock," you fell for the trap answer, choice H. Prepositional phrases, such as "of molten rock," rarely affect subject-verb agreement. Choice J unnecessarily changes the tense of the sentence. Be careful that your change makes your new sentence fit within the paragraph. The rest of the paragraph here is in the present tense.

33. **D.** The original is a fragment, an incomplete sentence. When you read it, you expect to hear something more at the end. Alter the *-ing* verb (often an indication of an error) to "built" to change the sentence to the simple past tense.

I hope that you didn't fall for choice B. The English language has no such word as "bilt." "Bilt" is not the past tense of "build." The past tense of "build" is "built." (Come, come now, don't leave in a huff over that cheesy answer. As Groucho Marx would say, "Wait a minute and a huff!")

34. **F.** *Like* compares similar objects. That is, *like* usually connects two nouns. *As* compares situations or actions. Eliminate choices G and H. Choice J changes the meaning entirely. *Likely* means probably; *like* means similar to.

35. **B.** The correct expression is "to mix one thing *with* another" not "to mix one thing *from* another."

36. **G.** This question tests whether you know a *cliché,* a common saying such as "more (something) than you can shake a stick at." For example, Chapter 4 has more good rules than you can shake a stick at. If you didn't know this saying, you would have been well advised to skip (or just guess at) this question.

Occasionally this exam expects you to know a proverb, a quotation, or a saying that is in common usage in English. If the saying is completely foreign to you (pun fully intended, I'm sorry to say), make a quick guess and go on.

37. **C.** The subject is *park,* which is singular and requires the singular verb *boasts.* This fact eliminates choices A and D. Did you fall for the trap I set? "Boast some," when read aloud, sounds like "boasts some," because of the *s* in *some.* Whenever a verb is underlined, check that the subject agrees with the verb. Choice B is wrong because it sounds as if the park is doing some boasting. The expression **boasts some of the** simply means ***is proud to have.*** You and your friends can boast some of the highest ACT scores around if you learn the tricks and the traps of the exam.

38. **F.** The correct construction is semicolon, coordinating conjunction, and comma, as used in the original. Choice G is backward. The semicolon should come before the comma. Choice H would make the sentence into a run-on with a comma splice (a comma is not strong enough to join independent sentences). Choice J has the colon used incorrectly. A colon usually indicates a sequence or series of items to follow. For example: Please learn the following rules: 1 . . . ; 2 . . . ; and so on.

    (I can never see a punctuation problem without remembering a really smart student who informed me, "Punctuation exacerbates my clinomania." As soon as he left, I looked up the word: *Clinomania* is an overwhelming desire to stay in bed!)

39. **D.** This passage is very straightforward. It discusses a certain geographical area, how that area was built, and what species of plants and animals and people live in that area. The passage is objective and neutral (as most passages are on this test), and the passage does not need humor. A cliché or slang expression, such as "more . . . than you can shake a stick at," is inappropriate (although you personally may be relieved to find even a glimmer of comic relief at this point).

    If you had trouble choosing an answer, use the process of elimination. Choice A is wrong because nothing in this sentence changes the meaning of the passage. The passage discusses species; this sentence talks about more species. Choice B is wrong; nothing new was introduced. Choice C can sound confusing. To *forestall* an opposing argument means to anticipate an objection and address it directly. No objections were discussed or anticipated here.

    This question is a good one to guess on. Fill in something, anything, because the ACT does not penalize you for wrong answers (random guesses). You just can't afford the time to go back through the whole passage and try to figure out this sentence's role in it.

40. **J.** Don't invest a lot of time and effort in this type of question; make a wild guess and go on. If English is not your native tongue, reading the passages is hard enough to do when the sentences are in the correct order and nearly impossible to do when the sentences are all jumbled up.

    If you decide to do this sort of question, the best place to begin is with the *topic* or *main idea* sentence. The subject of the paragraph is "the theory of plate tectonics," meaning that sentence 2 should come first. This positioning of sentence 2 eliminates choices F and J. Now, if you're really shrewd, you will simply look at choices G and H to determine which second sentence would come next. In choice H, the second sentence is number 5, which begins with "These become. . . ." Because nothing appears in sentence 2 for "these" to refer to, sentence 5 must not be second. Look at choice G. Sentence 3 says "pockets of molten rock result." Result from what? Sentence 2: "It penetrates deep enough into the earth to be partly remelted."

    This type of question is a major time-waster and is one of the most frequently missed questions. Unless you are very confident of your answer, you're better off not destroying any brain cells unnecessarily, but just guessing.

Chapter 22: Practice Exam 2: Answers and Explanations   317

41. **A.** "Because of" is correct. Choices B, C, and D turn the sentence into a fragment. If you selected any of these three choices, you didn't take the final, critical step: Reread the entire sentence with the new answer inserted. If you're going to answer a question, take enough time to do it right.

42. **F.** The sentence means to say that the Indians didn't leave many artifacts behind. Choice G changes the meaning (and the tense). Choices H and J turn the sentence into a fragment.

43. **C.** This last paragraph starts an entirely new train of thought. Previously, the passage gave a physical description of the land and discussed its plant life. This paragraph is the first time that you learn that humans inhabited the area.

Passage 4

44. **G.** Read a little bit ahead in the paragraph to learn that the writer is no longer a young boy. Therefore, the simple past tense "dreamed" is required. Choice J turns the sentence into a fragment.

   TIP: Remember, *-ing* words often make complete sentences into incomplete sentences or fragments. If you decide to choose an *-ing* verb, be sure to reinsert it into the sentence and reread the entire sentence.

45. **A.** You can immediately eliminate choice C because the English language has no such word as *its'*. *It's* means *it is,* and *its* is the possessive of it, but no *its'* exists. Choice D looks tempting because "of whom" is a proper formation (*of* is a preposition; *whom* is the object of the preposition). However, choice D, when reinserted into the sentence, destroys the structure of the sentence, as does choice B.

46. **F.** This question tests the use of prepositions. You can be fascinated by, enslaved by, captivated by, or enriched by something, but you are not enslaved *with,* or captivated *to,* or enriched *of* something. Choice J does not work when reinserted into the sentence (as an *-ing* word, it was dubious from the start).

   And speaking of enriching, did you ever hear John D. Rockefeller's three rules for becoming rich? (1) Go to work early. (2) Stay late. (3) Find oil.

47. **B.** This question is an interesting one because all of the answer choices are pretty bad. Your job is to choose the least awful among them. (Hmm: Sounds rather like a mixer dance, doesn't it?) The original creates a fragment: "A few miles past Naples, Italy along the slopes of Vesuvius." This fragment doesn't finish the thought. The same is true for the next part: "This city is found, which is much the same it was in A.D. 79. . . ." Choice B, even though it is in the passive voice (is found) rather than the active voice (we find), makes a complete sentence. (Active voice is usually preferable to passive voice because active voice is usually more concise, less wordy.) Choice C has an unnecessary colon. The colon usually introduces items in a series, as in "I want you to learn the following: . . . ." Choice D lacks a subject for the sentence (*who* finds the city?) and is a fragment.

48. **F.** For the ACT, you need to be very comfortable with all of the forms of the verbs lie and *lay*. *Lie* requires no object. You do not *lie something*. For example, you can say, "Studying for the ACT makes me so sleepy that I want to lie down." *Lay* requires an object. You'd say, "Now I *lay* me down to sleep." In this question, no object is supplied for the verb, meaning that the correct form is a conjugation of *lie*. This lack of an object eliminates choices G, H, and J.

   TIP: Can you list the conjugations of lie and lay? (See Chapter 4.) They are as follows:

   lie, lay, have lain

   lay, laid, have laid

49. **D.** If you got this question correct, congratulate yourself. Most people immediately misread "causally" as "casually."

Anytime you think that the sentence has no error, read *every* word carefully to ensure that you haven't automatically, subconsciously corrected the errors. If you selected NO CHANGE for 30 out of 75 questions, this automatic correction is probably a habit of yours.

50. **F.** "Anybody" is singular and requires a singular verb, "invites." Eliminate choices G and H immediately. Choice J is tempting, but omitting this portion destroys the meaning the author is trying to get across and deletes necessary punctuation.

Many students fall for the trap of choosing "OMIT the underlined portion" every time they see it. Sometimes an omission creates havoc with the sentence. If you decide to omit the underlined portion, be sure to reread the entire sentence with the portion omitted.

51. **C.** "Neither" is teamed with "nor" (and "either" is teamed with "or"). Whenever you see the word "neither," be sure that "nor" follows hard upon its heels.

When you find a simple grammar or diction error, change only that part and leave the rest of the sentence alone. In general, it's good to change as little of the sentence as possible.

52. **F.** Because the nonunderlined portion uses the past tense sat ("as he sat in his hotel room"), the underlined portion also requires the past tense "looked."

Trivia: You've probably heard about the ruins of Pompeii, but did you know that the courthouse was found full of arms and legs? Yeah, now that's clear evidence that the people had paid their lawyers' bills!

53. **B.** The original sounds as though Halliburton earns money simply by breathing and writing at the same time! (Only John Grisham, Tom Clancy, and Stephen King can do that!) The sentence means to say that the writing comes alive. However, it does not literally start to breathe; it simply becomes vivid, or lively.

54. **J.** The correct expression is "to relate to," not "to relate with," eliminating choice G immediately. Choice H becomes a run-on sentence. The comma is not sufficiently strong punctuation to separate independent clauses. The original is definitely a fragment. This portion has no conclusion, no verb, no complete thought.

Fun fact: Do you know the singular form of the word graffiti? It's graffito. I read all the graffiti on the walls regularly. My all-time sicko favorite graffito is "Join DAM: Mothers Against Dyslexia.")

55. **B.** "Perfect" is an absolute adjective. Something either is perfect or is not perfect. Perfect cannot be modified; for example, nothing can be *very* perfect or *completely* perfect, eliminating choices A and C. Choice D disrupts the flow of the sentence.

Although the shortest answer is often the best answer (because lengthy, verbose answers tend to be redundant or to add superfluous terms), if you decide to choose the shortest answer, check to be sure that it doesn't make the sentence awkward or difficult to read. This "flow" is one reason that I suggest rereading the sentences aloud. Of course, during the test you will not be able to shout out your answers, but you can always mutter under your breath.

56. **J.** The portion "Sure to inspire every young boy's imagination to feats of daring and bravery" is a sentence fragment, an incomplete sentence. Adding it to the previous noun ("gladiators"), which the clause modifies, eradicates this problem. Choice G makes a run-on sentence. A comma splice is not sufficiently strong to separate independent sentences. Choice H does not fit when reinserted into the sentence.

Chapter 22: Practice Exam 2: Answers and Explanations

57. **C.** The easiest way to answer an "order-of-sentences" question is to identify the topic sentence or the main idea. The main idea of this passage is Richard Halliburton, his writing, and his travels. It makes sense to begin the passage with Halliburton. Doing so immediately narrows the answers down to choices B and C. Next, look only at choices B and C to determine whether the second sentence should be sentence 3 (choice B) or sentence 2 (choice C). Because the first sentence has graffiti at its end, logic dictates that the next sentence should have graffiti at its beginning, which is the case with sentence 2.

58. **H.** The best way to answer this question is through the process of elimination. The article is too personal to be in an encyclopedia. It doesn't express an idea or argue an opinion the way an editorial would. Although choice J is tempting, the article discusses very little actual geography. The writing is more reminiscent, as if a man were writing of what influence Halliburton had on him.

    Personal aside: I've always wanted to write a travel memoir. I even have a title ready for the chapter about my trip through Egypt: *Ankhs for the Memories!*

59. **B.** Immediately eliminate choices C and D as negative. This passage is lightweight and charming, not somber and macabre. The purpose of questions is rarely to ridicule or to emphasize a negative point. Choice A is inane: Who cares about dental hygiene when you're dealing with a volcano?

    Riddle: How do you know that a dentist is sad?

    Answer: He's always looking down in the mouth!

Passage 5

60. **J.** The sentence as it is doesn't express a complete thought; it's a fragment. Leaving out the word "that" makes the sentence complete.

61. **D.** A routine is something that's set, that doesn't vary. Therefore, the original version is redundant and unnecessarily wordy. The author can make his point just as clearly with the one word, "routines."

62. **G.** Because dancers is plural, you need the plural verb, "appear."

    The word "some" is one of the "SAMAN" words (discussed in Chapter 4): words that are sometimes singular and sometimes plural. You need to look at what follows the some, which in this case is the plural form, "dancers."

63. **D.** The two sentences prior to this expression talk about the warlike, aggressive, charging actions of the birds. The author probably chooses the expression "pop out" to emphasize that sort of aggression.

64. **H.** If you missed this easy question, you probably were just careless.

    A common mistake in the English test is *anticipating;* that is, reading what you expect to see (the proper form of the word), rather than what's actually printed (a wrong word). My suggestion is that you make a habit of checking every NO CHANGE answer, just in case you automatically corrected what you were reading.

65. **D.** The original has the dreaded *-ing,* a form that should make you neurotic and suspicious every time you encounter it. While, of course, an *-ing* form is sometimes right, it's often used incorrectly, as it is here. Choice B is wordy; choice C is the wrong verb tense.

66. **F.** The original version, with the comment set apart in commas, is correct. Choice G would be inconsistent, with the first part of the comment set apart with a comma and the second part with a dash. Choices H and J have the commas in the wrong positions.

    To determine where to put a comma, read the sentence aloud and see where the natural pause is. A comma's function is to serve as that slight pause.

67. **C.** Items in a series must be parallel in form. For example, you wouldn't say "The ACT is thrilling, exciting, and a challenge." Instead, you'd say, "The ACT is thrilling, exciting, and challenging." Here, only choice C keeps the sequence of items in the same form. (Parallelism is covered in more depth in Chapter 4.)

68. **G.** It is safe to assume there are more than two types of birds and more than two types of bowers. Therefore, the superlative form most (used on three or more) rather than the comparative form more (used for two items) is necessary.

69. **B.** The iris is the colored portion of the eye. It's redundant to say "irises in the eye region," because you don't have irises in your ears or your tummy!

70. **H.** Use parallel structure on the verbs. The peacock *has* eyes on its feathers; the pheasant *has eyes* as well. Parallel structure or parallelism is discussed more fully in Chapter 4. Choice J is the trap. Inserted, it would make the sentence read, ". . . a pheasant also has them too." You don't need both also and too.

Be sure to reread the sentence with your answer choice inserted. Doing so may take a few seconds, but helps you prevent mistakes like this one.

71. **B.** The original version is wordy and awkward. Choose the most direct, straightforward answer to make the same point. Choices C and D are just as verbose as the original version. (Also, in choice C, just who are "they," these people naming the bird?)

Although the shortest answer is not always the best answer, it's always an answer worth checking out. I suggest plugging in the shortest answer first to see whether it works.

72. **F.** To *emulate* is to imitate. Humans, dressing to resemble birds and copying their dances, are emulating the birds. Choice G is wrong because initiate means to begin, as in you initiate your ACT studies as soon as possible. Choice H is the wrong verb number (singular when the plural noun dances requires a plural verb). Choice J is the passive voice (active and passive voices are discussed in Chapter 4) and is unnecessarily wordy.

73. **D.** The original version is a fragment, an incomplete sentence. It's missing a verb, which "take," in choice D, supplies.

Bonus trivia: Speaking of New Guinea, birds aren't the only interesting creatures there. Did you know that Papua, New Guinea, has several types of kangaroos that live in the top layers of trees? Just imagine walking along throughout the trees and looking up to see a kangaroo! (You'd probably think you were hallucinating from studying too much ACT!)

74. **G.** The passage most likely would continue with the last thought, which was about the dances the human males perform that are like those of the birds.

75. **C.** This type of question is very subjective, meaning it's as much opinion as fact. You may not want to spend a lot of time on this question, just guess and go. (Remember that the ACT has no penalty for wrong answers, so you never leave a question blank.) The passage talked about what male birds do to attract female birds, thus fulfilling the author's intention.

Mathematics Test

1. **D.** The official, algebraic way to do this is to let the amount each cheerleader gave be c and the amount each football player gave be f. Then $c = 2f$. Because there are five cheerleaders, their total amount was $5c$ or $10f$. The ten football players also gave $10f$. The final equation is $10f + 10f = 480$. $20f = 480$. $f = 24$.

Chapter 22: Practice Exam 2: Answers and Explanations

TIP

After you have finished the problem, double-check it by plugging in your answer and talking through the problem. This takes only a few seconds and can save you from yourself. If each football player gave 24, then the ten of them gave 240. Each cheerleader gave twice as much as each football player, or 48. First, $5 \times 48 = 240$. Then $240 + 240 = 480$.

TIP

The ACT was nice enough to give you answer choices; why not take advantage of them? You can do this whole problem without algebra by simply plugging in the answer choices. Start with the middle value. If the middle value doesn't work, you'll know whether the number must be greater or lesser than that choice. First, $22 \times 10 = 220$ and $44 \times 5 = 220$ and $220 + 220 = 440$. Because 440 is not enough, go to the next higher number, choice D. Begin with $10 \times 24 = 240$. Then $5 \times 48 = 240$. Finally, $240 + 240 = 480$.

2. H. Find the relationship between the first three terms: 2 plus 3 is 5. Then 5 plus 3 is 8. Keep going: 8 plus 3 is 11.

HEADS UP

If you thought this was too easy, keep in mind it was only question 2. Questions go from easier to harder, such that this was to be as simple as possible.

3. D. First, plug in -3 for x. Then $2x = 2(-3) = -6$ and $-3x = -3(-3) = 9$.

HEADS UP

The minus sign outside the parentheses changes the $+9$ to -9. (Remember that you have to distribute the minus sign through the parentheses.) You now have $-6 + -9 = -15$. The answers are narrowed down to D or E. Next, solve for y: $-3y$ plus $+4y = y$.

TIP

Make a habit of eliminating answers as you go. This method can prevent your working through an entire problem and then choosing the wrong answer because you forgot the first part of the problem by the time you did the second part.

4. F. If two sides of a triangle are equal, their angles also are equal. Because all three angles of a triangle total 180°, the two unmarked angles must be 60° total ($180 - 120 = 60$) or 30° each ($60/2 = 30$). Angles along a straight line are *supplementary,* or total 180°. Therefore, $180 - 30 = 150$. The exterior angle measures 150°.

TIP

The measure of an exterior angle is equal to the sum of the measures of its two remote interior angles. Here, the *remote* (in other words, "not next to") interior angles are NLM, which is 30, and LNM, which is 120, for a total of 150.

Did you notice that F is the only possible answer? It is the only choice greater than 120. Because exterior angle = the sum of two remote interior angles, it must be $120 + x$; x is not equal to 0. Therefore the exterior angle is greater than 120.

5. B. First, use your common sense to eliminate choices C, D, and E. If she can already assemble 300 widgets in one hour and is going to raise her rate and work eight hours, she certainly is going to assemble a lot more widgets than these answers show. Quickly narrow the answers down to choices A and B.

Next, find that 25% or ¼ of 300 is 75 — trap choice E, which you have already eliminated. (One good reason to eliminate choices as you go is to avoid falling for traps like this one.) If she increases her rate by 75, Jarnelle can now assemble 375 widgets in one hour (trap choice C). In eight hours, she can assemble 375×8 or 3,000 widgets.

Another way to estimate is to say that 375 is about 400 and $400 \times 8 = 3,200$. Only choice B is remotely close.

6. H. To solve a proportion, cross multiply: $3 \times 25 = 75$. $5 \times a = 5a$. Make the products equal: $75 = 5a$. Divide both sides through by 5; $a = 15$.

7. D. The sides of an isosceles right triangle are in the ratio side: side: side$\sqrt{2}$. The "side$\sqrt{2}$" is the hypotenuse. (If you forgot this formula, go to Chapter 10.) Each side or leg of the triangle, therefore, is 5. The area of a triangle is ½bh, one half *base* × *height*. In an isosceles right triangle, the two legs are the base and the height, making the area of this triangle ½ (5) (5) = ½ (25) = 12.5.

Choice B traps students who forget to multiply by ½. Choice E is the perimeter, not the area. Because answer choices often have such "variations" to trap a careless test-taker, circle what the question is asking for. Before you fill in the oval on the answer grid, refer to that circled info again to be sure that you're answering the right question.

Did the term "square units in the area" confuse you? Not to worry. Just think of it as the area.

8. **K.** Distribute the negative: When I was in school, I always inserted a 1 in front of parentheses. You can use that principle here and distribute the negative 1. A negative 1 times a is $-a$. A negative 1 times -3 is $+3$ (which immediately eliminates choices G and H). A negative 1 times $-a$ is $+a$. Combine like terms: $6a - a + a = 6a$.

When the answers are all "variations on a theme" like this, double-check that you are keeping your positive and negative signs correct.

9. **C.** First, find 25% or $\frac{1}{4}$ of 18,000: $\frac{18,000}{4}$ = 4,500 (trap choice E). Because that's the discount, subtract it from $18,000 to get $13,500 (trap choice D). Then take 5% of $13,500, which is $675. That's the luxury tax, so add it to $13,500 to get $14,175.

If you chose A, you added the sales tax to the original cost, not to the sales cost. If you chose B, you assumed that a discount of 25 percent and a tax of 5 percent is the same as a discount of 20 percent. The logic is superficially plausible but wrong because the percentages are percentages of different *wholes* (in the first case, the percent is of the original price; in the second case, the percent is of the sale price). Keep in mind, whenever you deal with percentages, that a percentage is part of a whole, and double-check that you have started with the correct "whole."

10. **G.** This is a relatively simple problem — easier than it looks. Draw a rectangle of width x and length $3x$ (because the problem tells you that length is 3 × width). Add all the sides to find the perimeter: $x + 3x + x + 3x = 8x$. The perimeter is 640, so $8x = 640$. $x = 80$. If x, the width, is 80, then $3x$, the length, is 240. The area of a rectangle is *length × width*: $80 \times 240 = 19,200$.

11. **D.** First, circle the words "closest approximation." That's a clue that the problem is going to be a pain in the posterior — that you will probably have some very weird numbers. More important, it's a clue that you don't have to work the problem through to the bitter end but that you can estimate a final answer.

Next, plug and chug. Put the numbers in and work the problem through.

$$\frac{3 + 10(3-10)^2(9-10)}{10(9-10)}$$

$$\frac{3 + 10(49)(-1)}{190}$$

$$\frac{3 - 490}{190}$$

$$-\frac{487}{190}$$

Here's where you estimate. -487 is about -500; 190 is about 200. Estimate $\frac{1}{4}$.

This type of problem is great to do whenever the word problems are hard for you. This question consists of numbers, numbers, and more numbers. However, this problem also lurks to catch those who are prone to making careless errors. The more calculations you do, the greater the chance of a careless error. Double-check work like this.

12. **K.** Angles along a straight line total 180°. Forget about all the fraction jazz; start off by plugging in nice, simple numbers. Say, for example, that $x = 1$ part. Then $y = 2$ parts and $z = 3$ parts. See how neatly things work out? You're often rewarded for plugging in

Chapter 22: Practice Exam 2: Answers and Explanations 323

simple numbers. Then you have $x + y + z = 180$, or $1 + 2 + 3 = 180$; 6 parts = 180; 1 part = 30. Then $x = 30$, $y = 60$, and $z = 90$. Yes, it works. Now just go back and answer the question: $z - x = 90 - 30 = 60$.

13. **A.** This problem looks a lot harder than it is; don't let yourself be intimidated. First, be sure that you get the wording straight. You're subtracting the first term from the second term. Think of this as "second term minus first term." If you overlook this wording, you may have fallen for trap choices D or E.

    Second, check that the variables are the same and are to the same power, or else you can't subtract them. For example, you can subtract $5a^3 - 3a^3$, but you cannot subtract $5a^3 - 3a^2$ (unless, of course, you know the value of a). Because the variables and exponents (powers) are the same, you can ignore them and just subtract the *numerical coefficients* (the numbers in front of the variables). $1 - 5 = -4$. (Because no number is in front of the a^3b^4, you assume a 1.) Now your answers are narrowed down to choices A and B. Subtract the coefficients in front of the a^2b^3: $-2 - 3 = -5$.

14. **J.** The sides of a 30:60:90 triangle are in the ratio side:2side:side$\sqrt{3}$. (If you forgot this ratio, flip to Chapter 10.) Draw the figure like this:

    You know the "side$\sqrt{3}$" is the base, opposite the 60° angle, and the "side" is the height, opposite the 30° angle. The area of a triangle is ½ *base* × *height*.

    $$\frac{1}{2}(10)(10\sqrt{3}) = 50(\sqrt{3})$$

15. **E.** This question is as much vocabulary as it is math. A *mean* is the average of numbers: Add the numbers together (420) and divide by the number of numbers (420 divided by 5 = 84). A *median* is the middle number when the numbers are put in order.

    If you chose D, you fell for the trap of thinking that 79 was the median because it was the "middle number." You have to put the numbers in order first: 75, 79, 82, 91, 93. Now you can see that 82 is the median. Subtract mean minus median: $84 - 82 = 2$.

    Bonus: While we're talking vocabulary, do you know what the mode is? A *mode* is the most repeated term, the one that shows up the most. For example, if the numbers were 2, 3, 2, 4, 5, the mode would be 2.

16. **J.** In this case, the diagonal with a length 6 splits a rectangle into two 30:60:90 triangles. The ratio of sides of a 30:60:90 triangle is side:side$\sqrt{3}$:2side. If the "2 side" is 6, then the "side" is 3, and the "side$\sqrt{3}$" is $3\sqrt{3}$.

    Add the sides to find the perimeter: $3 + 3 + 3\sqrt{3} + 3\sqrt{3}$.

17. **E.** This was a relatively simple question, but if you missed it, you probably got careless with an earlier answer. In choice A, while it's true that 24 is a common multiple of 4 and 6 (both terms divide evenly into it), it's not the least common multiple. The least common multiple is 12, as stated in choice E.

To find a least common multiple quickly, count by the largest number: 6, 12, 18, 24 . . . . Here, both 6 and 4 go into 12.

In Choice B, 4 is not a common denominator for 6. Choice C isn't even logical. All numbers can be factored down into prime numbers; that's what prime numbers are, the least positive integer factors. Choice D is wrong because least prime factor of 4 is 2. (If you thought it was 1, you need to flip to Chapter 12. By definition, 1 is not a prime number.)

18. **H.** Remove the parentheses: $3x^2y + xy^2 - 2x^2y + 2xy^2$.

The last term is added because of the negative sign in front of the second set of parentheses. Remember to distribute the negative sign throughout the parentheses.

$-1(-2xy^2) = +2xy^2$. Confusing signs is one of the most common careless errors in algebra problems.

Combine like terms: $3x^2y - 2x^2y + 2xy^2 = x^2y + 3xy^2$.

19. **E.** The key to this problem is knowing the formula for the TSA (total surface area) of a cylinder: $2\pi r^2 + 2\pi rh$. This formula is explained in detail in Chapter 9.

The $2\pi r^2$ represents the areas of the top and bottom circles: Here, $4^2\pi = 16\pi$. Add top and bottom: $16\pi + 16\pi = 32\pi$. The $2\pi r$ represents the circumference of the cylinder, which, if cut, would be the length of the base of a rectangle, like this:

The area of a rectangle is *length × width*. Here, that is $2\pi r$ times height, which is $(2)4\pi \times 10 = 80\pi$. Finally, add: $32\pi + 80\pi = 112\pi$.

20. **J.** All parallel lines have the same slope. Isolate the y value using the slope intercept formula: $y = mx + b$ (where m is the slope of the line). Given that $2x + 3y = 6$, subtract $2x$ from both sides. $3y = 6 - 2x$. Then to get rid of the 3, divide all variables by 3. You are left with $y = -\frac{2}{3}x + 2$. The slope is $-\frac{2}{3}$ because it is resting where the R is in the formula.

21. **D.** First, distribute the negative sign from outside the parentheses, making the second expression $-3a^2 + 2ab - 8$. Then combine like terms: $2a^2 - 3a^2 = -a^2$. Immediately your answers are narrowed down to choices D and E. If you're in a big hurry, quickly make a 50/50 guess.

Next, $ab + 2ab = 3ab$. Because you've already narrowed the answers down to choices D and E, only D works. (Finish up the problem: $-8 - 8 = -16$.)

22. **K.** To find Jessica's missing test score, write an equation that includes the fifth missing test score. $\frac{(93 + 92 + 90 + 100 + x)}{5} = 95$. Solve the equation for x and get $x = 100$. To find Josh's missing test score, write his equation and get $\frac{(95 + 97 + 89 + 94 + y)}{5} = 95$. Solve this equation and get $y = 100$. Therefore, 100 (Jessica's needed score) – 100 (Josh's needed score) = 0 (choice K). Because 95 is the average of the five scores, then the total must be $5 \times 95 = 475$.

If you chose F, you fell for the trap. The question asks you how many more points Josh needs than Jessica, which is zero.

23. **D.** Remove the parentheses. Remember that the minus sign in front means that you write the opposite of 4, which of course is –4, and the opposite of $-3y$, which is $+3y$.

Chapter 22: Practice Exam 2: Answers and Explanations 325

That means that 2y − (4 − 3y) + 3 becomes 2y − 4 + 3y + 3. Combine the 2y and the 3y to get 5y. Then −4 + 3 = −1. All together now, you have 5y − 1.

This problem is a great one if your first language is not English. This question has no confusing words and no tricky phrasing — it's just straightforward numbers. But be especially careful to keep the − and + signs straight.

24. **H.** A shaded area is what remains after you've subtracted the unshaded portion (the circle) from the entire figure (the square). If the shaded portion is 144 − 36π, the area of the square must be 144. A square's area is side times side: root 144 = 12. The two sides of a square make an isosceles right triangle with the diagonal of the square. The ratio of sides in an isosceles right triangle are side:side:side$\sqrt{2}$. If the side of the square is 12, the diagonal (which is the same as the hypotenuse of the triangle) is $12\sqrt{2}$.

All these formulas, area of a square and ratio of sides in triangles are found in Chapter 10.

25. **B.** First, solve for angle y inside the triangle. Because the angles of a triangle total 180°, y = 180 − (20 + 40) or 120. Next, the three x's and this y angle total 180° because they form a straight line. Therefore, 120 + 3x = 180 and 3x = 60 and x = 20.

Did you see the shortcut to completing this problem? An exterior angle of a triangle is equal to the sum of the two remote interior angles. In other words, this outside angle is the same as the sum of the two interior angles that are not adjacent to it. The exterior angle is actually 3x, and 3x = 60. So x = 20.

26. **H.** Sometimes the hardest part of a math problem is knowing where to start. Use the test answers to help you with this one and work backward. If the machine is losing half the ball bearings every cycle, double the answer five times to track it down. 11(end of fifth cycle) × 2 = 22 (end of fourth cycle), 22 × 2 = 44 (end of third cycle), 44 × 2 = 88 (end of second cycle), 88 × 2 = 176 (end of first cycle).

27. **B.** Note that the problem says each person wants to pay *under* $12, not exactly $12. This problem is relatively easy, if you plug in the answer choices instead of trying to make equations. Start in the middle with choice C. Currently, if the 5 friends pay $22.20 each, the total cost of the time is $111.00. If 4 more friends join them, for a total of 9 people, divide $111 by 9 which gives you $12.33 — just *over* $12. You know you must have more people, but probably just one more because you're so close. Plug in choice B. If you add 5 people, you have 10 people sharing the $111 cost. Divide 111 by 10 to get $11.10, which is under $12.

28. **J.** Cross-multiply to solve for a and b: $\frac{1}{a}$ = 4 so 4a = 1 and a = $\frac{1}{4}$. Because $\frac{1}{b}$ = 5, 5b = 1 and b = $\frac{1}{5}$. Therefore, 1/(ab) = 1/($\frac{1}{4}$) × ($\frac{1}{5}$) = 1/($\frac{1}{20}$) = 20.

If you chose F, you forgot to invert (turn upside down) and multiply. If you chose G or H, you added the 4 and 5 instead of multiplying them.

29. **D.** The circumference of a circle is 2πr. If the circumference here is 10π, then r = 5. The area of a triangle is ½ base times height. The base, AC, is two radii, or 10. The height, OB, is one radius, or 5.

If you chose E, you forgot that the area is one-half base times height, or ½ (5)(10) = 25.

30. **G.** You know that 4^3 = 64, but if you chose J, you fell for a cheap trick. Choice J would have 4^{-3}, or $\left(\frac{1}{4}\right)^3$ or $\frac{1}{64}$. You need x to be −3, such that (two negatives make a positive)

$4^{-(-3)} = 4^3$, or 64.

31. **B.** Do you remember that great saying that you learned in right triangle trig: SOH CAH TOA ("soak a toe uh")? This means

S = Sine	C = Cosine	T = Tangent
O = Opposite	A = Adjacent	O = Opposite
H = Hypotenuse	H = Hypotenuse	A = Adjacent

Here is an illustration:

$$\text{Opposite A} \quad \overset{C}{\underset{B \quad \text{Adjacent to A} \quad A}{\triangle}} \quad \text{Hypotenuse}$$

To find tan Z in this problem, identify the side opposite angle Z and the side adjacent to angle Z.

$$\overset{X}{\underset{Y \quad 24 \quad Z}{\triangle}} \quad 7 \text{ opposite} \quad 25$$

$$\text{Tan } Z = \frac{opposite}{adjacent} = \frac{7}{24}$$

32. G. When you deal with percentages, start by plugging in 100. Say that the slow reader originally read at 100 words per minute. Then when she increased her speed by 25 percent, she read at 125 words per minute (because 25 is 25% of 100). If she is only 50 percent, or half as fast as the fast reader, the fast reader reads 250 words a minute. The fast reader's speed, 250, is what percent of the slow reader's original speed, 100? Make the is/of fraction (250 *is* what percent *of* 100): $\frac{250}{100} = 2.5 = 250\%$.

If you chose D, you got careless and found what percentage the fast reader's speed is of the slow reader's *increased* speed rather than of her original speed. Circle precisely what the question is asking you so that you don't fall for traps like this one.

33. D. For every 2 yards (6 feet) that she swims, the swimmer actually progresses only 4 feet (because she loses 2 feet for every 2 yards). That means 1 yard swum = 2 feet covered. If 1 stroke is 5 yards, she goes 10 feet in that one stroke. The swimmer needs to cover 500 yards, or 1,500 feet, meaning that she has to take 150 (that is, $\frac{1500}{10}$) strokes.

This is a great problem to skip if English is not your primary language. The wording is quite confusing. In addition, the best way to solve this problem is not to use an equation but to talk it through. Word problems of this sort are very hard to get correct for native English-speakers and nearly impossible for others.

34. K. One easy way to do this problem is to plug in numbers. Let $x = 5$ and $y = 10$. The farmer can plow five rows in ten minutes or one row every two minutes. Therefore, the farmer can plow 30 rows in one hour (because one hour = 60 minutes). Let $w = 2$, such that the farmer works for two hours. If he can plow 30 rows in 1 hour, he can plow 60 rows in 2 hours. The answer to the problem is 60. Go through all the answer choices, plugging in your values for x, y, and w, to find which one works out to 60 (choice K).

$$\frac{60(5)}{10} \times 2 = \frac{300}{10} \times 2 = 30 \times 2 = 60$$

35. C. The only way to miss this problem is to intimidate yourself, to make the problem look harder than it really is. Even if you haven't studied functions in school (that's what the little *f* stands for, functions), you can solve this problem by "following directions." Talk your way through the problem. Say to yourself, "I have something in parentheses.

Chapter 22: Practice Exam 2: Answers and Explanations **327**

That means I cube the something, then add one." In this case, the "something," the *x*, is given as –5. So cube –5 to get –125. Then add 1 to get –124. That's all there is to it!

The answer choices are full of traps for the careless student. If you cubed –5 and got positive 125, then added 1, you got answer A. If you correctly cubed –5 and got –125, then added 1 and got –126 (!), choice E was waiting for you. And if you got choice B, you combined both mistakes, cubing –5 to get the wrong answer of +125, then subtracting rather than adding 1. **Remember:** Just because the answer you got is in front of you does not mean it is the right answer. The test-makers are aware of commonly made mistakes and put them on the test to tempt you.

36. **K.** An octagon has 8 sides. The formula for the total interior angle measure of a figure is (n – 2) 180, where *n* stands for the number of sides. (This formula is explained in detail in Chapter 10.) Here, 8 – 2 = 6 and 6 × 180 = 1080. Subtract 480 to get 600. There are 8 angles in an octagon. Two have been accounted for, leaving the remaining 6 to sum up to 600 degrees. Divide 600 by 6 to get 100.

37. **B.** The four sides of a square are equal, such that one side of square RSTU is 12. If points A,B,C,D are midpoints, then each one divides the larger square into lengths of 6 units. When you draw square ABCD you will notice that each side forms an isosceles right triangle. The ratio of the sides of an isosceles right triangle are side:side:side$\sqrt{2}$. That means the hypotenuse of (for example) triangle DRA is $6\sqrt{2}$. Add the four sides to get $24\sqrt{2}$.

If you chose A, you said that $\sqrt{2}$'s equaled 8, and added 24 + 8 = 32. You can't add square roots like that. (If you're confused, go back to the roots section of the math review.)

38. **K.** This problem is much easier than it looks. You don't have to find the lengths of each and every side. Just visualize that line FE is elevated to be at the same height as DC. That makes the long line FC the same length as the long line, AB. Visualize that the short side, ED, is shifted to the left and put on top of the short line AF. That makes the long line AD the same length as BC. You have 16 × 2 and 9 × 2, for a total of 50.

39. **B.** You get the largest product by using the middle or median terms. Here, 13 + 13 = 26, and 13 × 13 = 169, which is the trap answer.

If you chose A, you forgot the note that *a* is *not equal* to *b*. Therefore, you have to choose the next two largest terms, 12 + 14. Multiply 12 × 14 = 168.

40. **J.** Does this problem make you think of Egyptian hieroglyphics? Join the crowd. Instead of just saying, "That's history, Babe!" and guessing at this problem, make it easy to work through by plugging in numbers. Choose a number that has an easy square root. Make $x = 9$ (because $\sqrt{9} = 3$). Now solve the question:

$(\sqrt{9} + 2) \div (\sqrt{9} - 2) = (3 + 2) \div (3 - 2) = \frac{5}{1} = 5$

Keep in mind that 5 is the answer to the problem. It is not the value of *x*. Jot down the 5 to the side, draw a circle around it, put arrows pointing to it — do whatever it takes to remind yourself that the answer you want is 5. Now go through each answer choice, seeing which one comes out to be 5. Only choice J works:

$(\sqrt{9} + 4\sqrt{9} + 4) \div (9 - 4) = (9 + 4 \times 3 \div 4) = (9 + 12 + 4) \div 5 = \frac{25}{5} = 5$

Be very, very careful not to put 3 in for *x* in the problem because $x = 9$ and $\sqrt{x} = 3$. I suggest that you make a chart to the side simply writing down $x = 9$ and Answer = 5.

When you plug in numbers, go through every single answer choice, *soporific* (sleep inducing) though that may be. If you started with choice K, for example, and made a careless mistake, you would find that choices J, H, and G didn't work either . . . and probably choose F by process of elimination. If you take just a second to work out F, you'll see that it too is wrong, alerting you to the fact that you made a careless mistake somewhere.

41. D. Begin the steps for this problem with $64^{2/3} = \left(\sqrt[3]{64}\right)^2$. The cube root of 64 is 4, and $4^2 = 16$.

Exponents and bases are among the easiest things on the whole exam to answer correctly. If you are confused on how to work this problem, go to the exponents section in Chapter 11.

This type of problem, because it involves only numbers and no words, is perfect for students who get headaches just looking at some of those lengthy word problems.

42. H. A prime number has no positive integral factors other than one and itself. (Prime numbers are discussed in more detail in Chapter 12.) The prime numbers in Set A are 2, (did you forget 2? Two is the only even prime number), 3, 5, 7. Note that 9 is not prime, because it can be factored into 3×3.

Not all prime numbers are odd (2 is a prime) and not all odd numbers are prime (9 is not prime). The nonprime (also called composite) numbers from Set B are 6, 9, 12, 15. The sum of all these numbers is 59.

43. B. To find probability, use a fraction:

$$\frac{\text{The number of possible desired outcomes}}{\text{The number of total possible outcomes}}$$

There were originally 19 cookies, but 5 were eaten, leaving 14 total. That's the denominator. There were originally 9 chocolate chip cookies, but 2 were eaten, leaving 7. That's the numerator. The fraction $7/14$ reduces to $1/2$ or 50%.

If you chose E, you fell for the trap. The question asks for the *percent* probability. Choice E would be saying there is one-half of one percent, not 50 percent.

44. H. I sincerely hope that you didn't make an equation to solve this problem. There is a much easier way: Draw a simple diagram. Put dashes so that the 13th dash has a billboard, like this:

$$\underbrace{_____}_{1\ 2\ 3\ 4\ 5\ 6\ 7\ 8\ 9\ 10\ 11\ 12\ 13}\text{B}$$

Then counting backward with the billboard as the 14th, make a second diagram:

$$\text{B}\underbrace{_____}_{14\ 13\ 12\ 11\ 10\ 9\ 8\ 7\ 6\ 5\ 4\ 3\ 2\ 1}$$

Put the two together and count:

$$_____\text{B}_____$$

If you were careless and thought that you could just add, you probably chose J, 27. Invest a few moments to make a simple diagram and get the problem right.

45. B. Take this problem step by step. First, factor. You know, via FOIL (First, Outer, Inner, Last), that the first two terms have to come out to x^2, making them (x) and (x). You know that when you multiply the last two terms, you must get –8, which means that one term is positive and one is negative.

The middle two terms have to total + 7. How about + 8 and –1? That gives you $(x + 8)(x – 1)$. Quickly remultiply this to be absolutely sure that it equals the original, $x^2 + 7x – 8$. It does. All is well. Now that you know that $x^2 + 7x – 8$ factors into $(x + 8)(x – 1)$, add the two expressions: $(x + 8) + (x – 1) = x + 8 + x – 1 = 2x + 7$.

46. H. The wording "in terms of" can be very confusing — ignore it. You are simply solving for b. Do this problem the same way that you do any other algebra problem. First, get all the b's on one side and all the non-b's on the other: Subtract $3a$ from each side. $5b = 10 – 3a$. Next, divide both sides by what is next to the b:

$$\frac{5b}{5} = \frac{10 - 3a}{5}$$

$$b = 2 - \frac{3}{5}a$$

(Don't forget that $\frac{10}{5} = 2$.)

47. A. Get all the terms with x and y on one side of the equation and all the terms without x and y on the other side of the equation. You do this by first adding $4mx$ to each side: $-4mx - \frac{3b}{c} = 4my$. Next, $-4mx + 4mx - \frac{3b}{c} = 4mx + 4my$. $-\frac{3b}{c} = 4mx + 4my$.

To solve for x and y, factor out the $4m$ on the right. $-\frac{3b}{c} = 4mx + 4my$. Next, divide by $4m$: $-\frac{3b}{4mc} = x + y$.

If your English isn't up to solving word problems or story questions, this type of math problem should make your day. It's all numbers and variables without any confusing phrasing or terminology. If you're running short on time or patience, head for this type of question first.

The most common mistake that I see students making on this type of problem is confusing their – and + signs. As soon as you get an answer, turn around and double-check it *immediately*. You can be pretty sure that the test-makers will include whatever you get if you mess up the – and + signs as one of the answer choices.

48. H. First, multiply through the parentheses: $a(a + 4) = 12$, so $a^2 + 4a = 12$. Next, make everything equal to zero by moving the + 12 to the other side of the equal sign, remembering to make it –12 (forgetting to change the sign is a common mistake): $a^2 + 4a - 12 = 0$. Next, factor the expression down into $(a + 6)(a – 2) = 0$. Finally, make the parenthetical expressions equal to 0 and solve, $a = –6$ or $a = 2$.

49. A. First, multiply through the parenthetical expressions: $(3 + x)(4x) = 3 \times 4x = 12x$ and x times $4x = 4x^2$. Add 2 to get $4x^2 + 12x + 2$. Next, multiply everything by the x outside the brackets: x times $4x^2 = 4x^3$. Then x times $12x = 12x^2$. Next, x times $2 = 2x$. Finally, $4x^3 + 12x^2 + 2x$.

This problem is great to do if you are running short of time. It doesn't take much effort to understand what you are expected to do, nor much time to do it. The only mistake you are likely to make is a careless one, so be sure to double-check your work.

50. J. Get rid of choices F and G right away. These choices show that the distance equals 0 at one time beyond the starting time. The car never moves back to the initial designated point. Choice H does not feature an interval in which the car slows to 70 m/hr. Choice H shows that the car moved forward at a constant speed, stopped, and then resumed the constant speed. Choice J is correct. Choice K is close, but the gas/lunch interval (horizontal line) lasts too long.

51. D. To solve, factor $x^2 – 5x + 6$ by thinking of FOIL (First, Outer, Inner, Last) in reverse: $x^2 – 5x + 6 = 0$

$(x \underline{\quad})(x \underline{\quad}) = 0$

The missing numbers need to add to –5 and multiply to 6.

$(x - 2)(x - 3) = 0$

Check with FOIL: $(x - 2)(x - 3)$

$= x^2 - 3x - 2x + 6$

$= x^2 - 5x + 6$

To solve for x, make either expression inside the parentheses equal to 0.

$x - 2 = 0$ when $x = 2$

$x - 3 = 0$ when $x = 3$.

The solutions are $x = 2$ and $x = 3$. Check this:

$(2 - 2)(2 - 3) = 0$

$(3 - 2)(3 - 3) = 0$

These are okay. The sum of the solution is $2 + 3 = 5$ (choice D).

52. **F.** If $x + 1$ is less than or equal to 8, then x is less than or equal to 7 (subtract 1 from both sides).

If you chose choice G, you fell for the trap. You neglected to account for the "or equal to" portion of the inequality.

53. **C.** First, put the equation in slope-intercept form: $y = mx + b$. Then $x + 2y = 4 - x - y$ (distribute the – sign). Next, $3y = 4 - 2x$ (move the x's and y's to different sides of the equation). Then $y = \frac{4 - 2x}{3}$ (divide everything through by 3 to isolate the y). Finally, $y = \frac{4}{3} - \frac{2x}{3}$.

54. **F.** The key to answering the question is to remember that $\cos^2\theta + \sin^2\theta = 1$.

If you have trouble remembering this, think of a right triangle with a hypotenuse 1:

$x^2 + y^2 = 1$ (remember the Pythagorean theorem?).

Because $\cos\theta = \frac{adjacent}{hypotenuse} = \frac{x}{1} = \frac{opposite}{hypotenuse} = \frac{y}{1} = x$ and $\sin\theta = \frac{\sin^2\theta + \cos^2\theta}{\sec^2\theta} = \frac{1}{\sec^2\theta} = y$, then $x^2 + y^2 = 1$.

You can just rewrite this as $\cos^2\theta + \sin^2\theta = 1$

$\frac{\sin^2\theta + \cos^2\theta}{\sec^2\theta} = \frac{1}{\sec^2\theta}$

To get back to our problem, $\sec\theta = \frac{1}{\cos\theta}$, so $\sec^2\theta = \frac{1}{\cos^2\theta}$

Finally, substitute $\sec^2\theta = \frac{1}{\cos^2\theta} = \frac{1}{\sec^2\theta} = \frac{1}{\frac{1}{\cos^2\theta}} = 1 \cdot \frac{\cos^2\theta}{1}$

Chapter 22: Practice Exam 2: Answers and Explanations   331

If this problem is really, really tough for you, you're not alone. Many students find this jazz difficult. Keep in mind as you're going through these questions that you don't have to get all the problems right to get a very good score; you can afford to skip or miss several of them.

If you are an international student having a tough time with the word problems, brush up on your trig to be sure that you get this type of problem correct. If you can do this hard problem that's all numbers and symbols, you don't have to worry so much about the easy and medium story problems that are so confusing to you because of the wording.

55. E. Multiply both the top and the bottom of the fraction by $2 - \sqrt{3}$ (known as the *conjugate of the denominator,* just in case you care). Doing so makes the denominator equal to 1, so you can just ignore it from that point on.

This problem is great to do if you are short on time. It looks incredibly complicated, but all you have to do is multiply both top and bottom by the conjugate of the denominator.

56. F. The most straightforward way to approach this problem is to remember that slope is change in rise over change in run, or $\frac{y_2 - y_1}{x_2 - x_1}$. In this case, $y_2 - y_1 = -b - (-b)$. That comes out to be $-b + b = 0$. Next, $x_2 - x_1 = -a - 2a$, which comes out to be $-3a$. Substitute and you get slope = $\frac{0}{-3a} = 0$.

If you did this problem upside down, and got $\frac{3a}{0}$, you thought that it was undefined (because division by 0 is undefined) and chose choice K. You may have recognized that $y = -b$ in both points. This means that y is constant and the line is horizontal.

Horizontal lines have a slope of 0, reinforcing choice F as the answer.

57. D. Choice E is a sucker bet. Just because the problem multiplied both the number of painters and the number of rooms by 3 does not mean that you multiply number of hours by 3.

If three times as many painters are working, they can do the job in ⅓ the time just one painter takes. If you are confused, reword the problem in your own terms. Suppose that you take three hours to mow a lawn. If your two friends chip in and help you, the three of you can work three times as fast and get the job done in just one hour. The same is true here. Three times the number of painters (from 3 to 9) means that the job can be done in ⅓ the time: 1⅓ = 3⅓.

If you chose 3⅓, you didn't finish the problem. Nine painters would do the same job — that is, paint four rooms — in 3⅓ hours. But the number of rooms is three times what it was, so this factor triples the amount of time needed. Triple 3⅓ to get ten hours. Yup, you're back to the original amount of time, which unfortunately was probably the first answer your "common sense" told you to eliminate.

Think about this logically. The painters take ⅓ the time, but they do three times the work. The ⅓ cancels out with the 3 to get you right back where you started from.

58. F. First, write out each expression: 10.8 (10^{-3}) means to move the decimal point three places to the left. (***Remember:*** A negative power means the number gets smaller, shifting the decimal point to the left, not to the right.) That gives you .0108. Do the same for the denominator: 400 (10^{-5}) means to move the decimal point 5 places to the left, giving you .004. Next, divide .0108 by .004 to get 2.7. Finally, figure out which of the expressions is equal to 2.7. The expression .027 (10^2) means to move the decimal point two places to the right (a positive exponent makes the number larger, meaning the decimal point shifts to the right, not the left): 2.7.

This question is probably the easiest one to make a careless mistake on in this whole exam. If you are going to do a problem of this sort, be sure that you can commit the time to the problem. Do the problem carefully, double-checking your decimal point as you go, and then triple-checking it after you have finished.

59. **D.** Okay, you can make this easy, or you can make it hard. You want to do it the easy way, you say? Great: Plug in numbers. You can choose any numbers that your heart desires, but I suggest that you keep them small. Why waste time on a lot of multiplication? Let $q = 1$. Georgia buys 1 quart of milk. Let $d = 2$; the milk costs 2 dollars a quart. (It doesn't have to make fiscal sense; maybe this is rare yak's milk. You have better things to worry about.) Let $b = 3$. She buys 3 boxes of cereal at 3 dollars a box ($d + 1 = 2 + 1 = 3$). Now you can easily figure the total: 1 quart of milk at 2 dollars a quart equals 2 dollars. Three boxes of cereal at 3 dollars a box equals 9 dollars. Add them up to get 11 dollars. Plug the values for q, d, and b into the answer choices and see which one equals 11.

Keep two important concepts in mind when you plug in numbers: First, keep the numbers small and easy to work with. Second, jot down the numbers as you create them. That is, write to the side: $q = 1$, $d = 2$, and $b = 3$. It's very easy to get the numbers confused in the pressure of the exam and say that $d = 3$ or $b = 1$. Take just a nanosecond to put down the assigned values and refer to them constantly.

Here's the algebraic way to solve this problem: The amount spent for milk is (q quarts) (d dollars/quart) = Cancel the "quarts" and get qd. Then the amount spent for cereal is (b boxes) ($d + 1$ dollars/box) = cancel the "boxes" = $b(d + 1) = bd + b$. Add these together: $qd + bd + b$. Take out the d: $d(q + b) + b$.

If you think the algebra is straightforward, you're right . . . as long as you set up the original equation correctly. Unfortunately, too many people have no idea how to set up the equation and do it upside down, inside out, or whatever. If you plug in numbers, you can talk your way through this relatively difficult problem in just a few seconds.

60. **K.** The interior angles of any triangle add up to 180°. You are given two of the three angles of triangle GFX, 30 and 90. Solve 180 − (30 + 90) = 60. A 30:60:90 triangle has a special ratio for its sides: side:side$\sqrt{3}$:2side. The side GX here is the "2side" part (the hypotenuse or side opposite the 90° angle). That means that the other sides are 2 and $2\sqrt{3}$. (If this ratio is confusing to you, return to the triangles section of the math review.) If FXS is 2, then XB is 2, and FB sums up to 4. The height of the rectangle is 4. If side GF is $2\sqrt{3}$, then FE is also $2\sqrt{3}$, and the length of the rectangle is 2 ($2\sqrt{3}$) or $4\sqrt{3}$. The area of a rectangle is base times height (also called length times width): $4 \times 4\sqrt{3} = 16\sqrt{3}$.

Reading Test

Passage 1

1. **D.** A main purpose or main idea is by definition broad and general. An answer with the word "overview" is often correct, because it encompasses nearly everything. Choice A is wrong because prehistoric animals were barely mentioned. In Choice B, "refute," meaning to disprove, is rarely a correct answer (passages discuss or describe, they don't refute or criticize; Chapter 5 covers this concept in more detail).

It's irrelevant that Choice B may be a true statement (the cycad seeds were too large to be spread by birds). The mere fact that an answer is true doesn't mean it's the correct answer to the question. Choice C is overly broad. There is little discussion of current plant life, and the entire passage is limited to cycads, not to plants in general.

2. **J.** The line implies that the plants, although prehistoric, still exist today, telling you where they may be found. Choice F is exactly backwards; the plants are *not* extinct. Choice G is illogical in the context of the passage. Choice H is contradictory to the rest of the sentence, which tells you how widespread the plants are.

3. **A.** This question is about pure detail. Lines 13 and 14 state that scientists considered the widespread distribution of the cycad a mystery.

4. **G.** The sentence contrasts the wet tropical and semi-tropical habitats with the arid regions, leading you to conclude that arid must be the opposite of wet: dry.

5. **C.** A passage often suggests; it rarely refutes (to *refute* is to disprove). Pangaea, mentioned in paragraph one, was the one large Supercontinent that later broke into smaller continents, taking the cycad seeds and plants with them. This was mentioned as a possible way the seeds were distributed. Choice A is wrong; the cycad is not extinct today, but *extant* (still in existence). Choice B is going too far. Although you were told the plants in prehistoric times were huge, there was no mention or implication that the cycad was the largest plant.

6. **F.** The cycads provided sustenance to huge animals, who logically needed huge amounts of food. In addition, the rest of the paragraph discusses food, such that the first or topic sentence would probably do the same.

7. **B.** Paragraph two tells you that the seed cones are female and the pollen cones are male. The paragraph also warns of the cancer-causing properties of the seeds, but never mentions any medicinal properties.

A question like this requires an investment of time. Unless you're a reader who retains everything after one quick reading, you're probably wise to go back and double-check your memory. Look for the precise answer; don't depend on remembering everything.

8. **H.** Paragraph three states that the leaves of the cycad plant grow into a crown that makes people think the plant is a palm tree.

9. **B.** A question that begins "according to the passage" is a gift to you. It is a pure detail question that requires little thought. All you have to do is go back and find the answer in the passage, usually stated very clearly and directly. Here, paragraph three says that "the conversion of atmospheric nitrogen into ammonia is one way the cyanobacteria supply the cycad with inorganic nitrogen."

10. **F.** In line 55, the author states that it is fascinating to note that "even though" the cyanobacteria are in the dark underground, they have the same membrane structure and pigments of bacteria that thrive in the sunlight. From this you may deduce that the two bacteria don't usually have the same pigments.

Choice G goes too far in the reasoning. Just because the plants have been distributed in the past doesn't necessarily mean they will be "much" more widely distributed in the future. Choice H is nearly backward. The passage states that cycad seeds cause cancer, not that they may cure cancer. Choice J was neither mentioned nor implied in the passage. Palm trees and cycads may superficially resemble each other because of the crown of leaves, but there is no implication that the two species come from a common ancestor.

Passage 2

11. **B.** By rereading the first sentence carefully, you note that Mr. Casaubon in fact was full of jealousy and vindictiveness himself, eliminating choices A and D. The phrase "which compelled him to find other reasons for his conduct" tells you that he was trying to justify his jealousy and vindictiveness, sugarcoating them or calling them by other names.

12. G. Lines 11–13 say that "occasions might arise in which such possession might expose her to the more danger." The next few sentences talk about how men might prey upon her, allowing you to deduce that it is the money that turns Dorothea into the prey.

Choice F is such a '90s answer, don't you think (1990s, that is)? Nothing in the passage talks about Mr. Casaubon's having had a previous marriage or having had children. Choice H is exactly wrong. Mr. Casaubon argues to himself that his responsibility, in fact, is not to give Dorothea money, but to keep it from her, in order to keep her safe. If you chose J, you really are a cynic, aren't you? Although this brief excerpt makes you wonder what Dorothea ever saw in the man that she married, you have no real reason to assume that she was a *gold digger*, after only his money.

13. A. Lines 16–21 have an amusing sentence containing the following passage: "an animosity which he has constantly vented in ridicule, of which I am as well-assured as if I had heard it." If you read that carefully, you see that Mr. Casaubon has, in fact, not heard the man express any animosity at all. The sentence implies that this so-called animosity is all in Mr. Casaubon's head.

The other answers may or may not be true statements. For example, perhaps Mr. Casaubon has given the other man ample reason for animosity. (Just from reading this little bit, don't you get the idea that Mr. Casaubon is that type of man?) Maybe the other man, who wants to marry Dorothea, has dishonorable motives for doing so (he's after only her money). Maybe the other man vied with Mr. Casaubon for Dorothea's affections long ago. All those things may or may not be true; you just don't know. Be very careful not to read too much into the material.

14. G. By such sentences as "Such a marriage would be fatal to Dorothea" and "it is my duty to hinder to the utmost the fulfillment of his designs," Mr. Casaubon makes it clear that he believes — or at least wants to believe — that the responsibility to foil the other man's intentions to protect Dorothea is his. (You already discovered in question number 2 how easily Mr. Casaubon could convince himself that he is doing everything from the loftiest of motives, not out of petty jealousy and spite.)

Choice F may be a true statement. Maybe Mr. Casaubon believes the other man will "corrupt" Dorothea, given Mr. Casaubon's low opinion of the person. However, the primary theme of the indicated lines is not Mr. Casaubon's fears (those were expressed earlier) but his determination to hinder such an attachment. Be very careful not to choose an answer simply because the statement is true. Check that the answer directly answers the question.

15. C. All the other answers are too strong and include information that you have no way of knowing. Maybe Mr. C did believe Dorothea was marrying him only for his money. Maybe Dorothea was unaware of Mr. C's fears. (It sounds as if she'd have been crazy to marry the guy, had she known what he was really like!) Choice C seems logical; a man who has made "arrangements" that leave "strong measures open to him" sounds quite cautious.

In fiction passages, try to get a sense of the overall moral worth of the character and then answer questions based on that impression. For example, you can tell from a quick reading of the passage that Mr. C is a cantankerous old coot (at least in this excerpt). Most of the answers involving him will show him in a bad light. Dorothea is spoken of highly by the author. Therefore, anything said about her will probably be positive. Using this very simplistic "good guy/bad guy" concept can help you to eliminate at least a few of the answers, such as choices A and D (the passage sounds as if Dorothea were a pushover, a passive person, not one likely to "demand" anything).

16. H. You must take the sentence in the context of the entire passage, not just read it alone. The passage talks about Mr. C's concern over what will happen to his money — and incidentally, to his wife — when he dies. He therefore wants to have some idea of how much longer his life will be.

Chapter 22: Practice Exam 2: Answers and Explanations 335

Choice F is the cheesy answer. Just because the quote has the word *probabilities* in it does not mean the man is a gambler. Nothing in the passage even hints at such a possibility. While choice J is possible (the man cared more for how people would mock him than for his wife's future happiness, it seems), the answer is too strong, using dramatic words like "obsessed" and "no one else." Moderate, more temperate answers are more likely to be correct than emphatic answers.

17. **B.** This question was rather difficult. Lydgate was "conscious of an energetic frame in its prime," meaning that he knew what an energetic frame in its prime was. Lydgate is obviously a physician — this is the source of his knowledge — and he contrasted his vitality with the weakness of the man coming toward him.

Choice C is the trap answer. Yes, Lydgate felt pity, but pity for Mr. Casaubon, not for himself. And if you chose D, you went for the big, hard word on the principle of "if I don't know it, it must be the right answer" (we all have those feelings of insecurity, believe me). Usually, the most difficult word is merely a trap answer. Unless you can absolutely, positively eliminate the rest of the answers, don't choose a word you can't define.

18. **G.** The paragraph primarily describes how weak Mr. Casaubon is, contrasting that condition with both Lydgate's vitality and the beauty of the surroundings.

A *why* question like this one can be very difficult for international students. You are asked to understand not just the passage itself, but the motivation of the writer. If the correct answer doesn't immediately jump out at you, don't waste a lot of time on this sort of question. Make a quick guess (wrong answers are not penalized on the ACT) and go on to the next question.

Choice H is the trap answer. The paragraph talks about a *dirge,* which is a hymn sung at a funeral. If you knew that, you may have thought the purpose of this description was to predict a death. However, that may be going too far. If you have a choice between a moderate answer, such as contrasting *fit* versus *unfit,* and a dramatic answer — predicting death! — go for the more moderate of the two.

19. **D.** Eliminate choice C immediately. Very rarely is the correct answer negative in an ACT question. In this case, Lydgate is filled with compassion at seeing Mr. Casaubon and would be unlikely to be malicious. Choices A and B are possible, but D is more directly related to what the author specifically says: " . . . said Lydgate, filling up a pause." One fills up a pause by saying something when the silence becomes awkward.

20. **F.** The first half of the passage shows Mr. Casaubon in a very bad light, discussing how petty and jealous and vindictive he is. The last half of the passage elicits a feeling of compassion for a prematurely old man.

Choice G is exactly wrong. The reader becomes more tolerant of Mr. Casaubon when learning of his problems. Choice H is unlikely. Although Lydgate is introduced at the end of the passage, the focus is still definitely on Mr. Casaubon. Choice J goes too far. The reader may feel sorry for Mr. Casaubon but is even less likely than before to understand why Dorothea married him (the man is not only nasty but also unattractive and prematurely old).

If two answers are direct opposites, the chances are good that one of them will turn out to be the correct answer choice. Here, choices G and F are opposites, indicating that one of them is likely to be the correct answer. You have a 50-50 guess, almost a present from the test-makers.

Passage 3

21. **D.** The primary purpose of many passages is to describe, discuss, or explain something. Those three words are so often the correct answer to a "main idea" or "primary purpose" question that you should immediately give them serious consideration. (They're not *always* right, of course — but almost always.)

You should have dumped choice C right away. The ACT is not going to write a passage whose primary purpose is to trash (*denounce* means to put down, to bad-mouth) someone, especially a professional such as a child psychologist. Main-idea, primary-purpose, or best-title answers are almost always positive or neutral, not negative.

Choice B is tempting. The passage does mention self-esteem (and if you're smart enough to look at the attribution, you'll see that the excerpt, in fact, comes from a book on self-esteem), but it never mentions anything about *low* self-esteem.

Choice A is also tricky. It just sounds so pompous and correct: "provides the foundation for life." La-di-da. However, the passage discusses children up to the age of 16, well beyond "early childhood."

22. G. This question was an absolute gift to you. The answer is given specifically in the second sentence of the passage.

If you chose J, you fell for the trap. Yes, children work to achieve competence at various tasks throughout the stages of childhood, but all the tasks lead to the ultimate goal of selfhood. Don't choose an answer simply because it was mentioned in the passage. Be sure that the answer that you choose refers to the specific question asked.

23. C. Paragraph three mentions this cry of a child to make the point that he needs feedback, recognition of his achievements.

Choice A is a true statement, and it was discussed in the passage. However, choice A is not the answer to this specific question. Be careful that you don't choose a statement merely because it was true and was mentioned in the passage. Doing so is like saying, "There are 360 degrees in a circle," when the teacher asks you for the capital of Romania. Sure, the statement is true, but what does it have to do with the matter at hand?

Choice B is tempting, but parent-pleasing behavior was discussed later (in paragraph four) as typical of 5-year-olds.

24. J. This question traps rushed students who don't go back and see how the statement is used in the context of the passage. Lines 29–30 say that "the mother is the center of the child's world." True, the other answers mention games, but the phrase "the name of the game" was used metaphorically in this instance. To say that something is *the name of the game* means that it's the main idea, the point of the whole activity. For example, getting into college is the name of the game when studying for the ACT. If you didn't need a good ACT score to get into school, would you really go through all this mind-numbing studying? (You would? Just for our jokes? We're flattered, but whoa — get a life!)

If it appears that a question depends on your understanding of a slang phrase or saying, you may want to make a quick guess. Such phrases are especially difficult to nonnative speakers because such phrases are not literally translated. Don't waste a lot of time trying to understand the phrase; guess and go. Remember that the ACT does not penalize you for wrong answers, so guessing is always to your advantage.

25. D. The author states that this separateness is an important milestone in the children's development, indicating that this separateness is vital. (A *milestone* is an event marking a significant stage in life. For example, getting a driver's license is a milestone to teenagers.)

Did you notice that all the wrong answers were negative, and only the correct answer was positive? If you're guessing (and the ACT has no penalty for wrong answers, so a guess is always worthwhile), dump the negative answers and go for the positive. The ACT rarely trashes anyone or anything and is all sweetness and light.

26. G. The theme of the passage is the confusion between wanting two opposite things, such as demanding to have freedom from parents but being afraid to let go of them.

Every answer, obviously, comes right from the passage itself, so they all look familiar and "sound right." In a question like this one, I suggest that you ignore the answer choices at first. Reread the passage and identify its main idea to yourself. Then go back and find which answer best expresses that idea. If you look at the answer choices, every one looks good. Try to predict the answer first.

27. **D.** This should have been a pretty easy question. You want to examine more than just the indicated sentence; read the few sentences surrounding it. The next sentence tells you that, "He needs to ask what he is going to do with his life."

You didn't fall for the cheap trick in choice A, did you? A *vocation* is not the same thing as a *vacation*. And if you fell for choice B, you confused a *vocation* with a *location*. (Occasionally, I'll have a student come back after the test and exclaim, "There was a typographical error in the ACT, but I corrected it." Wrong. Although you may find a typo or two in this book — because I'm not perfect like the ACT — the ACT itself has none. If you think that you found a typo, you probably fell for the trap.)

28. **F.** Lines 90–94 mention that the convictions (which are developed at specific ages, statement II) will be influenced by the level of self-esteem (statement III), especially if a conflict exists among what a child believes, what he was raised with, and what his friends find acceptable. Nothing was mentioned about educational level.

When doing Roman numeral questions, focus first on the statement that you are most sure of. In this example, the author does, in fact, mention self-esteem. This fact means that you can eliminate any answer with III in it, choices H and J. As quickly as that, you've gotten the choices down to two. (You should always guess, because the ACT has no penalty for wrong answers; but a 50-50 guess is a real luxury.)

29. **C.** The passage discusses the various stages of children by their ages. ***Chronological*** means in order of time. If you didn't get this question, you outsmarted yourself and tried to make matters more difficult than they really were. Believe it or not, not every single question on the ACT is out to get you.

30. **H.** You could answer this question based on either the last paragraph or the first paragraph. The final paragraph discusses how the final stage of development is establishing total development. If that's the final stage, then the ultimate goal is that independence. The first paragraph also discusses how the purpose of childhood development is to achieve selfhood or self-knowledge.

Passage 4

31. **B.** The easy way to answer this question is to "plug 'n' chug." Plug each answer choice into the sentence and chug, or read through it. It makes sense to say, "Nearly any small child can recite quickly the twelve months of the year."

Choices A and D are traps. Yes, when you rattle something, you can shake it, or you can rattle someone and upset her, but those uses are not appropriate in this particular sentence. Words have more than one meaning. Your job is to identify which meaning works best in the context of the sentence.

32. **F.** The first paragraph specifically states that a piece of information is missing: how the names of the months came into existence. The majority of the rest of the passage explains the names.

If you chose G or H, you fell for the "But I know I read that!" trap. Just because something is mentioned in the passage does not mean that it is the main idea of the passage. A main idea is a general, underlying theme that runs through most of the passage. A good way to identify a main idea is to pretend that you are answering a buddy's question: "Hey, what did you just read?" In this case, you would respond with something like, "Oh, I read a passage about how the months got their names." Often, you can predict the correct answer to a main idea question before you ever read the answer choices.

33. **C.** Lines 18–20 state, "As the guardian of doors or gateways, he had to be vigilant for friends and foes coming from either direction." This should have been a very easy question for you. It is called a detail or fact question and simply asks you to find one fact from the passage. You don't have to interpret anything or draw a conclusion. It's important to recognize this type of question. If you're running short on time, or your brain cells are so scrambled that you know that you're missing most of the questions, this type of question is worth investing time in, because you can almost always get it correct.

338 Part VII: I'd Rather Wait for the Movie: Full-Length Practice ACTs

34. **F.** When a question begins with the words, "According to the passage," it is usually quite simple. The answer is given, almost word for word, in lines 26–28, which state, "This month's name came from the February 15 feast of purification." If you missed this question . . . well, hang your head in shame.

35. **A.** Paragraph 4 implies that because people know Mars was the god of war, they assume that the month of March got its name from warfare. Instead, the author states, the origin of the name actually referred to the fact that war was postponed until the springtime, and that Mars was also the god of springtime.

    Choice B is close but not quite right. The author discusses that most of the months are named after gods and goddesses but never states or implies that most people believe that all months are named for gods and goddesses. (Be careful not to read too much into the answer.) Choice C is definitely wrong. Paragraph five talks about how not every month's name has a definite **provenance,** or known origin. And choice D is off the wall: Nothing is mentioned in the entire passage about lunar cycles.

36. **G.** This question should have been relatively easy (unless you were too lazy to go back and look at how the expression is used in the passage). Plug the answer choices into the sentence and see which one works best. Here, it is logical to say, "In order to bring the Roman calendar back in line with the solar year. . . ."

37. **D.** The second-to-last paragraph states that Romans considered even numbers unlucky but never said why.

    Often, when a question asks which of the following is not discussed, the answer has a "why" in it. Passages often state facts but may not give the why and wherefore behind those facts.

38. **J.** Because the question asks for a main idea, look for the most general answer. Choices F and G are mentioned in the paragraph but are not its main point. A main idea usually is given in the topic or opening sentence of the paragraph, which here states, "Not every month has retained its original name over the years."

39. **A.** The author states that most people believe every fourth year is a leap year, but that's not the case. The century years are not leap years unless they are evenly divisible by 4. For that reason, statements I and II are wrong. Statement III takes a little more thought. If the millennium year were 1000 or 2000, both of which are divisible by 4, it would be a leap year. But if the millennium year were 3000, which is not evenly divisible by 4, it would not be a leap year. Therefore, statement III is not correct. (Give yourself a pat on the back if you got this question right.)

40. **H.** This question is very typical of "vocabulary in context." Sure, you know what *gloss* normally means, but the ACT rarely uses a word in its normal sense. In fact, the normal sense of the word is usually the trap. (Choice F and choice J here are the trap answers.)

    The key is to insert every answer choice into the sentence and see which one makes the most sense. The author is discussing how people don't realize something (that not every fourth year is a leap year), which means that they ignore a fact.

    Did you notice that choices F and J are basically the same? Because you can't have two right answers, both must be wrong.

Science Reasoning Test

Passage 1

Did you remember to slow down and think about the introductory material and examine the tables before you headed to the questions? You're normal if you want to get right down to business, but spend at least a minute going over the material you are given. You don't have to understand that material perfectly, but do at least identify what the study is about and the basic results.

Chapter 22: Practice Exam 2: Answers and Explanations 339

You've probably watched pole vaulting on television, right? When you're reading through this problem, try to visualize a pole-vaulter, running down the runway, planting the pole, zooming skyward, clearing (or crashing into) the bar, and finally, falling into the pit. The main point to get out of the intro to this problem is that the pole, as it unbends, forces the vaulter up.

Looking at the second paragraph and Table 1, you should note that a thick fiberglass pole is harder to bend than a thin fiberglass pole (logically enough), but the carbon fiber pole is harder to bend than a fiberglass pole.

Tables 1 and 2 combine to show that the more force required to bend a pole, the faster the pole bends back. Think of this relationship in another way: as a spring. You know that the harder a spring is to stretch, the more forcefully the spring recoils when released.

Okay, you now have the picture in mind and have evaluated the tables. Time to go on to the questions.

1. **B.** The answer to this question follows from the major relationship noted in the next-to-last paragraph of the analysis of this passage. Remember that the harder a spring is to stretch, the faster it will snap back to its regular position after it's released. Look at the two tables: Pole 3 requires the most force to bend but the least amount of time to snap back. Pole 1 requires the least force to bend but the greatest amount of time to snap back. Pole 2 is intermediate for both force and snap-back time. Choice B follows very cleanly from the numerical relationship shown in the two tables. The more force/less time relationship holds for all three poles, so you cannot justify choice D.

2. **G.** More force is required to bend a stiffer pole, as you are told in Table 1. In the introductory material before the tables, you find out that poles No. 1 and No. 3 have the same mass (no, you don't have to calculate mass; the mass is just given to you right out, as a gift) and that pole No. 2 has the greatest mass. Therefore, pole No. 3, the carbon fiber pole, which is one of the least massive poles, is the stiffest. Eliminate choice F. When looking at fiberglass compared to carbon fiber, this relationship doesn't hold. Eliminate choice H because with poles No. 1 and No. 2, the more massive pole is stiffer. To choose between choices G and J, look at poles No. 1 and No. 2, the two fiberglass poles. Because the table indicates that the most massive pole is the stiffest, G is the right answer.

3. **A.** This type of question is common in Research Summaries (the name of this style of passage). This question requires you to understand some fundamentals of experimental design. A controlled variable (also known as an independent variable) is a factor that the experimenter can directly control (duh!). Because you're often asked about controlled variables, you may want to identify them as you read through the experimental data upfront. In other words, as you read the problem, say to yourself, "Okay, what's different here? The two factors that are being fiddled with are the size of the pole and the material it's made of. Those, therefore, are the controlled variables."

In this study, pole dimensions and material (fiberglass or carbon fiber) are controlled variables. The experimenter can easily change the diameter or length of a pole to a specific value, or he can change the pole's material. Choices B, C, and D mention factors that result from the experiment, not factors that can be changed going into the experiment.

4. **G.** Don't despair; this question is not as tough as the terminology initially suggests. In fact, you can answer this question pretty much by using your common sense. What is "potential"? Potential is something that can happen but hasn't happened yet. (You have the potential to enjoy these questions . . . but that hasn't happened yet!)

The pole acts to transfer the energy produced while the vaulter runs into energy that lifts the vaulter upward. When bent, the pole has stored the energy gained from the running, but has not yet moved upward. At this point, the pole has the potential to move with much energy, but is not moving at the moment. Therefore, the pole has potential energy, but no kinetic energy.

5. **D.** The question tells you that the vaulter needs a pole that isn't too massive when it is very long. Home in on choices B and D because they focus on mass. Because low mass is the objective, D is correct.

6. **G.** This passage's introduction tells you that beginning vaulters need poles that are relatively easy to bend. Therefore, pole No. 1 is best for beginners, and choice J is out. The ideal advanced pole is one that quickly returns to a vertical position. That is, the pole quickly transfers the energy to a lifting force. Study 2 reveals that the best pole to transfer energy quickly to a lifting force is pole No. 3.

   Bonus! Did you see the second way to identify pole No. 3 as best for an experienced vaulter? The pole has a low density, meaning that the pole can be longer. If you remember question 5, vaulters like longer poles because they enable a vaulter to get closer to the crossbar.

Passage 2

Always begin by summarizing to yourself just what exactly the graph (or table, chart, or picture) indicates. This graph shows that the percentage of deaths grows with time. Well, duh! This relationship, of course, is what happens. The total number of deaths can never decrease. Fewer people may die in certain years, but when people die, the overall number of deaths goes up until 100 percent of the people are deceased.

Be careful not to interpret the graph as showing that more people die at the age of 100. Because the total number of deaths keeps growing, not only the number — but also the percentage — has to be higher at 100 years.

To get an idea of when most people die, look at where the graph makes the steepest climb. This increase appears to be between about 55 and 85 years. The percentage of people who have died grows from about 20 percent to about 80 percent over this time, so more than half the population dies between the ages of 55 and 85. Not too many people die at 100 because not that many people are left by that time. (They probably took too many ACTs, SATs, and various other agents of neurocellular destruction.)

The graph shows that a typical human being lives to be about 75. (Don't get too depressed. The mere fact that you bought this test-prep book rather than a more serious tome shows that you are definitely not typical.) Half the population dies in 75 years. The remaining half of the people die after more than 75 years pass.

7. **B.** Not to worry. This question is a basic test of graph reading skills, with a little twist thrown in. First, find 80 years on the horizontal axis. Go straight up from this year (your ACT answer grid can serve as a straight edge) until you hit the plotted curve. Next, go straight to the left to find the percentage of people who have died. But watch out: If you chose choice C, you fell right for the trap. The question is asking for the percentage alive after 80 years. You must subtract 60 percent from 100 percent to get 40 percent.

   Get into the habit of circling precisely what the question is asking for. In this case, circle the word "alive," so that you keep in mind that the percentage alive is what the question wants.

8. **J.** The percentage climbs from 0 percent to only 10 percent or so from 0 to 40 years, so choices F and G are out. A good look at later intervals shows much bigger increases in later intervals. The graph climbs from about 10 percent to 25 percent (an increase of 15 percent) between 40 and 60 years and from about 25 percent to 70 percent (an increase of 45 percent) between 60 and 80 years. (Just looking at the slope of the graph quickly provides the answer for this question.)

9. **A.** With no infant mortality, nobody dies just after 0 years. The graph will stay at 0 for a year or so and then start rising when children start dying from accidents, childhood diseases, brain explosion (from taking the ACT), and so on.

For choice B to be correct, more people would have to die in the first 20 years. With fewer people dying soon after birth, more people will likely be alive at 20 years, so the graph should be lower. Even if all the people who would have died as infants die before 20, the graph would be the same at 20. Additional people would have to die to make the graph higher.

Choice C is out because with more people surviving infancy, more people will have to die at later ages. The graph will be more, not less, steep in later years.

Choice D is unreasonable because those who survive past 1 year of age are almost certain to die before they reach 100. Most people survive infancy but still don't make it to 100. (Yes, of course, some people do live past 100, but you are not expected to think of remote possibilities. Curb your argumentative tendencies and go for the logical, common-sense scenario, unless a question specifically says otherwise.) Another reason to eliminate choice D is that it mentions a figure, 120 years, that is far beyond the range shown on the graph. For the graph to get to 120, a significant number need to live to 100. Only a small percentage of people die before 1. Why would keeping these people alive swell the number surviving past 100?

10. **H.** You can answer this question by process of elimination. The graph tells you that choices F and G are out. A clear majority of people live past 45, which means that the largest number of people have yet to die.

   Don't fall for choice J. More people die within 95 years than within 75 years, but this fact does not mean that more people die at age 95 than at 75. Only 10 percent of the people live to 90, so many people aren't left to die at 95 years. Only choice H is left.

11. **C.** At 15 years (choice A), less than 5 percent have died, so more than 95 percent are still alive. Just because a statement is correct doesn't make it the right answer choice. Note that the question asks you for the maximum number of years. Keep going to find out whether a larger number can be correct. At 35 years (choice B), more than 90 percent are still alive. This larger number eliminates choice A. Keep going. At 55 years (choice C), 20 percent have died, so 80 percent are still alive. This number is mentioned in the question. At 80 years (choice D), 60 percent have died, so this choice is out.

   Did you see the word *maximum* and immediately choose the largest number? Do you really think the ACT is that easy? By all means, check the largest number, but don't automatically assume that that number is right.

Passage 3

No, nuclear physics is not a required course for the ACT. Although this topic may seem incredibly advanced, the reading and interpretation are relatively straightforward. All you have to do is to realize that the radioactive substances change in a way that can be measured and that the rate of change slows down with time. The tables show these relationships: You can see that the disintegration rates consistently slow down as time goes on.

Be sure to notice that the time frames used for the two substances differ. Don't assume that Table A and Table B use the same frame of reference. Treat each table separately.

12. **H.** You can dump choice J immediately. If the substance is down to 125 after 16 hours, how can there be 200 after 20 hours? Use your common sense to eliminate illogical answers.

   Choice G penalizes the careless reader who looks at substance A rather than substance B.

   The most important thing to notice is that the disintegration rate is cut in half every four hours. After 20 hours (which is only one 4-hour segment after 16 hours), you can expect that the rate will be half of what it was at 16 hours. Half of 125 is 62.5.

13. **B.** The disintegration rate goes down because the number of radioactive atoms goes down as the substance disintegrates. (Actually, that's what "disintegration" is all about.) When fewer atoms are available to disintegrate, the disintegration rate naturally decreases.

So what does all this information mean to you? The number of atoms decreases in the same way that the disintegration rate decreases. At 15 hours, the disintegration rate is only 25/200 or 1/8 of what the rate was when measuring began. The number of atoms must be only 1/8 of the original 10,000,000. A little simple multiplication finishes the problem: 1/8 × 10,000,000 = 1,250,000.

14. **F.** Because wimpy or wishy-washy answers usually are better than dramatic or precise answers, eliminate choices G and J. Think about the choices as follows: If G is correct, the test-maker also has to accept choice F, which really wouldn't be wrong. However, choice F can be correct without choice G being correct. The same thing is true for choices H and J. If you're going to make a guess, guess F or H, the safer answers.

Just because 1,500 is halfway between 2,000 and 1,000 does not mean that the time has to be halfway between the times that are associated with 2,000 and 1,000. Take a look at Table 2. You'll notice that for every 4-hour interval, the decrease in millicuries is less. For example, the millicuries decrease 1,000 during the first 4 hours but decrease only 500 during the next 4 hours and decrease only 250 during the next 4 hours. You can conclude that more of a decrease occurs during the first 2 hours than during the second 2 hours. At 2 hours, the number of millicuries will be closer to 1,000 than to 2,000. You can conclude that 1,500 was reached a little before 2 hours, making choice F the safe bet.

Although this question is tough, thinking logically about how the test is constructed can help you narrow the field. *Remember:* The test-makers don't want to have to defend their answers. They're usually going to leave themselves some leeway by choosing less-precise answers.

15. **C.** The key is to look for which substance took less time for the disintegration rate (which is directly related to the number of radioactive atoms) to fall to one half of the original value. Substance A went from 200 to 100 in 5 hours, while substance B went from 2,000 to 1,000 in only 4 hours. Therefore, substance B has a shorter half-life, which narrows the field to choices C and D. Choice D is full of irrelevant garbage (just because the scientists decided to go home after 16 hours does not affect the half-life), while choice C actually reinforces the definition of half-life.

Choice A is misleading because the key is not the absolute amount of substance present but the amount of substance present relative to the starting amount. Choice B is simply wrong. The amount present after 25 hours is half the amount after 20 hours; the amount does not all disappear.

16. **G.** Hey, don't do too much work on this question. All you have to do is look at both tables and find the substance that has the lowest disintegration rate (which means a lower emission rate). You do not have to be concerned with the rate relative to the starting rate.

Because the disintegration rate is always lower after more time, knock out choices F and H right away. Table 1 shows that the rate for substance A after 20 hours is only 12.5 millicuries, while Table 2 shows 125 millicuries for substance B after 16 hours.

Passage 4

The key part of the introduction lies in the second paragraph, which tells you that the dispute involves whether the earth is getting too warm because of increases in carbon dioxide. Scientist 1 claims in the second sentence of her paragraph that it is. Scientist 2, on the other hand, professes very directly in the first sentence of his paragraph that it is not. You have, therefore, an obvious point of disagreement (as there should be, considering this type of passage is called Conflicting Viewpoints).

Both scientists use temperature evidence from the last hundred years to support their claims. Scientist 1 uses some numbers to propose that there has been some significant warming and that the trend has been most dramatic recently. Scientist 2 mentions the temperature

Chapter 22: Practice Exam 2: Answers and Explanations 343

numbers toward the end of the passage and asserts that the recent numbers show that global warming is under control. Although you shouldn't get hung up on details, note that Scientist 1 mentions an increase of 0.6°C while Scientist 2 comes in with 0.45°C for the overall increase in the past hundred years. To reason as a scientist does (remember that the test is entitled "Science Reasoning"), figure that such discrepancies suggest that the data are not clear.

HEADS UP

Did you notice the correct grammar: "The data are not clear," in this sentence? "Data" is a plural word, requiring a plural verb. I know, I know, it isn't fair to make you think of grammar in the middle of science . . . but I bet you'll remember this point now!

Scientist 1 cites computer models that indicate future global warming. According to Scientist 1 (don't you love those creative titles?), the increase in temperature will be significant if increases in carbon dioxide are stabilized and even more weighty if the carbon dioxide levels continue to increase. Scientist 2 casts doubt on the models. Don't try to follow all of Scientist 2's logic, but note that he says that the models don't account for key factors and that they have already been shown to have exaggerated increases in both carbon dioxide and temperature.

17. **D.** Look at the first two sentences of Scientist 1. She mentions a match between carbon dioxide and temperature variations, and then uses the recent large change in carbon dioxide levels as evidence that significant changes in temperature will occur. Scientist 1 goes on to discuss how continued sharp increases in atmospheric carbon dioxide will lead to similar dramatic temperature increases. Scientist 1 implies that the recent carbon dioxide changes have been unprecedented. The data during the past 160,000 years show a correspondence between temperature and carbon dioxide fluctuations but such a correspondence has occurred in the absence of the dramatic changes the earth is now and soon will be experiencing. For Scientist 1 to use the fluctuation correspondence as evidence for what will soon happen, she must assume that the correspondence will continue in light of current and near-future sharp changes.

Feedback factors are discussed by Scientist 2 in light of the computer models; right there is a good reason to eliminate choice A, because the question asks about Scientist 1. You may infer from Scientist 2's discussion that the main difference between the two scientists regarding feedback factors is that Scientist 1 thinks that they'll increase the carbon dioxide-related warming and that Scientist 2 thinks that they will minimize it.

Choice B is implied by Scientist 1 when she mentions that greenhouse gas concentration can be stabilized. Choice C is contradicted by Scientist 1 in that she mentions that a 0.5°C rise is significant.

18. **H.** Choice G is tempting in that only Scientist 2 questions the models currently being used. He claims that a model that appropriately incorporates feedback factors will show that global surface temperatures will not rise as high as models currently predict. The problem with choice G is not that Scientist 2's viewpoint is inconsistent with the article but that Scientist 1's viewpoint is also consistent. Scientist 1 relies on computer models. It could very well be that an updated model will make Scientist 1's case even stronger. You don't know exactly how those feedback factors will contribute to global warming. Don't take Scientist 2's opinion that the feedback factors will minimize warming as a fact. Although either scientist could turn out to be wrong in the face of a new model, both viewpoints are now consistent with the statement in the question.

19. **A.** As mentioned in the analysis of the passage, the discrepancy in the temperature figures suggests that calculating global temperatures is not a clear-cut process. Mean global temperature over 100 years entails gathering data from many sites for a long period of time. Some of these sites could have changed. It's also easy to envision that there is not one accepted way to average all these sites together so that they can represent what has happened around the entire world.

Choice B is wrong because a temperature measure is just that, a measure of temperature. The carbon dioxide is important only in that a change in carbon dioxide levels might account for why the temperature levels change. They are not included when numbers for temperature are taken and calculated.

Choice C is wrong because such an issue concerns only when the change in temperature occurred. Scientist 2 could very well also know about the hot years after 1980. The issue is simply how the present numbers compare to the numbers 100 years ago.

Choice D has to do with the consequences of increasing temperatures, not with the extent to which temperatures have risen.

20. **J.** The breakup of the ice sheet is indicative of global warming. Scientist 1 predicts greater global warming in the next hundred years, so she would expect there to be additional breaking up of Antarctic ice sheets. More breakup should lead to higher water levels and greater vulnerability to flooding.

Choice F is something that Scientist 2, who predicts minimal global warming in part because of feedback factors, would predict. Choice G is too exact. The passages discuss some numbers regarding the relationship between carbon dioxide and temperature, but even for those two variables there is no indication that the relationship is as precise as a doubling of one means a doubling of the other. There is no mention of the ice sheet in the passage, so eliminate choice G. Choice H may tempt you if you think that ice means cooling, but remember that the ice is melting in this case. The main problem with choice H is that, even if choice H were true, you would have to have some specific science knowledge to say so.

Remember that a correct answer on the ACT never depends on specialized scientific knowledge.

21. **A.** Choice A is a nice, noncontroversial statement with which both scientists would agree. Scientist 1 stresses that rising carbon dioxide is linked to higher temperature (another factor) while Scientist 2 discusses feedback factors, that is, factors that respond to carbon dioxide changes and will, in turn, affect the carbon dioxide. Scientist 2, who refers to improved energy technology, clearly disagrees with choice B but so does Scientist 1, who mentions the possibility that carbon dioxide levels will stabilize. Choice C is out because Scientist 2 discusses a slowing down in the rate of carbon dioxide level increase. Choice D, because of "directly," is too extreme.

Often, strong or extreme words are incorrect; view them skeptically. Scientist 2, by discussing feedback factors, certainly thinks that there is no direct link.

22. **H.** Scientist 1 asserts that a 0.6°C rise is significant because a 0.5°C change affected crop growth in the past. What if the 0.5°C change were a drop in temperature? It could be that increased temperatures will do nothing to the crops because the crops will do fine as long as temperatures stay above a certain level.

Eliminate choice F because carbon dioxide has to do with what may cause global warming. It determines what significance increased temperatures will have. In addition, the 150-year figure in this choice doesn't challenge the 100-year figure Scientist 1 presents about temperatures. The time periods still overlap, and there is general acceptance that both carbon dioxide and temperature are increasing. The big questions are to what extent the two are related and what the consequences will be.

Choice G is not very important, because it's clear that there have been higher temperatures toward the end of the 100-year period. It is not too important exactly which years had these higher temperatures. Because it's been only a little more than 20 years since 1980, there isn't too much room for variation anyway, so don't think less of Scientist 1 for omitting the exact years.

Choice J is out primarily because this choice has to do with the future, not the past hundred years. Also, Scientist 1 is free to predict a greater increase during the next hundred years because conditions are changing.

23. **B.** Scientist 2 mentions that water vapor and clouds make up 98% of the greenhouse effect, so it's reasonable to say that a change in water vapor will affect the greenhouse effect, which, in turn, will affect temperatures. In addition, Scientist 2 discusses how water vapor serves as a feedback effect, which contributes to temperature.

Choice A goes too far. Always be on the watch for answers that go beyond what you want, ones that are too extreme or continue past the point required. Scientist 2 mentions improved energy technology, implying that humans can handle some problems brought on by global warming, but you can't say whether Scientist 2 believes that humans can handle anything that comes our way.

Choice C picks up on the difference in figures mentioned at the end of the two Scientists' passages, but watch out for "never." Scientist 2 believes that the level will be below 1,100 parts per million in 2100, but he could feel that the level eventually will rise to 1,100.

Scientist 2 may believe choice D, but it is too extreme to say for sure. Scientist 2 believes that the rate of increase will slow and that the world will survive, but Scientist 2 could easily believe that such survival will occur even in the face of continually rising carbon dioxide levels.

Passage 5

Did you look at this experiment and mutter to yourself, "What a blooming mess!" If so, congratulate yourself: Your humor is becoming almost as sorry as mine. That aside, this passage isn't too bad. This passage doesn't shock the senses by introducing concepts unfamiliar to you. You've seen plants produce flowers at only a certain time of year. You know that the length of daylight is different throughout the year (longer days in summer, shorter days in winter).

After you've got the topic of this passage (the effect of the length of day on plants), you're ready to summarize each experiment. (You may want to write your brief synopsis in the margin.) Experiment 1 shows that interrupting the day has no effect.

Experiment 2 shows that interrupting the night changes the plants' responses, indicating that the plants may actually respond to the length of night rather than the length of day. An SD plant is actually a long-night plant, whereas an LD plant is a short-night plant.

Experiment 3 may sound complicated, but the gist is that, as with Experiment 1, manipulating the day has no effect on the plants.

In Experiment 4, as in Experiment 2, changing a nighttime factor affects the plants.

Taken together, these experiments suggest that the plants are sensitive to changes in the length of night, rather than the length of day. Don't economize on time here. Wanting to jump right into the questions is natural, but take a minute or two to think about what you just read. You don't have to be able to quote chapter and verse; you just have to know a little bit of what's going on. If you get confused here, you're likely to miss nearly every question.

24. **J.** Experiments 1 and 2 showed that only interruptions that occur during the night affect the flowering response. Eliminate choices F and H, which mention daytime hours. Choice J makes more sense than choice G because if the total number of hours are critical, a brief interruption would have very little effect. On the other hand, if the plants are somehow measuring the number of continuous nighttime hours, a brief interruption would affect the plant.

25. C. One major point of this passage is that SD and LD plants show opposite responses. This difference makes choices A and D unlikely. You can make a good guess at this point by choosing between choices B and C. Remember, the ACT does not subtract points for wrong answers, so guessing is always justified. Having a 50-50 choice is a real treat.

When the light is presented in the middle of the 16-hour night, the plants are exposed to only 8 hours of uninterrupted night hours. The plant that flowers when nights are short will start flowering. Which plant meets this criteria? The LD plant, which is spinach in this passage, flowers when days are long and nights are short.

You may be saying, "Yes, but what if . . ." Ah, Smart Students' Disease (in which you make things harder than necessary) is back. Don't be too concerned with the exact number of uninterrupted nighttime hours that spinach requires to flower. Although some LD plants may not flower until the number of uninterrupted night hours falls to, say, seven hours, the ACT will not pull this type of trick on you. The ACT does not expect you to memorize such obscure facts. What the ACT is testing is your understanding that a nighttime interruption effectively shortens the night and therefore leads to LD flowering.

The information presented in the first part of the passage reinforces choice C. The passage mentions that cocklebur does not flower until day length is less than 15.5 hours. This statement means that nighttime must exceed 8.5 hours (24 − 15.5 = 8.5) for cocklebur to flower. When the light is flashed in the middle of the 16-hour night, the night is effectively only 8 hours long, which means that the cocklebur will not flower.

26. G. The experimenter can easily choose another plant, keep the lights on or off at a certain time, or change the temperature. Whether the plants flower, on the other hand, has to do with how the plants respond to the conditions presented in the experiment. Flowering depends on what happens to the other variables. Such dependent variables are a step removed from the direct control of the experimenter.

27. C. In both sets of experiments, changing day conditions has no effect on the plants' responses, although changing night conditions does. Choice D acknowledges this consistency, but the reason focuses on how the experiments are set up, not on the results. In many biological experiments, the same organisms are used, but doing so does not guarantee similar results. (Imagine, for example, if you and your friend both had colds and both were given aspirin. The aspirin does not guarantee that both of you would have the same response to the medication.)

Choices A and B, besides being flat-out wrong from the start, also provide reasons that focus on the experimental conditions rather than the results. In addition, choice A may not even be correct because you have no information regarding the variety of plants used in Experiments 1 and 2. Choice B points out a key way that the sets of experiments differ, but the results are similar.

28. G. On the horizontal axes, day length increases to the right. The LD plant flowers during long days. This information means that high vertical values are associated with the right side of the graph. Eliminate choices H and J, in which flowering does not increase with the increasing day length.

Choice G is better than choice F because with LD plants, no flowering occurs until a critical day length is reached. (The experiments actually show that the LD plant responds when the length of night falls below a certain value, but associating an LD plant's flowering with long days is still okay.) In choice F, the graph continually rises, implying that flowering increases as day length increases from 0 hours. Choice G correctly shows that flowering does not occur when the day length is less than 15 hours.

29. C. So many questions are about SD and LD that you may have forgotten the third actor in this play, a DN plant. Look at the introduction, which defines a DN plant as one that is not sensitive to changes in day length. This type of plant should flower in any environment, including near the equator. (So you shouldn't be surprised that some weeds are DN plants.) Because IV is part of the answer, choice B is out.

Plants that require very long or very short days will probably not flower near the equator because the day length stays close to 12 hours and will not approach the number of hours necessary for flowering. This means that III is out. Such an SD plant will flower when days are less than 8 hours (and nights are more than 16 hours), which never happens near the equator. With III out, you can eliminate choice D, leaving you with only choices A and C.

Do I and II seem reasonable? Yes, because the day length varies slightly from 12 hours near the equator. Such changes are enough to produce flowering in plants that don't require much different from a 12-hour day/night. With statements I and II acceptable, you can eliminate choice A.

Passage 6

Even though you do not need outside knowledge to answer these questions, information you have gained over the years (along with just plain common sense) can be very helpful. The ACT does not try to trap or trick you by giving wrong science. What you have learned in school or from experience will remain valid and useful for the ACT.

Use your own knowledge. What's more spread out: a solid, such as a block of ice, or oxygen gas as it is sprayed from a tank into a room? You know or can visualize that in a gas, particles quickly spread out as much as possible.

Continue using your own knowledge. What happens when you heat ice? The ice melts and turns into liquid water. Further heating leads to boiling, and the water evaporates. These thoughts should help you grasp what's being stated in paragraph two.

The third paragraph is probably less familiar to you, but the figures should help. You can see from Figure 2, for example, that at 60°C and 0.20 atm, water is a gas, but at 60°C and 0.80 atm, water is a liquid. Try to summarize the information to get the gist or main point. The main point is that pressure affects phases.

The figures re-emphasize that high temperature is associated with a gas and that low temperature is associated with a solid. When pressure is high, a relatively high temperature is needed to turn a liquid into a gas.

30. **G.** This straightforward question simply tests your ability to read a graph. Look at Figure 2, which deals with water. Locate 60°C on the horizontal axis and then go straight up until you are even with 1.00 atm (on the vertical axis). You are in the liquid region.

31. **A.** You are looking for a point on one of the figures where a solid is next to a gas. Choice A looks good. In Figure 1 (bromine), –20°C and 0.05 atm is near the lower-left corner, where a solid and a gas are next to each other. Liquid is out of the way, up and to the right.

    Choice B is wrong because at 0°C and 0.80 atm, bromine is near the solid-liquid boundary. Water is also near that boundary at 0°C and 0.80 atm, so choice C is out. Choice D is way off because water is nowhere near a solid at 80°C and 0.50 atm.

32. **G.** The easiest way to do this question is to take a straightedge (your answer grid will work) and, on each figure, draw a vertical line from the 30°C mark. Now, for each figure, mark 0.6 atm and 0.3 atm on the line. On the bromine graph (Figure 1), 0.6 atm is in the liquid region, and 0.3 atm is in the gas region when the temperature is 30° C, so choice G is the answer. Don't be careless and pick choice F. The pressure is going down, so you're moving from the liquid to the gas, not from a gas to a liquid. The liquid region is generally higher than the gas region. On the water graph (Figure 2), you can see that both of your marks are in the liquid region, eliminating choices H and J.

Figure 1: Bromine Phases.

33. D. Your gut instinct should attract you to choices B and D because higher temperatures move particles further apart. If you are running out of time, go ahead and make a guess; 50/50 odds aren't that bad on this test, and remember: The ACT has no penalty for wrong answers. Choice D is correct because water at 100°C and 0.60 atm is a gas, while bromine at 50°C and 0.80 atm (choice B) is a liquid. Just to be certain, (good test-takers are always paranoid, but are you paranoid enough?), check choices A and C. In choice A, bromine is a solid. In choice C, water is also a solid.

34. H. You can probably eliminate choice F by using common sense: Higher altitudes don't necessarily mean your pasta freezes! When an answer seems illogical or even amusing, put it aside for a moment. If none of the other answer choices are correct, you can always come back to it. (For those of you who love Sherlock Holmes, you will recognize this strategy as a variation on his famous saying, which roughly goes, "When you have eliminated the impossible, whatever remains, however improbable, must be true.")

Go through the rest of the choices without wasting any time on choice F. Choice G is out because the water temperature (the spaghetti is in the water) is important, not the air temperature. A look at Figure 2 confirms the first part of choice H: At 1.00 atm, water becomes a gas. At 0.80 atm, water becomes a gas at about 90°C. With the water boiling at a lower temperature, there's less heat available to soften the spaghetti. The answer is probably choice H, but double-check choice J just to be sure. Choice J is contradicted by Figure 2 (think of how you analyzed choice H). Besides, in this problem, the water is already boiling, so the length of time required to boil water is irrelevant.

Passage 7

First of all, don't panic if the terminology is not familiar to you. You don't have to know what radon is to understand the introduction. Remember that the ACT does not presuppose any specific scientific knowledge on your part. Simply note that radon may have something to do with earthquakes and that scientists are going to check out this possibility.

Spend a minute or two looking at the charts. You don't have to understand the charts perfectly, and you certainly don't want to start memorizing the information given. Just realize that Figures 1 through 4 are basically maps. You can see the epicenters and note that wells around the epicenters have higher-than-normal amounts of radon emission.

Chapter 22: Practice Exam 2: Answers and Explanations 349

Figure 5 shows a systematic relationship (called a correlation) between earthquake magnitude and the differential, which is a measure of how much the radon emission exceeds normal. The rightmost point is the only one that bucks the trend. When you see something abnormal, something that doesn't follow the same pattern as the others, pay special attention to it. The chances are good that you will be asked a question about this aberration. Which earthquake site is represented by the rightmost point? The site had a magnitude of 7.9 and an average differential of 2.5. Scan Figures 1 through 4 and you will see that the point in question represents China. Note that China has two wells near the epicenter that were not much above normal. Perhaps these wells were measured inaccurately. Whatever the case, these wells may have something to do with why China is a little off in regard to Figure 5.

35. B. Choice A doesn't look right. All four sites had radon emissions that were greater than the normal amount found over the earth, making choice B look good.

You should have been leaning toward choosing B as soon as you saw the wishy-washy, wimpy language. A correct answer often has language that is not extreme, language that hedges a little bit. A conclusion that stated that an association is *definitely* present would be too strong unless a lot more data were collected.

None of the figures show wells that are 1,000 km (10 cm) away from the epicenter, so you can determine nothing about choice C.

The conclusion stated in choice D is also unjustified. For the most part, wells near the epicenters show higher emissions, but the numbers are not very close to 5 percent and no measurement was taken right at the epicenter.

36. H. The results of the studies indicate some association between earthquakes and radon emissions. Results that go along with the trend found in the studies strengthen the results and any claim derived from the results. Option I is one such result. You can already see that a higher-than-normal emission from all the well sites shown exists. With more evidence, the case becomes more compelling. Because statement I is true, you can immediately narrow the answers down to choices H or J. If you're in a huge rush, guess and go. *Remember:* The ACT does not subtract points for wrong answers. Guessing is always to your advantage.

Does statement II look good? It does if you remember the introductory analysis about China. The one point that is off in Figure 5 is the one from China. The finding cited in statement II would produce a point that would fall in line with the points from the other three sites. Because statement II is valid, choice J has been eliminated.

On the real test, you wouldn't even need to look at statement III. However, for you skeptics in the audience, I'll examine III. It does not provide enough information. What is needed are more quakes associated with high radon emissions. Simply having more quakes doesn't shed any light on the association between earthquakes and radon emissions.

37. A. You have to be careful when dealing with data that show an association (a correlation in more mathematical terms). Just because two things go together does not imply that one causes the other. For example, the number of skyscrapers in a city and the number of children who live in that city have a correlation. That is, in general, cities that have more skyscrapers also have more young people. Does this mean that young people are building the skyscrapers? Of course not. A more reasonable explanation is that when a city is large, it has many skyscrapers and youngsters. An underlying cause, namely overall city size, exists. Children do not cause skyscrapers or vice versa.

This study simply measured a correlation. This study was not designed to investigate any possible mechanism that would convert radon emissions into earthquakes, which knocks out choices C and D and narrows the field to choices A and B. Choice B is out because nothing in the study points to 4 percent as a magic number. This point is not true, but even if it were, you would not have to know this information from some specialized outside study, which is not required on the ACT.

38. J. When experimental results are obtained, the responsible factor is often unclear. For example, if a scientist wanted to study whether a new drug could increase ACT scores, he could give the drug to a group of students and then look at the scores. If the scores are high, the scientist could conclude that the drug had an effect. But what if the group studied included many people who have a history of scoring well on tests similar to the ACT? What if the students did better simply because they believed the drug would help them? By including a control condition, experimenters can rule out these possibilities. Experimenters can find a group that was equal to the drug group on previous test scores and then give these control students a placebo (a fake pill) but tell them that this pill is supposed to help raise ACT scores. If the drug group scores higher, experimenters can be more confident that the high scores weren't simply the result of using a high-achieving group or a psychological belief in the drug because the two groups were matched in terms of these factors. In this case, the chemicals in the drug more likely had something to do with the higher scores. The control condition helped rule out other possible factors.

In the earthquake studies, radon emissions were measured after earthquakes. The researchers obtained high values, but such values can occur even in the absence of an earthquake. Scientists would need to know the radon emission level that normally occurs in the sites studied.

In a sense, choices F and H mention conditions that are included in the studies. The studies compared the wells near the epicenters to worldwide values. Sites far from the epicenters or in virtually earthquake-free areas are included in the worldwide averages.

All choice G would do is add more data to what has already been found. Clearing up the graph in Figure 5 would be particularly helpful, but the condition is not a control condition.

39. A. Use common sense! If you want to predict an earthquake, you have to measure something *before* the earthquake occurs. The problem with the current studies is that scientists measured emissions after the earthquakes. Maybe the earthquakes caused the emissions, making radon pretty useless as a predictor. Choices B, C, and D wouldn't help unless measurements were taken before.

You aren't required to have specific science knowledge to answer an ACT question, but the test-makers do assume a level of common sense. The ACT does not teach or test false science (for example, you won't have an experiment with totally illogical results). This small act of kindness means that you can trust your common sense and general knowledge. The science portion of the ACT has very few traps or tricks in it. The science is pretty straightforward, as are the questions. Don't make these questions harder than they have to be.

40. H. What's so puzzling about choice F? One site had to have the strongest earthquake, so why not China? Choice G is logical. It's not surprising that the highest differential would be found near the epicenter of the strongest earthquake, given the trend shown in Figure 5.

Choice H is the strange one. At the other three sites, the wells closest to the epicenter had differentials that were among the highest found in the area. In China, the two closest wells had far lower differentials. Choice J is not puzzling. Why not measure from as many wells as possible? Besides, readings were taken from six wells in Chile as well as China.

Part VIII
The Part of Tens

The 5th Wave   By Rich Tennant

ACT overload

"We can't eat the pizza until Lamar determines the relationship of the 3 small wedges to the 2 larger ones."

In this part . . .

Party time! Sure, you can actually learn a few new things in these chapters, but you can also have a lot of fun with the ten hottest rumors about the ACT that absolutely aren't true, ten interesting differences between the ACT and SAT, and ten true horror stories about testing day.

Chapter 23

Ten Wrong Rumors About the ACT

In This Chapter
- Recognizing that not everything you hear is true
- Finding out what's true and what isn't

They're whispered in the bathrooms and written in notes passed in the classroom. What are they? They're the vile and vicious rumors about the ACT — rumors that seem to grow with each telling.

- "You can't use a calculator." (Wrong. You may use a calculator, just as you may use one on the SAT.)
- "They make you write an essay." (No. The essay is optional. You write an essay on the SAT II, but the ACT essay is optional.)

On the Friday night before the ACT, the phone rings off the hook. We spend hours reassuring students and their parents that the latest rumors they've heard about the ACT are completely false. Here are ten of the rumors you may have heard.

You Can't Study for the ACT

If you really thought that, why did you buy this book (not that we don't appreciate your purchase, mind you)? The ACT tests grammar; you can certainly refresh your memory of the grammar rules. The ACT has algebra, geometry, and arithmetic questions on it; you can certainly study formulas and rules in those areas. In addition, a little preparation can make you very comfortable with the format and timing of the test, helping to reduce test-taking anxiety and ultimately improve your score. This book, in particular, discusses tricks and traps that are built into the exam — gotchas! that we want you to be prepared for.

Different States Have Different ACTs

This rumor is based on the fact that the score sheet compares your performance to that of other students who have taken the ACT in your state. When you get back your ACT score, you are told your percentile rank nationally and within your state. However, all students in all states take the exact same ACT on any one test date. (Of course, the ACT changes from one date to the next; otherwise, you could keep retaking the same test. You'd be surprised how many students don't realize this and merrily say to us, "Oh, I remember the questions from last time, so I'll do great next time.") It will do you no good to fly to Rhode Island or Nebraska, thinking that you can get an easier exam there.

The ACT Has a Passing Score

There is no such thing as a passing or failing score on the ACT. By looking at the college bulletins of the schools you are interested in, you can, however, deduce your minimum entrance score based on your GPA. If you have a high GPA, your ACT score can be lower than if you have a low GPA. In fact, you may be pleasantly surprised how low your ACT score can be. Scoring on the ACT is not like scoring on high school exams, in which a 65th percentile is failing. If you score in the 65th percentile on the ACT, you may still be able to get into the college of your choice.

The ACT Tests IQ

The ACT is a college entrance exam. It tests your potential for doing well in college. If you are the type who normally studies hard for an exam, you will probably study hard for the ACT and do well on it, and then study hard for college exams and do well on them, too. The key is in the preparation. You have the same opportunity to do well on the ACT regardless of whether you're a SuperBrain or as cerebrally challenged as the rest of us. With this book, you can learn to improve your ACT scores with all sorts of tricks, tips, and techniques — something that is much harder to do on IQ exams.

If You Don't Know the Answer, Choose A or F

We're constantly amazed by how many people say they've heard this rumor. The answer choices on the ACT are A, B, C, and D, or F, G, H, and J. (*Note:* The one exception is the Mathematics Test. In that section, the answer choices are A, B, C, D, and E or F, G, H, J, and K.) Students repeatedly tell us that they've been told to guess an A or an F if they don't know the answer. This speculation is ridiculous. Every answer choice has the same possibility: one of four choices (or in the math section, one of five choices).

You Should Never Guess

Wrong, wrong, wrong. You should always guess on the ACT. This exam has no penalty for guessing. Never leave an answer blank. Fill in something, anything, on the chance that you may get lucky and get the question correct.

If you're also taking the SAT I, notice that the two exams are different in this respect. The SAT I penalizes you (either ¼ or ⅓ point, depending on the type of question) for each wrong answer, so that random guessing on that test is discouraged (except on the grid-in math portion). Random guessing on the ACT, however, can only help you.

The ACT Is Easier than the SAT I

Maybe. Maybe not. The ACT has no vocabulary on it, only English grammar. Obviously, if you are better at grammar than vocabulary, the ACT is easier for you. The math questions on the ACT are all straightforward multiple-choice with none of the tricky QC (Quantitative Comparisons) or grid-in questions featured on the SAT I. However, the ACT does feature a few trigonometry questions (only about four; don't sweat 'em) that are not on the SAT I. The ACT reading passages, both in the Reading Test and in the Science Reasoning Test, tend to be slightly longer than some of those on the SAT I but are not necessarily more difficult.

The ACT Is the Same as the Achievement Test

Many people, especially parents, confuse ACT with ACH. The Achievement Test used to be referred to as ACH. To confuse everyone totally, the test-makers have renamed the Achievement Test the SAT II. Got that? The regular old SAT is the SAT I; the former Achievement Test is the SAT II. Neither is connected with the ACT, which stands for American College Testing. SAT II consists of single-subject tests that require you to actually know things like Chinese verbs or botany rules. The ACT does not test single subjects, but it does test general knowledge and reasoning skills.

You Have to Write an Essay

No. You do not have to write an essay during the ACT. It is optional. However, within a few years, colleges will require this section and make it mandatory. In fact, some colleges are already requiring it. Taking this portion of the test is a good idea even though you really do not want to.

You Can't Take Both the SAT I and the ACT

Wrong, wrong, wrong. Many students take both exams. Usually, the ACT is offered a week or two after the SAT I. You may be burned out, taking two exams this close together or have trouble studying for both of them, but you certainly may take both tests. Some colleges require the SAT I. Other colleges will accept either the ACT or the SAT I. A few colleges accept the ACT only. When we tutor students, we suggest that they take both exams.

Chapter 24

Ten Differences between the ACT and the SAT

In This Chapter
- Identifying the different content of the ACT and the SAT I
- Recognizing the differences in how you take the ACT and SAT I

What's the difference between the ACT and the SAT I? Do they test different things? Do they require different study programs? Is it possible to know whether you'll do better on one test than the other? This chapter gives you the ten (well, actually only seven) primary differences between the SAT and the ACT.

The ACT Emphasizes English Grammar; The SAT I Emphasizes Vocabulary

The ACT requires that you know grammar rules, such as the distinction between *lie* and *lay* or *it's* and *its*. The SAT I doesn't test grammar. However, the SAT I has sentence completions that feature big, hard words like *pulchritudinous* and *pusillanimous*. The ACT doesn't test vocabulary.

The ACT Has an Optional Essay Question; The SAT I Has a Required Essay Section

The ACT has an optional Essay section. However, it appears that colleges and universities probably will require this section in the near future. The SAT I also has an essay question, but it is mandatory!

The ACT Questions Are All Multiple-Choice; SAT I Math Questions Aren't

All questions on the ACT have multiple-choice responses. The SAT I has ten questions (20 percent) that have no multiple-choice responses. You have to solve a math problem yourself and enter your answer in the bubble. In addition, the SAT I has a bizarre type of math question called the QC (or quantitative comparison). That style of question is not on the ACT.

The ACT Tests Science Reasoning; The SAT I Doesn't

One of the four tests on the ACT is Science Reasoning. The test features science reading passages, sometimes with charts or diagrams that you have to read and use to answer questions. You may be required to interpret an experiment or understand information in a table.

Don't worry, you're not expected to know scientific information on your own. That is, you don't have to have had physics to answer questions on a physics passage. The passage gives you all the information you need.

The SAT I has no science reasoning per se. However, one of the reading passages (called Critical Reading on the SAT I) is usually on a science topic.

The ACT Doesn't Penalize You for Guessing; The SAT I Does

The ACT allows you to guess your brains out. When taking it, you don't receive any penalty for missing a question, so never leave anything blank. On the SAT I, however, you lose either ⅓ or ¼ of a point for wrong answers (depending on the question style).

The ACT Has Five Long Sections; The SAT I Has Ten Short Sections

The ACT has one 60-minute section, one 45-minute section, two 35-minute sections, and one 30-minute optional writing section. The SAT has seven 25-minute sections, two 20-minute sections and one 10-minute section (one of which is equating, or experimental, and doesn't count).

The ACT Has No Experimental Sections; The SAT I Has One

On the ACT, everything counts. The SAT I has a 25-minute section (either math or verbal) that doesn't count toward your score. No, you won't know which section it is. If you did, you wouldn't take it seriously, now would you? The SAT I test-makers are using you as a guinea pig to try out new questions.

Index

• A •

ACH *versus* ACT, 355
ACT. *See also* Practice Exam; test center
   versus ACH, 355
   breakdown, by section, 9
   breaks, 9
   compensating for poor score, 22
   importance of, 21
   learning disabilities, 11
   as measure of IQ, 354
   military duty, 11
   number of questions, 9
   passing scores, 354
   physical disabilities, 11
   religious obligations, 11
   repeating, 13, 22
   rescheduling, 11
   rumors about, 353–355
   versus SAT I
     college planning, 22
     difficulty, 354
     summary of differences, 357–358
     taking both, 355
   state variations, 353
   studying for, 353
   subjects tested, 12–13
   time limit, 9
   timing yourself, 11
active voice, 73
acute angles, 79
adjectives, 30–31
admission ticket, 10
admissions essays, 23
adverbs, 30
affect/effect, 33
algebra
   See also geometry
   See also math review
   See also Mathematics Test
   See also trigonometry
   bases, 99–101
   exponents, 99–101
   factoring, 108
   FOIL method, 106–108
   Mathematics Test, 131–132
   numerical coefficients, 101
   order of operations, 106–108
   powers, 99–101
   radicals, 108–110
   ratios, 101–102
   reciprocals, 100
   roots, 108–110
   solving for x, 105–106
   symbolic values, 102–105
all, subject-verb agreement, 28
among/between, 34
amount/number, 33–34
angles
   acute, 79
   around a point, 81
   complementary, 80
   exterior, 82
   fractional, 79
   in isosceles triangles, 82
   negative, 79
   obtuse, 80
   reflex, 81
   right, 80
   straight, 80
   supplementary, 80
   transversal, 81
   trigonometric ratios of, 115–116
   zero, 79
answer choices, English Test, 42
answer grid, 17, 18–19
anxious/eager, 34
any, subject-verb agreement, 28
arcs in circles, 96–97
areas
   circles, 95
   parallelograms, 88
   rectangles, 88
   rhombuses, 88
   sector of a circle, 98
   squares, 88
   trapezoids, 88
   triangles, 85
arithmetic. *See* math review; Mathematics Test; *specific topics*
assure/ensure, 34
averages, 118–120

• B •

bases, numeric, 99–101
between/among, 34
books, during the test, 10
both, subject-verb agreement, 28
box questions, English Test, 42–43, 46
breaks during the test, 9
breathing exercises, 15
Bulgarian language, 125
bumper stickers, 49
but also construction, 31

• C •

calculator, for test, 10
calculus, 132
careless mistakes. *See* mistakes
case (grammatical), pronouns, 30
center of circles, 94
central angles, 95–96
change for the sake of change, 46
charity work, importance of, 23
charts. *See* coordinate geometry
cheating, 19
checking your work
   answer grid, 17
   careless mistakes, 16–17
   common sense answers, 16
   context, 17
   decimal places, 17
   diction, 17
   exponents, 16
   grammar, 17
   -ing words, 17
   mistakes
     answer grid, 18–19
     box questions, 46
     change for the sake of change, 46
     cheating, 19
     college planning, 24
     English Test, 46
     failure to double-check, 20
     listening to others, 20
     losing concentration, 18
     missing the big picture, 46
     NO CHANGE option, 46
     OMIT... option, 46
     rubbernecking, 19
     second guessing, 20
     superfluous information, 45

checking your work, mistakes *(continued)*
    transferring information, 20
    traps, 46
    wasting time, 18
    worrying, 19–20
    Writing Test, 55–58
  operations signs, 17
  political correctness, 17
  twosomes, 17
chords in circles, 94
circles
  arcs, 96–97
  area, 95
  area of sectors, 98
  center, 94
  central angle, 95–96
  chords, 94
  circumference, 94
  degree measure, 96–97
  diameter, 94
  inscribed angle, 95–96
  perimeter, 94
  radius, 94
  sectors, 98
circumference of circles, 94
clothing, for test, 10
club, subject-verb agreement, 28
collection, subject-verb agreement, 28
collective nouns, subject-verb agreement, 28
college planning. *See also* ACT, *versus* SAT I
  admissions essays, 23
  charity work, importance of, 23
  choosing a school, 24
  common mistakes, 24
  compensating for poor ACT score, 22
  importance of the ACT, 21
  interviews, 23
  recommended high school classes, 22–23
  repeating the ACT, 22
  sports, importance of, 23
  what colleges look for, 21
common mistakes. *See* mistakes
common-sense answers, 16
comparisons, 32–33
complementary angles, 80
complement/compliment, 35
composite numbers, 123–124
compound subjects, subject-verb agreement, 28

concentration, mistakes, 18
conclusion, Writing Test, 71–72
context, checking your work, 17
controversy, Writing Test, 57
coordinate geometry, 93, 132
cosines, 114
counting numbers, 122
creativity, Writing Test, 56
cubes
  polygons, 91
  TSA (total surface area), 92–93
  volume, 91
cylinders
  TSA (total surface area), 92–93
  volume, 91–92

• D •

Data Analysis, Science Reasoning Test, 162–163
Data Representation, Science Reasoning Test, 160–163
decimal places, checking your work, 17
degree measure of circles, 96–97
denominators, 110
detail questions, 148
diameter of circles, 94
diction
  checking your work, 17
  grammar review, 33–39
diction-type questions, 44
directions to test center, 10
D.I.R.T. math, 117–118
distance, time, rate calculations, 117–118
double checking your work. *See* checking your work; mistakes

• E •

each, subject-verb agreement, 28
eager/anxious, 34
editing, Writing Test, 58, 72–73
effect/affect, 33
either/or, subject-verb agreement, 29
eminent/immanent/imminent, 35
English Test. *See also* grammar review; Writing Test
  answer choices, 42
  box questions, 42–43, 46

change for the sake of change, 46
diction-type questions, 44
format, 41–42
grammar questions, 44–45
guessing, 45
missing the big picture, 46
mistakes, 46
NO CHANGE option, 46
OMIT... option, 46, 48
overview, 12
passages, 41
Practice Exam 1
  answers and explanations, 227–235
  questions, 185–194
Practice Exam 2
  answers and explanations, 311–320
  questions, 269–279
practice questions, 47–51, 185–194, 269–279
questions, 42
speed *versus* thoroughness, 45
superfluous information, 45
test strategy, 44–45
traps, 46
usage questions, 43
ensure/assure, 34
equilateral triangles, 82
essays for ACT. *See* English Test; Writing Test
essays for college admission, 23
every, subject-verb agreement, 28
every day/everyday, 35
exams. *See* ACT; Practice Exam
expectation of perfection, 57
exponents, 16, 99–101
exterior angles
  definition, 82
  polygons, 90
  triangles, 83
eyeglasses, for test, 10

• F •

factoring, 108
farther/further, 35–36
faze/phase, 38
few, subject-verb agreement, 28
fewer/less, 37
flaunt/flout, 36
flounder/founder, 36
FOIL method, 106–108

Index

four-sided figures. *See* quadrilaterals
fractional angles, 79
fractions, 128–129
further/farther, 35–36

• G •

gender, pronouns, 30
geometry
  See also algebra
  See also math review
  See also Mathematics Test
  See also trigonometry
  angles
    acute, 79
    around a point, 81
    complementary, 80
    exterior, 82
    fractional, 79
    in isosceles triangles, 82
    negative, 79
    obtuse, 80
    reflex, 81
    right, 80
    straight, 80
    supplementary, 80
    transversal, 81
    zero, 79
  area
    parallelograms, 88
    rectangles, 88
    rhombuses, 88
    squares, 88
    trapezoids, 88
    triangles, 85
  circles
    arcs, 96–97
    area, 95
    area of sectors, 98
    center, 94
    central angle, 95–96
    chords, 94
    circumference, 94
    degree measure, 96–97
    diameter, 94
    inscribed angle, 95–96
    perimeter, 94
    radius, 94
    sectors, 98
  coordinate, 93
  largest angle, 83
  Mathematics Test, 132
  point of origin, 93
  polygons *See also* quadrilaterals; triangles
    cubes, 91
    cylinders, 91–92
    exterior angle measure, 90
    interior angle measure, 90–91
    perimeter, 90
    rectangular solids, 91
    regular, 90
    TSA (total surface area), 92–93
    volume, 91–92
  quadrilaterals *See also* polygons
    definition, 87
    eccentric shapes, 89
    parallelogram, 88
    rectangle, 88
    rhombus, 88
    square, 87–88
    trapezoid, 88–89
  shaded-area problems, 89
  similar figures, 84
  triangles *See also* polygons
    area, 85
    equilateral, 82
    hypotenuse, 85
    isosceles, 82
    largest angle, 83
    lengths of sides, 85
    measure of exterior angle, 83
    perimeter, 85
    Pythagorean theorem, 85–87
    right, 85–87
    scalene, 83
    sum of interior angles, 83
    sum of length of two sides, 83
  x-y axes, 93
ghost words, Writing Test, 72
good/well, 36
government, subject-verb agreement, 28
grammar review. *See also* English Test
  adjectives, 30–31
  affect/effect, 33
  amount/number, 33–34
  anxious/eager, 34
  assure/ensure, 34
  between/among, 34
  checking your work, 17
  comparisons, 32–33
  complement/compliment, 35
  diction, 33–39
  eminent/immanent/imminent, 35
  everyday/every day, 35
  farther/further, 35–36
  flaunt/flout, 36
  founder/flounder, 36
  good/well, 36
  hardly, 39–40
  hopefully, 40
  if/whether, 36–37
  if...would construction, 40
  imply/infer, 37
  it's/its, 37
  less/fewer, 37
  lie/lay, 37–38
  parallelism, 32
  phase/faze, 38
  prescribe/proscribe, 38
  principle/principal, 38
  pronouns, 29–30
  questions, English Test, 44–45
  in regards to...in regard to construction, 40
  rise/raze/raise, 39
  run-on sentences, 31
  sentence fragments, 32
  sentence structure, 31–32
  stationary/stationery, 39
  subject-verb agreement, 27–29
  where...that construction, 40
  who/whom, 39
graphs. *See* coordinate geometry
group, subject-verb agreement, 28
guessing, 12, 354

• H •

handwriting, Writing Test, 73
hardly, 39–40
high school classes, recommended, 22–23
hooking the reader, Writing Test, 67–68
hopefully, 40
humanities, Reading Test, 145
hypotenuse of triangles, 85

• I •

if/whether, 36–37
if...would construction, 40
imply/infer, 37
in regards to...in regard to construction, 40
indecisiveness, Writing Test, 57, 67
infer/imply, 37
-ing words, checking your work, 17
inscribed angles, 95–96
integers, 122

The ACT For Dummies, 4th Edition

interest problems, 124–125
interior angle measure, 90–91
interior angles, sum of, 83
interviews, college planning, 23
introduction, Writing Test, 70
IQ, measuring with the ACT, 354
irrational numbers, 123
isosceles triangles, 82
it's/its, 37

• L •

largest angle of triangles, 83
latter/last comparison, 32
lay/lie, 37–38
learning disabilities, 11
length, units of measure, 127
leotard, inventor of, 28
less/fewer, 37
lie/lay, 37–38

• M •

main idea questions, 148
many, subject-verb agreement, 28
map to test center, 10
math review. *See also* Mathematics Test
 algebra
  bases, 99–101
  exponents, 99–101
  factoring, 108
  FOIL method, 106–108
  Mathematics Test, 131–132
  numerical coefficients, 101
  order of operations, 106–108
  powers, 99–101
  radicals, 108–110
  ratios, 101–102
  reciprocals, 100
  roots, 108–110
  solving for x, 105–106
  symbolic values, 102–105
 averages, 118–120
 composite numbers, 123–124
 counting numbers, 122
 D.I.R.T. math, 117–118
 fractions, 128–129
 geometry
  acute angles, 79
  angles, 79–82
  arcs, 96–97
  area, 85, 88, 95, 98
  central angles, 95–96
  chords, 94

circles, 94–98
circumference of circles, 94
complementary angles, 80
coordinate, 93
cubes, 91
cylinders, 91–92
degree measure, 96–97
diameter of circles, 94
eccentric shapes, 89
equilateral triangles, 82
exterior angle measure, 90
exterior angles, 82
fractional angles, 79
hypotenuse, 85
inscribed angles, 95–96
interior angle measure, 90–91
isosceles triangles, 82
largest angle, 83
Mathematics Test, 132
negative angles, 79
obtuse angles, 80
parallelograms, 88
perimeter of circles, 94
perimeter of polygons, 90
perimeter of triangles, 85
point of origin, 93
polygons, 90–93
Pythagorean theorem, 85–87
quadrilaterals, 87–89
radius of circles, 94
rectangles, 88
rectangular solids, 91
reflex angles, 81
rhombuses, 88
right angles, 80
right triangles, 85–87
scalene triangles, 83
sectors, 98
shaded-area problems, 89
similar figures, 84
squares, 87–88
straight angles, 80
supplementary angles, 80
transversal angles, 81
trapezoids, 88–89
triangles, 82–83, 85–87
TSA (total surface area), 92–93
volume, 91–92
x-y axes, 93
zero angles, 79
integers, 122
interest problems, 124–125
irrational numbers, 123
mixed numbers, 129

mixture problems, 124
mnemonics, 126
number sets, 122–123
percentages, 120–122
prime numbers, 123–124
probability, 110–111
PRTI formula, 124–125
rational numbers, 122–123
real numbers, 123
statistics, 111–113
time, rate, distance calculations, 117–118
trigonometry
 cosines, 114
 Mathematics Test, 132
 questions in the ACT, 113
 ratios of angles, 115–116
 sines, 113–114
 SOH CAH TOA, 113–116
 tangents, 114
units of measure, 126–127
whole numbers, 122
work problems, 125–126
Mathematics Test. *See also specific topics*
 arithmetic, 131
 breakdown, 131–132
 calculus, 132
 content, 132
 coordinate geometry, 132
 do's and don'ts, 135–136
 elementary algebra, 131–132
 format, 131–132
 geometry, 132
 grid-ins, 132
 guessing, 135
 intermediate algebra, 132
 overview, 13
 plane geometry, 132
 Practice Exam 1
  answers and explanations, 235–248
  questions, 195–202
 Practice Exam 2
  answers and explanations, 320–332
  questions, 280–287
 practice questions, 137–142, 195–202, 280–287
 pre-algebra, 131
 quantitative comparisons, 132
 recommended approach, 133–134
 timing, 134–135
 traps, 132
 trigonometry, 132

Index 363

median, 112
military duty, 11
missing the big picture, 46
mistakes
  answer grid, 18–19
  box questions, 46
  change for the sake of
    change, 46
  cheating, 19
  checking your work
    answer grid, 17
    careless mistakes, 16–17
    common sense answers, 16
    context, 17
    decimal places, 17
    diction, 17
    exponents, 16
    grammar, 17
    -ing words, 17
    operations signs, 17
    political correctness, 17
    twosomes, 17
  college planning, 24
  English Test, 46
  failure to double-check, 20
  listening to others, 20
  losing concentration, 18
  missing the big picture, 46
  NO CHANGE option, 46
  OMIT... option, 46
  rubbernecking, 19
  second guessing, 20
  superfluous information, 45
  transferring information, 20
  traps, 46
  wasting time, 18
  worrying, 19–20
  Writing Test, 55–58
mixed numbers, 129
mixture problems, 124
mnemonics, 126
mode, 112
modifiers. *See* adjectives;
  adverbs
most, subject-verb
  agreement, 28

• N •

natural sciences, Reading Test, 145
negative angles, 79
negative questions, 149
neither/nor, subject-verb
  agreement, 29
NO CHANGE option, 46

not only construction, 31
note paper, for test, 11
notes, during the test, 10
nouns, subject-verb agreement, 28–29
number sets, 122–123
number/amount, 33–34
numbers. *See also* math review;
  Mathematics Test; *specific topics*
  composite, 123–124
  counting, 122
  irrational, 123
  mixed, 129
  powers of, 99–101
  prime, 123–124
  rational, 122–123
  real, 123
  whole, 122
numerators, 110
numerical coefficients, 101

• O •

obtuse angles, 80
OMIT... option, 46, 48
operations signs, checking your work, 17
order of mathematical
  operations, 106–108, 126
organization, subject-verb
  agreement, 28

• P •

parallelism, 32
parallelograms, areas, 85
passages, English Test, 41
pencils, 10
percentages, 120–122
perfection, in 30 minutes, 57
perimeter
  circles, 94
  polygons, 90
  triangles, 85
phase/faze, 38
photo ID, for test, 10
physical disabilities, 11
plural subjects, subject-verb
  agreement, 28
point of origin, 93
political activism, Writing Test, 57
political correctness, checking
  your work, 17

polygons
  cubes, 91
  cylinders, 91–92
  exterior angle measure, 90
  interior angle measure, 90–91
  perimeter, 90
  rectangular solids, 91
  regular, 90
  TSA (total surface area), 92–93
  volume, 91–92
positive thinking, 16
powers of numbers
  (exponents), 99–101
Practice Exam 1
  answer key, 225
  answer sheet, 182–183
  English Test
    answers and explanations, 227–235
    questions, 185–194
  exam conditions, 181
  Mathematics Test
    answers and explanations, 235–248
    questions, 195–202
  Reading Test
    answers and explanations, 248–254
    questions, 203–210
  Science Reasoning Test
    answers and explanations, 254–264
    questions, 211–222
  scoring key, 223–224
  subscores, 223
Practice Exam 2
  answer key, 310
  answer sheet, 266–267
  English Test
    answers and explanations, 311–320
    questions, 269–279
  Mathematics Test
    answers and explanations, 320–332
    questions, 280–287
  Reading Test
    answers and explanations, 332–338
    questions, 288–295
  Science Reasoning Test
    answers and explanations, 338–350
    questions, 296–307
  scoring key, 308–309
  subscores, 308
  test conditions, 265

practice questions
  English Test, 47–51, 185–194, 269–279
  Mathematics Test, 137–142, 195–202, 280–287
  Reading Test, 151–155, 203–210, 288–295
  Science Reasoning Test, 169–177, 211–222, 296–307
prepositional phrases, subject-verb agreement, 28
prescribe/proscribe, 38
prime numbers, 123–124
principal/principle, 38
probability, 110–111
pronouns
  case (grammatical), 30
  definition, 29
  gender, 30
  grammar review, 29–30
proofing, Writing Test, 72–73
proscribe/prescribe, 38
prose fiction, Reading Test, 145–146
PRTI formula, 124–125
public, subject-verb agreement, 28
punctuation, Writing Test, 73
Pythagorean theorem, 85–87

• Q •

quadrilaterals. *See also* polygons
  definition, 87
  eccentric shapes, 89
  parallelograms, 88
  rectangle, 88
  rhombus, 88
  square, 87–88
  trapezoid, 88–89
quantities, units of measure, 127
questions, practice. *See* practice questions

• R •

radicals, 108–110
radius of circles, 94
raise/raze/rise, 39
range (statistical), 112
rate, distance, time calculations, 117–118
rational numbers, 122–123
ratios, 101–102
ratios of angles, 115–116

raze/raise/rise, 39
Reading Test
  detail questions, 148
  humanities, 145
  main idea questions, 148
  natural sciences, 145
  negative questions, 149
  overview, 13
  Practice Exam 1
    answers and explanations, 248–254
    questions, 203–210
  Practice Exam 2
    answers and explanations, 332–338
    questions, 288–295
  practice questions, 151–155, 203–210, 288–295
  prose fiction, 145–146
  question types, 148–149
  reverse questions, 149
  scoring, 146
  social studies, 145
  strategies, 146–147
  timing, 146
  tips, 149–150
  tone, attitude, and inference questions, 148–149
  topics, 145–146
  traps, 149–150
  vocabulary in context questions, 149
real numbers, 123
reciprocals, 100
rectangles, areas, 88
rectangular solids
  polygons, 91
  TSA (total surface area), 92–93
  volume, 91
reflex angles, 81
regular polygons, 90
reiterating the question, Writing Test, 66–67
religious obligations, 11
remembering your readers, Writing Test, 57
repeating the test, 13
repetition, Writing Test, 58, 72
rescheduling the test, 11
Research Summaries, Science Reasoning Test, 163–165
reverse questions, 149
reviewing your work. *See* checking your work; mistakes
rhombuses, areas, 88
right angles, 80

right triangles, 85–87
rise/raze/raise, 39
roots, 108–110
rubbernecking, 19
rumors about the ACT, 353–355
run-on sentences, 31

• S •

S.A.M.A.N., 28
SAT I, *versus* ACT
  college planning, 22
  difficulty, 354
  summary of differences, 357–358
  taking both, 355
The SAT I For Dummies, 132
scalene triangles, 83
Science Reasoning Test
  conclusion, 167
  conflicting viewpoints, 165–166
  Data Analysis, 162–163
  Data Representation, 160–163
  format, 159–160
  overview, 13
  Practice Exam 1
    answers and explanations, 254–264
    questions, 211–222
  Practice Exam 2
    answers and explanations, 338–350
    questions, 296–307
  practice questions, 169–177, 211–222, 296–307
  question styles, 166–167
  Research Summaries, 163–165
scoring
  and college admissions, 21
  description, 11, 12
  guessing, 12
  passing scores, 354
  Reading Test, 146
  subscores, 223, 308
  Writing Test, 58
scratch paper, for test, 11
second guessing, 20
sectors of circles, 98
sentence fragments, 32
sentence structure, 31–32
several, subject-verb agreement, 28
shaded-area problems, 89
similar figures, 84
sines, 113–114

singular subject, subject-verb agreement, 27
slang, Writing Test, 57
snacks, during the test, 10
social studies, Reading Test, 145
SOH CAH TOA, 113–116
solving for x, 105–106
some, subject-verb agreement, 28
speed *versus* thoroughness, 45
spelling, Writing Test, 72
sports, importance of, 23
square roots, 108–110
squares, 87–88
stationary/stationery, 39
statistics, 111–113
straight angles, 80
stress management, 15–16
stretching exercises, 15
studying for the ACT, 353
subjects tested, 12–13
subject-verb agreement, 27–29
superfluous information, 45
supplementary angles, 80
symbolic values, 102–105

• T •

tangents, 114
test center, 9–11. *See also* ACT
thinking positively, 16
thought diarrhea, 56
ticket to the test, 10
time
  English Test, 185
  Mathematics Test, 195
  Reading Test, 203
  Science Reasoning Test, 211
  speed *versus* thoroughness, 45
  units of measure, 127
  wasting, 18
  Writing Test, 56
time, rate, distance calculations, 117–118
time limit, 9
timing yourself, 11
tone, attitude, and inference questions, 148–149
total surface area (TSA), polygons, 92–93
touch method of editing, Writing Test, 72
transitions, Writing Test, 71
transversal angles, 81
trapezoids, 88–89

traps
  English Test, 46
  Mathematics Test, 132
  Reading Test, 149–150
triangles. *See also* polygons
  area, 85
  equilateral, 82
  hypotenuse, 85
  isosceles, 82
  largest angle, 83
  lengths of sides, 85
  measure of exterior angle, 83
  perimeter, 85
  Pythagorean theorem, 85–87
  right, 85–87
  scalene, 83
  sum of interior angles, 83
  sum of length of two sides, 83
trigonometry
  See also algebra
  See also geometry
  See also math review
  See also Mathematics Test
  cosines, 114
  Mathematics Test, 132
  questions in the ACT, 113
  ratios of angles, 115–116
  sines, 113–114
  SOH CAH TOA, 113–116
  tangents, 114
TSA (total surface area), polygons, 92–93
twosomes, checking your work, 17

• U •

union, subject-verb agreement, 28
units of measure, 126–127
usage questions, 43

• V •

verbs, subject-verb agreement, 27–29
visualization technique, 16
vocabulary
  in context questions, 149
  Writing Test, 56–57
volume, polygons, 91–92

• W •

watch, for test, 10, 11
well/good, 36

where...that construction, 40
whether/if, 36–37
whole numbers, 122
whom/who, 39
work problems, 125–126
worry, 19–20
Writing Test. *See also* English Test; grammar review
  active voice, 73
  common mistakes, 55–58
  conclusion, 71–72
  controversy, 57
  creativity, 56
  editing, 72–73
  essay examples, 58–63, 75–76
  essay organization, 70–72
  expectation of perfection, 57
  failure to edit, 58
  first sentence, 66–67
  ghost words, 72
  handwriting, 73
  hooking the reader, 67–68
  indecisiveness, 57, 67
  introduction, 70
  judges' expectations, 65–66
  making a judgment, 65–66, 67
  mandatory essay, 355
  offering examples, 69
  overview, 13
  paragraph examples, 70–71
  planning your approach, 56
  political activism, 57
  proofing, 72–73
  punctuation, 73
  reiterating the question, 66–67
  remembering your readers, 57
  repetition, 58, 72
  scoring, 58
  slang, 57
  spelling, 72
  thought diarrhea, 56
  time constraints, 56
  touch method of editing, 72
  transitions, 71
  vocabulary, 56–57

• X •

x-y axes, 93

• Z •

zero angles, 79

BUSINESS, CAREERS & PERSONAL FINANCE

0-7645-5307-0 (Grant Writing For Dummies)
0-7645-5331-3 *† (Home Buying For Dummies)

Also available:
- Accounting For Dummies †
  0-7645-5314-3
- Business Plans Kit For Dummies †
  0-7645-5365-8
- Cover Letters For Dummies
  0-7645-5224-4
- Frugal Living For Dummies
  0-7645-5403-4
- Leadership For Dummies
  0-7645-5176-0
- Managing For Dummies
  0-7645-1771-6
- Marketing For Dummies
  0-7645-5600-2
- Personal Finance For Dummies *
  0-7645-2590-5
- Project Management For Dummies
  0-7645-5283-X
- Resumes For Dummies †
  0-7645-5471-9
- Selling For Dummies
  0-7645-5363-1
- Small Business Kit For Dummies *†
  0-7645-5093-4

HOME & BUSINESS COMPUTER BASICS

0-7645-4074-2 (Windows XP For Dummies)
0-7645-3758-X (Excel 2003 All-in-One Desk Reference For Dummies)

Also available:
- ACT! 6 For Dummies
  0-7645-2645-6
- iLife '04 All-in-One Desk Reference For Dummies
  0-7645-7347-0
- iPAQ For Dummies
  0-7645-6769-1
- Mac OS X Panther Timesaving Techniques For Dummies
  0-7645-5812-9
- Macs For Dummies
  0-7645-5656-8
- Microsoft Money 2004 For Dummies
  0-7645-4195-1
- Office 2003 All-in-One Desk Reference For Dummies
  0-7645-3883-7
- Outlook 2003 For Dummies
  0-7645-3759-8
- PCs For Dummies
  0-7645-4074-2
- TiVo For Dummies
  0-7645-6923-6
- Upgrading and Fixing PCs For Dummies
  0-7645-1665-5
- Windows XP Timesaving Techniques For Dummies
  0-7645-3748-2

FOOD, HOME, GARDEN, HOBBIES, MUSIC & PETS

0-7645-5295-3 (Feng Shui For Dummies)
0-7645-5232-5 (Poker For Dummies)

Also available:
- Bass Guitar For Dummies
  0-7645-2487-9
- Diabetes Cookbook For Dummies
  0-7645-5230-9
- Gardening For Dummies *
  0-7645-5130-2
- Guitar For Dummies
  0-7645-5106-X
- Holiday Decorating For Dummies
  0-7645-2570-0
- Home Improvement All-in-One For Dummies
  0-7645-5680-0
- Knitting For Dummies
  0-7645-5395-X
- Piano For Dummies
  0-7645-5105-1
- Puppies For Dummies
  0-7645-5255-4
- Scrapbooking For Dummies
  0-7645-7208-3
- Senior Dogs For Dummies
  0-7645-5818-8
- Singing For Dummies
  0-7645-2475-5
- 30-Minute Meals For Dummies
  0-7645-2589-1

INTERNET & DIGITAL MEDIA

0-7645-1664-7 (Digital Photography For Dummies)
0-7645-6924-4 (Starting an eBay Business For Dummies)

Also available:
- 2005 Online Shopping Directory For Dummies
  0-7645-7495-7
- CD & DVD Recording For Dummies
  0-7645-5956-7
- eBay For Dummies
  0-7645-5654-1
- Fighting Spam For Dummies
  0-7645-5965-6
- Genealogy Online For Dummies
  0-7645-5964-8
- Google For Dummies
  0-7645-4420-9
- Home Recording For Musicians For Dummies
  0-7645-1634-5
- The Internet For Dummies
  0-7645-4173-0
- iPod & iTunes For Dummies
  0-7645-7772-7
- Preventing Identity Theft For Dummies
  0-7645-7336-5
- Pro Tools All-in-One Desk Reference For Dummies
  0-7645-5714-9
- Roxio Easy Media Creator For Dummies
  0-7645-7131-1

* Separate Canadian edition also available
† Separate U.K. edition also available

Available wherever books are sold. For more information or to order direct: U.S. customers visit www.dummies.com or call 1-877-762-2974.
U.K. customers visit www.wileyeurope.com or call 0800 243407. Canadian customers visit www.wiley.ca or call 1-800-567-4797.

WILEY

SPORTS, FITNESS, PARENTING, RELIGION & SPIRITUALITY

Golf For Dummies
0-7645-5146-9

Parenting For Dummies
0-7645-5418-2

Also available:
- Adoption For Dummies
  0-7645-5488-3
- Basketball For Dummies
  0-7645-5248-1
- The Bible For Dummies
  0-7645-5296-1
- Buddhism For Dummies
  0-7645-5359-3
- Catholicism For Dummies
  0-7645-5391-7
- Hockey For Dummies
  0-7645-5228-7
- Judaism For Dummies
  0-7645-5299-6
- Martial Arts For Dummies
  0-7645-5358-5
- Pilates For Dummies
  0-7645-5397-6
- Religion For Dummies
  0-7645-5264-3
- Teaching Kids to Read For Dummies
  0-7645-4043-2
- Weight Training For Dummies
  0-7645-5168-X
- Yoga For Dummies
  0-7645-5117-5

TRAVEL

Hawaii For Dummies
0-7645-5438-7

Italy For Dummies
0-7645-5453-0

Also available:
- Alaska For Dummies
  0-7645-1761-9
- Arizona For Dummies
  0-7645-6938-4
- Cancún and the Yucatán For Dummies
  0-7645-2437-2
- Cruise Vacations For Dummies
  0-7645-6941-4
- Europe For Dummies
  0-7645-5456-5
- Ireland For Dummies
  0-7645-5455-7
- Las Vegas For Dummies
  0-7645-5448-4
- London For Dummies
  0-7645-4277-X
- New York City For Dummies
  0-7645-6945-7
- Paris For Dummies
  0-7645-5494-8
- RV Vacations For Dummies
  0-7645-5443-3
- Walt Disney World & Orlando For Dummies
  0-7645-6943-0

GRAPHICS, DESIGN & WEB DEVELOPMENT

Creating Web Pages All-in-One Desk Reference For Dummies
0-7645-4345-8

PHP & MySQL For Dummies
0-7645-5589-8

Also available:
- Adobe Acrobat 6 PDF For Dummies
  0-7645-3760-1
- Building a Web Site For Dummies
  0-7645-7144-3
- Dreamweaver MX 2004 For Dummies
  0-7645-4342-3
- FrontPage 2003 For Dummies
  0-7645-3882-9
- HTML 4 For Dummies
  0-7645-1995-6
- Illustrator cs For Dummies
  0-7645-4084-X
- Macromedia Flash MX 2004 For Dummies
  0-7645-4358-X
- Photoshop 7 All-in-One Desk Reference For Dummies
  0-7645-1667-1
- Photoshop cs Timesaving Techniques For Dummies
  0-7645-6782-9
- PHP 5 For Dummies
  0-7645-4166-8
- PowerPoint 2003 For Dummies
  0-7645-3908-6
- QuarkXPress 6 For Dummies
  0-7645-2593-X

NETWORKING, SECURITY, PROGRAMMING & DATABASES

C++ For Dummies
0-7645-6852-3

Hacking For Dummies
0-7645-5784-X

Also available:
- A+ Certification For Dummies
  0-7645-4187-0
- Access 2003 All-in-One Desk Reference For Dummies
  0-7645-3988-4
- Beginning Programming For Dummies
  0-7645-4997-9
- C For Dummies
  0-7645-7068-4
- Firewalls For Dummies
  0-7645-4048-3
- Home Networking For Dummies
  0-7645-42796
- Network Security For Dummies
  0-7645-1679-5
- Networking For Dummies
  0-7645-1677-9
- TCP/IP For Dummies
  0-7645-1760-0
- VBA For Dummies
  0-7645-3989-2
- Wireless All In-One Desk Reference For Dummies
  0-7645-7496-5
- Wireless Home Networking For Dummies
  0-7645-3910-8